SEXTON FOR GOD

TIM ROLLS

SEXTON FOR GOD
Copyright Tim Rolls 2021
ISBN: 979-8493264665

THE MORAL RIGHT OF THE AUTHOR HAS BEEN ASSERTED
Apart from any fair dealing for the purposes of research or private study, or criticism or review, as permitted under the Copyright, Designs and Patents Act 1988, this publication may only be reproduced, stored or transmitted, in any means, with the prior permission in writing of GATE 17, or in the case of reprographic reproduction in accordance with the terms of licenses issued by the Copyright Licensing Agency. Enquiries concerning reproduction outside those terms should be sent to the publishers.

Twitter: @tim_rolls
Cover Design: Nicki Rolls
www.gate17.co.uk

CONTENTS

INTRODUCTION 1
ACKNOWLEDGEMENTS 5
PRELUDE: The Doc's Legacy 9
CHAPTER ONE: 1967-68 – Steadying The Ship 14
CHAPTER TWO: 1968-69 – 'We Can Do Better' 54
CHAPTER THREE: 1969-70 – Southern Softies No Longer 99
CHAPTER FOUR: 1970-71 – European Conquest 184
CHAPTER FIVE: In Hindsight 248

APPENDICES *(all cover Sexton's arrival 23/10/67 to end 1970-71 season)*
APPENDIX A: Player Profiles 266
APPENDIX B: Chelsea Appearances And Goals For Each Player 270
APPENDIX C: Chelsea Season-By-Season Overall Record 271
APPENDIX D: Chelsea Transfer Activity 272
APPENDIX E: Listing of Chelsea Transfer Rumours 274
APPENDIX F: Listing of Televised Chelsea Games 278

BIBLIOGRAPHY 281

INTRODUCTION

For supporters of a certain age, regardless of the silverware garnered during the Ken Bates and particularly the Roman Abramovich eras, the Chelsea team that won two cups at the turn of the 1970s will always be remembered with supreme fondness, for the quality of football, the ability of the players and the charismatic nature of the club.

Yet just a few years earlier, after popular if volatile manager Tommy Docherty had summarily left the club, the side was in 19th place in Division One, the highest profile player was telling anyone who would listen that they would be relegated and a train carriage containing Chelsea board members was attacked by disgruntled supporters after a horrendous 7-0 defeat.

How did this transformation come about? How did Dave Sexton come into a club in crisis, steady the ship, strengthen the team and win the FA Cup and the European Cup-Winner's Cup?

This book looks at the period from him joining the club in October 1967 to his greatest triumph, winning the European Cup-Winner's Cup in Athens less than four years later, having won an epic FA Cup Final the previous season. It examines the man, his methods, his personality, the players he inherited, those he bought, the youngsters he brought through and the established stars he sold. It also looks at why, in that era, despite Chelsea having such a strong side capable of feats of enormous doggedness and spirit, a concerted challenge for the League title never took place and whether this constituted underachievement.

Sexton was the opposite of his mercurial predecessor. Quiet, methodical, guarded. Yet he managed, during the period covered by this book, to get the freer spirits at the club buying into his ideas and tactics, with mutually beneficial results. Those he inherited included the stoic and hardworking (Peter Bonetti, Ron Harris, Eddie McCreadie, John Hollins, Marvin Hinton, Peter Houseman, John Boyle, Bobby Tambling, Tommy Baldwin) and the flamboyant (Peter Osgood, Charlie Cooke). He bought well (Alan Birchenall, David Webb, Ian Hutchinson, John Dempsey, Paddy Mulligan), sold assiduously and, critically, introduced two young players, Hutchinson and Alan Hudson, who both had a transformative effect on the side.

Sexton was not afraid to drop underachievers, and could be ruthless with poor performers, or those he perceived as not putting the necessary effort in. He had to deal with cases of player indiscipline, though nothing on the scale of the latter part of his Chelsea career, a period covered in '*Stamford Bridge Is Falling Down*'. What he did, though, that should never be forgotten, was win major trophies. He won the supporters over, and by the time of Athens was revered by them. The book details how he did this, and why he deserves to be high on the list of great Chelsea managers.

The idea for this book came when regulars at the *cfcuk* stall opposite Fulham Broadway tube entrance asked why I had written about Chelsea's history from 1961-67 (in *'Diamonds, Dynamos and Devils'*) and 1971-75 (in *'Stamford Bridge Is Falling Down'*) but not the period between the two when Chelsea actually won trophies. The more I thought about it, the more I realised it made sense to write the middle and final (if that makes sense) part of a trilogy covering Chelsea from 1961 to 1975.

As with my other two books, I write this as a matchgoing Chelsea supporter but not one who regularly watched that side. I have seen nearly 1,500 Chelsea games and been a Stamford Bridge regular since 1976, but in the late 1960s and early 1970s had to content myself with a few games a season. Objectivity is not always easy, especially when supporting the club you are writing about, but I have attempted to utilise evidence uncovered rather than emotion aroused.

The 203 competitive first-team matches between October 23rd 1967, when Sexton was appointed Chelsea manager, and May 21st 1971, when captain Ron Harris lifted the European Cup-Winner's Cup, are covered, but the book aims to be much more than just a series of match reports. Chelsea were highly newsworthy and high-profile personalities, especially Osgood and Cooke, had plenty to say. Their comments, interviews and features are analysed. Football was changing, top stars were starting to earn very good money and the lifestyles of some of Sexton's squad reflected this. Osgood's travails as he tried to win a place in the 1970 Mexico World Cup squad are covered, as is the persistent, premeditated brutal fouling he and Hutchinson had to suffer from cynical opposition hard men. His struggle to avoid retaliating, and the price he paid when he failed, are detailed.

If your memory of events differs from those I describe then I apologise. Events that occurred half a century ago are almost always open to interpretation and memory blurring. I have used a myriad of contemporary newspaper reports, articles and interviews as my main source of information, backed up with a series of biographies, autobiographies, Chelsea histories and websites. I accept that newspaper articles are not always accurate, that they are subject to speculation and axe grinding, but by using multiple sources I have hopefully reduced the impact of this. All these sources are credited at the end of the book. I have also picked the brains of a number of supporters who watched the club in those days.

In some cases, there is a consensus about events and individuals, in other cases, an unsurprising dissension. I have attempted to show both sides of arguments and, where appropriate, to draw my own conclusions. Though I have tried hard to minimise factual inaccuracies, any which appear are my responsibility and I apologise for them.

Transfer fees, especially large ones, are notoriously difficult to report with accuracy. Where there is a generally accepted fee involved, I have used that. Often newspapers reported different fees for the same deal, so I have tried to go with the most commonly used. Any assumptions made have been detailed.

An ongoing theme in the book is the players Chelsea were linked with, or squad members potentially being sold, most of which did not come to fruition, but I felt it interesting to see names the club could potentially have bought. Transfer speculation, especially that with little basis in reality, has always fascinated me and Appendix E lists every transfer rumour which never went anywhere in the Sunday tabloid press, whether incoming or outgoing, for the four seasons under review.

Average matchday attendances have been taken from Brian Tabner's *Through the Turnstiles* and matchday ones from *'Chelsea - The Complete Record'*. Occasionally there are slight, usually insignificant, variations in average attendances given by different sources.

The title of this book comes from a banner displayed on Fulham Road during the 1970 FA Cup victory parade.

ACKNOWLEDGEMENTS

As with my two previous books, I have a large number of people to thank.

My wife Nicki, for not only providing ongoing moral support during the 18 months it took me to research and write this book but also designing and painting the book cover. I am more grateful than I can say.

My late father, Peter, who took us to three successive Chelsea v Manchester United games in the period covered in this book, sell-out games that whetted my appetite for the big occasion.

Mark Worrall at Gate 17 for supporting, producing, formatting and publishing the book. He also came up with the title, as he did for '*Stamford Bridge Is Falling Down*'.

Martin, Hugh and Graham, who I have been going to Chelsea with since 1976.

John McKinnon, for running the coach from Camberley that took me to my first Chelsea game, against Stoke City in September 1967, age 10. He also ran coaches I went on to half-a-dozen of the games featured in this book.

Chelsea authors including Rick Glanvill, Clayton Beerman, Chelsea Chad, Stuart Deabill, Neil Fitzsimon, John King, Martin Knight, Mark Meehan, Walter Otton and Neil Smith for their advice, support and encouragement.

John Boyle for his time, company and openness when I interviewed him in 2017.

Supporters Bob Barlow, Terry Cassley, Tony Foss, Brian Gaches, David Gray, Peter Gray, Steve Hodder, Barry Holmes, Martin Horne, Geoff Kimber, Jonathan Kydd, Julian Patten and Bob Ruthven for sharing their memories and thoughts of those far-off days with such clarity and energy. Paul McParlan of These Football Times for such distinct memories of the 1970 Burnley FA Cup replay. Rodney George for the use of his comprehensive list of televised Chelsea games.

The British Library Newsroom staff for their politeness and efficiency.

Everyone who bought one, or both, of my previous books, providing me with the encouragement to write this one and those people who helped me promote the crowdfunding exercise.

Tim Rolls
London 2021

'Sexton For God' is dedicated to Peter Bonetti, Tommy Docherty, Joe Fascione, Peter Houseman, Ian Hutchinson, Brian Mears, Peter Osgood, John Phillips, Dave Sexton, Ken Shellito, Ron Suart, Keith Weller and Allan Young. *They all feature in this book but are sadly no longer with us. RIP*

PRELUDE
The Doc's Legacy

Farewell To The Doc

The manner of Tommy Docherty's departure from Chelsea Football Club in early October 1967 was unexpected, but a high-profile parting of the ways was always likely to happen. A volatile, passionate, inspirational manager, 'The Doc' was loved by many supporters, and certainly transformed the club from the footballing backwater it had become in the latter days of his predecessor Ted Drake.

He had been at the club since 1961, cleared out the deadwood, been relegated, promoted and, largely using young players who had come through the youth system, allied to some extremely shrewd acquisitions like Eddie McCreadie and George Graham (who cost just £5,000 each), had built an exciting, highly promising team. The team arguably underachieved in 1965 when, chasing a realistic treble, they won just the League Cup. Team morale was not helped when The Doc sent home eight first-team squad members after they returned to their hotel in Blackpool late at night. Some of those sent home never forgave him.

Key players, including Terry Venables, Barry Bridges and Graham, departed after falling out with the manager and most of the rest of the squad had issues with Docherty at one time or another, including club loyalists Peter Bonetti, Eddie McCreadie, John Hollins and Bobby Tambling.

Docherty had an excellent, mutually respectful working relationship with chairman Joe Mears but after his tragic and untimely passing just before the 1966 World Cup, the role was taken by vice-chair Charles Pratt, whose dealings with the mercurial Docherty were less than harmonious. Public rows over ticket allocations and squad bonuses culminated in a fall-out just before the 1967 FA Cup Final, which an insipid Chelsea lost 2-1 to Tottenham. That summer the team went on tour to Bermuda, Docherty was involved in rows with match officials and the Bermudan FA, eventually, reported the matter to the Football Association.

Chelsea's start to the 1967-68 season was abysmal, the low point being a humiliating 6-2 home defeat by Southampton, and at the end of September they were languishing in 19th place after ten League games, just two points and two places above the relegation zone. Home crowds were below 30,000, well under the 40,000 average the board thought achievable, and there seemed a palpable sense of uneasy drift around the club.

When the FA were officially advised of the incidents in Bermuda in early October, they suspended Docherty, long a thorn in their side, from all football activities for 28 days. He was given no chance to present his side of the story to what amounted to a kangaroo court. Sensing an opportunity, Pratt and the board met with Docherty and, though there are differing versions of exactly what happened, the upshot was that the club dispensed with his services, with immediate effect, that day, Friday October 6th.

Docherty had transformed the club, but six years of a man with his restless personality at the helm was probably enough, and it was time for a new man to take over and steer the ship back on course. More detail on Docherty's time at Chelsea, his departure, and the reasons for it, is given in '*Diamonds, Dynamos and Devils*'.

The Team Docherty Left Behind

Docherty had inherited a bunch of talented youngsters from Ted Drake in 1961 and was happy to give them first-team opportunities. Barry Bridges, George Graham, Bert Murray and Terry Venables all departed in 1966 but a core of homegrown talent remained.

Goalkeeper Peter Bonetti was in the England squad for the 1966 World Cup and generally recognised as the second best English goalkeeper after Gordon Banks. Utterly fearless and nicknamed 'The Cat' because of his agility, he had been a regular in the team since 1960 and was a cornerstone of the side. *1966-67 - 38 League games.*

Captain Ron Harris, nicknamed 'Chopper' because of his uncompromising tackling style, could play full-back or centre-back. His fearless defensive capabilities and leadership qualities more than compensated for his limitations in passing and attacking. *1966-67 - 42 League games, 0 goals.*

An overlapping left-back with a crunching tackle, Crowd favourite Eddie McCreadie was bought from East Stirling in 1962 for just £5,000, a brilliant piece of business. *1966-67 - 38 League games, 1 goal.*

Marvin Hinton was a footballing centre-back bought from Charlton Athletic four years earlier for a bargain £35,000. He was a natural sweeper, comfortable on the ball and a skilled passer but, when in combination with Harris, weak in the air against powerful centre-forwards. *1966-67 - 38 League games, 0 goals.*

A hugely energetic, positive midfielder with an eye for goal, John Hollins came through the ranks, was in the side at 17 and had been a regular for three seasons. He had won his first England cap earlier that year. *1966-67 - 39 League games, 2 goals.*

A versatile, competitive and committed young midfielder or full-back, John Boyle had held down a first-team place for most of the past two seasons. *1966-67 - 36 League games, 5 goals.*

Hugely talented winger Charlie Cooke had signed from Dundee the previous year. He had fantastic dribbling ability and was beloved by the supporters but was occasionally prone to showing flashes of individual brilliance without creating an end product. *1966-67 - 33 League games, 3 goals.*

A regular in the team for seven years, Bobby Tambling was the club's record goalscorer. Very quick and a natural marksman, he had in some ways been taken for granted by Docherty. *1966-67 - 36 League games, 21 goals.*

The charismatic, hugely gifted Osgood competed with Cooke for the title of the most talented team member. In the side at 18 and probably the best young player in the country after George Best in early 1966, He broke his leg that October when Chelsea were top of the League and missed the rest of that season as the team slumped to an eventual ninth place. He could seemingly without effort run with the ball, beat men and make breath-taking passes. Crucially he was also a natural goalscorer. Against that he was sometimes seen as moody and lazy. *1966-67 - 10 League games, 6 goals.*

Hardworking forward Tommy Baldwin was a perfect foil for Osgood. He was supposedly the makeweight in the deal that took George Graham to Arsenal but was an excellent piece of business by Docherty. *1966-67 - 30 League games, 16 goals.*

Diligent winger Peter Houseman was an excellent crosser of the ball, but Docherty had been loath to use him regularly, which he admitted later was a mistake. He sometimes lacked confidence in his own ability. *1966-67 - 18 League games, 1 goal.*

Summer centre-half signing from Bury, Colin Waldron, had struggled since his arrival and was substituted at half-time in a League Cup defeat at Middlesbrough. Full-back Geoff Butler had arrived from Middlesbrough in September, having impressed in that game. Jim Thomson and Joe Kirkup were also squad full-backs but neither had made a first-team place their own. Winger Joe Fascione had been in and around the fringes for a few years without ever fully establishing himself. Youngsters Barry Lloyd (midfield) and Ian Hamilton (forward) had played a few first-team games without making compelling cases for a regular place and Stewart Houston (defender) was knocking on the first-team door.

Of Docherty's final back four against Coventry - Thomson, Waldron, Harris, Butler - only Harris was at the club a year later. The side was weak in the air defensively and needed strengthening at full-back but, in general, the new manager would inherit a pretty decent squad that, with a few additions and better organisation, should be competing for honours.

The Board And Club Administration

After the untimely death of the hugely respected Joe Mears, Chelsea chairman and FA chairman, at the end of June 1966, he was replaced by vice-chair Charles Pratt, who struggled to fill his predecessor's shoes. Other board members were vice-chair Leonard Withey, Viscount Chelsea, Joe's son Brian and Brian's cousin Leslie Mears.

Chelsea Secretary John Battersby had worked in football since 1934 and been at the club since 1949. He was widely respected throughout the English game and a very influential voice at the club, the board habitually relying on his sound advice.

The Ground

Stamford Bridge needed significant refurbishment. The West Stand was 18 months old, but the rest of the stadium was aged and inadequate, something the more progressive members of the Chelsea board were acutely aware of. The greyhound track round the pitch meant the stands were a long way from the action which impacted on atmosphere, especially as, apart from The Shed, which covered part of the Fulham Road end, neither terrace was covered. The North Stand, next to the East Stand but completely different in appearance, was an architectural oddity that looked as though it was likely to fall down any minute.

Capacity was around 60,000 but there were only 15,500 seats (including 3,500 benches at the front of the West Stand), and the terrace layout meant that on occasion the gates were shut below capacity, as gangways were blocked when space still existed on the terracing.

A complication was that the stadium was owned by the Mears Trust, not Chelsea Football Club, and two Chelsea directors were beneficiaries of that trust. Decision making with regard to ground improvements and who should pay for them was therefore more complicated. To add to the complexity, Stamford Bridge was shared with greyhound racing, who obviously had different needs and desires when it came to the stadium.

The Supporters

In the title-winning 1954-55 season, Chelsea's average crowd was an impressive 48,260, the highest in the League, which showed the potential the club had to draw consistently large attendances. By the 1961-62 relegation season, however, the average had fallen to just 27,000. By 1964-65, when for some time the treble looked a realistic prospect for Tommy Docherty's side, it had increased to 37,054. In 1966-67 Chelsea's average was 35,526, though the view at the club was that with any sort of success then average attendances in excess of 40,000 should be achievable.

The crowds for the biggest games - Manchester United, Arsenal,

Tottenham Hotspur, Liverpool - often exceeded 55,000 but there were occasions when, with less attractive opponents, they could struggle to reach a third of that. The potential was undoubtedly there for regular 40,000+ attendances, but for that to be achieved, the team would need to produce entertaining, winning football on a consistent basis.

The Shed was named after diehard supporter Clifford Webb had a letter on the subject printed in the Leicester City home programme in September 1966. It had become a congregation point in the ground for a growing number of young supporters who could sing, chant, sway and surge to their heart's content. It was also the only part of the terracing that was under cover so not all the noise was lost, though it was still a long way from the pitch so, from the players perspective, the atmosphere was rarely as vibrant as at more compact, covered grounds like Upton Park.

The number of travelling supporters had increased during the early and mid-1960s and, by 1967, clubs like Chelsea were regularly followed on their travels by thousands and those die-hards were making their vocal presence felt. In March 1965, Chelsea chants can clearly be heard on *Match Of The Day* coverage of the 4-0 defeat at Manchester United and, the following season, loud renditions of Chelsea terrace classic 'Zigger Zagger' are a feature of the West Bromwich away game coverage on the same programme.

CHAPTER ONE
1967-68
Steadying The Ship

October 1967

24 hours after Tommy Docherty left his job, the club, inevitably in a state of flux, faced what was always one of their hardest games of the season, at Leeds United. Don Revie had built a formidable team over the previous few years, and there was still much bitterness in Yorkshire about Peter Lorimer's controversially disallowed goal in the last minute of the FA Cup Semi-Final that April, which would have equalised Tony Hateley's header.

Ron Suart had been Docherty's deputy since earlier that year and was the obvious acting manager while a new man was sought, though he naturally had ambitions for the post on a permanent basis. An experienced football man respected by the players, he had previously been Blackpool boss.

The first, short-term issue was to stabilise the team, and that was down to Suart. The second, more far-reaching and strategic, was the appointment of a permanent replacement for Docherty. If he did well in the interim role then Suart was clearly a contender. Others mentioned in the press on the day of the Leeds game, while Docherty's departure was front-page news, included highly respected managers Bill McGarry of Ipswich and John Harris of Sheffield United, the latter a well-regarded ex-Chelsea stalwart and a regular in the 1954/55 League-winning side. The *Daily Telegraph*, who thought Harris the favourite, pointed out that 'the board must allow the manager to manage' but that the manager 'must recognise that the board also has responsibilities'. Common sense but not always the case at Chelsea in Docherty's latter days. They also thought Suart's chances might be hampered by being a club official 'during the past months of crisis'.

The mood of the players travelling to Elland Road was not exactly positive. Peter Osgood told anyone who would listen, including journalists, that he thought the team would be relegated, which earned a rebuke from Suart. Unsurprisingly, others who had been developed by Docherty were also shocked and saddened by his departure.

If the pre-match mood was negative, the performance during the game was utterly shambolic. 4-0 down at half-time, the team were crushed 7-0. Apart from the ever-loyal trio of midfield dynamo John

Hollins, hard-man captain Ron Harris and hardworking utility man John Boyle, no player was exempt from press criticism and the *Daily Telegraph* called the team 'a ragged collection of misfits'. Chelsea chairman Charles Pratt told the *Daily Mail* 'the events of the past 24 hours have nothing to do with this result. We were simply beaten by a much better team'. Like a number of Pratt's comments, this one stretched credulity more than a bit. Yes, Leeds were high-quality but 7-0 was the team's worst result since an 8-1 thrashing at Wolverhampton Wanderers in September 1953. Suart packed the defence and tried a short-passing, close-marking game, with a marked lack of success. Five goals came down the right flank, where recent signing Geoff Butler was overwhelmed. Left-back Eddie McCreadie was a fish out of water in a forward position.

The departure of Docherty had clearly had a massive impact on those loyal to him and, given the League position (19th), it was imperative that the situation was stabilised, and quickly, if an unthinkable fight against relegation was to be avoided.

The Leeds debacle was probably the end for Suart's realistic chances of getting the job on a permanent basis, possibly unfair but in a results-driven world, a hammering on that scale was unacceptable, regardless of circumstances. Headlines like the *Daily Mail's* 'They Didn't Even Seem To Mind Losing...' showed how low team morale had become. It was to Suart's great credit that he had stepped up to the role on the Friday, as his mother had died earlier that week and he only returned to the club that day.

The frustration of a number of young supporters with the Docherty departure and the shambolic performance boiled over on the train home and there was an attempt to attack the carriage reserved for the Chelsea directors. If chairman Charles Pratt, understandably shaken by events on the train, had not previously been aware of Docherty's popularity with the more vocal among the club's support he was now, and this hiatus only reinforced the imperative of steadying the ship.

Pratt woke the following morning to a volley of critical match reports and a host of speculative articles about the identity of the next manager. The *Sunday Mirror* identified three favourites. McGarry, Harris and Arsenal coach Dave Sexton.

Sexton, a highly respected coach and tactical innovator, was Chelsea coach under Docherty from 1962 to 1965, leaving in January 1965 to become Leyton Orient boss. There was a school of thought that felt that if he had stayed, then Chelsea may well have won more than just the League Cup that 1964/65 season. His calm, phlegmatic, serious nature was a highly effective counterpoint to the volatile Docherty, and he was still highly thought of by the club hierarchy and the players. A week earlier Hugh McIlvanney, one of the most perceptive sports writers in the country, interviewed Sexton in *The Observer* and opined 'it is clear (he) will soon be persuaded to return to management'.

The *News Of The World* was clear who they expected to get the job. Under a 'Harris Set For Chelsea' headline, they opined it was likely the Sheffield United boss would be offered the post because of his 'long friendship' with Pratt, which apparently made his appointment appear almost inevitable. They argued he would be the logical choice of the board, though their writer Reg Drury, clearly with sources in the dressing room, felt the team wanted Sexton.

Any hope that the players might pull together in this time of crisis were dispelled when a seemingly well-informed *The People* article headlined 'Osgood Next - He'll Demand A Quick Break With Chelsea' detailed how the forward hoped to be the next man to depart. As the star of the team, aged only 20 and after nearly a year out recovering from a broken leg suffered at Blackpool in October 1966, the team, the club and the supporters all desperately needed his talent and charisma. However, even after eleven first-team games that season, he had not regained full fitness and sharpness after his injury, a factor in the series of dismal team displays. He was 21 the following February and therefore automatically entitled to a new contract.

Massively skilled but on occasions infuriating, a Leeds match report referred to Osgood strolling through the game 'showing no purpose or intensity', so getting him motivated and actively contributing was clearly a priority for the new man. Suart told the *Daily Mail* 'I have had a bit of a go at Osgood. He has a fantastic talent, but he has got to buckle down if he is to become as good a player as he should be'. He made it clear he wanted the job permanently, thought the squad was better suited to a more attacking 4-2-4 than a 4-3-3 formation and wanted to bring in another winger to augment Houseman, seeing Cooke as a midfielder.

The Chelsea board did the decent thing and, publicly at least, gave the temporary manager a chance to prove himself. Pratt told the *Daily Mail* 'We must let Mr Suart have a short spell to see how he measures up. He deserves that much before we think about a permanent solution'. He said the club would not rush into a decision. He admitted 'we are friendly with Johnny Harris...but that doesn't mean we just have the right to ring him up and offer him the job'. On players leaving, he was clear. 'Nobody is going to leave here, especially now. I know that there are stories about Nottingham Forest wanting Hollins, and many other (stories)...but it would be unfair to release players, even if we could spare them, before we decide about a new manager. Whoever the new man is, he must be left with the best staff we can provide'. Fringe men Joe Kirkup, Joe Fascione and Allan Young were taken off the transfer list. Suart said there had been enquiries for all three but 'the players will certainly not be leaving until things settle down'. Brighton and Northampton had spoken to Young.

Pratt also said that if good players were available, they could be bought before the new man arrived, though whether that was sensible, given a newcomer would definitely have their own ideas about squad strengthening, was debatable.

The following day's *Daily Mail* featured a picture of first-team squad members at Mitcham getting a 'pep talk' from Suart, who commented 'Chelsea's future is very much at stake. The immediate aim must be to restore the team's confidence and spirit'. Keen to lose the 'acting' tag, he needed things to go very well, very quickly. He opened peace moves to persuade Hollins, a key team member, to end his pay dispute with the club. Coventry, supposedly set to appoint Manchester City coach Malcolm Allison as their new boss, approached Chelsea about signing striker Bobby Tambling and were willing to pay £80,000 to sign him, though any possible deal was frozen when Docherty left. Arsenal had also expressed an interest in him. Revealingly, there was no press speculation about the extrovert, outspoken and exceptionally talented Allison getting the Chelsea job (in the end he stayed at City). Given these were personality traits he shared with Docherty, it was pretty clear that the board were looking for a significantly different personality.

Docherty said farewell to the squad at the Mitcham training ground. Suart commented 'Tommy said goodbye to the players collectively and individually. These goodbyes are always sad but now we have got to get down to work. I told the players that they are fighting to save Chelsea Football Club. In a way the 7-0 defeat at Leeds was a good thing'. Exactly how one of Chelsea's worst ever results was a 'good thing' is hard to comprehend, as their lowly position hardly indicated anyone at the club could have been complacent about the situation before the game.

In '*Chelsea - The Official Biography*', Chelsea official historian Rick Glanvill recounts how *The Times* of October 11th carried an unusual obituary, placed presumably by a disgruntled supporter. '*IN MEMORIAM. Chelsea Football Club which died 6 October 1967, after five proud and glorious years*'.

The London Challenge Cup was a competition Chelsea usually fielded reserves and youngsters in. Suart decided to give some of his off-form players a run out at Brentford in midweek. He was also keen to quickly return Osgood to full match-sharpness by giving him as many matches as possible. First-team squad members Osgood, Tambling, Kirkup, Fascione, Jim Thomson, Colin Waldron and Peter Houseman all turned out in a 2-0 win, where a rugged Chelsea were booed and slow-handclapped for time-wasting. Tambling, after a clash of heads, went off with concussion and needed stiches, so the hope of playing him back into top form was dashed.

Later that week the *Daily Mirror* carried a 'Players Want Sexton As Boss' headline. A 'senior Chelsea player' said 'the possibility of Dave returning has been discussed very seriously by a few of us. We want to emphasise that this means no disrespect to Ron Suart whom we all like. But if the club plan to appoint a new manager from outside we would like Dave to be considered. A lot of the lads have a tremendous respect for him. We have discussed a petition, but we will wait until we can get all the players together to go into it more fully'. This was a pretty clear message to the Chelsea board. The rarely-reticent Pratt was for once unavailable for comment but given the need to steady the boat, the sentiment of squad members must have been hard to ignore.

A piece of good news was John Hollins signing a lucrative new contract, having been in dispute with the club since his 21st birthday that June, ironically with Docherty publicly supporting the player's wage demands, and in doing so going against the club hierarchy. This ended the talk of the midfielder leaving and, as he said, 'now that we have settled our differences, I can get on with the serious business of playing football'. Hollins was clearly a key part of Chelsea's future, and it was clearly good news to have such a key man content and fully focussing on his job. Tambling, previously unsettled, was also happy to stay. 'I had the feeling I wasn't really wanted but that has all changed'.

To the credit of Suart and Pratt, that was the focal point of the midfield and the previous season's leading scorer both sorted out. Though Osgood's apparent discontent was still a concern, the new manager, whoever that was, was certainly inheriting a more settled squad. The *Chelsea News*, often well-informed, reckoned that Eddie McCreadie, who had submitted a number of transfer requests could go to Sunderland and that Boyle (21 on Christmas Day) and Houseman were both apparently expected to leave. Thankfully, In the end all three stayed but this reveals some of the challenges the new man faced.

Bonetti was in positive mood. 'You will see a new Chelsea tomorrow. This week has brought a big lift in the atmosphere. We had been getting mixed up for weeks tactically. Confidence and spirit had been sagging'. There was clearly a feeling that, for all the affection many held for Docherty, his departure had cleared the air and reduced tension around the club.

Suart had the week to work with the players before the Saturday visit of Everton. He was not helped by the absence of Hollins with a knee strain. Thomson was the only man dropped after the Leeds debacle, with Butler moving to right-back, McCreadie to his usual left-back role and Houseman coming in as Chelsea lined up:- Bonetti; Butler, Hinton, Harris, McCreadie; Cooke, Boyle, Osgood; Houseman, Baldwin, Tambling.

The Everton programme contained a letter to supporters from Pratt. Lacking grace, it pointedly failed to thank Docherty, though the chairman was right when pointing out the lack of success in the League since the middle of the previous season. 'We can all help by eager, loyal and tolerant support of the Team during the next few weeks' he reasoned. The *Daily Telegraph* hoped the supporters would back the club and the team. 'Docherty has gone, and no amount of chanting will bring him back'.

The stadium announcer said 'Chelsea will need your support today.

Can I ask for a real cheer, not only when they come out but for the whole game' and the support that day was certainly generally positive. What the chairman thought, though, when Docherty's name was chanted by The Shed, who also regaled him with 'Pratt Must Go', is easy to imagine.

Alan Ball put Everton ahead, but an extremely late Baldwin equaliser earned a hard-fought point against a very decent opposition. As the match programme said, 'there was a big improvement in work-rate and all-round teamwork'. Chelsea were less frenetic than under Docherty but the spirit was widely praised. Suart, who thought the display 'not perfect, but encouraging', felt Osgood, who played in midfield, had his best game since his comeback.

John Arlott was one of the great cricket writers and broadcasters of the age. Turning his hand to football, in *The Observer* he wondered whether Docherty 'may have burnt out the side's highest pace'.

Despite the managerial uncertainty there was a host of transfer speculation in the Sunday tabloids. *The People* reported that Nottingham Forest were expected to make a club record bid for Osgood, who 'fancies a break with Chelsea'. He apparently wanted European football which Forest could offer him immediately. They allegedly understood Chelsea were in the mood to sell him, but the reality was the club were unlikely to part with one of their star attractions, and definitely not before a new appointee arrived and took stock. Take Osgood out of the equation and, apart from the erratic Cooke, there was little genuine flair and creativity in the team.

Suart apparently convinced the board a traditional winger was needed. He had supposedly ordered scouting reports on Scottish wingers Peter Cormack (Hibs), Arthur Duncan (Partick Thistle), Tommy McLean (Kilmarnock) and Alex Edwards (Dunfermline), and was also potentially interested in highly-rated wide-man Len Glover of Charlton.

A free week due to Home International matches gave Suart a clear run to work with the players and the board time to decide who they wanted to manage the club long-term - him, Sexton, Harris, McGarry or anyone else. In the next round of the London Challenge Cup, at Millwall, Osgood managed to get himself booked for a comment to the referee, indicative of his growing ability to fall out with officials. As three bookings could lead to a suspension, it was a trait he could do with losing. Although the club had in the short-term banned transfers out, Aston Villa watched Kirkup and Fascione.

19-year-old centre-half Colin Waldron, bought by Docherty from Bury for £25,000 that summer, had struggled to settle at the club, had been withdrawn at half-time in the League Cup defeat at Middlesbrough and not selected since. Stories appeared regarding him being unhappy both about being dropped and the crowd reaction to his performances, and him having talks with Suart as a result. Burnley were interested in signing him, and it appeared possible that his mutually agreed departure might not wait for a permanent manager to be appointed.

As it happened, the managerial appointment was extremely imminent. On Monday 21st October, Dave Sexton was duly appointed Chelsea's seventh permanent manager, age just 37. Arsenal Secretary Bob Wall gave the move his blessing. 'It is obvious that a man of his calibre and ability could not be held as a Number Two for long, but we had hoped it would have been longer'. Pratt, unsurprisingly, was extremely pleased to make the appointment, telling the *Evening Standard* 'we are absolutely delighted. We have the greatest respect and admiration for him and regard him as the best man in the world for getting the team going'. A contract had yet to be signed, and a duration agreed, but it was clear all parties were happy. There is a photograph of Sexton and Pratt taken that day, standing on The Shed terrace, looking very relaxed.

Negotiations had begun between the two chairmen the previous week and Sexton made his decision over the weekend. It was believed his salary would be around £5,000 a year. 'It was not easy. Arsenal are a very good club and looked after me very well. I had three happy years at Chelsea and that swayed my decision. My aim is to get co-operation on and off the field, so that everyone gives something extra'. He talked about blending people together and making sure they were fit enough. 'My immediate job is to work on spirit and morale'. The fact that the squad clearly wanted him must have helped Pratt and his board decide he was the right appointee. Ron Harris was clearly pleased, commenting 'we gained a lot of respect for Dave when he was our coach, and he had a great deal to do with our success during that period'. He stressed that the players did not directly approach the directors about him as had been stated. 'We felt that it was not our place to do so because it is their job to make decisions like that'.

After the high-maintenance Docherty, it was clear that Pratt and the club hierarchy were delighted to have appointed a more considered, reserved man, who dealt with the press as part of his job but did not thrive on creating headlines in the way his predecessor did. Although Sexton had resigned from Leyton Orient after less than a year as manager, his coaching record at Chelsea, Fulham and Arsenal had earned him great respect within the game and it was therefore no surprise to see him taking a managerial role at a First Division club. His playing career at Crystal Palace had been curtailed through a cartilage injury, he was seen as a talented, forward-thinking coach and he had worked with many of the current squad.

Suart was naturally disappointed, having hoped he would have longer to prove himself, but agreed to continue as assistant-manager. Sexton made it clear he was happy to assess the squad before deciding if new blood was needed, though clearly given the position in the table and the 32 goals conceded in 12 League games, with only 15 scored, reinforcements were likely to be essential. Pratt advised that 'money is always available and if Dave wants new players, he can have them' though Chelsea had consistently made a transfer surplus during Docherty's reign, so the new man would have been under no illusions about the need to balance the books.

That evening Chelsea played at Derby County in a testimonial game for their ex-players Jack Parr and Ralph Hann. This was a perfect opportunity for Sexton to look at his new charges in a non-pressurised match environment. He chose a strong team, though after McCreadie damaged his hamstring playing for Scotland, the full-backs were Butler and Thomson, neither previously assured of a regular place. The return from injury of Hollins was welcome and he scored in a 2-1 defeat. Tambling had to be substituted for Fascione and this was to be his last appearance for two months as he became troubled by what was initially seen as a mystery stomach injury. Later that week he was taken into hospital for observation, worrying for both player and club.

Wheels had been set in motion to sell Waldron to Burnley and Sexton saw no need to intervene. He played just ten games, including the 6-2 home thrashing by Southampton where he was seen as particularly culpable. Though he might well have improved, and indeed he went on to enjoy a very decent career at Burnley, he clearly did not fit at Chelsea. He was sold for £30,000, useful money in the bank.

The new manager did not have to wait long for his first serious test, a League visit to Leicester City on the Wednesday. In the absence of Tambling he replaced Houseman with Fascione but chose the core of the side who had underperformed for much of that season. His first selection lined up:- Bonetti; Butler, Hinton, Harris, McCreadie; Hollins, Boyle; Fascione, Osgood, Baldwin, Cooke.

The visitors took the lead through a Willie Bell own-goal, doubled it through John Boyle and looked good for a very welcome three points, forcing Peter Shilton into a series of saves. Leicester made a tactical change, moved centre-half Bobby Roberts up front and he scored two in three minutes, emphasising to Sexton that he had much work to do. As he said after the game 'we should have won...I am confident we can do a lot better'. Importantly, though, he 'was delighted by the spirit the boys showed' though the *Daily Mail* thought that at times there were signs of 'disturbed morale, tactical confusion and utter bewilderment in Chelsea's ranks'. Butler was praised for fitting well into the defence.

Osgood, picked for England Under-23's a year earlier before his leg break, was selected for the game against Wales the following week, alongside Alan Birchenall of Sheffield United and Manchester United's Brian Kidd. He had bulked up a bit during his layoff and had yet to return to peak form, but hopes were high that, if he could regain it, the sky was the limit.

The match programme for the next game, at home to West Ham three days later, welcomed Sexton's appointment. 'The general acclaim with which his arrival has been received is, in itself, a true guide to the esteem in which Dave is held...Dave himself would be the first to say that he has not come back to Stamford Bridge to be popular...Rather will success be his yardstick'. It mentioned the regard the squad held him in. Sexton commented 'the immediate job is to get down to work with the players - every day, every hour is important'. He showed the team the classic Hungary v Portugal game from the 1966 World Cup to emphasise how 4-2-4 should be played. The *Daily Mail* quoted him stressing 'you will not be seeing ultra-defensive methods. We will not be packing the penalty area'.

West Ham were below Chelsea in the table, and had yet to win an away game, but beat an unchanged Chelsea 3-1. Osgood equalised Brian Dear's opener, leaving four men, including goalkeeper Bobby Ferguson, floundering in the mud in a wonderful 30 yard run before slotting the ball home. A programme photograph shows him jumping for joy as the ball enters the net, the grounded Ferguson a forlorn figure.

A failure to create chances, coupled with struggling to deal with goalscorers Geoff Hurst (despite a series of rugged challenges on him) and Martin Peters, consigned the home side to comprehensive defeat. Osgood was praised, but there were concerns in the press about Butler's performance. Sexton was disappointed, concerned about fitness and worried about some poor marking. Supporter Geoff Kimber remembers 'kamikaze' Chelsea defending.

Sexton gave a pragmatic message to the *Daily Mail*. 'First priorities? Fitness and organisation...speed of reaction and thinking. I was pleased with the effort, but it is still a fact we lost half chances because we didn't react quickly enough...The new Chelsea I want won't come overnight, nor will it necessarily mean the team looks or plays the same as when I was Chelsea's coach'. He stressed the importance of organisation which he thought had become 'a little slack'. There was clearly a lot of work to be done on the training ground, his natural habitat. He praised Cooke's 'exceptional skill' and saw his own role as getting over the basics then thought it was 'up to the very good players to show me their interpretation of that basic demand'.

Harris was injured so had to drop out of the Under-23 side, though Hollins was called up to accompany Osgood. The *Evening Standard* felt both had started the season indifferently, though Hollins' contract dispute may have affected him. Osgood's work rate was criticised (not for the first or last time) and they felt that 15 games in, he should have recovered full match fitness.

Manchester United were interested in buying Tambling despite his recurring stomach problem. United boss Matt Busby was supposedly ready to pay £80,000 and spoke to Suart who said Arsenal and Coventry were also interested in the forward, but stressed he was not for sale. It was thought United might follow up their interest when he regained fitness.

Boyle and Thomson were both unhappy with their basic wage offer so declined new contract offers for their 21st birthdays, even though they were on a £30-a-point bonus. Pratt told the *Daily Mail* that the club could not change contracts in mid-season, though the bonus system might be changed, though in the end several established players received new contracts as the club tried to tie down key squad members.

The Chelsea youth production line was by no means as prolific as six or seven years earlier, when the likes of Bonetti, Terry Venables, Barry Bridges, Tambling, Ken Shellito, Allan Harris and Bert Murray all came through to be first-team regulars within a couple of years of each other, followed a couple of years later by Ron Harris, then Hollins, then Osgood and Boyle. There were promising youngsters, certainly, but none considered ready for Division One. Alan Cocks, a 16-year-old centre-forward from Burscough in Lancashire, signed amateur forms with a view to signing as a professional when he was 17.

Chelsea ended October still in 19th place but, in the eyes of the board if not the supporters, the boil had been lanced. Sexton had a tough job on his hands but as a hard-working, diligent coach he had every chance, given time, of turning things around. He would need board support to strengthen the squad but, given that, there was room for optimism.

Leicester City	p14	11pts
West Ham United	p14	10pts
Chelsea	**p14**	**10pts**
Coventry City	p14	9pts
Sheffield United	p14	8pts
Fulham	p14	7pts

November 1967

Sexton, keen to optimise time spent on the training ground with his new squad, was fortunate in that there were only four games scheduled for November, Chelsea's League Cup run having ended in embarrassing style at Second Division Middlesbrough in September. His forward choices were reduced by the news that Tambling was likely to be out for several weeks after a successful stomach operation.

Peter Osgood's confidence was boosted by scoring one goal and making the other for Don Rogers in a 2-1 win for England Under-23's at Wrexham. A mix of squad members, reserves and youngsters beat Millwall 3-2 to reach the London Challenge Cup Semi-Finals.

A trip to Burnley, for whom Colin Waldron made his home debut, proved highly controversial, but at least demonstrated there was nothing wrong with Sexton's team spirit. Joe Kirkup came in for Geoff Butler, the only line-up change. Osgood put Chelsea ahead in an ill-tempered, highly physical game with just seven minutes to go. Five minutes later he had another disallowed, despite protests. In the last minute, a Willie Morgan free-kick was swung over and Peter Bonetti, under pressure from Willie Irvine, dropped the ball over the line. Cue apoplectic protests as a swarm of visiting players argued with referee Keith Styles that the goalkeeper had been unfairly jostled, but to no avail.

Captain Ron Harris led the protests, and a picture shows John Boyle, Eddie McCreadie, Charlie Cooke and John Hollins also berating the hapless Styles, who stumbled after being jostled. A policemen had to go onto the pitch to restore order. Harris was booked and Styles advised he was also reporting a number of others. 'One is Harris, but I cannot reveal the number or identity of the other players. I think their behaviour was ungentlemanly and completely pointless because the match was over'. Styles actually checked with a linesman before confirming the goal. Bonetti, not a man prone to over-reaction, complained 'it was one of the most blatant fouls I have ever suffered'. Harris added 'Peter was blatantly charged in the back just as he was picking the ball out of the air. It was a diabolical goal'. The *Daily Telegraph* thought the behaviour deplorable, and Burnley chairman Bob Lord, a man with a historic dislike of the visitors, criticised their defensive tactics.

Although the draw meant ten matches without a win, Chelsea's display was encouraging, their 4-3-3 system seen as 'flexible and impressive'. The *Daily Mail* thought it their best performance of the season and, though the incidents at the end drew unfavourable newspaper headlines, it seemed Sexton had a group who were prepared to fight for the cause.

Losing 1-0 to non-League Dagenham in the Semi-Final of the London Challenge Cup was chastening, given that five men with first-team experience played, and maybe demonstrated that there was insufficient challenge to the established first-teamers from within the club. Worse, full-back Jim Thomson was sent off for dissent, ludicrous behaviour in such a relatively unimportant match.

Another week on the training ground reaped dividends when the long winless run ended in some style with a 3-0 dismissal of Sheffield Wednesday. Boyle had an excellent game, making a goal for Hollins after two minutes and adding a well-taken second. A back-to-form Osgood wrapped things up with a well-taken third, a 'He's Peter Osgreat' headline in the *Sunday Mirror* summing up a classy individual display that promised much for the future. Ken Jones in the *Daily Mirror* described 'a team that had lost its desire to run and the spirit that made it tick. A month ago Peter Osgood was still groping for his form in a gloomy comeback. But this was more like the old Chelsea and, almost as important, a sign of a new Osgood...With sterner training, the edge is returning to his skill'. McCreadie was able to attack, almost at will, as a 'fast, clever, aggressive' Chelsea controlled the game. The *Sunday Mirror* felt the defence, keeping its first clean sheet since the opening day of the season, had not 'looked as tight and confident for a while'. The press praised Chelsea's spirit and how Sexton seemed to have already transformed morale. The newcomer was understandably delighted. 'Now they know they can do it, the confidence will return. Now we can start to move'.

The fall-out from the Burnley game continued, as five players were reprimanded by the FA for 'ungentlemanly behaviour' after the highly-disputed late equaliser. As well as the booked Harris, referee Styles also reported Bonetti, Kirkup, McCreadie and Osgood.

The following Saturday Chelsea travelled to London rivals Tottenham Hotspur, their conquerors in the FA Cup Final the previous May. The game was played against a backdrop of crowd disorder at the Park Lane End which caused referee Mr J.E. Carr to briefly hold up play. On the pitch, Tottenham dominated, winning 2-0, though Chelsea did create chances and Harris did his usual effective marking job on Jimmy Greaves.

The final November game was the visit of table-topping Manchester United. Denis Law was out injured but Bobby Charlton and George Best, two massive crowd-pullers, were playing, helping guarantee a huge attendance for what was always one of the very biggest games of any season at Stamford Bridge.

Interviewed by the *Daily Mail* a bullish Sexton emphasised 'I believe in a positive approach to these games. I would not destroy the shape and style of my side to counter what someone else is planning. That is the negative way, the way of people who haven't confidence in their players. There will be a lot of good players on this pitch. They'll have to think about Osgood and Cooke just as much as we will about Best and Charlton'.

The club reckoned they could have sold the 12,000 seats three times over. Chelsea tried to stop supporters climbing into the game by covering fences and railings with non-drying paint. Stadium capacity was officially 60,000 so it was something of a surprise when the gates were locked well before kick-off with just 54,712 inside. Supporter Brian Gaches remembers the crush in an uncontrolled seething mass on the concourse outside The Shed turnstiles at this match, and other big games around this time. Clubs, and not just Chelsea, took crowd safety far less seriously in those days. This was the author's second Chelsea match and the enormous mass of people on the Fulham Road at midday, the crush both to get in and on the terraces all stay with him 54 years later.

The game, a cracking match between two enterprising sides in an electrifying atmosphere, ended a 1-1 draw, and both sides were praised for their performances. Baldwin's spectacular header following a flowing move was enjoyed by millions on *Match Of The Day*, Brian Kidd equalising before half-time.

Charlie Cooke, given a roving role, gave a display that Hugh McIlvanney, in *The Observer*, felt was his finest and most effective at Stamford Bridge to date, overshadowing even the impressive Osgood. *The People* headline 'Swinging Osgood Knocks Best Off Top Spot' emphasised neatly how the pair were arguably the most glamorous figures in English football at that time.

McIlvanney argued that 'Chelsea's superior pace and more animated aggression might easily have left the champions clearly beaten'. United's main threat, Best, endured the close attentions of Harris who was booked. Best was booed for supposed play-acting but had to endure 'the recurring cruelty of Harris's fouls'. Fringe players Kirkup and Fascione were picked out for having achieved a new lease of life under Sexton, and Hollins for driving the team on. Although still 18th in the table, the mood around the club was increasingly positive. Supporter Geoff Kimber thought that game a turning point in the season, an impressive display the prelude to brighter times ahead.

The Sunday tabloid papers had their usual speculative sweep through transfer rumours. Suart travelled to Glasgow to see if any Scottish clubs were interested in doing a swap deal involving Jim Thomson. Greenock Morton and Kilmarnock were supposedly interested. Rumours persisted that Chelsea would go back in for Kilmarnock's Tommy McLean, who had turned them down that summer as he preferred home life in Scotland but had apparently changed his mind. *The People* reported that Chelsea were supposedly interested in Darlington striker Bryan Conlon, though Sexton may well have been setting his sights higher.

A number of papers reported that Newcastle were ready to make a bid for Cooke, although Sexton was not interested in selling the skilful Scot. Butler had lost his place in the team and West Bromwich were apparently willing to bid £60,000 for him. If the manager did not rate the full-back, then a deal of that size must have attracted him.

The purchase that did happen was a big one, passing all the Sunday paper transfer experts by, when highly-promising Sheffield United striker Alan Birchenall signed. The cost, £100,000, equalled Chelsea's highest ever fee paid for Tony Hateley a year earlier. United wanted to swap Birchenall for Cooke who, as he revealed in '*The Bonnie Prince*', was angry and 'crushed' as he felt the manager, in offering him the chance to talk to United manager John Harris, was ready to sell without giving him a chance. Sexton later told the Scot he had not wanted him to leave, but it was surprising he did not summarily turn Harris down.

Birchenall seemed a shrewd signing, a hard-working goalscoring striker who would strengthen attacking options. Whether this would mean Tambling, the subject of interest from a number of clubs, would be sold was a matter for conjecture. In '*Bring Back The Birch*', Birchenall described how he went from earning £30 a week and £5 appearance money in Sheffield to £60 a week and £10 a point at Chelsea, a significant increase. Sexton announced his new signing would go straight into the team at Sunderland.

So, a month into Sexton's reign, Chelsea had won just once,

against a poor Sheffield Wednesday side, but had given good accounts of themselves against Burnley and Manchester United. Importantly, the shoal of negative stories about the club had ended, as the board had hoped and expected, and though it would clearly take time, there was confidence that the new man could turn things round.

Leicester City	p18 14pts
Chelsea	**p18 14pts**
Fulham	p17 13pts
West Ham	p17 11pts
Sheffield United	p17 11pts
Coventry City	p17 10pts

December 1967

Two days after signing, Alan Birchenall duly made his debut at Sunderland. Not unexpectedly, Joe Fascione was the unlucky player to make way, after performing well in six successive games. Manager Sexton sympathised. 'It really hurts me to tell Joe he is out of the side. I want to let him down gently because he has done so much for me and the side since he came in. He is a hard worker and a great fighter. Joe has done an excellent job, and this is by no means the end of his first-team appearances. I cannot praise him too highly and leaving him out was a difficult decision'. That may well have been the case, but the reality was that Fascione never began another first-team game for the club.

Birchenall started with a bang, netting after four minutes with his second touch. Charlie Cooke scored a second and it looked as though Chelsea would win comfortably. Defensive frailties let Colin Todd and Neil Martin score for the home side, though they sandwiched a third for the visitors through Tommy Baldwin. Chelsea ran out 3-2 victors, impressing with their speed, teamwork and skills, and deserving a more comfortable victory.

Cooke, again, stood out from the rest and Geoff Butler, in for the injured Hinton, had a decent game. New boy Birchenall, predictably, was delighted, advising *The People* 'I was thrilled to bits to score the early goal, but let's face it I should have had two more'. His beaming positivity was obvious. 'This is what I have wanted all my life – to play in a side like Chelsea'.

Osgood, critical to Sexton's plans and keen to gain international recognition, was in negotiation for a new contract and was ready to tie himself to Chelsea for two years plus the option of two more. 'I am happy at the Bridge. There is no question of wanting to leave Chelsea. But I feel that a three-year contract with a similar option is a little too long. It is really great here now and I am enjoying my football. Dave Sexton has made a tremendous difference to the side. Some of his coaching ideas are out of this world - simple...but so effective'.

Sunderland approached Chelsea about buying Butler, who impressed against them. He cost £60,000 so Chelsea were looking for £65,000. He received a £3,000 signing-on fee on joining and, should he move, would be in line for another, as he had not asked for a transfer. The *Daily Mail* reported that the club needed to recoup some of the Birchenall fee if Sexton was to further strengthen the squad. This policy would be in line with recent seasons when the club regularly recouped more from transfers than it spent.

Sexton insisted he did not want to sell Butler. 'It's true we have received an enquiry, but there has been no firm bid and anyway I want Geoff to stay'. He was selected for the Wolverhampton Wanderers home game scheduled for Saturday December 9th, but the match was postponed due to snow.

Chelsea were planning to play Bobby Tambling three times in the reserves in a week in a bid to get him match-fit after his stomach operation. After two weeks without a game, and hard work on the training ground, Sexton was clearly disappointed to be well-beaten, 3-0 at home by West Bromwich, in an unbelievably 'dull, dreary and depressing' performance. The *Daily Telegraph* criticised Chelsea, presumably particularly aiming at Osgood and Cooke, as 'top-heavy with dribblers...they contrived to make the simple things look horribly difficult...Too many Chelsea players clearly regarded possession as a means of self-advancement'.

Only 27,739 turned out, ten days before Christmas admittedly, but still low considering Chelsea's recent improvement. The *Daily Mail* criticised those who did turn up for their lack of support. 'The encouragement they were prepared to give was almost non-existent, even in the early stages, when Chelsea were at their brightest...Nowhere does there seem less of a bond between players and 'supporters''. Hundreds left when they conceded a third. Sexton admitted 'we were sluggish' and he was right. A bad day all round, leaving Chelsea in 18th place with just four wins in 20 League games.

There were mitigations for the display. Birchenall, who had a goal disallowed and whose effort was praised, played with a heavy cold. Osgood hurt his ankle early on (sufficiently badly to miss the England Under-23 game the following midweek) but refused to go off. While he was on the ground injured and his teammates were desperately trying to get play stopped, Albion played to the whistle and Clive Clark scored their opener.

Worryingly, the defence - Butler, Kirkup, Harris, McCreadie - was completely unable to cope with bustling, excellent-in-the-air centre-forward Jeff Astle, and it was apparent Chelsea needed strengthening defensively. One bit of good news was John Boyle signing his new contract on reaching his 21st birthday, beaming 'I'm delighted to stay'.

Next up was a local derby at Fulham. Osgood was passed fit, and the return of Hinton at centre-back allowed Sexton to move Kirkup to his normal right-back position and drop Butler to substitute. Tambling was close to match-fitness but was not risked for that one. A decent attendance of 33,500 turned out despite the game being two days before Christmas. Chelsea raced to a 2-0 lead through Cooke and Baldwin but allowed Joe Gilroy and Robert Moss to earn their local rivals a welcome point in their seemingly perennial relegation struggle. A point thrown away. Hollins limped off, and was doubtful for Arsenal on Boxing Day, but all other squad members were due to train on Christmas Day.

Despite an anti-social kick-off time, 11.30 on Boxing Day, 51,700 crowded into Stamford Bridge for the Arsenal game. Half-price admission, withdrawn after youngsters broke the crossbar in a September friendly against a British Olympic XI, was reinstated. Tambling played his first game for ten weeks, replacing the injured Hollins as Boyle moved into midfield.

Arsenal were mid-table. Obviously, Sexton knew a lot about them and must have been especially pleased to beat them 2-1, his tactical plans triumphant as Alan Birchenall scored both. Tambling was unsurprisingly a bit rusty but he, Osgood and Birchenall were praised for their defensive work when it was necessary. Almost inevitably there was bad blood between the teams. In a highly physical game, referee Arthur Diamond was indulgent towards Harris and Arsenal hard-man Ian Ure 'though both tackled like threshing machines' according to the *Daily Mail*. Ex-colleagues George Graham and Hinton threw mud at each other, and Graham seemed to butt Hinton, but no action was taken. Fog caused problems for spectators at both ends and some apparently tried, unsuccessfully, to get their money refunded as they could not see.

The Arsenal return game was four days later. Chelsea, still missing the indefatigable Hollins, earnt a hard-fought draw through a disputed Osgood penalty in another competitive game. They set out for a point, with a very defensive display which involved Cooke and Osgood in withdrawn roles, but the manager would have been heartened that the team worked so hard, and defended so fiercely, conceding just once, to John Radford.

The Arsenal home programme included a revealing interview with Sexton. 'I aim for a fluid, all-purpose team, with players able to fulfil a variety of roles, sometimes even in the same match...it helps to have players in the side who can adapt themselves'. He took skill for granted at that level. 'I regard the ability to concentrate - in training and in matches - as the most important part of a player's make-up. He builds his game from that. It is also essential to be professional in outlook seven days a week'. He reiterated that he saw his first priority 'to work on club spirit and morale'. A scouting network had been reintroduced, having unwisely been scrapped a few years earlier. For a man so tactically astute, he was reticent about the use of substitutes by choice, having failed to use one in his first two months at the helm. In the *Daily*

Telegraph the manager further expounded his approach to his job. 'My job is to direct and jog memories, to suggest what might happen, but that is all. I can't play the game in advance. I can do nothing on the field. Football is for players. They must do it'.

A feature in that Arsenal programme stated Chelsea had sold 302,547 programmes to total crowds at 11 home games of 368,642, the average of 82% 'well up on previous seasons'. The programme had rightly won awards, with interesting features and no adverts, unlike many club's offerings which could be read inside ten minutes.

Terry Venables, ex-Chelsea captain, had been dropped by Tottenham and rumours appeared in various papers that Sexton had expressed interest and he was bound for Stamford Bridge, having worked with the manager during his previous spell at the club. An intelligent, self-confident, ball-playing midfielder, Venables fell out with Docherty and may have fancied linking up with his successor, but nothing came of the stories.

Inconsistency still abounded and the defence was still leaking too many goals but, though the team ended the year in a precarious 16th place, just four points off the relegation places, things definitely seemed on the up as 1968 began. The *Daily Telegraph* was full of praise for Sexton but, presciently, felt that 'Chelsea need a couple more years to become a power in the land and challenge in Europe'.

Chelsea	**p23 20pts**
Southampton	p23 19pts
Leicester City	p23 18pts
Sunderland	p23 18pts
Sheffield United	p23 18pts
Fulham	p22 16pts
Coventry City	p24 15pts

January 1968

The New Year started well for Peter Bonetti, John Hollins and Peter Osgood when all were called up for an England get-together later that month. 35 men were called up, and it was assumed that those attending were in Ramsey's mind for the World Cup in Mexico two years hence. Given how well Birchenall had started his Chelsea career it was slightly surprising he was not in the group.

The *Evening Standard* reported that Jim Thomson had turned down a new contract offer on his 21st birthday in October as he wanted to return to Glasgow and was being watched by Glasgow Rangers. The contract would have given him an extra £15 a week. He had made 36 appearances in seven different positions for Chelsea since May 1966 without ever establishing himself in the side.

More worrying, *The People* ran a headline story **'Osgood: I Want**

More Cash'. Despite his positive words only a few weeks earlier, the club were apparently facing a showdown with a player who was 21 in February and therefore entitled to a new contract. Player and board were seemingly some distance apart. 'The feeling at Stamford Bridge is that Osgood, although rich in potential, is not producing the consistency to merit a huge pay rise'. He said he would wait and see what the club offered but, asked what would happen if they turned down his demands, said 'you know as well as I do'. This may well have been a negotiating tactic, but was not what the supporters, their affection for the player undimmed by his inconsistency since returning from his broken leg, wanted to read.

The first game of the New Year was at Southampton, renowned for their highly physical approach. Bonetti missed out with flu, giving Tommy Hughes a rare first-team game. Chelsea conceded three goals, though Hughes was blameless and considered to have had a solid game. Luckily, the forwards scored five in an impressive attacking effort, gaining a form of revenge for the 6-2 home thrashing in September. Charlie Cooke, Tommy Baldwin, Bobby Tambling, John Boyle and Osgood all netted as the goals were shared around. Cooke shone, despite the muddy pitch, scoring one and making two, supporter Barry Holmes remembering him playing in a freer, deeper midfield role and dominating the game. Birchenall, too, was praised for tormenting the home side, even though he did not score. The defence again struggled in the air, against Martin Chivers, Ron Davies and Mike Channon, and the need for a tall, assertive centre-half was becoming ever more urgent despite the win. Boyle, seemingly happier after signing his new contract, again impressed, wearing the No.4 shirt in the absence of the injured Hollins. Holmes felt this game was the first real sign of a fresh beginning under Sexton.

Tambling was punched on the jaw and knocked out as Southampton again demonstrated their tendency to employ football's dark arts. 'My jaw is not so sore, and the swelling has gone down. I feel much better' he bravely commented afterwards.

Geoff Butler duly signed for Sunderland for £65,000, a few weeks after the move was first mooted. He only started eight games for Chelsea, and clearly suffered homesickness. 'I just didn't like London. The Chelsea lads were smashing (but) the place is so vast that your colleagues live miles away…Not being in the Chelsea team regularly did not help'. The board originally rejected the idea but changed their minds at that week's board meeting, presumably after the manager confirmed he was comfortable to lose him. The manager did not say whether the sale meant a purchase was imminent. The *Sunday Mirror* reported a strange tale. Butler was apparently promised a £1,000 loan for accommodation by Tommy Docherty. After The Doc went, club officials said they knew nothing about it. He went to see Butler and offered to loan him the money himself. In the end the club came to an agreement with the player, who admitted he was glad to move on. The move certainly suited both parties, though it did mean Chelsea were light of full-back cover.

The Liverpool home match on Saturday January 13th was postponed because of snow, meaning a fortnight break after the Southampton trip before another match, at Stoke. Hollins returned, but not in midfield, where Boyle kept his place, reward for his excellent form, but at right-back. He replaced Joe Kirkup, who as it turned out never made a League start for Chelsea again.

Birchenall scored four minutes from the end of a 'tepid, thoroughly disappointing clash' to earn a welcome 1-0 victory, after England goalkeeper Gordon Banks inexplicably dropped the ball. Chelsea were accused of setting up over-defensively and applying an over-vigorous approach, but given that Stoke were no strangers to a rigorous physicality themselves, Sexton will have lost no sleep over any criticism, the two points being the primary issue as he looked to continue the rise up the table. A concern was Osgood's poor form, his contract negotiations continuing without resolution.

Chelsea had drawn Ipswich Town, at home, in the FA Cup Third Round, and were quoted at 16-1 for the cup. Manchester United were 8-1 favourites. Chelsea trained for FA Cup-ties that season at Brighton, as they had the previous year. As well as being a welcome break from routine for the squad, it was handy for Sexton who lived close by.

A decent attendance of 42,986, paying £13,241, watched a comfortable 3-0 home victory in a game they dominated, despite Ipswich's defensive tactics. Kirkup came in for Hinton, who hurt a knee in training. Birchenall scored two classy goals and Tambling scored his 23rd FA Cup goal, setting a club record. Birchenall and Cooke came in for particular praise, the former having only been on the losing side once since his arrival and netting a highly encouraging six goals in eight matches. Tony Pawson, in *The Observer*, praised Birchenall's aerial ability, his power and his finishing. He also felt that Cooke was 'as clever a dribbler as Stanley Matthews ever was'. Praise indeed. The *Kensington Post* called it 'a rare clean game', in an era when many encounters descended into excess physicality and bad temper.

The game kicked off at 2.30 as Fulham were at home as well, to non-League Macclesfield, kicking-off at 3.30. Supporters got there late, some of the turnstile staff were working at Fulham so not all the gates were open, and there was significant congestion outside at kick-off. These problems were entirely predictable and did not reflect well on club organisation. Supporter Barry Holmes remembers that after Chelsea's game had finished, he and his friends rushed down to Craven Cottage to watch the second-half, joining hundreds of others who had the same idea because Fulham were losing. With a cup upset on the cards they all became Macclesfield fans for 45 minutes, until Johnny Haynes 'started to take it seriously' and Fulham went on to win 4-2.

Chelsea drew Norwich City or Sunderland at home in the Fourth Round, making the possibility of a good FA Cup run a very real one. They were still only 12-1 to win the cup, which half a century later looks a decent bet.

Juniors Ian 'Chico' Hamilton and Ken Halliday, both 17, signed professional terms. Chelsea were linked with St Mirren centre-half Andy McFadden and speculation continued that Terry Venables was likely to return to Stamford Bridge. Bristol City were the latest club supposedly interested in signing Joe Fascione.

The club announced that they had sold a record 5,000 seat season-tickets, meaning only 7,000 stand seats, plus the 3,500 unreserved bench seats, went on general sale for every League game. There were no terrace season-tickets in those days.

Chelsea ended January in 14th place in the League and with a positive chance of reaching the FA Cup Fifth Round. They were unbeaten in six games with Birchenall's signing quickly paying off. There was still the Osgood contract issue to resolve of course, but generally the situation was significantly more positive than when Sexton had arrived.

February 1968

Another month with just the four scheduled games beckoned, including the rearranged visit by Liverpool and the FA Cup-tie against Norwich. It started with a potentially difficult home encounter with Nottingham Forest. Peter Osgood headed a superb winner in a tough 1-0 victory, from a Charlie Cooke corner. The *News Of The World* pulled no punches. 'A savage, ugly game which threatened frequently to explode into open warfare was won the hard way by Chelsea'. Only the excellence of Forest goalkeeper Peter Grummitt stopped Chelsea achieving a comfortable win as Cooke, in front of Scotland boss Bobby Brown, turned in an illuminating display. Supporter Geoff Kimber remembers one run where he beat six men. Alan Birchenall had to go off with a damaged ankle after a hard challenge by Terry Hennessey, who was booed by an incensed home crowd for the rest of the match. Hennessey responded by accusing opposition players of trying to get him sent off, claiming they were responsible for 'starting the rough stuff' and concluding that 'both sides did things they shouldn't have'.

Three clean sheets in a row were testament to Sexton's coaching and organisational skill. Though Hinton returned against Forest, it was evident that he needed a commanding centre-half. John Hollins and Osgood played for the England Under-23's in Glasgow that midweek, both seen as having the chance to establish themselves in the senior squad.

A trip to Coventry City, trapped in the relegation zone, seemed an opportunity for two more points and to extend the seven-match unbeaten run, despite the absence of Birchenall (replaced by Peter Houseman), more so when Tambling put the dominant visitors 1-0 up from 25 yards. The missing of several chances seemed unimportant until Coventry stepped things up after half-time. The midfield missed Hollins, miscast at full-back, Hinton struggled at centre-back (*The People* argued he was 'really a full-back'), the defence looked increasingly uncertain and allowed Gerry Baker and Ernie Hannigan to grab an unexpected victory. The team as a whole looked lethargic and the *Sunday Mirror* summed it up nicely as 'first-half dictators and second-half runners'. This type of casual inconsistency and throwing away of points infuriated Sexton and needed resolving if the quest for honours was to be a serious one.

Linked with a litany of lower-League defenders - Blackpool's Graham Rowe, and Halifax pair Malcolm Russell and Ivan Hampton - what Chelsea actually needed, and quickly, was someone who could come straight into the team at centre-back. High-class talents like Bonetti, Hollins, Cooke, Osgood and Birchenall were of reduced value if the back four could not be relied on.

The team's inconsistency manifested itself spectacularly two days later, with a 3-1 defeat of title-chasing Liverpool in arguably Chelsea's best home performance that season. This despite 18-year-old debutant Stewart Houston having to mark Tony Hateley, a relative flop at Chelsea before being sold earlier the previous summer and hence a man with a point to prove. Houston, normally a full-back, made his debut at centre-half. The *Daily Mail* headline 'Liverpool Legend Is Destroyed – Ruthless Chelsea Hand Out The Hiding Of The Season' summed the display up. Liverpool were 'made to look like a team who have been too long at the top'. Cooke, Osgood and Tambling, who scored twice, tormented the opposition, the absence of Birchenall being barely felt, with Baldwin netting the other. Chelsea competed fiercely and a defence of Hollins, Houston, Harris and McCreadie restricted Liverpool to a single goal, scored by England winger Peter Thompson. A 6-1 scoreline would have not flattered a totally dominant Chelsea.

Scotland manager Bobby Brown, returning to watch Cooke again, much have been again impressed by a virtuoso display that 'was his finest since he moved south' according to the *Evening Standard*, despite him suffering a stomach upset on the day of the game. Geoff Kimber remembers an 'electric atmosphere', which he thought was almost as good as that against Bruges three years later.

In a *Daily Mail* article in the aftermath of the Liverpool victory, Sexton was praised by his players for his impact. Harris commented that 'the difference (he) has made is fantastic. As a team we are playing better now than when we reached Wembley last year'. Optimism abounded before the Norwich FA Cup-tie, as the squad again spent the week training in Brighton.

Sexton observed 'when you are in trouble you must start tightening from the back – like we did...Now we are going well up front too, and Monday's performance against Liverpool was our best all round of the season. That pleased me a lot'. Birchenall was the only new arrival, but the manager stated 'we are now playing the game in different shapes'. He saw Tambling regaining fitness as a big boost. The Mail identified that 'since Sexton took over, he has brought silence to the club of a thousand headlines' a comment that the Chelsea board must have appreciated.

The youth team won 3-0 at Ipswich in the FA Youth Cup. It is instructive to look at the team Chelsea fielded and realise that only Kingsley Whiffen (one game) and Ian Hamilton (five games) ever saw first-team action, and it both cases that was the previous season. There was no wide pipeline of young talent coming through.

Second Division Norwich took around 10,000 supporters to the FA Cup-tie, appetites whetted by a famous 1967 Fourth Round victory at Old Trafford. The lure of the FA Cup was sufficient for the gates to close on 57,987 spectators, the biggest of the day, paying £16,237 and creating a superb atmosphere according to Geoff Kimber, who was there. Again, the attendance was well under stadium capacity when the gates were closed. With Fulham at home in the cup as well, the authorities again tried to spread the load on underground and on the roads, the games kicking off at 2.30pm and 3.30pm respectively. Supporters wore stickers proclaiming 'I'm Backing Chelsea For The Cup', paying homage to the 'I'm Backing Britain' campaign which reached its peak early that year.

In 'a physical and desperately disappointing tie' Chelsea were 1-0 victors, Charlie Cooke scoring from outside the area in the first-half. After the game, which they completely dominated until late on, Chelsea players called Norwich 'bruisers'. Given Hinton had a black eye and damaged cheekbone (later diagnosed as a hairline fracture), Bonetti a bruised hand and Hollins went off with a twisted ankle, they had a point. Norwich striker Hugh Curran, who had an equaliser ruled out for handball, took a different view. 'They had one or two players who dished it out. If they can't take it in return, they shouldn't squeal'. The *Sunday Mirror* called some of Norwich's tackling 'intimidating and dangerous' and it is to Chelsea's credit that they attempted to play football in those circumstances. Boyle, no shrinking violet, observed 'I thought we were supposed to kick the little white round thing'. *The Observer* identified that Boyle had 'emerged from near-anonymity to a mobile all-round ability, while Cooke now employs his ball skills to clear and valuable purpose'. The *Daily Mail* also thought Cooke the key man, reporting that he had lost over a stone in just over three months. 'It was hell. I almost stopped eating…it was my own idea…Luckily it didn't leave me weak, but it was really hard work'.

The Fifth Round draw was not particularly kind to Chelsea, giving them a trip to Sheffield Wednesday, FA Cup opposition for the third year in a row. They were 10-1 to win the competition.

The following weekend was a blank one, the home match with Leeds United postponed as both teams had stars involved in the

Scotland v England game, **Cooke starring in a 1-1 draw.** Sexton was still busy, however, and in a transfer deal arguably as good as has ever been done by the club, bought 21-year-old centre-back David Webb from Southampton, Joe Kirkup going the other way. Chelsea also had to pay £10,000. Webb was valued at £40,000 which, with the benefit of hindsight, was a magnificent piece of business. Sexton had him under his management at Leyton Orient and knew what an asset he was getting.

Kirkup, though letting nobody down, had not been a first-team regular for some time and had started just ten of 28 League matches so far that season. In total he made 69 appearances for the club in the two years since his arrival from West Ham. The *Evening Standard* were underwhelmed and factually wrong regarding the deal, their headline advising readers 'Southampton Sign Kirkup - Chelsea Get Ex-Orient Back And Cash In Exchange'. They described Webb as a utility defender, which was certainly more accurate, though somewhat underplayed the impact he was to have at his new club.

Chelsea official historian Rick Glanvill recounts in *'Chelsea: The Complete Record'* how Webb went to watch the Liverpool game earlier that month and bought tickets for the game from famous ticket tout Stan Flashman outside the ground. Webb was impressed with what he saw, could not wait to join Chelsea and actually took a pay cut from £85 to £65 a week to do so. At one stage it seemed as though it might be Hinton who Chelsea swapped for Webb, but he wanted more money than Southampton were offering.

The crying need for a dominant centre-back had hopefully been answered, though cover at full-back was reduced with Kirkup's departure. Chelsea were apparently interested in teenage keeper Derek Crampton of non-League Spennymoor United though, as with so many of these Sunday paper nuggets of speculation, it came to nothing. The *Chelsea News* reported that wingers Brian Hill of Huddersfield Town and Carlisle United's George McVitie were being watched. Ipswich had a £25,000 bid for the displaced Joe Fascione turned down. George Luke, signed from Newcastle the previous season and a regular in the reserves, sought a move.

Osgood was called into the England party against Scotland that month as a replacement for Manchester United's David Sadler, but was never likely to play. Bonetti had to drop out through injury.

Chelsea ended February in twelfth place, testimony to Sexton's hard work and diligence, and the team's positive response to his coaching ideas. Though European football the following season seemed a long shot, depending as it did on becoming top London club and probably finishing in the top five, they were still in the FA Cup and Webb's arrival would hopefully end one major weakness in the side, aerial defending.

March 1968

David Webb's first game for Chelsea was as tough as it got, at champions Manchester United, who had not lost at home in almost two years and had just beaten Gornik Zabrze 2-0 in the first-leg of the European Cup Quarter-Finals. Though they had slipped slightly over the last month, United were three points clear of Leeds at the top of the table with 13 matches to go and clear favourites for the title.

Eddie McCreadie, hurt playing for Scotland against England, and Hinton, whose hairline cheekbone fracture was likely to keep him out for a month, were both missing so Sexton had to field a John Boyle, Ron Harris, Webb, Jim Thomson defence, the latter's first game since the rout at Leeds in October. Given Hollins was also missing, on paper it looked as though that defence may struggle against a forward line including George Best, Bobby Charlton and Brian Kidd.

In one of their very best performances of that era, the visitors rocked United's title hopes with a spirited, comprehensive and fully deserved 3-1 victory. The *Sunday Mirror* felt United were 'thrashed by a far superior outfit' and could not cope with Chelsea's fast-moving football. They argued that Chelsea 'tackled quickly and hard. Too hard at times', with Harris, taking time off from a highly effective man-marking job on Best, booked for 'a wild tackle' on Charlton, the third time his name had been taken that season in days when bookings were comparatively rare and meaning a likely suspension loomed. Referee Maurice Fussey was criticised for leniency in the face of visiting physicality, but as Sexton delightedly observed, there was now a tremendous confidence for the forthcoming cup-tie.

Charlie Cooke was again the best player on the pitch and Sexton was effusive in his praise. 'Charlie's real value is showing now because we are playing him in a different position practically every week. He has the talent to succeed anywhere'. He was also pleased with reserves Thomson and Houseman for their contributions to a highly efficient team display. Webb and Harris were also widely praised, the new boy defending stoutly and finding time to make the second goal for Tommy Baldwin. Cooke beat three men setting up Bobby Tambling's first, which Kidd equalised, and Peter Osgood rounded off the scoring. Best missed a penalty at 2-1 but Chelsea comfortably hung on.

Chelsea approached the upcoming FA Cup-tie in Sheffield in fine fettle. The mood improved still further with the news that Osgood had signed a new contract after a fortnight's negotiation since his 21st birthday. It was only for two years but Chelsea could exercise a two-year option. Sexton, unsurprisingly, felt 'I am very happy that we have reached agreement'. Tieing down his most valuable player was hugely important for the manager, though what he also needed were consistent top-class displays from someone who had been erratic for much of the season. Cooke and Osgood were Chelsea's two game-changers, and though the Scot was now performing at a consistently high standard, Osgood was not.

For their biggest game so far that season, Chelsea were weakened defensively by the absence of the cup-tied Webb and the still-injured Hinton, so Thomson played centre-back. Hollins and McCreadie returned and Chelsea set-off like a house on fire in front of 49,100 spectators, including a large contingent from London (12 Chelsea Supporters Club coaches were filled), with four corners in the first three minutes. A full-blooded, classic attacking cup-tie ended in a 2-2 draw. Wednesday twice led but Baldwin and Tambling forced a replay the following Tuesday, Chelsea choosing not to risk chasing a winner. Wednesday captain Don Megson felt they treated Chelsea with too much respect and saw his side as favourites in the replay.

As Chelsea recovered from the Saturday game and prepared for the replay, they heard that, should they go through, their Quarter-Final tie would be at Arsenal or Birmingham City, who drew at Highbury and were replaying the same night. Chelsea were unbeaten in 11 replays at Stamford Bridge since 1931. Thomson remained at centre-half and Peter Houseman came in for the injured Baldwin. The gates were again closed, this time ten minutes before kick-off. 55,013 spectators, again well under capacity, paying £15,818.

Clubs were reluctant to make games all ticket unless absolutely necessary, because of the administrative effort required and inconvenience to supporters, but if it had been all-ticket then an extra 5,000 tickets could have been sold. Add those to the 2,000 extra that could have been admitted against Norwich and that is extra revenue of 7,000 terrace tickets at 2/6d (12.5p) or c£850, surely worth a bit of extra administrative effort and ticket office overtime.

The replay was comfortably won 2-0, with excellent goals from Osgood and Tambling, whose fast, swerving free-kick for the second attracted especial praise, bamboozling Wednesday goalkeeper Peter Springett. Cooke's 70 yard run, leaving four defenders in his wake, was a memorable addition to the entertainment. The skills of Cooke and Osgood, allied to the pace and strength of Houseman and Tambling, made a potent combination that evening.

Birmingham surprisingly beat Arsenal and the sixth-round tie at St Andrews was promptly made all-ticket. Chelsea were 5-1 third favourites for the FA Cup behind Leeds and Liverpool and, as supporter Geoff Kimber recalls, 'all Chelsea fans fancied their chances of a second successive Wembley appearance'.

The manager's star continued to rise with a 4-1 demolition of Leicester City. Goals from Baldwin, two from Tambling and an Osgood penalty in the first hour made Chelsea extremely comfortable, before they eased up. *The Observer's* **'New Look Chelsea Impress'** headline summed up the afternoon. The forward line were all the subject of praise, particularly Cooke, who had the crowd chanting his name. John Arlott reckoned Sexton had 'changed the character, but not the characters, of the side. They now play with an air of mutual trust, confident rather than desperate'. Two new players had been bought but most of the side were indeed inherited by the manager, who deserved enormous credit for the clear improvement in performances and results. Webb made his home debut, and it was already clear that he would be a significant asset, his aggression, commitment and bravery making an immediate difference. As the *Chelsea News* observed, he 'seemed a strong and fearless player'. The seventh successive home win was a post-war club record.

Before the Leicester game there was a minute's silence in memory of ex-chairman Charles Pratt, who had passed away earlier that day. He had been a club director for 32 years, was appointed vice-chairman in 1952 and chairman in mid-1966 after the untimely death of Joe Mears. Although not as strong a chairman as Mears, it was still the loss of more valuable board experience - Pratt had been working on a new tenancy agreement for Stamford Bridge. Board member Leonard Withey was made acting-chairman.

The Observer carried a Hugh McIlvanney interview with Cooke, who had lost 16lb since pre-season started. He had put on weight when he joined in 1966, during a period of enforced idleness, and had struggled to lose it. He made it clear he had total faith in Sexton and realised his previous approach 'has been dilettante'. He had a 'brilliant' game for Scotland against England two weeks earlier. He had worked hard on delivering an end product, a shot or a cross, but was worried that 'the way the side is developing I feel that Dave may find eventually that I am a bit of a luxury. He may have to give me the elbow'. Given Cooke's form at that time that seemed unlikely, though the anxiety evident is one so talented shows the pressure he felt under.

A midweek home encounter with Leeds United, third in the table and just a point behind leaders Manchester City and Manchester United, was a good test for tenth place Chelsea. Leeds were unbeaten in 20 games and Chelsea had been defeated just once in 15 matches. Leeds would go top if they won, whereas Chelsea would rise to sixth should they prevail. In the event, it was a hugely competitive 0-0 draw, The *Birmingham Daily Post* wryly commented that there were more fouls than goal chances and the *Daily Telegraph* observed that '**no long-lasting friendships were struck up last night**'. Cooke, on fire for the first 30 minutes and inevitably the target of the hard men among Don Revie's side, was booked for retaliation on Terry Cooper, his fourth that season, meaning he and Harris could in theory miss the FA Cup Semi-Final if Chelsea beat Birmingham in ten days' time.

The draw was a very decent result for Chelsea which, taken with their defeats of Liverpool and Manchester United, were a strong indicator of developments under Sexton, who, it should be remembered, had been in post less than five months. The *Evening Standard* had a special feature by Bernard Joy on the changes implemented by the new man, with a 'Chelsea 'Kids' Grow Up' headline. 'They have achieved the tactical revolution Docherty wanted...Osgood, Hollins and Boyle have come of age within the last eight months'. He felt they continued to be competitive and well-organised, with a high work rate and individual ability, but their assets were now harnessed to a higher productivity. He saw them as a good bet for the FA Cup. He reckoned 'it was a failure in temperament, rather than lack of ability or fitness' that led to the 1965 and 1966 Semi-Final and 1967 Final defeats, crediting Sexton with 'the sharp rise in form and optimism', having won 12, drawn 7 and lost 4 of his 23 games in charge. He 'has made the vital contributions of encouraging a player to the limit of his resources, his colleagues to cover his weaknesses, and of cementing everyone together'.

Sexton felt the team were 'merely finding their own level', and that they were climbing the table to where they should be. 'The remarkable thing about the side is the wonderful amount of experience, despite including so many young players'. Two 21-year-olds, Hollins and Boyle, had 319 first-team appearances between them.

Two leading players were also expressed understandably positive views. Osgood commented 'our attack is a blend of individuals of different types. Tambling is a goal-snatcher, Baldwin takes the weight off the others by his front running, Cooke and myself take on opponents and Birchenall gets goals as well as beating opponents'. Harris observed 'we used to field an extra defender and so hand the initiative to the opposition. We have cut this policy out and are going for goals, with the result that we are showing more consistent form at home'.

The games were coming thick and fast, and three days later a trip to relegation-threatened West Ham produced a 1-0 victory, Osgood netting in the fifth minute in one of his finest displays of the season. Tactically Sexton got it spot on. The fit-again Hinton played alongside Harris, Webb omitted as he was cup-tied for the Birmingham game. Harris man-marked Geoff Hurst, who had dominated in the encounter at Stamford Bridge in October, though the rigour with which he did this meant he was probably lucky not to pick up yet another booking. A '**Harris Blunts the Hammers' Menace**' headline in *The Observer* emphasised what a strong performance the captain gave. The team defended as a unit and Bonetti was on top form. Supporter Geoff Kimber was there, stood on the North Bank with his father and remembers a dreadful crush leaving the ground. This was not uncommon at big matches and, frankly, it was a miracle there were not more serious incidents at football in those days.

The *Sunday Mirror* reflected a wider positive mood about the sterling work the manager was doing. 'Chelsea didn't ooze flair. What they did show was solidness everywhere...(Sexton) has worked a Stamford Bridge miracle in fewer months as manager than I have fingers on one hand'.

Chelsea put their allocation of tickets for the Birmingham cup-tie on sale the following day, warning supporters not to camp out all night.

Regardless, all 13,000 sold that morning. There were later complaints that letting those queuing buy two tickets, without having to produce any vouchers, meant that many fell into the hands of the touts. The club's facile, hand-washing, response to this last point was 'don't buy from them'. The game was a 52,500 sell-out. Six special trains were running in, at that point, one of the biggest ever exoduses of Chelsea supporters out of London outside an FA Cup Semi-Final.

Chelsea trained that week in Bournemouth. The routine was training in the morning and golf in the afternoon, in an attempt to reduce tension, and Brian James of the *Daily Mail* thought it was the most relaxed training camp he could remember.

Sexton commented 'home or away, we play to win...I believe in letting players enjoy the game but only as long as it is within the framework of the team'. He told the *Daily Mirror* 'I would be happier if we were playing at home, but it doesn't mean we are going to Birmingham to play for a draw'.

The *Daily Mail* revealed that the day he was appointed, he handed each squad member a list of his 11 football principles. He would not share them with the press but clearly they include getting men behind the ball when not in possession. He also admitted that he was nervous for his first Quarter-Final. 'I am nervous, they (the players) are not'.

Many thought Chelsea a good bet for the cup, as they had come into form at the right time, though the absence of Webb was a concern. Baldwin, who missed West Ham with a worrying shin problem, did not travel to Bournemouth but eventually won his fitness fight and was selected for St. Andrews. There was less good news about John Boyle, hospitalised after a car crash and needing a skin graft on his face. He was in hospital for a few days but expected to be out for at least a month. This was awful news for both club and player, as he was playing as well as he ever had, allowing Hollins to move to full-back in recent weeks.

A confident Harris, talking to the *Evening Standard*, warned Birmingham that 'we are a better team than when we reached the Semi-Finals in the last three seasons'. Harris, along with Bonetti, Hinton, Hollins and Tambling had appeared in all three. 'We have a lot more method, the team, spirit and atmosphere are first-rate, and we are more consistent'. On his hard-man reputation he was unequivocal. 'I am a hard player, but I never complain. If I am fouled, I don't roll over and lie down in order to get others into trouble'.

In the absence of Boyle, Cooke played in midfield, Hollins remained at right-back and Houseman came in. Chelsea were widely expected to win but, in the event, they lost 1-0, to the better team on the day, a massive disappointment to players, manager, board and the travelling hordes.

The Observer reflected the critical press coverage. 'Chelsea will find it difficult to remember a game in which they made fewer openings or had fewer direct attempts on goal...(An) inability to win the ball regularly in the tackle'. Cooke, lacking Boyle's attributes, could not compete physically with his home counterparts. Dreadful marking allowed Fred Pickering to head the only goal, after which the resolute home defence could not be broken down. Sexton got his tactics wrong, the midfield without Hollins or Boyle lacked the necessary bite, Hinton had a nightmare trying to mark Pickering and veteran Birmingham captain Ron Wylie was allowed to be the most effective man on the pitch. Thomson substituted for Houseman, finally letting Cooke to go further forward, but to no avail. The *News Of The World* felt Chelsea 'failed miserably' and were 'outfought rather than outplayed' as ex-Chelsea stars Barry Bridges and Bert Murray shone in the home attack.

Osgood, Cooke and Tambling were all criticised, but the *Daily Mirror* sought a scapegoat and, probably unfairly, found one. Marvin Hinton. Under a 'Cup Defeat The End for Hinton?' headline, they predicted he would be dropped for the cup-tied Webb for the matches ahead, but you hardly needed to be Nostradamus to realise that was likely to happen anyway. Hinton had rejected the swap move to Southampton and commented 'the fact that I was asked to go to Southampton suggests that Chelsea felt they could do without me. It's not easy to work out what will happen now we are out of the cup'. The way Hinton and centre-back partner Harris struggled against Pickering emphasised how much Webb's aerial capabilities were needed. Stung by press complaints about playing Cooke so deep, the manager observed he did not hear the same criticism when the Scot was used in that role in games against Liverpool, Manchester United, Sheffield Wednesday, Leicester City and West Ham (all of which were won, Wednesday after a replay).

Bonetti, Hollins and Osgood were all selected in England's squad of 22 for the Nations Cup Quarter-Final first-leg against Spain at Wembley on April 3rd, though none were likely to play. Hollins was getting married on the Sunday then planning to report for international duty.

Thomson was still homesick for Glasgow, the Scot missing his girlfriend, and had not signed the new contract offered to him the previous October when he turned 21. Sexton commented 'he wants to do well and if a first-team place does not make him want to stay, I don't know what will'. He was adamant he wanted to leave as he could not settle in London. 'I am not enjoying life, I just want to go home...I think the manager is great. I hung on another four months because he asked me for a chance to change my mind. The whole Chelsea club have been wonderful'.

Sad news emerged that Paul McMillan, 17-year-old centre-back who had played in the 6-2 defeat against Southampton, had to give up the game through ill-health. Young full-back Brian Brown was transferred to Millwall. Chelsea were in discussions on transfer deadline day with St Mirren over inside-forward Jim Blair, but the deal broke down. England left-back Keith Newton, of Blackburn Rovers, almost signed for Nottingham Forest for £100,000 and the thought occurs that a player of his quality would have been an excellent signing for Chelsea, but no serious move was made.

That month *The People* carried an expose of ticket touts, with the hardly revelatory news that one of their source was footballers. The most famous tout, Stan Flashman, was featured and was pictured with Osgood at the opening of a London restaurant. The paper had somehow got a transcript of a phone conversation between the pair about selling tickets. The player told the paper that the practise went on a lot less than it had in the past, but it was clear that players providing match tickets to touts was still widespread at many top clubs.

A story appeared in the *Daily Mail* that near-neighbours Queens Park Rangers might ask Chelsea whether they could groundshare Stamford Bridge if they were promoted to Division One, as Loftus Road would be inadequate and discussions with White City Stadium had broken down. Given the likely large rent increase payable by Chelsea if the Greyhound Racing Association moved out, as was rumoured, it was thought sharing might work well economically, though in the end the conjecture came to nothing.

Although bitterly disappointed at being summarily dumped out of the FA Cup, Chelsea's season was not yet over. The surge up the table suddenly meant European qualification in fifth place was a real possibility if the good run continued. Only one side per city could qualify, but Chelsea had every reason to believe they could make it. Although ninth in the table, they were just three points behind fifth-place Tottenham with a game in hand, and the North London outfit had to visit Stamford Bridge in mid-April for what was shaping up to be a crucial local derby.

April 1968

The *Sunday Mirror* contained a long interview with Sexton, clearly seen as a coming man. Chelsea supporters, appreciative of the improvement he had produced, had chanted his name during the win at West Ham which he thought was 'very nice (but) a compliment to my players'. Now the FA Cup had gone in such disappointing fashion, he was aiming for Europe. He accepted he could not ask young players 'to be completely adult' but he did ask that they 'are sensible and, most of all, enthusiastic'. He had said to Charlie Cooke and Peter Osgood 'as long as you do your whack for the team when you're off the ball, carry on with your own natural brilliance when you're on the ball'. He praised Peter Bonetti, Ron Harris and John Boyle 'who are just as important to me and who don't get as much credit'.

In terms of extra-mural activities, the manager felt 'all I ask from the players is two hours of complete concentration and dedication every day plus an hour and a half on Saturdays...outside of those hours they can, within reason, do as they wish'. In his later years at Chelsea a number of squad members were to test his patience with regards to 'outside of those hours' activities.

In the build-up to a League trip to Sheffield Wednesday, Cooke was fined £25 and severely censured by the FA for his first three bookings that season but avoided a suspension. Given the brutal punishment he regularly took from defenders it is hardly a surprise that he reacted occasionally, but in the late 1960s referees were extremely lax when it came to protecting skilful players.

Sexton moved Harris to right-back and paired David Webb with Marvin Hinton. This made sense, given Hinton's adept reading of the game and sweeping qualities and Webb's bravery and aerial abilities. Cooke played in a wide role, replacing the dropped Peter Houseman. All seemed well as a dominant Chelsea took a comfortable 2-0 half-time lead through John Hollins and Tommy Baldwin, but complacency set in and Wednesday drew level in the last 17 minutes through defensive lapses, Johnny Fantham's injury-time equaliser the result of a rare Bonetti error as he missed a corner. 'Bonetti Boob Costs Chelsea A Wednesday Treble' as the *Daily Mirror* headline starkly put it. A point wasted against opposition still threatened by possible relegation.

Harris had his FA Disciplinary Committee personal hearing postponed as some witnesses were unable to attend. With Boyle still recovering at home in Scotland from his car crash, Harris's tough tackling was even more essential to the side, though his suspension was just deferred, not cancelled.

The next match, on Good Friday, was at Manchester City, two points behind joint leaders Manchester United and Leeds United, with a game in hand on their local rivals. Liverpool were level with City but with a further game in hand, so four clubs had realistic title ambitions. Chelsea were still eighth, though a strong run might still see them finish fifth. Tottenham were now four points ahead, having played one more match, so consistently good performances were needed in the last nine games.

A 1-0 defeat at Maine Road, through a Mike Doyle volley, was no disgrace and a string of chances to level, or even win, a turgid game were missed. Tambling had to be substituted by Fascione after suffering more worrying stomach pains.

The following day Tottenham visited Stamford Bridge for a match Chelsea simply had to win to have any realistic chance of qualifying for Europe. In a reunion for ex-Southampton men Webb and the man he marked, Martin Chivers, Chelsea were bolder, quicker, fitter and always in control, winning more easily than the 2-0 score suggested. Webb marked Chivers out of the match and was widely praised, boosting his rising reputation as Chelsea's new defensive strong-man. Meanwhile, Harris took care of the ever-dangerous Jimmy Greaves, as he had done a number of times over the past few years, with effective man-marking and a series of strong tackles. The whole defence - Harris, Hinton, Webb and McCreadie - had excellent games and Bonetti had little to do.

Houseman, in because Tambling was still unwell, scored the first and Baldwin netted the second as the visiting defence capitulated.

Chelsea supporters mocked their rivals, many of whom departed early, with chants of *'easy, easy, easy'*. The Tottenham programme announced that following the sad death of Charles Pratt, Leonard Withey was now Chelsea chairman with Brian Mears vice-chairman. In that programme, Sexton and the players were praised 'for all (that they) have done towards restoring us in the eyes of the football world, bearing in mind the perilous state to which our playing fortunes had descended'.

The home return encounter with Manchester City three days later was crucial for both sides. To beat the title contenders 1-0 through an Alan Birchenall goal was a notable achievement, cemented by effective, resolute defending against a team missing their orchestrator, Colin Bell. The *Daily Mirror* headline 'Chelsea Near A Fairs Cup Spot' summed up what a vital win it was. Chelsea were still in ninth place but had games in hand on many of the teams above. The 'one club per city' rule might also help, potentially excluding a Manchester club and/or one from Liverpool, meaning sixth or seventh place might feasibly be enough. City's League title chances now depended on Manchester United and Leeds dropping unexpected points. For Chelsea to beat Liverpool, United and City, and draw with Leeds, in the previous two months clearly showed that they could compete with the best in England.

Tambling, whose stomach pains were causing concern given his recent problems, was having an exploratory operation and was likely to miss the rest of the season but there was better news on Boyle, who appeared in the reserves as part of his recovery from the car crash.

The *Illustrated London News* carried an interview with Harris, talking about money. 'Clubs will pay (£120 or £140) a week...Not so long ago the most a player could earn was £20 a week, which created the situation where clubs were giving them money under the counter or offering them huge amounts to make a transfer. But that's all finished now'. He was proud that Chelsea were one of the highest paying clubs in the country. 'To survive in first-class football required a combination of complete dedication, ability and good luck'. He coached at a London grammar school three afternoons a week. An interesting perspective, though possibly naïve if Harris really thought there were no under-the-counter payments in the English game.

A setback to European hopes was suffered at Goodison Park the following week, Everton winning 2-1. Chelsea's scored through an Osgood penalty and only great work by home goalkeeper Gordon West prevented Chelsea from at least equalising as Baldwin and Birchenall worked the home defence hard.

The relentless schedule meant that two days after the Everton defeat Chelsea hosted Burnley, welcoming back John Boyle who had recovered from his car accident and had been much missed. The versatile Scot and his teammates triumphed 2-1, though on a rainy day against unattractive opposition only 23,494 spectators turned out, less than half the attendance against Manchester City six days earlier. Two early Baldwin goals were enough to earn the points, though Andy Lochhead's late headed goal caused a few palpitations, especially as Birchenall had just had a penalty saved by Harry Thomson after potential hat-trick merchant Baldwin unselfishly refused an offer to take it. The *Daily Telegraph* noted that Chelsea lost momentum, Osgood playing deeper and deeper until substituted 'apparently injured' with ten minutes left. Chelsea had now won 10 and drawn one of their last 11 home matches, conceding just four goals.

The FA Disciplinary Committee reconvened with the relevant witnesses and Harris, unsurprisingly, was suspended for seven days and fined £50, meaning his run of 136 consecutive first-team games would come to an enforced end.

The Burnley programme contained a survey on whether there was sufficient interest for standing season-tickets to be sold for the enclosure at the front of the East Stand. The programme was voted best in the country by the 6,000 members of the Football Programme Club, due credit for the hard work of editor Albert Sewell.

Chelsea were in seventh place, two points behind Tottenham with both teams having four matches left. Sunderland were defeated 1-0 in a tedious encounter, the crowd a more respectable 33,086, with Osgood heading the winner, from a Cooke free-kick, for an 11th win in 12 home games. With 18 chances to Sunderland's four, the victory should have been a lot more comprehensive, but the two points were all that really mattered. Bonetti had an untroubled afternoon, commenting 'I've known easier games. But I can't remember them'. Boyle gave an excellent display, reminding supporters how his midfield bite was sorely missed at Birmingham.

For their seventh game in 17 days, and last home game of the season, the opposition were Wolverhampton Wanderers, just above the relegation zone and desperate for points. Hinton came in for the suspended Harris, the first match that the captain had missed since December 1965. It was a fractious affair, with Birchenall losing two front teeth and damaging a shoulder in a collision with goalkeeper Phil Parkes, who was in outstanding form. It looked as though Chelsea had wasted a point until a last-minute Osgood finish, set up by Boyle, grabbed a vital win and meant the club ended the season with an unbeaten home run of 13 games, giving hundreds of youngsters a chance to celebrate by running on the pitch after the goal.

The Wolverhampton programme announced that George Thomson had joined the board of directors, the numerical replacement for Charles Pratt. Chelsea's most promising youngster, local lad Alan Hudson, played in the South-East Counties Final first-leg, his first game since April 1967, having been ordered to rest because of a knee condition. The programme promoted Ken Shellito's testimonial against Queens Park

Rangers the following week. His career had been damaged by a serious knee injury against Sheffield Wednesday nearly five years earlier, when the sky seemed the limit for him, both for Chelsea and England. The programme described him as 'one of the most loyal and courageous players in the club's history, a man who has won a five-year fight against injury to stay in the game'. He appeared in 26 reserve matches that season.

Chelsea had a week to recover before their next match, a return at Wolverhampton. After discussions with Sexton, reserve full-back Jim Thomson, getting married in the summer, was persuaded to stay and his girlfriend was moving to London. Though the manager commented 'I am glad Jim has had second thoughts. He is much too good a player for us to lose' the reality was that, though Thomson came on as substitute in both Wolverhampton encounters, he never started a game for the club again.

There was paper talk about Hinton moving to Queens Park Rangers if they achieved promotion, but Sexton told the *Daily Mail* that he would not be leaving the club, pointing out 'he is a valuable member of our first-team squad'. Though Webb had come straight in at centre-half, and strengthened the team, Orient's young centre-half Tommy Taylor was watched, together with Tottenham reserve inside-forward Dennis Bond. Two Chelsea youngsters were involved in the forthcoming Little World Cup tournament, Ian Hamilton was in the England squad and Brian Goodwin a member of the Scotland one.

Ludicrously, there was still no clarity over how many English clubs would be allowed to compete in the following season's Fairs Cup. All Chelsea could do was optimise their points haul and wait and see what the European powerbrokers decided.

In the Sunderland programme it was announced that home terrace, seat and season-ticket prices would go up the following season, increased costs being blamed. Terrace admission would be 5/- (25p).

Manchester City	p40 54pts
Manchester U.	p40 54pts
Leeds United	p39 53pts
Liverpool	p39 51pts
Everton	p39 47pts
Tottenham H.	p40 47pts
Chelsea	**p40 46pts**

The disappointment of the FA Cup defeat at Birmingham had been cast aside and Chelsea finished April in seventh place, with two games left, with a realistic chance of overtaking Tottenham, who were one point ahead. Stamford Bridge had seemingly become a fortress and, regardless of the outcome of the matches at Wolverhampton and Sheffield United, Sexton could look back on his six-month tenure as manager with great pride, and the board could congratulate themselves on a very astute appointment.

May 1968

Two games of a long season to go, with two wins needed to optimise the chance of European football. To lose 3-0 at Wolverhampton, therefore, was a real shock. Frank Wignall, who did not play at Stamford Bridge, netted a hat-trick as the home outfit guaranteed their First Division safety in fine style. The *Daily Mail* reported that Marvin Hinton was marking Wignall and had a nightmare as the striker was unmarked for each goal. The whole team was shambolic, the defensive cohesion miserable, though John Boyle and Eddie McCreadie were exempted from press criticism. David Webb, who fought a 90 minute duel with Derek Dougan, and Peter Osgood were both booked for crude tackles. Wolves faced Tottenham the following week and Sexton desperately needed them to put in a similarly inspired effort to keep European hopes alive.

Ken Shellito's testimonial attracted a very decent turnout of 20,890 to see Chelsea beat Queens Park Rangers 6-3, earning the full-back £5,572. Liverpudlian comedian Jimmy Tarbuck substituted for Alan Birchenall at half-time, some of the crowd chanting 'Tarbuck for England'. Rangers put out a decent side, slightly surprising given they had a crucial promotion game at Villa Park five days later. The respect for Shellito was clear. As supporter David Gray remembers, he was a fine player at his peak, speedy and intelligent, and would have won many more England caps if his career had not been so cruelly cut short.

The Shellito programme reported that there was insufficient demand for East Stand enclosure season-tickets, though maybe if the club had asked the question in a programme for a crowd bigger than the Burnley one, (the second smallest gate of the season), they might have had more interest, as it seemed such a logical idea.

Peter Bonetti, replacing the injured Gordon Banks, hurt his knee playing for England against Spain in Madrid, so Tommy Hughes came in for the final must-win game of the season at Sheffield United, who needed the points themselves to try and avoid relegation.

Mick Hill put Sheffield United ahead, Osgood equalised as the United defence panicked and presented him with the ball. Though Chelsea did not play well and relied heavily on Hughes' goalkeeping talents, it was no surprise when Baldwin netted the winner with 12 minutes to go, heading home Osgood's cross after a counter-attack. As United were digesting the fact that a win would have kept them up and sent Coventry down, news came through that Tottenham had lost 2-1 at Wolverhampton and Chelsea finished top London side, and sixth in the League. At this point it was, ludicrously, still unclear whether three or four English sides would appear in the Fairs Cup the following season. If it was four then qualification was certain. If it was three, then qualification relied on Manchester United winning the European Cup Final against Benfica at Wembley later that month.

Two days after Sheffield, Chelsea ended their season with a 2-1 win over just-promoted Queens Park Rangers in a reciprocal testimonial game for Mike Keen. The match was most notable for the substitute appearance of 17-year-old midfielder Alan Hudson for his first-team debut.

The usual batch of end-season transfer rumours surfaced. Once again, Marvin Hinton to Queens Park Rangers was floated, and interest was reported in highly-talented Blackpool inside-forward Tony Green, who was being courted by a number of clubs.

Season Summary

Manchester C	p42 58pts
Manchester U	p42 56pts
Liverpool	p42 55pts
Leeds United	p42 53pts
Everton	p42 52pts
Chelsea	**p42 48pts**

Chelsea finished in sixth place, top-placed London side, a remarkable achievement given that when Sexton arrived they were already seven points behind Tottenham and six behind Arsenal, after just 12 matches. He had bought well, though the popular and hard-working Alan Birchenall ended up with just five goals from 22 League games. Birchenall praised the manager for developing his skills and there was optimism that he would fully flourish the following season, Webb was clearly an extremely shrewd signing, tightening the defence and inspiring others through the force of his positive personality. In 'A History Of Chelsea', Ralph Finn argues that 'Webb was the missing link the team needed. Ruthless with abundant power in the tackle and...great ability in the air'.

Peter Osgood was Chelsea's leading League scorer across the whole season with 16, one ahead of Tommy Baldwin. Bobby Tambling, who suffered injury for a significant chunk of the season, netted 12 from 24 games. A defence that let in a frightening 32 goals in the first 12 League matches conceded just 36 in the remaining 30, a step change that spoke volumes for Sexton's coaching. The final goal difference of -6 made 6th place even more remarkable. The home League record since he took over was laudable - 12 wins, 2 draws, 2 defeats.

The regular team, in terms of most League games played under Sexton that season, was :- Bonetti; Boyle, Hinton, Harris, McCreadie; Cooke, Hollins; Baldwin, Birchenall, Osgood, Tambling. Sub. Webb.

The side still suffered from bouts of occasional inconsistency and under-performance, most starkly manifested in the dismal display at

Birmingham in the FA Cup, a competition they looked eminently capable of winning. Against that, though, Sexton had tightened the defence, and got more out of his midfield and forwards, particularly Cooke. The stability he brought was especially praiseworthy given relegation looked a grim possibility when he arrived.

Cooke won the 'Player Of the Year' award from Chelsea Supporters Club. Bonetti, winner the previous season, was voted runner-up.

Supporter Barry Holmes, a regular match-goer that season, makes an interesting point. He feels that season was the start of the media's campaign to label Chelsea as the 'soft, Southern glamour boys', a tag the supporters simply did not recognise.

It is worth pointing out that, at just 38, Sexton was younger and a lot less experienced than peers like Matt Busby, Bill Nicholson, Harry Catterick and Bill Shankly. Don Revie, at Leeds, was only three years older but had been in charge for seven years. This comparative lack of experience made his first six months in charge even more impressive. His style was not to make tactical or personnel changes during matches unless forced, as evidenced by the fact that he only used his substitute seven times in 30 League games.

The season's average attendance of just under 36,000 was slightly up on 1966-67 but it was generally recognised that success on the pitch could significantly increase attendances and, hence, revenues.

Given the performances put in against the top four sides under Sexton, there was every reason for considerable optimism about the coming season. Picking up 39 points from 30 games after his arrival was certainly a very sound basis to build on.

Season Overview 1967-68

(from Sexton's appointment as manager on 23rd October 1967. 30 League games)

League Appearances (inc sub) (top 11 players) – Cooke 30, Osgood 30, Baldwin 28, Bonetti 28, Harris 28, McCreadie 28, Hollins 26, Boyle 25, Hinton 22, Birchenall 21, Tambling 14

League Goals (5+) – Osgood 13, Baldwin 12, Tambling 7, Birchenall 5
League Clean Sheets – 9
Biggest League Win – 4-1 v Leicester City (H), 16/03/68
Worst League Defeat – 0-3 v West Bromwich Albion (H), 16/12/67. 0-3 v Wolverhampton Wanderers (A), 04/07/68

Final League position – 6th
League Record –
Home W10 D2 L2 F22 A11. *Away* W6 D5 L5 F25 A25. Pts 39

Hat-Tricks – None

Sending Offs – None

Biggest Home League Crowd – 54,712 v Manchester United, 25/11/67
Smallest Home League Crowd – 23,494 v Burnley, 22/04/68
Average Home League Crowd – 38,038 (14 games)

Cup Performances –
FA Cup – 6th Round.
League Cup – Already eliminated in the 2nd Round.
Europe – n/a

Chelsea League Debuts – Alan Birchenall, Stewart Houston, David Webb

Player Of The Year – Charlie Cooke

Close Season

Three Chelsea players were involved in Under-23 activity in the close season. Tommy Baldwin scored twice as Young England beat England 4-1 in a pre-Cup Final fixture. John Hollins and Peter Osgood also played in that team, Bonetti for the full side. Baldwin, Ron Harris and Alan Birchenall were selected for the Under-23 tour of Italy, Hungary and West Germany. The *News Of The World* called Baldwin 'the type of brave front runner so rare in top-class football and (he) could be the successor to Roger Hunt' but he never made a representative appearance again after that summer, and neither did his two colleagues.

In some controversy, Hollins had dropped out of that tour, writing to England boss Sir Alf Ramsey saying he had only been married six weeks and needed to sort their new house out. Ramsey said he understood. In late May, *The People* featured an interview with him and wife Linda, scotching rumours that she stopped him training with the England team in March and had forbidden him from golfing with his teammates.

Manchester United duly won the European Cup so Chelsea were therefore guaranteed European football the following season, due reward to Sexton and his squad for their tremendous efforts since October. In mid-June it was announced that Leeds United, Liverpool, Chelsea and Newcastle United would be the four English representatives in the Fairs Cup. Everton, Arsenal and Tottenham were all excluded from the competition because of the 'one-club-per-city' rule. At one stage UEFA talked about only one club per country being allowed in the competition, an idea fiercely opposed by Football League supremo Alan Hardaker, who rightly thought the tournament benefited English clubs both football-wise and financially, and also gave clubs extra reason to enter the League Cup.

Charlie Cooke played for Scotland in Amsterdam at the end of May, but two weeks later it was reported in the *News Of The World* that he had made a transfer request, 'the result of a dispute between him and Chelsea over his wage packet for the coming season'. When signed, he was on just £40 a week plus an annual £1,000 payment, plus incentives. He had been voted Chelsea's 'Player Of The Year' and unsurprisingly wanted an increase. He denied he wanted to join a Scottish club, though Glasgow Rangers admitted they were 'very interested' in him. Any decision was delayed until Sexton returned from holiday.

Cooke was exceptionally talented and highly popular with the supporters, and it seemed beholden on the board and manager to resolve the issue without losing him. He had, however, only scored nine goals in 91 Chelsea first-team appearances. Sexton kept a player analysis chart noting goal-makers as well as goal-scorers, Cooke apparently featuring prominently on neither.

As well as Rangers, Arsenal were interested in Cooke and were supposedly keen to swap him for midfielder Jon Sammels. Maybe because of the Cooke situation, Chelsea were also interested in unsettled Burnley winger Willie Morgan, but he joined Manchester United. Bobby Tambling was granted a testimonial for the following season, and it was hoped that Glasgow Rangers would be a possible opposition.

David Webb was suspended for seven days for 'dangerous play' at Wolverhampton on May 4th. Luckily for him, the first match of the season, at Coventry on August 10th, was postponed until September as their stand had been wrecked by fire and the ground was not going to be ready. His suspension therefore applied to a period when there was no League game. The same good fortune applied to Chris Cattlin of Coventry. Webb would miss the planned friendly at Waterford in Ireland, a stroke of luck for player and manager.

CHAPTER TWO
1968-1969
'We Can Do Better'

Pre-Season

The air of confidence that Dave Sexton and his squad could build on the highly encouraging previous season was evidently shared by supporters as £70,000 in seat season-ticket sales were reached in early July, already a club record. Stamford Bridge had 12,000 stand seats, and 3,500 unreserved bench seats. To put this in context, sales were higher than champions Manchester City (£50,000 so far) but, surprisingly, below Coventry City's £100,000. By the time the season started, Chelsea's sales exceeded £80,000. Clearly, a redeveloped stadium with more seats would give significant scope for the club to increase season-ticket sales, extremely useful close-season income.

The League season made its earliest ever start because the Home International Championship was to be held in one week at the end of it. Chelsea's first League match was a home encounter with Nottingham Forest.

The pre-season friendly schedule, just three first-team games, was significantly less than in the Docherty era when half a dozen or more matches were commonplace. Bobby Tambling returned to training early to try and achieve full fitness after his stomach operation. Unluckily, he promptly damaged a knee trying to prove his fitness, a real blow especially as he had lost a stone in weight and was eager to regain peak form.

Sexton had high hopes of 17-year-old midfielder Alan Hudson, who had just signed professional forms, having missed much of the previous season through injury. The flow of young talent into the first-team had dried up in recent years, but there was real optimism that Hudson would be ready to breakthrough in the next year or so. Chelsea signed raw 20-year-old centre-forward Ian Hutchinson from Cambridge United for an initial £2,500 fee. Wing-half Brian Turner, who had arrived on trial from Auckland, signed professional forms, as did forward David Bibby. Chelsea gave trials to 450 schoolboys that July. Sexton commented 'it is time well spent. Remember John Boyle walked in here and asked for a trial, and we got Peter Osgood because someone recommended him'.

The Charlie Cooke situation seemed to be resolving itself. In early July, the Scot said 'I shall be having another talk with Dave Sexton this week. But I shall be staying at Chelsea'. Unfortunately, a couple of weeks later the Scot chipped an ankle bone and tore ligaments in training, and had to have his leg put in plaster, so was likely to miss the opening games. Sexton was keen for him to score more goals. 'I'm convinced that Charlie has not yet fully exploited his talent...I believe that with his control and acceleration he's a better player than Best'. Praise indeed. Talk about Marvin Hinton moving on if he did not get a regular first-team place persisted, Crystal Palace being the latest club supposedly interested in signing him.

The club announced that six executive boxes were to be installed in the West Stand. Chairman Leonard Withey proudly commented 'they have boxes at the Derby, at Ascot and Lords'. They were planned to be ready for the Tottenham match on August 31st. The following day, Chelsea Secretary John Battersby announced a waiting list was already in place as all six had been taken in a couple of hours. The cost was £500 a season (including cup-ties) for a glass-fronted box containing six easy chairs, thick carpeting, central heating and a drinks cabinet, with a waiter serving throughout the game.

At the end of July, Sexton told the *Daily Mirror* he had set an ambitious 105 goal target for his forwards. 25 from Peter Osgood and Tommy Baldwin, 20 from Bobby Tambling and Alan Birchenall, 15 from Charlie Cooke. The previous season Osgood had scored 17, Baldwin 16, Tambling 15, Birchenall 7 and Cooke just 5. In early August, Tambling had fully recovered from his injured left knee and Cooke had the plaster removed from his left ankle.

The three pre-season friendlies were against Crystal Palace at Selhurst Park, a trip to Germany to face Kaiserslauten and a visit to Irish side Waterford. Before all of those was a 3-0 win behind closed doors at Brentford. The Palace match on July 31st was a physical 1-1 draw, Osgood netting for Chelsea. Pleasingly, Tambling's knee came through the test without problems. The result in Kaiserslauten three days later was a disappointing 1-0 defeat. Birchenall was omitted, having only played a total of 45 minutes in the Brentford and Palace games, and was clearly in a fight for his place, probably with Tambling.

Baldwin, Birchenall, Joe Fascione, Hinton and Osgood were fined £50 each by the club following what were described as 'off-field incidents' after the game at Kaiserslauten. According to the *Daily Telegraph* and the *Evening Standard*, this involved Osgood, Birchenall and Hinton missing a 1am team bus back to their hotel so they had to get a taxi there, with Baldwin and Fascione having a row with a hotel manager while trying to obtain a meal. In '*Ossie The Wizard*' Osgood reveals they 'went on the razzle' and, perhaps unsurprisingly, thought Sexton saw him as the ringleader. The manager's disciplinary action, which he communicated individually and in no uncertain terms to the five miscreants, showed that the players should not mistake his quietness for a lack of courage, especially as he had the full and public backing of his board. That such antics took place less than two weeks before the season was clearly a disappointment to him.

The *Daily Mirror* went to town. Under a 'Sexton Faces New Storm Over Fines' headline, they reported that Chelsea 'could be heading for another crisis' following the disciplinary action. At least two of the stars fined over the weekend were supposedly considering asking for a transfer. One anonymous player complained 'I think we have been treated unfairly. We didn't do anything that would warrant such a large fine. The fines were a blow to us all and have caused us to do a lot of deep thinking'. Another claimed 'Fifty pounds is a lot of money. All we did was miss the team coach by ten minutes. I'm unhappy about it'. It was not to be the last time the manager had issues with the off-field exploits of some of the men fined.

While the first-team were facing Kaiserslauten, a reserve/youth XI was playing at Wealdstone, David Gray's local team. As he says, little did anyone know that within 18 months the mercurial number 8 (Hudson) and the gangling No.9 (new signing Hutchinson) he watched would go on to great heights and become club legends.

There were no last-minute moves before the League season began. Huddersfield Town bid for reserve goalkeeper Tommy Hughes, who had a transfer request rejected by the board, and Norwich City tried to buy winger Peter Houseman, but Sexton rejected both offers. Of the young players released that summer, Warren Tennant had moved to Guildford City and Kingsley Whiffen was on trial at Plymouth Argyle. Paul McMillan, who so sadly had to retire for health reasons, was trying to make a comeback with Clydebank. Brian Goodwin and Roy Summers had been released but had no club as yet. In addition, young half-back George Luke had joined South African club Durban City and apprentice Geoff Idle joined Tennant at Guildford City. The *Chelsea News* reported interest in three Scottish players, Queen of the South forward Lex Law who they had been interested in buying the previous year, inside-forward Jim Blair of St Mirren, nearly bought a few months earlier, and highly-rated forward Peter Cormack of Hibernian.

The final pre-season game, a charity friendly at Waterford, resulted in a comfortable 5-2 victory, Birchenall returning to the team and scoring. Bobby Tambling was back to fitness and a stone lighter after two stomach operations, telling the *Evening Standard* 'I feel all the better for it. I am much livelier and faster'. He played in all three friendlies and only Cooke's injury prevented Sexton having a full squad to choose from.

Stamford Bridge had been shared with greyhound racing since 1933, but that summer it was announced that the Greyhound Racing Association were pulling out, giving Chelsea the opportunity to plan to significantly redevelop the stadium. This could include extending the terraces nearer the pitch, which would help the atmosphere, long a bugbear of players, managers and supporters.

In the Nottingham Forest programme, chairman Leonard Withey

wrote to supporters. He pointed out that as the greyhounds had gone, Chelsea's outgoings would increase and that stadium improvements 'cannot be carried out as speedily as one would wish and must be related to the tenure of the new lease...I would ask you to bear with us during the period of continued negotiation'. The stadium was dilapidated in places and needed significant work, but because of the complexities involved in negotiation with the freeholder, the Mears Trust, this was unlikely to be straightforward.

That programme also contained an article from Sexton encouraging the supporters to continue to get behind the team. He felt their encouragement was a big factor in the excellent post-Boxing Day home record. He accepted Stamford Bridge did not 'contain' the noise as well as some other grounds but was clear what was needed. 'We want success. This is how you can share our efforts to achieve it. Good shouting, and thanks from us all'.

The Forest programme also listed all the professionals and apprentices on Chelsea's books. There were only two professional goalkeepers - Peter Bonetti and Tommy Hughes. This was a risk given that Bonetti's astonishing bravery made him prone to injury. Right-back Ken Shellito was still on the books but had not made a first-team appearance since December 1965 and, realistically, it was unlikely he would ever be a regular first-teamer again. Given the other two full-backs listed were Jim Thomson, who had never established himself as a regular and Eddie McCreadie, it seemed as though further strengthening the squad with a specialist in that position made sense, though Webb, Hinton, Harris, Hollins and Boyle could all play there. Alan Hudson was very highly thought of, but none of the other homegrown youngsters listed, who had turned professional having come through the ranks, ever became regulars.

The season ahead was a crucial one for Chelsea. The team had improved significantly under Sexton but needed to turn that into something concrete and to challenge seriously for honours. The squad had plenty of depth which he told the *Evening Standard* he saw as 'a healthy state of affairs for the club' though he was obliged to point out that 'it gives me a headache in trying to fit everybody in'. The first-team players were on a £30 a point bonus. This only applied to those in the team, so being injured or dropped could prove expensive. It was a very decent motivation, as a regular in a successful side could well earn £1,500 in point bonus payments alone.

The press saw Chelsea as the best London bet to challenge the Northern dominance, reflected in their 12-1 price for the title. With Manchester United, Manchester City, Leeds United and Liverpool all expecting very strong showings, and Everton ever-improving, such a challenge was clearly going to be a tough one, however. The *Daily Telegraph* thought Sexton was doing an exceptional job and saw them as real contenders 'if this dedicated manager can overcome the dressing-room difficulties that have plagued Chelsea for years'. Given the fines imposed in Germany, this was clearly an unresolved issue.

August 1968

Charlie Cooke, who told the *Daily Mail* 'I fancy us a bit for the League', was still not available for the opening Forest game on August 14th, despite the four extra days to recover from his ankle problem.

Sexton fielded a strong team:- Peter Bonetti; Ron Harris, David Webb, John Boyle, Eddie McCreadie; Peter Osgood, John Hollins; Peter Houseman; Tommy Baldwin, Alan Birchenall, Bobby Tambling. They lined up in a 4-2-4 system, as opposed to the 4-3-3 formation used much of the previous campaign.

A 1-1 draw was a disappointment to the decent 36,517 crowd. It could have been worse as Ian Moore gave Forest a first-half lead before Tambling equalised. Forest goalkeeper Peter Grummitt broke a thumb, centre-forward Joe Baker going in goal for the last 12 minutes, but Chelsea could not take advantage, in a slow, flat start to the season, the forwards lacking sharpness.

Three days later a better team performance at home to West Bromwich, with the forwards looking far more effective, resulted in a 3-1 victory against an outfit who had not lost at Stamford Bridge in their previous five visits. Cooke's return, at the expense of Houseman, was loudly cheered. Tambling scored neatly after a minute to settle the side's nerves. Baldwin, the 'least-publicised but hardest-working member of a Chelsea attack loaded with talented individuals' as the *News Of The World* put it, scored either side of half-time and though Tony Brown pulled one back from a free-kick, Chelsea were in control. The *Evening Standard* observed that 'Cooke's dribbling often delighted the crowd, but usually his colleagues were marked by the time he passed', not the first time this point had been made about the hugely talented but occasionally frustrating Scot. Baldwin, Tambling and Birchenall were all praised and, crucially, David Webb dominated bustling and dangerous Albion centre-forward Jeff Astle, a sign of just how important he had become in only his 15th game for the club.

Because the season was finishing in mid-April, there was a glut of games in the early weeks. Chelsea had 11 League matches, plus at least one League Cup-tie and a Fairs Cup first-leg, scheduled before the end of September. The next week brought two difficult trips, to fellow Fairs Cup contenders Newcastle United, and to European Cup holders Manchester United.

2-0 up at half-time at St. James' Park through Tambling and Birchenall, with both goals created by Osgood, Chelsea looked comfortable. Inexplicably, they took their collective feet off the pedal, assumed Newcastle would not threaten them and paid the price as they caved in after the interval. As the *Newcastle Evening Chronicle* put it, 'the classical football artists went in 2-0 at half-time and were then ripped apart' by a totally committed, never-say-die home side. 'Pop' Robson, to play for Chelsea over a decade later, scored twice, home debutant Tommy Gibb the other. A massive disappointment and an indication that maybe the defence was still a long way away from impregnability.

Houseman came in for the injured Cooke at Old Trafford in the only change from the trip to Tyneside. Possibly apprehensive that their woeful second-half at Newcastle may portend a tough afternoon, Chelsea set off like a house on fire, Baldwin scoring after 42 seconds, and the team never looked back, kept up the momentum for the whole match and put on one of their very finest displays of that era. A 4-0 victory in no way flattered the visitors who defended superbly, negating the impact of George Best and Bobby Charlton through effective shackling by Harris and Hollins. The *Daily Mail* 'Jailer Harris Keeps Best In His Cell' headline spoke volumes.

The team built moves effectively with Osgood playing deep to great effect, attacked quickly and finished clinically. Houseman was involved in three goals and caused endless problems for a struggling United defence. It was a tactical triumph for Sexton, especially considering the slack second-half performance days earlier, and demonstrated how good the team could actually be, inflicting United's worst home defeat for six years. Chelsea were in seventh after four games but had a game in hand over most of their rivals.

Next opponents Sheffield Wednesday were in a surprise third place and travelled to Stamford Bridge with a degree of confidence. Chelsea missed chances and had Bonetti to thank on a number of occasions in a tight encounter, but a Tambling 30-yarder before half-time resulted in the only goal. The now-slimline forward had now scored in each of the first five matches of the season and was clearly fully fit. The forwards had the chances to put the game to bed but failed to take them and the side were hanging on at the end.

The last August game, at home to Tottenham, attracted 48,412 spectators though, given Chelsea's form and the fierce rivalry, it is surprising the attendance was not higher. The *Sunday Mirror* were less than impressed with a frenetic, niggly encounter, calling it 'ugly, often brutal'. Referee Harry New had problems keeping order, Tottenham bitterly disputing a penalty award. Birchenall and Osgood, from the spot, twice gave Chelsea the lead but goals by ex-Blue Jimmy Greaves and Cliff Jones ensured a point for the visitors, who finished the month in a lowly 19th place. Tambling hurt his back colliding with goalkeeper Pat Jennings and had to go off, Houseman coming on, the first time that season Sexton had used a substitute. Tambling was hit so hard that trainer Harry Medhurst at first thought his back may have been broken. Luckily, it was only bruised, but Jennings' challenge infuriated the home players, and the match became increasingly fractious from that point. An 'amateurish' punch-up between the rarely-riled Cooke and Joe Kinnear, which could have led to both being dismissed, summed the afternoon up. Chelsea ended August in fifth place. Apart from a lacklustre opening game against Forest and a slipshod second-half against Newcastle, performances, both individually and collectively, had generally been decent. Ten men had played every game, only Cooke and Houseman playing less than all six. Reviewing the month, the *Daily Telegraph* felt they were over-reliant on Tambling for goals, with others needing to convert more chances. This was slightly unfair, as Baldwin had netted four and Birchenall three, though Osgood had just the one, a penalty.

There was also a *Daily Telegraph* observation of the type that only seemed to be made about Chelsea's squad. 'Meanwhile the quiet, but firm, manager Dave Sexton must guard against those dressing-room upheavals that have ruined quite bright prospects of success for Chelsea in recent seasons'. The manager revealed that he was hoping to film all first team games commenting 'we hope to learn from our mistakes and the things we do well'. He must have wished he could keep cameras on the more errant members of the playing staff.

Arsenal	p7	12pts
Leeds United	p6	11pts
West Ham	p7	11pts
Sheff. Wed	p7	9pts
Chelsea	**p6**	**8pts**
Everton	p6	8pts

September 1968

John Boyle, whose performances in defence were testament to his multi-positional abilities, had suffered from a back injury since the previous season, which hurt him late on in games. Trainer Harry Medhurst thought it might be a slipped disc and Boyle saw a specialist, but it did not affect him sufficiently to be left out of the side. Sexton, appreciative of what the Scot brought to the team, told the *Daily Mail* he saw Boyle and Hollins as 'my warriors in attack and my trojans in defence'.

In midweek, Chelsea travelled to Birmingham City for a League Cup Second Round tie, a chance to extract revenge for the shock March FA Cup defeat, a result the manager saw as the low point of that season. A bizarre own-goal by centre-half Winston Foster from a Boyle cross put the visitors through 1-0. The defence again struggled in the air against Fred Pickering and old-boy Bert Murray hit the bar, but the visitors held on. Five visitors limped away from another physical encounter. Ron Harris hurt his back and was expected to miss a couple of matches, Marvin Hinton stepping in and Eddie McCreadie taking over as captain. Two games a week was tough enough, two hard and bruising games a week would inevitably take its toll in terms of tiredness and injury.

The visit of Everton brought potential title contenders to Stamford

Bridge, though only 42,017 turned out to watch an equally disappointing game, two defensive sides cancelling each other out. *The Observer* headline summed up the game as '**Unreal, And A Boring Failure**'. Johnny Morrissey gave Everton an early lead after a Peter Bonetti misjudgement and Everton might have been in total control just after half-time but for Bonetti making amends with a majestic penalty save from Alan Ball after David Webb had fouled Joe Royle. Peter Osgood equalised from the penalty spot late on but had a poor match, the nadir being miskicking in front of an open goal, Sexton opining 'he didn't run enough' and supporters occasionally getting on his back.

The Observer explained that 'Chelsea's intensely dedicated young manager, made it clear…that in his opinion there were deeply satisfying technical and tactical niceties to be observed by the professional eye'. This was all very well, and Chelsea clearly possessed an extremely talented technical coach, but such niceties were not at the forefront of thinking of many of the supporters present (including the author) who spent 90 minutes waiting in vain to be entertained.

Midweek brought a trip to Coventry City for the game rearranged from the first day of the League season. Harris was still out injured so Hinton kept his place. Heavy rain made the pitch a quagmire, which gave the visitors their goal in a hard-fought 1-0 win, when a Maurice Setters back-pass stuck in the Highfield Road mud and Osgood, who had another quiet match, struck the ball home. Bonetti again saved Chelsea with a series of important saves and his teammates played their regular away tactics of massed defence and swift counter-attack, though they were hanging on grimly by the end. Chelsea had now reached the heady heights of fourth place, meaning the team were due a 'position' bonus on top of their salary and £30 a point bonus.

The games were relentless, and four days later there was a trip to Loftus Road for an all-ticket local derby against Queens Park Rangers, strangely their first ever meeting in a competitive match. Rangers opened their new South Africa Road stand, though with temporary staircases and an incomplete roof. The visitors were given 6,000 tickets, almost all of which were allocated to season-ticket-holders but, as was to regularly happen in the future at Loftus Road, there was away support all around the ground. Harris returned for Hinton and captained opposite his older brother Allan. In the end, only 26,358 turned up to see a complete mismatch as Chelsea comfortably won 4-0, easing up. Tommy Baldwin scored twice, Alan Birchenall also netted, and Osgood converted his third penalty in five matches.

One unnamed Chelsea player, slightly cruelly, told the *Daily Mirror* 'I can't see them staying up. They are just a bad side'. Another commented 'we have a tough European match on Wednesday, and it wasn't much of a work-out'. Chelsea were fitter, tactically more astute and technically more competent, Cooke and Osgood producing some sublime football. Geoff Kimber remembers 'The Loft' end of the ground being absolutely full of visiting supporters and thinks this was the first time those supporters gave a rendition of 'La-la-la la-la-la-la la-la-la-la Chelsea' to the sound of 'Hey Jude' by The Beatles, which had topped the charts that week, and is still heartily sung at Chelsea matches over 50 years later.

After an easy game, it was assumed that the Fairs Cup First Round, first-leg against Greenock Morton, at home, would be similarly straightforward, though supporter Brian Gaches recalls that the press tried to build it up as an England v Scotland clash. Bob Barlow remembers the visitors wore a striking fluorescent yellow kit, which was apparently a talking point among the home support. They had lost seven of eight matches that season, scoring just four times, so were hardly in top form. Competition rules decreed that two of the three named substitutes could be used, in theory giving managers more flexibility, though Sexton was not one for tactical substitutions. Chelsea superstitiously chose not to use the No.13 shirt.

Though Morton matched their opponents for much of the first-half and Boyle had to clear off the line, two goals in the two minutes before the interval changed things completely. Osgood, Birchenall, Charlie Cooke, Boyle and John Hollins all netted in a 5-0 thrashing to practically ensure progress to the Second Round. Pre-match, the manager had said he wanted home form to improve (after two wins and three draws) and he got his wish, though against hardly imposing opposition. The *Evening Standard's* Bernard Joy felt it was Osgood's finest game since he broke his leg and thought him the nearest thing in English football to Alfredo Di Stefano. This comparison seems more than slightly hyperbolic given the mediocre opposition and Di Stefano's unchallengeable status as one of the greatest stars ever, but does indicate just what Osgood was thought capable of.

The club earned around £10,000 from a crowd of 28,736. As all money stayed with the hosts in European games, this demonstrated the financial benefits of a long European run, because as the team progressed, and played more attractive opposition, attendances would inevitably increase. Each player received a £2 bonus per 1,000 spectators for European home games, a total of £56 a man.

58,062 crowded into Stamford Bridge, three days after the Greenock Morton game, paying record Chelsea home League receipts of £20,282, to watch the third-place side take on fourth-place West Ham. After some of the drab or one-sided fare of recent weeks, this was an excellent match, Scotland manager Bobby Brown thinking it one of the best club matches he had ever seen. 'This was soccer at its best with two talented teams giving a splendid exhibition of speed and skill' opined Tony Pawson in *The Observer*. Bobby Tambling scored after just two minutes (his 200th first-team career goal) and Chelsea had their chances, but Martin Peters equalised after half-time. David Webb close-marked Geoff Hurst to the point of ineffectiveness and Cooke's passing was much praised, particularly one mazy 70-yard run. Osgood spent much of the afternoon playing very deep but pushed up towards the end and immediately caused the visiting defence problems, but they held on for a 1-1 draw.

The first of two more games that month, against Derby County in the League Cup, attracted 26,975 and produced receipts of £10,116, both competition records for Stamford Bridge. Derby, going very well in Division Two under young manager Brian Clough, and marshalled on the pitch by the indominatable Dave Mackay, defended stoutly. Cooke went off with a badly twisted ankle, Chelsea could not break them down, the visitors gave an excellent account of themselves (their supporters were even chanting 'easy, easy' at one point), arguably deserved to win and the resultant 0-0 draw meant an unwanted trip to the Baseball Ground for a replay the following Wednesday. Ludicrously, Chelsea had to travel to Burnley on the Saturday, Greenock Morton on the Monday and Derby on the Wednesday before a home match with Ipswich Town three days later, as fixture congestion threatened to swamp the side.

Cooke was on crutches, his ankle sufficiently problematic that he was expected to miss eight games. Sexton admitted to the *Daily Mail* that there was not a direct replacement but 'I shall be looking for more from Peter Osgood. I think a lot more responsibility will be put his way because Charlie is out, and I am hoping he will respond to it'. A hugely frustrated Cooke commented 'I am sick that this has happened just when things were going right for me'.

Despite signing a new contract Jim Thomson had never really settled in London, so it was no shock when he was sold, though given his reported homesickness it was slightly surprising that, rather than returning to Scotland, he went to Burnley for £40,000, a record fee for that club. Given he cost the club nothing, it was good business for Chelsea. The deal was done on the understanding he could not appear against them later that week. Sexton was initially reluctant to sell because of the fixture pile-up, but Burnley boss Harry Potts persisted, and he relented.

Given the fixture congestion, what Chelsea did not need was a League game at Burnley described by the *Daily Mirror* as 'a sickening first-half of roughhouse tactics'. The injured Cooke was replaced by Peter Houseman. Boyle had to go off after a particularly brutal tackle by Dave Merrington and was expected be out for a couple of weeks. Osgood was similarly rough on Colin Blant but did little else. The match itself was almost an afterthought at times, but Burnley won 2-1, with two goals by 17-year-old winger Dave Thomas. Tambling deserved his goal, but it was scant consolation in a disjointed team performance that meant an end to a ten-match unbeaten run. In *'Ossie The Wizard'* he revealed that afterwards Sexton said 'ten of you were trying out there, one wasn't…I knew he was talking about me. He was right, but I couldn't put my finger on what was wrong'. The manager would not tolerate perceived lack of effort for long.

The 15th match in under seven weeks, and the final one in September, took Chelsea to Greenock Morton, after a weekend spent recovering from the Burnley game at Largs, where the Scottish team trained. Young midfielder Alan Hudson was in the party of 14 as Boyle and Cooke were out, but he did not start. Hinton came in at full-back, Harris reverting to centre-back. Baldwin gave Chelsea an early lead, but the complacent visitors then almost inconceivably conceded three goals before the half-hour as Morton dominated play and Chelsea's defensive weakness was exposed. Shocked but not panicking, goals by Birchenall, Houseman and Tambling eased them through 9-3 on aggregate. A perplexed Sexton commented 'we learnt that sometimes even a five-goal lead is not enough to keep you out of trouble'.

Cooke continued to garner press attention. In an article on flair players, the *Sunday Mirror* waxed lyrical. 'Cooke is fast becoming one of the game's solo personalities. He has not developed enough exuberant 'devil' as yet to annoy crowds like Osgood sometimes does…one of the most fascinating dribblers of a ball since Stanley Matthews'. He was certainly not fully effective every appearance, but then neither was George Best, one of very few with Cooke's ability in English football.

That month, in a slightly strange piece of business, young Ian Hamilton was sold to Southend United for just £5,000. He was once seen as highly promising within the club, with two League goals from five appearances the season before last, but had made no first-team appearances since. He was obviously well down the striking pecking order, especially after summer signing Ian Hutchinson had scored five in five reserve games, but it did seem a desultory price. West Bromwich clearly thought so, unsuccessfully bidding £30,000 for him just weeks later. A couple of years later Hamilton recounted how he was on the coach back from Plymouth when Ron Suart told him Southend had bid £5,000 for him, and was he keen to go? 'I was sick.' He felt he could have made the First Division grade and went on to have a decent career with Aston Villa, Sheffield United and Minnesota Kicks.

Chelsea were supposedly interested in highly-rated John Dempsey of Fulham and were ready to make an opening bid of £60,000. They were also reported to be watching Darlington winger Harry Kirk and strikers Hugh Curran of Norwich and Bristol City's John Galley.

Arsenal	p11 17pts
Liverpool	p11 16pts
Leeds United	p10 16pts
West Ham	p11 15pts
Everton	p11 14pts
Chelsea	**p11 14pts**

September ended in sixth place, three points behind leaders Arsenal.

The team were still in Europe, though faced a tough replay at Derby if they were to progress in the League Cup.

October 1968

Another month, another bout of fixture congestion, with eight games scheduled including the replay at Derby and both legs of the Fairs Cup Second Round against DWS Amsterdam. In the Greenock Morton programme, supporters were advised that, after pitch invasions at recent matches, half-price juvenile admission would be withdrawn for at least a month. This step had been taken a couple of times previously, though it never seemed right that youthful exuberance, which is what it was, should be punished in such a draconian manner. Such a price hike inevitably stopped some youngsters attending, quite possibly losing a proportion of them to the club for good.

The game at Derby, Chelsea's tenth in a month (with Peter Bonetti, Eddie McCreadie, John Hollins, David Webb, Alan Birchenall and Peter Osgood playing in all ten) was a predictably challenging one in front of a capacity 34,346 all-ticket attendance. Young centre-forward Ian Hutchinson, in for the hurt Tommy Baldwin, made his first-team debut. His manager commented that 'Ian is himself only just fit after a week's absence with a knee injury...There have been good reports about his reserve performances' and felt 'as a centre-forward has dropped out, it is only right that we should bring in (another one)' even though they were quite different sorts of player.

Birchenall, who had a fine game, put the visitors ahead but an increasingly-dominant Dave Mackay, belying his 34 years, equalised with 13 minutes to go after bursting through from midfield and, in a frenzied atmosphere, Chelsea capitulated to late goals from Alan Durban and Kevin Hector as a frustrated Osgood ended up brawling with Willie Carlin. So one chance of a trophy that season had already gone, and to a Second Division side (albeit a particularly good one). There was one bright spot, the encouraging debut by Hutchinson, but apart from a strong Bonetti display there was little else to be positive about.

The *Daily Mail* ran a feature on Houseman. Sexton enthused that 'he's in the team to stay this time. Peter has always been around when we wanted him because someone else has been injured. But his play in the last three away games has proved to me he deserves a place in his own right. His skill and effort were top rate'. The manager made it clear that Houseman would keep his place when others were fit again, putting the likes of Cooke and Osgood under pressure.

Hutchinson kept his place for the Ipswich home match three days later as Cooke, Baldwin and John Boyle were still missing. The newcomer nearly scored twice in the first few minutes but had an ace up his sleeve, a remarkably long throw-in, which Ipswich knew nothing about. Neither did the home supporters, as according to David Gray and

Geoff Kimber there were gasps when he launched his first one. Bob Barlow has vivid memories of that throw. 'I remember his home debut and as he came over to take a throw in in front of me, well a dog track away, there was smattering of boos and the cry of "*Olly 'Olly 'Olly*' as John Hollins was our long throw specialist. Hutch did his normal rubbing of the ball and threw it in to the far post like a rocket. The crowd was silent momentarily and burst into a huge roar. Hutch had arrived'.

Though Ray Crawford put the visitors ahead, Hutchinson's long throws caused panic and from his second, hapless and flummoxed centre-half Bill Baxter headed into his own net. Goals from Hollins and Birchenall clinched a comfortable win. Hutchinson explained to the *Daily Mirror* 'we have scored four goals in the reserves from my throws. It's not something I've practised specially. It's just something I can do'. As the *Daily Mail* pointed out 'his remarkable long throws sealed his appeal to the crowd' and he had a highly encouraging League debut. Houseman, too, continued his pleasing run of form.

There was much press comment about Osgood, who was substituted for young midfielder Barry Lloyd. Sexton explained 'I have been forced to play Peter in several different roles (up front and in midfield)...It has been very hard on him' and the manager felt it had a negative impact on his game. Building on the theme, he told the *Daily Mail* 'I feel it is my fault he is having a bad time because I asked him to play in different roles'. Osgood commented 'It is good of Mr Sexton to say that, but I can't let him take the blame'. He felt sluggish but could not explain why. 'This was going to be my season and I have really set my heart on doing well. But for some reason it just isn't happening....The way things are going I wouldn't blame Mr Sexton if he dropped me. In fact, though it is not for me to pick the team, I wish he would leave me out. I feel really low, tired and off-colour and perhaps a rest would help'.

Lloyd had withdrawn a transfer request, submitted through frustration at lack of opportunity. He had been selected as substitute three times in a week and saw a potential gateway to the first-team, though the impending return of Boyle and Cooke would presumably have limited future chances. He scored a hat-trick in a 3-3 London Challenge Cup draw at West Ham to demonstrate his improved form.

On the Monday, normally a squad day off, Osgood was ordered in to see Sexton to discuss his loss of form. Manager, trainer Harry Medhurst and club doctor Paul Boyne were all there. He complained to the *Daily Mirror* of 'being too tired and sluggish to play properly'. He went fishing on the Sunday. 'I...thought about it all. My form is so bad it isn't true, and I don't know what the answer is. I've been unable to sleep nights worrying about it. I have certainly lost my appetite for the game...But I don't want to leave Chelsea. I have a four-year contract and I intend to see it out'. Lethargic displays were hardly likely to attract a big club to bid a large fee for him, anyway.

The following day the *Daily Mirror*, under a 'How Soccer's Problem

SEXTON FOR GOD

Boys Were Sorted Out Yesterday - It's Pep Pills For Sleepy Peter' headline showed a staged picture of Osgood yawning on the treatment table. Medhurst had put him on a course of iron pills. A perplexed manager told the *Daily Mail* 'I've known Peter since he was 16. I like him and I want him to stay here....As far as I'm concerned, he's a good player having a bad time'. In fairly dramatic terms, the article referred to 'the latest episode in the sad story of Peter Osgood' and reckoned the club were 'distinctly unsympathetic' to his plea to be dropped. Sexton explained 'I don't know what the medical trouble is with Peter, but reserve football won't help him'. For one of his two most talented players to be suffering from fatigue was a concern, though surely the workload of two or three matches a week had something to do with it.

The manager was thinking of keeping him in the team for the midweek trip to Sheffield Wednesday but only because of injuries. In the end Osgood was dropped, Sexton selecting a Baldwin, Tambling, Hutchinson, Birchenall and Houseman forward line. Baldwin netted after 77 uneventful minutes but Chelsea were unable to hold on and Jack Witham equalised. Hutchinson, who had taken to the first-team remarkably well considering he had only been at the club a few months, gave another encouraging display. The dropping, inevitably, was big news. The *Daily Mirror* headline exclaimed 'I Want To Play My Way Back Insists Osgood', dropped for the first time in his Chelsea career and undertaking extra training. 'I have been happier since I started this course of tablets and I want to play my way back into the first-team'. The following weekend he told *The People* he was on iron tablets and tonics to recapture strength and lost form and reiterated 'I'm on a four year contract and happy to stay four years'. In the Everton programme the following season, he explained 'I had a bad patch...I was sluggish and began to dread going out on a Saturday afternoon. I was left out for three games and went on a course of pick-me-up tonics'.

Cooke returned, replacing Hutchinson, after missing five matches through his damaged ankle and gave an impressive display at Wolverhampton three days after the draw at Hillsborough. Boyle was still out, and Osgood was again omitted, though he did travel with the party. In recent games Chelsea had demonstrated a worrying inability to hold onto a lead and this failing reared its ugly head again at Molineux. Tambling, playing in midfield, netted after 88 minutes but there was still time for Peter Knowles to equalise. Chelsea played the game tight and would probably have settled for a draw before it started, but the two dropped points from Wolves and Sheffield Wednesday, and the cup elimination by Derby, would all have been avoidable if the team had shown better concentration and resolve. Fifth place, four points behind leaders Leeds United, was by no means a disaster, but those extra two points would have halved the deficit.

An enhanced reserve side, including Osgood, lost 4-2 after extra-time in the London Challenge Cup at West Ham. The star ran 60 yards to score a majestic opener after three minutes, but faded, as did his side.

After the first match-free midweek of the season, lowly Leicester, with one point from seven away games, visited Stamford Bridge. They made a dozen back-passes to keeper Peter Shilton inside 20 minutes and home supporters were showing signs of unrest when Baldwin scored before half-time. After the interval he netted twice more for his first League hat-trick and also had two more goals disallowed as Chelsea ran in easy 3-0 winners. Cooke was fully recovered from injury and back to his best, but Osgood was the unused substitute. For a man used to supporter adulation, and being at the centre of events and attention, this must have been exceedingly difficult. Boyle returned after five matches out, replacing Hinton at full-back.

The home leg against DWS Amsterdam followed on the Wednesday. Their manager, Englishman Les Talbot, praised Cooke and knew he had his work cut out to devise a plan to keep the Scot quiet. Pre-match, Sexton said he rated DWS as solid defensively and stressed the importance of getting a good lead at home but not conceding, as away goals counted double in the event of a tie after both legs. DWS had just eight points from nine games in the Dutch League so were hardly on top form. Eight of the Chelsea team had appeared in the European campaign three seasons earlier, Webb, Baldwin and Birchenall being the exceptions.

In the event, Chelsea could only manage a woeful 0-0 draw ('dreadful' as supporter Bob Barlow remembers it) in front of a smaller-than-expected 28,428 attendance. 'Chelsea Facing A Real Fight For Survival' ran the *Daily Mirror* headline. 'The performance (was) as disappointing as the result'. DWS played a very tight 1-4-4-1 formation, operating a highly effective sweeper system. The crowd became frustrated by the defensive Dutch tactics and Chelsea's inability to overcome them, and broke into sporadic slow-handclapping. Spurning the best chance, Tambling put a 19th minute penalty a yard wide, leading to chants of 'We Want Osgood', who duly came on for the errant penalty taker after 58 minutes to 'the biggest cheer of the night'. Chelsea had the vast majority of play, plenty of chances and 14 corners to nil, but lacked the necessary urgency and imagination to make this superiority count, an inability to step things up against supposedly weaker opposition an old failing. Sexton poured his heart out. 'It was frustrating. You've got to get the first goal to break the ice in a game like this'. A very tricky encounter in Holland awaited seven days later, though the thinking was that DWS would need to come out of their shell in front of their supporters, giving the visitors space and opportunity.

Before the Dutch trip, though, came an away match at Stoke City. Hollins was injured so Osgood returned, and Cooke went into midfield, though he played so deep as to be ineffective. The players seemed jaded after their midweek exertions, maybe with one eye on the second-leg in four days' time, and were well beaten 2-0 through David Herd and a late effort by Peter Dobing, who ran 50 yards through a tired defence. The *Daily Telegraph* was scathing, describing Chelsea as disorganised at the back and lazy in midfield, with a lack of incisiveness and pace up front. On the returning Osgood, they were equally dismissive. '(He) showed his skills, but as he so often does, he seemed intent on proving how easy the game is, and failed'. Ouch.

Hollins and Houseman missed the DWS second-leg through injury but the team, with Osgood back in the fold despite concerns about his hamstring, should have been good enough to go through, though the fact that Chelsea had never won a European game outside Britain was highlighted in the press.

The second-leg followed the pattern of the first, the English side dominated much of the play but could not break down the obdurate defence as their hosts refused to take any risks, though Chelsea needed to defend more than at Stamford Bridge. Dutch international winger Rob Rensenbrink caused havoc, embarrassing Harris to such an extent that he had to swap sides with McCreadie inside 30 minutes. What the *Daily Telegraph* euphemistically called 'solid tackling' eventually reduced Rensenbrink's effectiveness and he had to go off after the game went to extra-time.

After two hours of goalless tedium the captains had to toss a coin, this being in the days before penalty shoot-outs. The *Daily Mirror* 'Tails! Out Go Chelsea' headline said it all, as Harris wrongly called heads. A tossed coin had worked in their favour against Milan in 1966 but had bitten them hard this time.

Nobody gave DWS a realistic chance of going through. Their team included a café owner and a masseur, they were 13th in the Dutch League which, apart from Ajax, Twente Enschede and Feyenoord was not supposedly blessed with quality sides. The result was a massive disappointment and the sense of missed opportunity, of failure to achieve potential, was a very real one. Ron Harris, in '*Soccer The Hard Way*' reckoned DWS's sole objective was to prevent Chelsea scoring. To their credit, they succeeded.

An utterly dejected Sexton was defiant. 'I am not going to buy fresh players. I am satisfied with those I have got. Just because you lose one match everyone puts the pressure on' but clearly 210 minutes with no goals was a concern, regardless of how organised and resolute the opposition was, and it was evident a number of men were out of form. Baldwin worked hard, as ever, but missed the best chance near the end of normal time, the manager admitting afterwards that he needed 'a commanding header in the middle' to convert Houseman and Cooke's crosses. Despite his inexperience, Hutchinson could have fulfilled that role.

The players lost a £75 win bonus, and the attendance bonus from the next round (which was potentially £120 on a 40,000 attendance) as well as any chance of European glory. Had they gone through, Chelsea would have met Glasgow Rangers in the next round, a certain money-spinner. The financial loss to the club was a significant one. They earned £78,000 from their home games in their run to the 1966 Fairs Cup Semi-Final and early elimination meant under £20,000 had been earned from this truncated European campaign.

Transfer talk that October was relatively quiet, though it was recognised the manager would be looking to strengthen his squad given the lack of quality cover in a few positions. Promising young Charlton centre-half Paul Went was signed as a schoolboy by Sexton when he was Leyton Orient boss and could have provided necessary defensive cover, but the interest never went anywhere. 17-year-old defender Derek Vaughan, previously on the books as an amateur, signed professional terms.

So in the same month Chelsea had been knocked out of two competitions by supposedly inferior sides and had failed to score in their last three matches. League form had been inconsistent, though they were in fifth place, just three points off the top, and had lost just three of their last 16 League games. Until the FA Cup started in January, the focus could be 100% on Division One, trying to put a run together such that a real challenge for the title was a possibility.

Liverpool	p16 23pts
Everton	p16 23pts
Leeds United	p15 23pts
Arsenal	p16 22pts
Chelsea	**p16 20pts**
West Ham	p16 19pts

November 1968

With no midweek games, November was in theory a less demanding month for the players, though with Manchester City, Liverpool, Arsenal and Leeds United to face there was no shortage of tough matches to look forward to.

In the build-up to the home clash with the League champions, City boss Joe Mercer wondered whether Chelsea would suffer a hangover after the shock European exit. Osgood started the game, but was wearing the No.4 shirt, playing in midfield and deputed to look after City danger-man Colin Bell. This was certainly an imaginative move by Sexton, though not without risk as if Osgood had been in lackadaisical mood, the midfield could have been over-run.

Mercer was soon proved wrong as Tommy Baldwin gave Chelsea an early lead. The afternoon exploded into life before half-time when John Boyle tackled City winger Tony Coleman hard then kicked the ball at him, provoking a wild kick in retaliation before Ron Harris sent Coleman flying. Boyle was promptly sent off by referee Rex Spittle, limping off with an outsized lump on his knee. Spittle and Coleman, who was highly fortunate to receive no punishment for his part in the incident, were roundly booed for the rest of the game and the latter spent much of the time avoiding retribution from Boyle's incensed colleagues. The normally placid Sexton had an altercation over the matter with less placid City coach Malcolm Allison at half-time.

Despite being down to ten men Chelsea fought hard, particularly David Webb who clashed with Mike Summerbee, and it was to their great credit that they scored a second, a seemingly rejuvenated Osgood rounding goalkeeper Harry Dowd and netting, before he had to go off with a pulled muscle. This was a magnificent performance against the champions, cheered to the rafters by the home support, in need of a pick-up after the disappointment of Amsterdam. Sexton said he intended to ask for a personal hearing after Boyle's sending off, and Chelsea said they might use the *Match Of The Day* television pictures in his defence. Those BBC pictures were the first time football highlights had been shown on British television in colour. The move of Osgood to midfield had worked, he found and used space to great effect, and certainly gave Sexton interesting options. If the role utilised his manifest talents effectively, then the boost it would give could be significant.

For the trip to second-place Liverpool, Chelsea, in fourth, had no reason to be intimidated. Baldwin was out with a poisoned foot, Osgood stayed at No.4 after his hugely encouraging display against Manchester City, Barry Lloyd coming in for his first full senior game for over a year. Within four minutes Lloyd had set up Birchenall to put the visitors ahead and the team performed heroically, seemingly in control until a Bonetti error minutes before half-time let Ian Callaghan equalise. Worse, just before the interval Houseman gave away a penalty and Tommy Smith put the home team ahead. There were no further goals. The *Daily Mirror* headline 'Sexton Is Right To Be Proud Of These Fighters' spoke volumes and the manager was pleased with his side, if disappointed with the result, later describing it as one of their best displays of the season. Chelsea refused to be intimidated by Liverpool's hard men, Harris and McCreadie in particular giving as good as they got.

Unsurprisingly, given his two highly effective games in the position, the manager planned to keep the resurgent Osgood in his new midfield role. Sexton enthused that 'Ossie's form has been a revelation since the switch. I'm keeping him there now. It seems we've at last found his right position. He is facing the play all the time and breaking from midfield just when he has taken the ball off an attacker - which is when he is most dangerous. He does well defensively and is also making chances'. A relieved player commented 'I've felt a lot happier, and I've got a lot of my confidence back'. In '*Ossie The Wizard*' he said Liverpool manager Bill Shankly bid £100,000 for him the day after the game. The player was briefly potentially interested in moving, but he was never going to be allowed to leave.

Chelsea had a proud record of 26 home matches without defeat, stretching back to West Bromwich the previous December, going into the game against Southampton. Hollins returned and slotted in at right-back, Boyle demoted to substitute. Southampton were in the lower half of the table with one win and seven goals in nine away trips, so their 3-2 victory was therefore something of a surprise. Chelsea went 2-0 down to a Ron Davies goal, a ludicrous mix-up between Bonetti and Hollins led to the latter's own-goal and though the ever-industrious Baldwin pulled one back, Davies headed another. Birchenall reduced the arrears but though they poured forward, they lacked the guile to equalise. Davies had caused massive problems the previous season, and it seemed Chelsea had yet to work out a way to deal with him and his partner Mike Channon, as Webb and Harris were led a merry dance.

On this occasion, when the strikers were missing chances, Osgood seemed wasted in midfield. Sexton glumly observed 'we still have to get the right balance between attacking football and winning football', as Southampton were highly effective on the break. Worse, McCreadie went off after 30 minutes with a twisted knee, though substitute Boyle performed well, showing he had been unlucky to be dropped. The crowd, including the King of Norway, was just 31,325, disappointing given the home record and fifth place in the table.

The Chelsea board made a strange, unexplained decision that week and sacked club doctor Paul Boyne, and replaced by Dr. G. Dymond, who had held the position before Boyne's appointment five years earlier. Boyne, medical man on the last England Under-23 tour, and also England's youth team doctor would not comment except to say 'the news came in a letter on Thursday. I was due at the ground on Friday'.

Bobby Tambling had scored just once in 12 games, but it was still a surprise when he was dropped for the forthcoming trip to fourth-place Arsenal, a club he had a strong scoring record against. He was philosophical about the decision, admitted he had been out of touch, stressed it was up to him to fight his way back and made it clear he preferred to play in the reserves rather than sit on the touchline. Lloyd replaced him with a strong managerial endorsement. 'He has matured a lot and been playing very well'.

Chelsea had slipped to eighth when they visited Highbury and were now a worrying six points off joint leaders Liverpool and Everton. The hosts were unbeaten at home, so it was an excellent result for the visitors to win 1-0, through a glorious Houseman goal, created by Lloyd. Houseman spent the match in a bruising battle with hard-man Peter Storey and the goal was just reward for his courage. Both sides looked to counter-attack, making for an extremely tedious stalemate until the goal. Bonetti was widely praised for his efforts in repelling Arsenal's forwards as they came into the game after half-time. Osgood revealed a new-found physicality in his new midfield role, an attitude he was to regularly display in the years ahead. Boyle and Frank McLintock took physicality a stage further, both being booked after a flare-up.

Cooke had a quiet game against Arsenal and admitted to the *Daily Mirror* that he was worried about his 'drastic' loss of form. 'I am going through a bad spell, and I don't know why it is. It may be more of a mental problem than anything else'. He had talked it over with Sexton and admitted it was playing on his mind. 'I am training hard enough. In fact, I am doing more to try to put things right.' He was the third senior player that season, after Osgood and Tambling, to suffer a loss of confidence but retained his place in November's final match, a tough home encounter against Leeds United.

Interviewed beforehand, Leeds boss Don Revie thought Chelsea would be involved in the latter stages of the title race and praised their ability to bounce back from disappointment. McCreadie returned after missing the Arsenal encounter, Boyle moving to stiffen the midfield to replace Lloyd, who was substitute. The result was a 1-1 draw, with two extremely late goals from Mike O'Grady and Osgood, Chelsea for once coming from behind. Osgood thrived in his new midfield role and the first half-hour was full of high quality football. After a bad foul by Harris on Terry Cooper, however, the mood changed, physicality came to the fore and the trainers were kept busy tending a string of injured players. Paul Reaney and Webb were booked but at least six others could have been.

As was not unusual after games with Leeds, trainer Harry Medhurst was busy in the following days. Birchenall (who had limp off to great applause, after enduring a series of nasty tackles), Boyle, Houseman and Harris all picked up knocks and were doubtful for Sunderland away the following Saturday.

McCreadie marked Lorimer out of the match, but Bremner did the same to Cooke, who gave another poor display, out of form and without any obvious answer to massed defences. The Scot told the *Daily Mirror's* Ken Jones 'it isn't easy to see a way clear. I have tremendous respect for Dave Sexton, and I want to do well for Chelsea. I am fit and I have the ability to do certain things well. But it's just not going right for me'. He admitted he needed to improve his final pass. Jones felt 'his major problem may well lie in the critical self-analysis to which he exposes himself. Best's temperament means he can shrug off a bad game, but Cooke finds it more difficult', a perceptive view of one difference between arguably the two most skilful players in English football at that time.

Chelsea were heavily linked with Tottenham right-back Joe Kinnear, as Boyle, Hollins and Harris had all been forced to play at full-back recently. A figure of £65,000 was mentioned and player-exchange was also suggested. Sexton wanted to bring Allan Harris (twice on their books and a 1967 FA Cup Finalist) back from Queens Park Rangers but his board vetoed the idea. They supposedly watched Barnsley centre-half Eric Winstanley and made another bid for St Mirren forward Jim Blair, though that approach went nowhere. They were also keen on centre-half Liam O'Kane of Derry City, but he signed for Nottingham

Forest in December. Lots of rumours, no deals, as was so often the case. Tommy Docherty was the new Queens Park Rangers manager and was expected to bid for Hinton who he rated highly. Luton were the latest club supposedly interested in reserve forward Joe Fascione, who was also linked with a loan move to Brighton.

Osgood appeared for the Football League against the Irish League in Belfast - a welcome return to representative football, having been omitted the Under-23's earlier that month. Delighted to be back in the international picture, he agreed that he deserved to be dropped a few weeks earlier, admitted he hadn't wanted the ball and said he relished his new midfield role. He made the only goal, for Geoff Hurst, and was hopeful of more chances as the season developed.

Excitement reigned in Peter and David Gray's house as their sister, Maureen, took over the running of the official John Hollins Fan Club. For 2 shillings (10p) per year members would receive photos and a regular newsletter about him. One evening John phoned their house. David answered it. 'You can imagine how excited as an 11 year old I was to speak to him! My sister received some weird letters whilst doing this role; one person wrote that 'John's form has deteriorated rapidly since he was married'. I was not sure what my sister was meant to do about that? Tell him?'.

Chelsea's average home League attendance after 11 games was 39,330, the highest at that stage for nine seasons. Crowds so far were up 63,991 on 1967-68, from 368,642 to 432,633. This was encouraging, though still several thousand less than Manchester United and the two Merseyside clubs.

So Chelsea ended November, and halfway through the 42-match First Division season, in sixth place, losing touch with leaders Liverpool. Although they had faced four highly-rated teams that month, it was the disappointing performance against Southampton that demonstrated once again the infuriating inconsistency that seemed likely to prevent a serious title challenge for another season.

Liverpool	p21 32pts
Everton	p21 30pts
Leeds United	p20 30pts
Arsenal	p20 27pts
West Ham	p20 26pts
Chelsea	**p21 25pts**

December 1968

December in theory brought with it an easier run of games, and it was essential that Chelsea picked up a decent haul of points or the League leaders would disappear over the horizon and the chance of Fairs Cup qualification would also reduce. Having gone out so meekly, Sexton was determined to return to European competition as soon as possible, and to do markedly better.

The first December game, at 15th place Sunderland, should have been a chance to build some momentum. Charlie Cooke was omitted, telling the *Daily Mirror* 'I was dropped and that's that. I've nothing more to say about it...I don't know what the trouble is. I have trained harder and even done extra work, but I cannot find the answer. It must be in my mind'. Bobby Tambling returned after a spell in the reserves, coming on as substitute for Barry Lloyd, who was making what turned out to be his last appearance for the club.

The encounter was an exciting one, but poor defending contributed heavily to an unexpected 3-2 defeat. Ron Harris gave away a penalty for the first, scored by Calvin Palmer, Colin Suggett netted a second and Tommy Baldwin pulled one back before a defensive shambles, caused by a bad Hollins back-pass, let in George Mulhall for the third. Alan Birchenall netted for Chelsea but to no avail. Sunderland's tallest forward was a mere 5ft 8 ins, but they still caused the visitors problems in the air.

Defensive frailty was regularly causing points to be lost and a 1-1 home draw with mid-table Wolverhampton Wanderers a week later was not what the doctor ordered, either. Cooke was recalled, after a strong game for Scotland in Cyprus, replacing Houseman, but had another quiet match. Tambling replaced Lloyd. It was another attractive game, on a rock-hard, icy pitch, but another point was wasted. Harris gave away another penalty, this one scored by Mike Kenning. Osgood had one saved by Alan Boswell but luckily had another opportunity from the spot, in the last minute, and coolly equalised. Chelsea now had just one win in five, only five in 19, clearly unacceptable for any side with serious trophy aspirations.

Some good news in midweek when the FA Disciplinary Committee held a personal hearing, where they found that John Boyle's controversial sending off against Manchester City was 'sufficient punishment'. He used the *Match Of The Day* film to successfully argue that no further action should be taken against him. A host of Chelsea representatives attended the hearing in support of Boyle, including Sexton, trainer Harry Medhurst, Harris and Birchenall. The versatile Scot would have missed League matches against Ipswich Town and Stoke City as well as the FA Cup-tie against Carlisle, so the finding was a great relief to Sexton. The committee were unable to consider whether other incidents in the game, including Tony Coleman's retaliation on Boyle, were worthy of punishment.

A trip to struggling Leicester City looked an opportunity to rediscover winning form, and so it proved. Despite going behind early on to a Mike Stringfellow goal, Chelsea rallied, Osgood equalised and in the last ten minutes they over-ran their opponents, scoring three more, through Osgood, Birchenall and Tambling. Birchenall was widely praised, as was Cooke, making three of the goals despite a sticky pitch which should theoretically have hindered him. Rarely so far that season had Cooke, Osgood and Tambling, each having suffered a serious loss of form, all played well in the same match, but that day they all clicked.

Boxing Day brought a trip to lowly Ipswich Town. Stewart Houston made his first senior appearance for nearly a year, and only his second ever, replacing McCreadie, out with a gum infection. David Webb, it seems hard to believe in retrospect, had not scored in two years. He certainly made up for it that afternoon, with a remarkable, and most unlikely, hat-trick from centre-back. Two headers from set pieces taken by Tambling and a drive from the edge of the box did the trick in a comfortable 3-1 win. Supporter Barry Holmes recalls that 'his third was treated with wild celebration. Like a Tiller Girl, he came skipping back down the full length of the ground towards us fans waving his usually redundant left leg in the air to show us all which foot had secured his treble'. Bizarrely, no photos of the hat-trick apparently exist, as the Chelsea photographer was given Christmas off. Chelsea's task was made easier when Derek Jefferson, already booked for fouling Birchenall with whom he continually niggled, kicked him and was sent off after an hour. Leading scorer Tommy Baldwin had to go off having damaged his right knee ligaments and was expected to be out for a few weeks.

The scheduled home game two days later against Stoke City was postponed, meaning a very uncluttered New Year period for the players, as the next match, a Third Round FA Cup-tie against Carlisle United from Division Two, was not until Saturday January 4th.

A *The People* feature on the most promising youngsters of 1969 included Barry Lloyd but not Alan Hudson or Ian Hutchinson, arguably even better prospects. The list - Lloyd, Dave Thomas, Steve James, Alan Foggon, Keith Dyson, Paul Richardson and Asa Hartford - is interesting in that only two (Thomas and Hartford) became full internationals, though the others all had decent-enough careers.

Sexton had decided that the centre-half he wanted to sign was Fulham's John Dempsey. *The People* said he opened negotiations by offering two players in exchange. One was Lloyd, the other presumably Marvin Hinton, who would have been supernumerary. Lloyd had been available for £15,000 earlier in the season, but his value had gone up after a few decent first-team appearances. This offer was turned down, but Fulham apparently told Dempsey they would accept £75,000 - the Chelsea board had to decide whether they could afford that amount. The paper implied the manager had been frustrated by lack of available funds in his quest to strengthen the team. He was also having Greenock Morton midfielder Preben Arentoft, who had impressed in the two European games, watched, and highly-rated Orient defenders Dennis Rofe and Tommy Taylor were also monitored.

Centre-half Allan Young, 27, was likely to move to Torquay in the terms were right. After seven loyal years at Chelsea, almost always a permanent reserve, he understandably wanted first-team football and turned down a loan move to Bristol City as, for family reasons, he wanted a permanent move. To replace him Chelsea looked at Charlton Athletic's Paul Went, with winger Joe Fascione possibly going in the other direction. 21-year-old South African forward Derek Smethurst signed for the club on a permit from Durban City and scored on his reserve debut against Swindon Town.

A frustrating month, with unnecessary dropped points and a winnable game postponed. Chelsea ended it in fifth place, League glory looking an increasingly distant prospect. The FA Cup, the last realistic chance of silverware that season, loomed large.

Liverpool	p26 39pts
Leeds United	p24 37pts
Arsenal	p24 35pts
Everton	p25 35pts
Chelsea	**p25 30pts**
West Ham	p25 28pts

January 1969

The manager had a rare midweek day off, his first since taking over, and talked to the *Daily Mirror* about the Carlisle FA Cup-tie. 'I am more confident about my team now than at any other stage of the season. Peter Osgood's form has given us height in defence, he tackles well, and his distribution and ball play are first-class. In the nine games he has played in midfield, his standard has not dropped'. It is interesting that he saw Osgood's height, presumably primarily at set pieces, as such a useful defensive tool. Baldwin's knee problem was not progressing as hoped, and he was out of the Carlisle tie, but Eddie McCreadie had recovered from his gum infection and played, as did Alan Birchenall, recovered from flu.

Chelsea were quoted at 12-1 for the FA Cup, with Liverpool 8-1 favourites. Carlisle sold all 3,000 seat tickets they were allocated, FA regulations meaning visiting teams were allocated 25% of tickets. It was just as well there was a healthy representation from Cumbria, as a disappointing crowd of 37,322 (paying £14,451) turned out to see Chelsea comfortably win 2-0 in an uneventful game, Tambling and Osgood both netting just before half-time. Their Second Division opponents were unable to cope with the quality of the likes of Cooke and Osgood. A magnificent display by goalkeeper Alan Ross was widely praised, preventing a much higher score, and he rightly received an ovation at the end. Webb, inspired by his hat-trick at Ipswich, looked more threatening than Tambling or Birchenall.

Chelsea drew a trip to Second Division Preston North End in the Fourth Round and were made 11-1 sixth favourites. Before then they had two tough matches. A trip to champions Manchester City, strangely languishing in a mediocre 14th place, followed by the visit of League leaders Liverpool.

Peter Houseman gave Chelsea a 24th minute lead at Maine Road and they defended well until Neil Young equalised before half-time. After the interval, the visiting defence struggled as City scored three without reply, running out comfortable 4-1 winners, the first time Chelsea had lost by three goals for over a year. Bobby Owen, in for the injured Mike Summerbee, scored his first two goals for City and Stan Bowles, a substitute for the hurt Colin Bell, caused all sorts of problems. The visitors, particularly Cooke and Osgood, actually played quite well and the team were praised for some magnificent football, but marking was erratic, chances were missed, and a 4-1 defeat was undeniably a poor result.

The centre-back partnership since mid-November had been Webb and Harris, the fullbacks Hollins and McCreadie. Harris's strength was not in the air and Hollins was wasted at right-back, so defensive strengthening was required, arguably both at centre-back and full-back. Cover became more important when Allan Young left for Torquay. He had been at the club since November 1961 but had only made 26 first-team appearances. The Liverpool programme praised him for helping so many young players in the reserve side. The programme also announced that gates had been installed behind the East Stand to prevent supporters changing ends at half-time, after concerns about them doing this to confront rivals. Previously a line of police had attempted to do this.

Liverpool, amazingly, had not won on any of their previous 14 visits to London. Tommy Hughes came in for the injured Bonetti, his first senior game that season. Hughes broke his nose in a collision with Birchenall and played on in agony, which made his mistake for Liverpool's first goal, dropping Peter Thompson's cross at Roger Hunt's feet, understandable. In scoring, Hunt broke Gordon Hodgson's Liverpool League scoring record of 223 goals. Alun Evans scored a second and though Tambling pulled one back after Webb was moved up front, it was not enough, Webb having a late effort cleared off the line by Ron Yeats. Again, it was an excellent game which the inventive hosts played a full part in but failed to get anything from, watched by Sir Alf Ramsey and Scotland boss Bobby Brown. Sexton criticised his defence for becoming 'loose' after Hunt opened the scoring and the team missed Baldwin's non-stop industry.

The loss of Young, and the fact that Hinton had not started a first-team game since the DWS Amsterdam away tie in October, emphasised the urgency of signing an experienced, high-quality centre-half. After months of rumour that issue was eventually, and effectively, resolved when 22-year-old John Dempsey was finally signed from Fulham. Barry Lloyd (valued at £30,000) went the other way, as did £40,000. Lloyd wanted first-team football, so it was a good move for him. Sexton observed that having Harris and Dempsey as his centre-back partnership and playing Webb at right-back allowed the latter to attack more and let Hollins, who had made ten appearances at right-back that season, return to midfield.

The cup-tie at Preston therefore became even more important. Stewart Houston played at right-back, replacing Houseman in a reshuffled XI as Bonetti returned. Dempsey had joined the club before the Preston away tie but could not play, despite a bout of flu meaning he had not been cup-tied with Fulham, because new signings were ineligible to appear in the FA Cup for 14 days. Given the nose operation endured by Hughes, if Bonetti had not recovered from his sore leg then apprentice Alan Dovey would have been called into action. Fortunately, that was not necessary.

The result at Deepdale was an uninspiring 0-0 draw though the visitors would have won but for the wonderful goalkeeping of Alan Kelly. *The Observer's* 'Casual Chelsea' headline spoke volumes as they failed to impose their superiority. They opined that 'Chelsea needed a sense of urgency, not complacency' and thought Osgood seemed wasted in midfield, though supporter Barry Holmes recalls a superb 'long, mazy run …which reminded me of his early days before he broke his leg'. Seven visiting players were hurt in a brutal encounter, including the unfortunate Birchenall who was twice kicked in the head. Osgood collided with Webb and damaged his thigh.

The replay, on Wednesday January 29th, has gone down in club history, but not for positive reasons. Young centre-forward Ian Hutchinson came in after two reserve goals against Tottenham and Chelsea were two up, through Hutchinson and Birchenall, and coasting with just 16 minutes left. The floodlights then suddenly flickered and dimmed. Referee Ken Burns hesitated a moment and waved play on but a minute later the pylons down one side went off leaving the pitch in semi-darkness. Burns led the teams off to jeers. Shortly afterwards the PA announcer said 'we are doing what we can to put things right' so the crowd cheered and hung around but, after a desperate attempt to fix the problem, the match had to be abandoned, hugely frustrating for the 44,239 spectators who had paid £16,142.

Hutchinson's first senior goal for Chelsea was therefore chalked off. It was also supposedly Peter Bonetti's 400th first-team game, which would now be the visit to Southampton. An incandescent manager commented 'this is terrible luck…in a match that was clearly ours'.

An investigation revealed there had been a fire in a junction box caused by overheating, which was extremely embarrassing for the club. The *Daily Mirror* ran a 'Chelsea's Bonus For Lucky 5,000' headline with Secretary John Battersby bemoaning the fact that season-ticket-holders would not have to buy replay tickets and that the club would contribute the balance to the receipts to ensure Preston and the FA got their proper share.

The fault clearly ultimately lay with the club, but there was no apology to the other 39,000 spectators who had paid good money and would have to pay more good money to watch the rearranged tie, assuming they could get there. Because the floodlights could not be guaranteed to work, the game was scheduled for 15.00 the following Monday afternoon, meaning many supporters would in theory be unable to attend.

The sad but inevitable news broke that Ken Shellito had to retire, after five years and four operations battling a knee injury. He had made 12 reserve appearances that season but had broken down again in October and was scouting future opponents for Sexton.

Cooke was fined £75 for a booking incurred playing for Scotland against Austria. The disciplinary hearing also considered a previous international booking and one against Tottenham the previous August. The *Daily Telegraph* thought he presumably avoided suspension as two of the bookings were happened while not appearing for Chelsea, so the club would have lost the player through events beyond their control.

Not for the first time, it was reported that Sexton was interested in Fulham winger Les Barrett and had also expressed interest in Queens Park Rangers inside-forward Alan Glover.

Chelsea had played just two First Division games in January and lost both but remained in fifth place, although European qualification was the best they could now aim for. The FA Cup was the only potential source of a trophy and, assuming Preston could be disposed of in the replayed replay, the visit of Stoke City awaited in the Fifth Round.

Liverpool	p28 43pts
Leeds United	p27 42pts
Everton	p28 40pts
Arsenal	p26 37pts
Chelsea	**p27 30pts**
West Ham	p26 29pts

February 1969

February started with a trip to Southampton followed, 48 hours later, by the rearranged Preston replay. John Boyle, Charlie Cooke, Peter Osgood, Tommy Baldwin and Peter Houseman were all injured for the Southampton game and doubtful for the cup-tie. There were fears that Baldwin might need a cartilage operation but in the end his leg was put in plaster, and it was hoped he would be back by March.

'*Kings Of The King's Road*', possibly using understatement, described Sexton as 'unhappy' that week when Cooke, Osgood, Boyle and Birchenall stayed drinking in nearby Barbarella's restaurant rather than report back to Stamford Bridge for treatment on their injuries after lunch. In '*The Bonnie Prince*' Cooke reckons it was him, Baldwin, Boyle and Osgood who were the miscreants, whereas the *Daily Mail* and *Evening Standard* named Osgood, Cooke and Boyle. Whoever was involved they received a club fine, a one-week suspension and severe managerial displeasure. Although clearly annoyed, the manager publicly described it as a 'minor internal matter' and said as far as he was concerned the incident was closed. He did make the point that senior players had to learn they were expected to set an example to others.

New signing John Dempsey made his debut at Southampton and 20-year-old centre-forward Ian Hutchinson made his first appearance since October, the original Preston replay not appearing in the record books, though Sexton had praised his performance that day. Stewart Houston continued at right-back and Joe Fascione, who had not appeared for the first-team that season and was the subject of ongoing transfer speculation, was on the bench. It was Bonetti's 400th first-team game, the abandoned Preston tie again not counting.

Also making his Chelsea first-team debut that day was hugely-promising 17-year-old midfielder Alan Hudson. The *Daily Mail* interviewed him, and he explained how tough it was sweeping the dressing room as he was unable to train for seven months of the previous season, during which time he was worried he was not going to be offered a contract. He was in the team because of injuries but Sexton made it clear that 'he isn't in on sentiment but because he is a fine young player - the way he organises things in midfield is first-class'.

All the changes created uncertainty and Chelsea found themselves 3-0 down at half-time, eventually lucky to escape with a humiliating 5-0 defeat after 90 minutes of disjointed ineptitude. David Webb, captain for the day against his old club, had a nightmare capped off with an own-goal, leaving The Dell with bruises, stiches and a black eye as his ex-colleagues continued their bid to be the most physical outfit in the division. They committed 20 fouls that afternoon, the most of any top-flight team that weekend. Ron Davies, a thorn in Chelsea's side in the past, scored twice. His team had now scored 17 goals against them in four matches, of which he had scored nine. He was generally recognised as the best centre-forward in Britain, but Sexton must have been tearing his hair out at the red carpet his defence put down for him. The *Daily Telegraph* thought **Hudson showed confidence and control on his debut, and felt sympathy for him, for making it in 'such a mass of mediocrity'.**

Hutchinson suffered bad bruising of both his kidneys and his hip after a sustained hammering from the Southampton defence and missed the Preston replay two days later. Osgood, Boyle, Webb and Cooke all came in for another momentous cup-tie. 36,522 supporters turned out, excellent considering the Monday afternoon kick-off time, a 'surreal' time to play a game, according to supporter Terry Cassley. Presumably, a range of excuses were given for those absent from work or school for the afternoon. Brian Gaches, who missed school for the match, remembers a **'24 hour stomach upset'** sweeping across West London. Chelsea were obviously favourites, but confidence must have been knocked back by the debacle at Southampton. The club economised on seat ticket costs by overprinting 'FA Cup' on unused League Cup Round Four tickets.

The hosts looked a long way below par. Preston took the lead after 15 minutes through Gerry Ingram and looked fairly comfortable as the game wore on. Archie Gemmill hit the bar after 75 minutes and the subdued crowd of truants and absentees watched with mounting concern as the favourites dithered and floundered. Osgood was thrown up front but to little avail and it seemed like a shock was about to occur. As ninety minutes were up, sections of the home support had started drifting away but Chelsea never gave up, and after Boyle had a back-heel kicked off the line and with the referee continually looking at his watch, Webb headed an equaliser. Sixty seconds later, Cooke hit the unlikely, and probably undeserved, winner, turning home Birchenall's cross shot. Preston were utterly mortified, Chelsea jubilant. A mightily relieved manager commented 'I came down from my seat upstairs to the touchline just in time to see those goals go in, but I had just about given up hope'.

Osgood was extremely grateful to the supporters. 'The fans kept us going more than anything else during those desperate closing minutes. Without their help, I doubt if we would have made it'. Supporter Barry Holmes remembers leaving his spot in The Shed to return to work after 90 minutes, missing Webb's equaliser. He, and hordes of other departees, rushed back just in time for Cooke's winner, though in the chaos of some spectators leaving at the same time, he missed the goal itself. Brian Gaches remembers car horns sounding up North End Road after the win in celebration. A hugely relieved Chelsea had got out of jail and had five days to recover before the next round against Stoke City. The three Preston encounters attracted total crowds of 112,368 and total receipts of £37,679.

Webb had ignored the various injuries he picked up at Southampton to play against Preston. Sexton paid tribute to his centre-back, only at the club a year but already indispensable. 'He's a tough character all right. A lot like (Arsenal's) Frank McLintock. He keeps going every minute of every game'. Although he had been poor at The Dell there was real optimism that his partnership with Dempsey would, in time, flourish, giving a settled defence of Webb, Dempsey, Harris and McCreadie. The new man was very keen to play in the cup-tie, against a Stoke side unbeaten in nine matches, now he had completed his 14-day FA Cup qualifying period. In the end, though, Sexton went with a Houston, Webb, Harris and McCreadie back four, with Hollins, Osgood and Boyle in midfield and Tambling, Birchenall and Cooke up front. The unlucky Baldwin broke down in a reserve appearance, his knee badly swollen, and it looked like he was going to be out for a further significant period.

The tie, scheduled for Saturday February 8th was postponed until the Tuesday because of snow, and then a further 24 hours to allow three inches of snow to be removed from the pitch. Secretary John Battersby had the repaired floodlights fully tested and they were passed, to enable them to be used with confidence.

In a surprisingly open encounter, Birchenall and Osgood put a dominant Chelsea two up after 32 minutes but Harry Burrows pulled one back early in the second-half. Osgood restored the two goal lead, but Peter Dobing's goal kept Stoke in the game. Chelsea hung on, Bonetti making a critical late save from Alan Bloor, and the home support let out a massive roar at the final whistle. Stoke were less than happy, arguing both Osgood's goals were offside. The crowd of 39,191, paying £15,010, was a decent one considering the game had been twice rearranged. West Bromwich Albion awaited in the last eight, their visit to Stamford Bridge bound to be a sell-out. Chelsea were now 6-1 third-favourites to lift the cup. Supporter Geoff Kimber remembers raucous singing on the tube back to Earl's Court, relieved supporters confident of cup success.

Osgood was praised for the quality of his goals and told the *Daily Mirror* how happy he was. 'Since breaking my leg I found I could not go past opponents like I used to. But in those days I was playing for myself, now I like to think I'm very much part of the team'. He generally played midfield in away games but in a more forward role at home and commented 'this suits me fine'. Sexton was equally positive. 'Ossie, for all his skill, is a difficult player to place in the team. But his performances lately have given Chelsea new strength. I would like to see him win an England cap. He deserves it'. He and Hollins were in the Under-23 squad for the Scotland clash the following week, though had the Stoke cup-tie gone to a replay they would have had to withdraw.

Dempsey came in for the next game, at Leeds, and played in the remaining 15 that season. Houston, who had let nobody down, returned to the reserves. Kick-off was delayed 15 minutes as straw was being cleared from the pitch, which was a mixture of grit and sand after heavy frost. Dempsey and Webb were praised for their efforts as Chelsea looked to play tight defence and try to catch Leeds on the counter-attack, two of the few chances falling to Tambling, who could not convert them. A 1-0 defeat, to a Peter Lorimer goal, was disappointing but no disgrace. The *Kensington Post* praised the highly professional performance under a 'Defeat, But Chelsea Don't Need To Worry' headline. There was no shame in losing to a team that in the end won the title by six points, winning 18 and drawing three of their 21 home League games. The degree of physicality was less than in some recent encounters, though Harris was booked near the end for a challenge on Mike O'Grady. Leeds boss Don Revie praised Bonetti for his agility and anticipation, seeing him as more adept at starting an attack than any other keeper in Britain, which enabled Chelsea to break quickly.

Though the FA Cup Quarter-Final was not until March 1st, there was already huge interest in the tie. West Bromwich sold all 13,880 allocated tickets and Chelsea put 32,000 terrace tickets on sale the previous Sunday morning. The clash was certain to be a 52,200 sell-out, though given the capacity was 60,000 (a figure reached against Manchester United two weeks later) the club must have been disappointed that the agreed ticket limit was 7,800 less, meaning the two clubs missed out on potential extra revenue between them of nearly £2,000.

Before that came a home encounter with lowly Sunderland, a chance to get their League campaign back on track after four successive defeats. Jimmy Greaves had already scored four against them for Tottenham that season, and Geoff Hurst six for West Ham, so it was not entirely unexpected that Bobby Tambling should make hay, scoring four second-half goals in a runaway 5-1 victory after Birchenall had given Chelsea the lead. Colin Suggett's goal was scant consolation for the visitors.

Osgood ran the match, and Houseman's wing play caused no end of problems and led to three of the goals. The dominant display and goal rush was certainly food for thought for the watching West Bromwich manager Alan Ashman and his squad, their game with Ipswich being postponed. Tambling looked as sharp as ever, happier to be back to his normal weight of 12 stone after falling almost a stone below that after his operation. His goal-hungry efforts took his Chelsea career goal total to 199. As David Gray recalls, there were fears that injuries had put his hero's first-team spot at risk, at the age of only 27, so for him to get four goals was a massive fillip for both player and support, his popularity with supporters undimmed. Despite the weak opposition, fellow supporter Brian Gaches remembers his 'fantastic' performance and it is clear that, to so many supporters of that era the humble and self-effacing Tambling was, and remains, an absolute hero.

Renowned *Evening Standard* writer Bernard Joy interviewed Osgood who revealed 'I am one of those players who need a jerk now and again. I lose interest quite easily'. Joy saw him as 'at the crossroads' and needing to 'take the road of devotion and hard work to reach the very top'. He had a reputation as a practical joker from earlier in his career but commented 'I believe that I'm more responsible'. Sexton felt his move to right-half had improved his play enormously, the star unsurprisingly agreeing.

In an interview in the *Coventry Evening Telegraph*, Cooke claimed he felt 'more at home at Chelsea then ever he did with Aberdeen'. This was good news indeed, reflecting the strong club spirit that existed at Stamford Bridge and Cooke's confidence in the side's ability to stay among the leading clubs. The *Sunday Mirror* ran a feature on Osgood under a 'England Soccer Needs A Player With Flair' headline. They saw him as 'first the wonder-boy, then a problem boy and now once more a pin-up boy' but stressed he needed more consistency. Baldwin had his plaster removed but was still some way from match-fitness.

Osgood, Hollins, Tommy Hughes and Boyle all missed out on caps when the England v Scotland Under-23 game at Sunderland the previous Wednesday was called off. Webb and Harris had already received two bookings that season, one more and a trip to the FA Disciplinary Committee would beckon. Testimonials for Tambling and Charlton Athletic's Brian Kinsey were arranged for the end of the season, Chelsea scheduled to be playing Charlton twice.

Sheffield Wednesday offered money plus big centre-forward John Ritchie, valued at £70,000, for Birchenall, but Chelsea turned the bid down. Assistant-manager Ron Suart informed the player of Wednesday's bid, and also of Newcastle's expression of interest. Birchenall commented 'I don't mind at all. It would have been nice if a bit ironical...to play for Wednesday having left United. But I'm not too bothered, for I'm enjoying football...as much as I have done at any time in my career', hardly demonstrating a desperate commitment to remain at Chelsea.

Wing-half John McHugh of Clyde was watched. Portsmouth were interested buying Hutchinson but there was no way Sexton would sell him, given he was developing so well, so quickly. An old story revived itself, with a report in *The People* that Queens Park Rangers were expected to bid £25,000 for Hinton. 17-year-old defender Michael Maskell signed full professional terms that month.

Chelsea, despite only gaining two points from three games in February, remained in fifth place at month-end. One serious problem with regard to European qualification was that Arsenal were eight points ahead with just 12 matches left and massive favourites in the League Cup Final against Third Division Swindon Town.

Leeds United	p31 50pts
Liverpool	p31 46pts
Everton	p29 42pts
Arsenal	p29 40pts
Chelsea	**p30 32pts**
Southampton	p31 32pts

March 1969

The consensus was that a draw would be a decent result for mid-table West Bromwich. Their captain Doug Fraser warned that they would provide stiffer opposition than Sunderland (which was not saying much) and was unworried about them being seen as underdogs. Chelsea approached the game with great confidence, the fifth year in a row they had reached the Quarter-Final, with no home FA Cup defeat since Huddersfield Town in 1964. Harris commented that 'the FA Cup is all we have left to play for. We mean to win'. The squad watched film of their opponent's 1968 FA Cup Final win over Everton. The *Daily Telegraph* correctly observed that Chelsea had 'a remarkable cup record in recent seasons, but they have always met late disappointment'. John Boyle was substitute despite being fit, as Sexton picked the attacking line-up that had taken Sunderland apart. Eddie McCreadie, after four years of disappointment, thought 'it must be our year'. 52,285 paid £19,700 to find out if he was right.

David Webb netted after ten minutes with a clever flicked header and John Dempsey missed a wonderful chance to head a second. Chelsea looked completely on top early on, Dempsey keeping danger-man Jeff Astle quiet. Inspired by midfielder Tony 'Bomber' Brown, however, Albion came back into the match as the hosts appeared complacent and Brown took advantage of defensive hesitancy to equalise before half-time.

An Astle goal was disallowed after the interval as Ron Harris had handled the ball, and the linesman had already flagged for a penalty, before Astle headed the ball in. West Bromwich players rightly complained that the advantage should have been played by referee Jim Finney. Peter Bonetti brilliantly saved Brown's penalty, and the game looked as though it could go either way. Tambling had a decent shout for a penalty turned down by Finney and argued after that he was tripped. Finney was equally adamant afterwards that 'he was not tripped, he fell'. The visitors immediately broke away and Astle scored, Bonetti fumbling and failing to stop his shot, while his furious forwards were still at the other end of the pitch, appealing in vain for the penalty. Chelsea missed chances, Houseman unfairly became the butt of the crowd's ire and the forward line, together with midfield lynch-pin Osgood, were unable to make effective headway.

As the hosts became increasingly frenzied, Boyle was thrown on for Osgood with a minute to go and was almost immediately booked after appearing to kick at Albion goalkeeper John Osborne, sparking a goalmouth punch-up involving 15 players. Albion held on for a famous victory and Chelsea were out. The defence was criticised for mistakes and an inability to deal with Astle and Brown, the midfield berated for lack of energy and ideas and the forwards slaughtered for missing a host of chances.

West Bromwich certainly played in a physically assertive style and The Shed can be heard on the *Match Of The Day* footage bellowing '*dirty, dirty ba**ard, la-la la-la lah-la-lah*' at John Talbut after he clattered Cooke, who, unusually, lost his temper and struck the defender. It seemed as though their players just wanted it more than some of Chelsea's did, and old criticisms about freezing in big games duly resurfaced. The *News Of The World* made pertinent, damning, biting comment. 'There can be no doubting the ability in the side but there is an outsize question mark about the determination and dedication of some of their star players'. The *Daily Mail* headline 'Chelsea - You Chucked It' spoke volumes. They scathingly observed that 'it is the lack of sustained efficiency that makes Chelsea promise so much yet disappoint so badly...Talent does not bring concentration. Style cannot conceal the cracks in their application'.

A massively disappointing result for everyone involved in the club. West Bromwich were a decent team but had just three away League wins from 15 games and Chelsea should have been well capable of beating them, but failed when it mattered most, as their opponents showed greater fight and resilience. The side now had little to play for, given they were out of all three cup competitions and had little chance of qualifying for Europe.

Sexton limited the number of changes he made for the rearranged Stoke City home match the following Wednesday. Ian Hutchinson had fully recovered from the bruised kidneys sustained against Southampton, but Baldwin had broken down in training, having not played since Boxing Day. In the end he chose the same side, giving the FA Cup flops the chance to partially redeem themselves.

The sense of anti-climax and FA Cup hangover was palpable, only 19,856, the lowest attendance of the season at Stamford Bridge to date by some 6,000, turning up to watch Webb score the only goal of a tedious game in near silence, many leaving before the end. **Osgood went off at half-time with a recurrence of his knee problem, substitute Hutchinson adding weight, impetus and aggression after the interval. The programme referenced his long throw as 'The Hutchinson Hurl'.**

For the League visit to West Bromwich three days later, Cooke was dropped for Boyle. Osgood was out with a heavy cold, meaning the two most creative players at the club were missing, and Hutchinson came in. He was to remain in the side for the rest of the season. An extremely comfortable 3-0 victory was an excellent result, but miniscule consolation for the FA Cup elimination. Boyle and Hutchinson, both with something to prove, had excellent afternoons and scored, the latter's his first in senior football. Houseman, the butt of supporter frustration in the FA Cup, beat three men for the other and produced an inspirational performance. The Daily Mail reckoned he had set a managerial poser. Going forward, did he go with the mercurial Cooke or the steady and reliable Houseman?

Cooke was philosophical about being dropped, telling the *Daily Mirror* 'I'm not a bit surprised. I am badly out of form. The reason? I don't know. I'll have to play myself back into form (in the reserves)'. The manager explained 'Charlie has had a number of indifferent games. He is no longer enjoying his football. We shall have to see what this break will do'. In the event, he only started one more first-team match that season whereas Houseman missed just one and, in essence, had clinched a regular starting place for the next few years.

Two days later an even smaller attendance than for the Stoke game, just 17,639, saw relegation-threatened Coventry go behind after two minutes to Tambling's 200th Chelsea first-team goal, a marvellous achievement from a loyal one-club man. Hutchinson scored his first home League goal and, though Neil Martin pulled one back, an unchanged side held out to win 2-1, their supporters whistling desperately for the referee to end the match. Hutchinson again impressed and it was clear he was likely to become a regular, putting pressure on Birchenall, Tambling and, when he returned, Baldwin. Supporter Peter Gray remembers the weather was terrible, which did not help the attendance, the atmosphere or the quality of the football.

The fifth game of a busy, if sadly inconsequential, month saw the visit of Manchester United, always a huge attraction. This was no exception, despite United going into the match in 17th place, underachievement for a team that had won the title and the European Cup in the previous two seasons. Due to the clash with the League Cup Final between Arsenal and Swindon Town, all other games in London that weekend were moved to the Friday night, but it is hard to see why, unless a lot of London supporters were likely recipients of Wembley tickets, as the tie was not live on television.

The gates were closed at 14.40, with 60,436 packed in, Chelsea's largest Stamford Bridge crowd since the visit of Liverpool four seasons earlier, when both were active title contenders. It made the gate closure in the same game the previous season, with under 55,000 inside, even more remarkable. Supporter Peter Gray, locked out with an estimated 10,000 others, vowed to buy a season-ticket to ensure that never happened to him again.

Osgood returned, having only been on the bench against Coventry, but it was Birchenall, not Hutchinson, who was omitted to accommodate him, ending a run of 54 consecutive appearances and flagging that Hutchinson was clearly a very real threat to his place. In a rousing encounter on a really muddy pitch, Webb gave Chelsea an immediate lead, his seventh goal since Christmas, and Hutchinson doubled it after an excellent cross by John Boyle and a one-two with Tambling. Steve James pulled one back before half-time, but Tambling scored a superb third. Denis Law's penalty was mere consolation as Chelsea deservedly saw the game out for a magnificent 3-2 victory, their fifth League win in a row and enjoyed by millions watching *Match Of The Day*. United's defence struggled to cope with Hutchinson's power, Tambling's speed and Houseman's control and, at the back, Webb and Harris's physicality and diligence kept Law and George Best relatively quiet.

The press picked up on the fact that Hutchinson was still part-time, as he was working as an apprentice engineer half the week. His cost, £2,500, would be doubled when he made ten appearances and an extra £2,500 added if he won an Under-23 cap, as seemed increasingly likely. 'I don't bother about who I'm up against, just on concentrating on the job I've got to do' was his admirably calm perception. He was praised by United's England star Nobby Stiles and described, accurately, as the 'bargain buy of the season' by the *Sunday Mirror*. The *Kensington News* headline 'Hutchinson Swagger Stuns United' spoke volumes.

Though there were moves to scrap the daft Fairs Cup 'one club per city' rule, it was highly likely to still be operating the following season. Chelsea's chances of qualifying were increased when Arsenal, unexpectedly, deservedly and utterly humiliatingly, lost the League Cup Final 3-1 to a Don Rogers-inspired Swindon Town. Sexton's men still had to overhaul The Gunners in Division One and though they were just two points behind with eight games left, Arsenal had four in hand.

The European cause was not helped by a 1-0 defeat at Tottenham where Chelsea set up to catch the home side on the break but were unable to do that effectively in a heavy wind, missed chances and conceded a late Neil Johnson goal. Harris did his usual tight marking job on Jimmy Greaves, the latter, unusually, eventually losing his cool and the pair of them having a scrap.

Osgood, playing in midfield, and Bonetti were in an experimental Football League line-up against the Scottish League at Hampden Park. Bobby Tambling, who had not been part of the international set-up for three years and was an unlikely prospect for the Mexico World Cup, was added to the side though Harris sat on the bench, unused. England won 3-1 and Tambling scored the second goal. Sexton told his Scotland counterpart Bobby Brown that he intended fielding Cooke and McCreadie against Arsenal in mid-April, two days before Scotland met West Germany in a crucial World Cup qualifier.

Earlier that month Chelsea had been knocked out of the FA Youth Cup 2-1 at home to West Bromwich. Of that side, just two ever played League football for Chelsea, Alan Hudson, who carved a niche in club history and Tony Potrac, who made just one appearance. Similarly, the reserve team at Bournemouth the following week contained Potrac, three who had first-team experience (Tommy Hughes, Stewart Houston and Joe Fascione) and Derek Smethurst, who came from South Africa, broke through a couple of seasons later and played 19 first-team games. The other six never made it at Chelsea. This lack of youngsters coming through was a growing concern and was going to cause problems a few years later. Interestingly, earlier that season the *Evening Standard* interviewed ex-chief scout Jimmy Thompson, who brought the likes of Jimmy Greaves, Barry Bridges and Bobby Tambling to Chelsea. He revealed that a few years ago, the club had turned down the chance to sign Trevor Brooking of West Ham (who was at the club for three months) and Luton's Bruce Rioch (who scored six goals in a trial), both of whom went on to have successful club and international careers.

The final encounter of a very mixed March was a trip to meet an Everton side that were a place ahead of Chelsea in the table, had not lost a home game for seven months but had recently been shattered by their last-minute FA Cup Semi-Final defeat by Manchester City. The match kicked off at 19.30 to avoid a clash with that afternoon's Grand National and Chelsea started like the winner, Highland Wedding, finished. Hutchinson, impressive again, beat two England men, Brian

Labone and Tommy Wright, before scoring. A Joe Royle penalty equalised before half-time but Birchenall, in for gastric flu victim Tambling, won the points with a quality header from a Hollins cross. The visitors were organised in defence and swift on counter-attack, exactly as Sexton wanted them to play away, and the *Daily Telegraph* thought them the most efficient visitors to Goodison Park that season.

The *Kensington Post* featured an article on Chelsea's young players. They thought Hutchinson, Hudson, Joe Cruickshank and Michael Maskell were seen as 'stardom-bound' but felt that, as a result, the club might have a problem with some of the established stars. Cooke and Birchenall had been left out in recent weeks and would not be happy with that for long. The two would be in demand and the paper thought maybe this was the time to cash in and free up some money to strengthen the squad. An interesting perspective, and certainly Hutchinson's sudden emergence as a genuine star prospect (he was again the subject of much newspaper praise, after both the Tottenham and Everton games) had re-ordered the striking pecking order. Baldwin was still injured, though there was optimism he would be back before the end of the season. His fitness routine was broken up by a court appearance for drink drinking in January, when out injured, which resulted in him being fined and banned from driving.

It was a quiet March for transfer speculation, though Ipswich Town's unsettled Irish winger Danny Hegan and, once again, £40,000-rated Orient centre-half Tommy Taylor were apparently on Chelsea's radar.

A month when Manchester United and Everton had been beaten should have been considered a very decent one but the dismal cup exit, coupled with defeat by Tottenham, left a sour taste. The team was clearly capable of extending the best but was also prone to losing to sides they should have been able to overcome. Overtaking Arsenal to be the top London club was possible but difficult, and there was also a danger that West Ham, with games in hand, could overtake. Against that, there was still the possibility the one-club-per-city rule could be changed so every point could be vital. It did not help that the matter would not be discussed, and voted on, by the Fairs Cup Executive in June.

Leeds United	p34 55pts
Liverpool	p33 50pts
Arsenal	p33 47pts
Everton	p32 44pts
Chelsea	**p36 42pts**
West Ham	p34 40pts

April 1969

Six League games to go, including potentially crucial London derbies against West Ham and Arsenal. First up was a Good Friday home match against surprise Fairs Cup Semi-Finalists (and eventual winners) Newcastle United, in front of a very decent 42,078 crowd. The in-form Ian Hutchinson converted a John Boyle corner, but Bryan 'Pop' Robson equalised from a penalty a minute later, after handball by Eddie McCreadie, the fourth penalty Peter Bonetti had faced in five weeks, maybe hinting at defensive indiscipline. Supporters became disenchanted as a poor game petered out to a 1-1 draw, chanting for the recall of Charlie Cooke.

For the home clash with Burnley 24 hours later, Sexton rang the changes. Peter Osgood and Alan Birchenall were dropped, Cooke and Bobby Tambling replacing them. The attendance, 12,000 down on the previous day but not bad considering the relatively unattractive opposition, witnessed an exciting, but again overly-physical, encounter. Tambling scored before half-time but had to go off at the interval after a particularly bad challenge by Colin Waldron, a teammate less than 18 months earlier, and possibly still bearing a grudge with his old club. The *Kensington Post* was unimpressed. 'Waldron returned and showed the crowd how lucky Chelsea are to be rid of his violent services...He launched an assault on Tambling that ended only when the winger was carted off with a damaged leg'. They felt he was extremely lucky to only be booked.

The *Daily Mail*, under a 'Waldron Sorry For Being Hateful' headline, interviewed the miscreant. They reckoned he hurt Boyle (twice), Houseman, Hutchinson and Cooke in the first-half as well as Tambling but was only booked only for the latter 'appalling' tackle. Waldron apologised for his behaviour, which by any rational judgement would have resulted in an early bath and a long suspension. 'I don't know what got into me. I wanted to do something special to show the crowd. They hated me when I was here. I don't blame them all that much, I was playing some terrible stuff...I was really keyed up, but I didn't want to get involved in all that bother. I didn't intend to play like that, it just happened....I was too intense...I feel terrible. I bet they don't think much of me here now'. The paper blamed him for an escalation in the feuding, though they concluded that, in the end, 'Chelsea were as bad as Burnley, finally, as the football faded to nothing and kicking and hacking went relentlessly on'.

Waldron was booed for the rest of the afternoon, a sound he had heard before at Stamford Bridge, and rounded his day off with an 'ugly gesture' to the furious home support at the final whistle. He had the last laugh as his team achieved an unlikely 3-2 win, surprising as they had previously scored just 15 away goals all season. Tambling put the hosts ahead, but Dave Thomas equalised direct from a corner before half-time. Hinton came on for Tambling with Webb moving up front, which made life easier for Burnley's forward line, and though Hollins restored Chelsea's lead, Doug Collins netted twice to give the visitors two points.

Hutchinson, not for the first or last time, was targeted for rough treatment, ending with a badly bruised leg and thigh after an ongoing duel with Waldron, but was booked for retaliation on Collins. Cooke, returning after missing six games, played so deep he was less than fully effective and, all in all, it was a highly unsatisfactory afternoon, which coupled with Arsenal's 3-1 win over Wolverhampton, effectively meant no European football at Stamford Bridge the following season unless the rules changed.

A midweek trip to Nottingham Forest proved far more satisfactory in terms of result. Osgood came back in, Houseman dropping out. Birchenall was recalled for Cooke and celebrated by scoring. Hutchinson, who made that one, netted the other in a welcome, if possibly irrelevant, 2-1 win as the visiting defence limited Forest to a Barry Lyons goal. This was enjoyable revenge for a youngster who two years earlier, when playing for International Combustion FC in Derby, was turned away when he turned up at Forest's training ground.

Three games to go, all London derbies. First up was a trip to West Ham, often an attractive encounter but not this time as the result was a disappointing 0-0 draw, Chelsea seemingly happy with a point against opponents who had now been involved in three successive goalless home matches. One bright spot was Osgood, the *Kensington News* noting that his confidence and enthusiasm were returning. They argued he 'is rapidly approaching greatness, the greatness we always knew he had, but feared he would never realise' which, if true, boded well for the following season.

After the low-key Upton Park encounter, the visit of Arsenal two days later was anything but. McCreadie and Cooke were with the Scotland squad and Boyle and Hollins were out injured. Tommy Baldwin was welcomed back after 14 weeks out, Bobby Tambling came in and Marvin Hinton made only his sixth League start that season, highly effective in his role as sweeper.

Beating Arsenal 2-1, only the second side to do the double over The Gunners that season, was a very decent result even if only 37,890 turned out to watch. As was often the way when these sides met, physicality was the order of the day, and this bruising battle was no different. McLintock butted Harris just before half-time, referee Norman Burtenshaw missing that incident and also Osgood bringing down McLintock in retaliation. Hutchinson's throws made both goals, for Webb and Baldwin, and desperate but effective defending limited their rivals to a David Court goal. Bitterness continued after the match and Arsenal coach Don Howe had to intervene to prevent a brawl in the tunnel.

For the season's final Division One game, against relegated West London rivals Queens Park Rangers, the crowd was 41,263, 3,400 bigger than the very disappointing gate against Arsenal. The match itself was dull fare, old-boy Barry Bridges putting the visitors ahead but Baldwin scoring twice in a 2-1 victory, with another three goals disallowed for offside, to end the season with a very decent run of seven points from four games and fifth place. Supporters spent the last 20 minutes chanting Cooke's name, and he finally replaced Osgood with eight minutes left.

13,565 turned up for Bobby Tambling's testimonial two days later, Chelsea beating Charlton Athletic 5-1. In Brian Kinsey's game at the Valley four days later, Charlton won 1-0.

The Observer carried an interview with Cooke by Hugh McIlvanney, who was getting to know his fellow Scot quite well. Cooke, as ever, was considered and interesting in what he said. 'In this game you can still be an adolescent at 30. Everything is done for you…everything is organised for you. You don't live your own life at all'. He realised he was recognised as one of the 22 best players in Scotland without being recognised as one of Chelsea's best 11 and had the dark suspicion that he was a hero without a role. 'I'm worried about now, and whether the whole thing is worth the candle'.

He recognised the paradox that a player may get his head down, and another will have 'pi**ed it up' and the one who has behaved badly may be the one that has played well. He was none too optimistic about making a quick return to the Chelsea team. McIlvanney felt that 'as usual Cooke is too pessimistic. Sexton is in a genuine dilemma about how and where Cooke can be accommodated. But Sexton appreciates that Chelsea, and indeed the game of football, cannot afford to leave such a talent on the sidelines'. The *Kensington News* complained about his 'negligible work rate' and felt he was 'a luxury that Chelsea can ill-afford'. The sadly retired Ken Shellito took on a role assisting Frank Blunstone with the youth team.

Supporters were asked through the programme to vote for 'Chelsea's greatest ever player' and the result was:- 1. Peter Bonetti 17% of the votes; 2. Jimmy Greaves 13%; 3. Roy Bentley 12%.

As supporter David Gray points out, the likes of Osgood, Tambling, Cooke, Frank Blunstone and Terry Venables did not even make the top ten.

Forward Alan Cocks signed professional forms that month. There was talk that Liverpool's Bill Shankly was prepared to offer £150,000 for Osgood, having had a bid turned down earlier in the season. That was unlikely to succeed but there might have been more traction in a bid by ex-manager Tommy Docherty, now in charge at Second Division Aston Villa, who was keen to buy the out-of-favour Cooke and willing to pay £100,000 to buy him. The deal came to nothing, but there must have been temptation in the Chelsea boardroom to try and cash in. Tottenham had also expressed an interest. Not for the first or last time, Sexton was supposedly keen to sign Fulham winger Les Barrett.

With the Mexico World Cup just a year away, Osgood hoped to go on the England tour of South America, but he ended up being chosen for the Under-23 party to tour Europe post-season, with Chelsea assistant-manager Ron Suart in charge of the party. In the end, Osgood was unable to travel, having had his tonsils removed, to his massive disappointment.

Season Summary

Leeds United	p42 67pts
Liverpool	p42 61pts
Everton	p42 57pts
Arsenal	p42 56pts
Chelsea	**p42 50pts**
Tottenham H.	p42 45pts

Another season of promise and, ultimately, frustration. The club would not know until June whether they were in Europe the following season. Fifth place was an improvement of one place on the previous season but still 17 points behind champions Leeds United, a chasm that would be hard to cross without serious player investment, something the board seemed reluctant to sanction without raising the money through sales. Chelsea finished one place behind Arsenal who qualified for the Fairs Cup and won it, which makes one wonder what if... Of course, European football would have meant a more crowded fixture list, which might have compromised the 1970 FA Cup run.

The European campaign had ended disastrously, the FA Cup run little better, the League Cup run never got going. Despite this, Cup competitions seemed a better bet, given an ongoing lack of consistency and the presence of Osgood and Cooke, who on their day were as talented as any players in the country with the exception of George Best. The manager admitted to the *Daily Mail* that 'it is our job to win things and we haven't. We can do better'.

One massive plus was the emergence of Ian Hutchinson as a potentially international-class centre-forward, quickly established in the latter months of the season as an integral part of the team. As *Goal* magazine said, Hutchinson was 'all punch and power...one of the finds of the season'. With the astute signing of John Dempsey the squad was definitely stronger than a year earlier, with greater competition for places.

David Webb was rightly voted 'Player Of The Year' by Chelsea Supporters Club, Birchenall came second and Bonetti third. It is interesting that the perception was very much that the supporter favourites were Cooke and Osgood, yet neither made the top three. Votes were cast by CSC members every 5-6 weeks throughout the season through a form included in their 'Chelsea Blue' magazine, to get a more rounded view of the whole nine months.

Bonetti was generally recognised as the second best goalkeeper in the country after Gordon Banks and had saved four out of eight penalties he faced that season. The first choice defence - Harris, Webb, Dempsey, McCreadie - was as tough as teak, though 53 goals conceded was the worst in the top eight League finishers, which showed that improvement at the back was still needed.

Osgood's conversion to midfield had generally worked very well, though his craft was missed further forward. Hollins, as ever, was a rock of energised dependability and the emergence of Houseman as a more regular first-teamer provided stability and consistency, though he would never have the eye-catching flair of the erratic Cooke. There was a feeling in some quarters that Sexton was still not getting the best from his two most skilful players, trying to force them into a system unsuited to best utilising their talents. There was an over-reliance on the mercurial duo for craft and creativity, the need for a clever ball-player evident. Alan Hudson was pushing hard for a first-team place, and it was hoped he could plug that creative midfielder gap.

The regular team, in terms of most League games played, was:- Bonetti; Boyle, Harris, Webb, McCreadie; Hollins, Cooke, Houseman; Birchenall, Osgood, Tambling. Sub. Baldwin.

The strikers failed to reach Sexton's target of 105 goals set in pre-season. He had wanted 25 from Osgood and Baldwin, 20 from Tambling and Birchenall, 15 from Cooke. He actually got 67. Osgood scored 13 (though to be fair he was in midfield for much of the season), Baldwin 17 (though he was injured for much of the second half of the season), Tambling 19 (many from the wing, a considerable achievement), Birchenall 16 and Cooke just 2. Hutchinson added 6 in 15 games but with Houseman adding 4 and Hollins just 3, the 8 netted by the indefatigable Webb were certainly welcome.

Chelsea scored 73 League goals, only bettered in Division One by Everton, so the goals were there, but the feeling persisted that if all the forwards contributed to the maximum, then there were plenty more to be found. Osgood was effective in midfield and enjoyed his role, facing play, but his absence from the forward line left a gap that would need filling if he was to continue in that role. Cover at full-back and on the wing would also be useful but generally the squad had much to commend itself. Hinton and McCreadie were the oldest members, at 29, so unlike Manchester United, age was not catching up with the side. There was much to look forward to in the following season.

Their average League attendance, 37,613, was fifth best in the country, behind Manchester United, Liverpool, Everton and Arsenal, and a welcome increase of 1,600 on the previous season. Ticket prices for were unchanged despite an inflation rate of 5%, a decent gesture by the club.

Season Overview 1968-69

League Appearances (inc sub) (top 11 players) – Webb 42, Bonetti 41, Harris 40, Birchenall 39, McCreadie 38, Hollins 37, Tambling 36, Osgood 35, Boyle 34, Houseman 32, Cooke 26

League Goals (5+) – Tambling 17, Baldwin 16, Birchenall 12, Osgood 9, Hutchinson 6, Webb 6
League Clean Sheets – 10
Biggest League Win – 5-1 v Sunderland (H) 22/02/69
Worst League Defeat – 0-5 v Southampton (A) 01/02/69

Final League position – 5th
League Record –
Home W11 D7 L3 F40 A24. *Away* W9 D3 L9 F33 A29. Pts 50

Hat-Tricks – 3
Baldwin (3) v Leicester City (H) Division One 19/10/68 Webb (3) v Ipswich Town (A) Division One 26/12/68 Tambling (4) v Sunderland (H) Division One 22/02/69

Sending Offs – 1
Boyle v Manchester City (H) Division One 02/11/68

Biggest Home League Crowd – 60,436 v Manchester United 15/03/69
Smallest Home League Crowd – 17,639 v Coventry City 10/03/69
Average Home League Crowd – 37,613

Cup Performances –
FA Cup – 6th Round
League Cup – 3rd Round
Europe (Fairs Cup) – 2nd Round

Chelsea League Debuts – John Dempsey, Alan Hudson, Ian Hutchinson
Player Of The Year – David Webb

Close Season

Chelsea bought nobody in the close season, but the press rumour mill was as busy as ever. One name that regularly popped up was Terry Venables, who manager Bill Nicholson had said could leave Tottenham. As an ex-Chelsea captain, and highly-talented midfield lynch-pin there was some merit to the link, but nothing became of it. Youngsters David Bibby, Ken Halliday, Brian Turner and Steve Hipwell were all released, Turner quickly joining Portsmouth. Southampton and Leicester City both tried to sign winger Peter Houseman but were rebuffed by Sexton, who saw him as far too valuable and integral to his plans. Birmingham City boss Stan Cullis told *The People* that Tommy Baldwin and Alan Birchenall, men he was potentially interested in, were not on the list of available Chelsea players.

Chelsea were one of a number of clubs interested in £150,000-rated Allan Clarke of relegated Leicester City. Sexton supposedly contacted manager Frank O'Farrell and was interested in a player-plus-cash deal, possibly involving Alan Birchenall. This came to nothing, though ironically two years later Birchenall did sign for Leicester, after O'Farrell had moved on. The thought of Clarke appearing alongside Hutchinson is a mouth-watering one and from a distance of 50 years it seems a pity it was not pursued. At the other end of the scale, a link with 17-year-old Cliftonville goalkeeper Irwin McKibben came to nothing.

A late-May trip to Mozambique for two friendlies against a Mozambique XI had been organised. A match was also originally planned against Slovan Bratislava, but they failed to turn up. The players returned from their summer break for five days of pre-tour training. Hollins missed the trip to Mozambique under somewhat bizarre circumstances, tripping over his dog and scalding his foot with a hot lemon drink meant for his wife.

Chelsea won the first game 9-3 but, ludicrously, Harris got sent off for clashing with an opponent and Cooke for arguing with the referee, in shades of the controversial tour of Bermuda two years earlier. The second game resulting in a calmer 2-1 win. Trainer Harry Medhurst picked up a blood infection on the trip, spent 14 days in hospital and weeks later was still troubled by the bug.

Before the Mozambique trip, the *News Of The World* headline 'Angry Webb Wants To Quit Chelsea' worried supporters. The 23-year-old, an ever-present the previous season and current 'Player Of The Year', slapped in a transfer request before leaving for Mozambique. He complained 'it is now a matter of principle with me. I understood contracts were being reviewed and I was being recommended for a rise' which he did not get. He had one year of his contract to run, and the request was likely to be turned down, but he had made himself arguably the most important player in the team and to aggravate him in that manner reflected badly on the club.

The UEFA meeting in Budapest in mid-June decided the 'one-club-per-city-rule' should be retained so Everton (3rd) and Chelsea (5th) were out and Southampton (7th) and Newcastle (9th) in. Chelsea did not help their cause by failing to send a representative to the UEFA meeting so could not vote on the motion. The *Daily Mail*, under a 'Chelsea's £100,000 Cup Blunder' headline, reported at the end of July that in Chelsea's absence, the vote was 22 to 12 in favour of allowing more than one club from a city to complete, just under the 2/3 majority required for change. Chairman Leonard Withey explained that they wanted to send a delegate but Secretary John Battersby was ill, and his assistant had left the club. Arsenal could not attend as they failed to pay the SF100 fee but in their absence, all Chelsea would have needed to do was work on one delegate to change their mind, the motion would have been carried and the club would have been back in Europe. Incomprehensively they failed to send anyone and, given the potential income a cup run in Europe could generate, quite literally paid the price.

CHAPTER THREE
1969-70
Southern Softies No Longer

Pre-Season

A possible home friendly against Glasgow Rangers on July 30th was vetoed as the Metropolitan Police were not happy about the prospect of trouble, after highly-publicised crowd problems at their visit to Newcastle in the Fairs Cup. Just three pre-season friendlies were organised - in late July at Bristol City and Crystal Palace, and in early August at West German outfit Alemannia Aachen.

In early July, Division Two club Aston Villa bid £100,000 for Charlie Cooke, who had started just one of the last 11 games of the previous season, and Chelsea made the bid public. Villa chairman Doug Ellis, one of the pricklier, more pompous figures in an industry well populated with them, was unimpressed, feeling Chelsea were trying to invite an auction, and rang vice-chairman Brian Mears to express his concerns. Diplomatically choosing not to tell Ellis exactly where to get off, Mears assured him that neither he or his board had given permission for it to be disclosed and were sorry it had been. Sexton was emphatic that the club could not afford to let Cooke go, as 'there are too few players around with his ability'. Villa boss Tommy Docherty, who took Cooke to Stamford Bridge, made it clear through the press that he was happy to pay up to £125,000, but Chelsea remained uninterested.

David Webb's transfer request was to be considered by the board at their meeting in the middle of July, though it was surely inconceivable he would be allowed to leave. Tommy Baldwin and Alan Birchenall made it clear they, too, were unhappy with their contract offers and wanted to talk to Sexton. Birchenall was likely to find it hard to get a regular first-team place with Baldwin, Hutchinson and Tambling in the squad, even with Osgood seen as a midfielder. If Birchenall had become available Everton, Wolverhampton Wanderers and Birmingham City were all reported as being keen to sign him.

Assistant-manager Ron Suart turned down the chance to manage Norwich City, but loyal forward Joe Fascione, who made just 34 first-team appearances in five years but was unlucky to be dropped when Birchenall was signed, was allowed to join Durban City. Goalkeeper Alan Dovey, half-back Tony Frewin and right-winger John Ware all signed professional terms.

As training began and the friendlies loomed, the fitness of two key defenders was a concern. McCreadie was seeing a specialist about a pain in his knee that prevented him from twisting and turning, while Webb had a groin operation and did not know when he would be starting training. The *Chelsea News* reported the manager was putting his players through extremely strenuous physical work, including cross-country runs, and felt 'he is determined to toughen up on discipline'.

Chelsea claimed their new floodlights would be Britain's best during the coming season, seven times brighter than the previous Stamford Bridge lights. Many would just have settled for complete reliability after the Preston fiasco just months earlier. The new lights cost nearly £30,000 and supposedly made their predecessors look like 'candlelight'. Secretary John Battersby claimed 'we believe we are the only club in the world with them, and they make us suitable for colour television'.

In the days before the first friendly, Webb withdrew his transfer request, the directors having promised to review his wages the following year. The remarkably philosophical star, arguably the heart of the team, laudably commented 'if you are in dispute with the club, you cannot concentrate 100% on soccer. I will try to do twice as well this season so that I have a strong case to negotiate a better contract'.

In the first friendly, at Bristol City, Tambling scored but John Galley, a potential target a year earlier, equalised. Two days later, the National Recreation Centre in Crystal Palace was the venue for the Palace friendly, in aid of the National Sports Development Fund. Pre-match, Sexton pointed out to the *Daily Mail* that teams must be at 'a peak of readiness' from the first League game so friendlies had by necessity become more competitive. He argued that the squad system meant fewer players were automatic choices, so they were playing for their place pre-season. Certainly, it was looking hard for men like Tommy Baldwin (still occasionally feeling his knee ligament injury), Bobby Tambling, Birchenall and Cooke to try and secure regular first-team places.

Chelsea won 2-0, goals coming from a Tambling penalty and John Hollins. Young South African reserve Derek Smethurst, signed on permit from Durban City in December 1968, who went on as substitute in Mozambique but had never played a competitive game for the first-team, was a surprise inclusion in the side. Osgood was badly fouled by Palace's new centre-half Roger Hynd and had to go off, not what player or manager wanted less than a fortnight before the League season started. Webb went on as substitute, but McCreadie was not ready to appear.

Neither Webb nor McCreadie featured in a fractious, niggly 3-1 defeat against Alemannia Aachen five days later, Hollins scoring the only goal in a defeat where Sexton's men struggled to put together coherent football. Cooke, captain Ron Harris and Stewart Houston (who played in all three friendlies as McCreadie's deputy) were all booked. Baldwin pulled a muscle and had to be replaced by Ian Hutchinson. Tambling, Hutchinson and John Boyle all needed treatment in a bid to get fit for the tough opening game at Liverpool.

More bad news was that combative midfielder John Boyle was probably out for the first six matches, the cartilage previously operated on had swollen up after the Aachen friendly and he needed to rest it for three weeks. McCreadie was having cortisone injections to speed up recovery from a knee strain and Webb was having treatment for his groin problem. Not ideal with nine games in the first month.

Birchenall, who did not play against Palace, was not keen to go to Aachen as his wife was expecting a baby, appearing for the reserves at Enfield instead. He was unlikely to be match sharp for the trip to Anfield.

The season previews made interesting and, in some cases, uncomfortable reading. In the *Evening Standard*, Sexton talked about the 'embarrassment of riches' in his squad. The paper pointedly commented 'it is a pity the stern competition for places does not lead to supreme dedication among all the players. The only thing which prevents men like Osgood and Cooke reaching the very top is their own casualness'. Ouch. The *Sunday Mirror*, on a similar theme, argued that **Chelsea** needed to find 'a way of producing a consistent level of performance from those who brush the fringe of genius - notably Osgood and Cooke - and grafting it successfully onto the well-drilled fitness of the rest'. There was yet more in the same vein from the *Sunday Telegraph* 'I fear Sexton may again experience difficulty in persuading some of his stars to make best use of their gifts'. The authoritative *Football Monthly* magazine repeated the message in their season preview. 'Some of the zest has gone from their game and the wayward performance of players like Osgood and Cooke, together with the surprisingly jaded form of Hollins, does not augur well for an improvement. They may well slip back a few places'.

Chelsea had two game-changers they needed to effectively utilise this special talent consistently, not sporadically as in recent seasons and the widespread criticism must have hurt the pair. Hollins, too, needed to be at his absolute best, though he could certainly never be accused of less than 100% effort. Sexton had high hopes of youngsters Alan Hudson and Houston breaking through and certainly any pressure that youth products could put on established stars was to be welcomed.

Osgood, under pressure to perform as World Cup year began, gave an upbeat and positive interview to the *Evening Standard*. He admitted he had lost confidence when he returned after breaking his leg. 'I really love (playing in midfield). As a striker you get marked tight. Now I have the freedom to create...I'm not playing for myself anymore. I'm a team player now and more conscious of the responsibility involved'. In the season just finished 'I was more concerned with marking than creating in midfield...I'm hoping to play a slightly different role this season with more freedom to create chances. After all, that's my strength'.

Claiming he had trained harder in pre-season than ever before,

Osgood was confident about the coming season and praised Hutchinson who he thought showed tremendous promise. The article concluded if he made the World Cup party 'then that midfield switch will have paid off for Chelsea's golden boy'. At the start of the summer Liverpool boss Bill Shankly had bid £150,000 for the star, but detailed discussions never took place. There was also talk that he could be swapped for midfield schemer Terry Venables, the ex-Chelsea captain unhappy at Tottenham, plus a cash adjustment, but Sexton was extremely unlikely to agree to any deal that involved Osgood leaving.

Osgood's autobiography '*Ossie The Wizard*' was close to completion and the *Chelsea News* reported that 'stories about some of the wilder moments of Peter Osgood's controversial career have, I hear, been censored by Chelsea's board of directors. The amendments deal chiefly with Osgood's off-the-pitch activities'. It seems strange that the player could say what he liked in the press but not in a book, though maybe the club thought they were saving him from himself, if the censored sections were particularly lurid.

August 1969

For the League opener at Liverpool, Sexton, missing key defenders David Webb and Eddie McCreadie, was forced to move midfield engine John Hollins to right-back, partnering the inexperienced Stewart Houston. John Boyle was out injured, and Alan Birchenall dropped but Charlie Cooke, omitted for much of the latter part of the previous season, was back.

The team lined up:- Peter Bonetti; John Hollins, John Dempsey, Ron Harris, Stewart Houston; Charlie Cooke, Peter Osgood, Peter Houseman; Tommy Baldwin, Ian Hutchinson, Bobby Tambling. Sub Alan Birchenall.

Even from a distance of over 50 years that midfield looks light in terms of tackling and dynamism, the full-backs ill-equipped to deal with the high-class wing-play of Ian Callaghan and Peter Thompson. And so it proved, as Liverpool won extremely comfortably, 4-1.

Osgood, who had an ineffective afternoon, and Hollins were booked as Chelsea struggled to stamp any authority on proceedings, the latter struggling against the excellent Thompson. Hutchinson scored the equaliser but, him apart, there was little threat up front as Birchenall, who had missed just three League games the previous season, sat forlornly on the bench.

A dismal start but, 48 hours later, the chance to remedy the situation with a trip to London rival West Ham United. Houston picked up an injury at Anfield, but McCreadie was welcomed back. Baldwin was relegated to substitute to allow Marvin Hinton, out of favour for most of the previous season, to come in alongside Dempsey as sweeper, Harris moving to full-back.

Chelsea gave an improved first-half display but conceded goals by Martin Peters and Geoff Hurst after the interval. Hutchinson limped off with a twisted ankle, having accredited himself well against England captain Bobby Moore, much of the fight upfront disappearing with him. Harris bravely struggled through the latter stages with a calf problem, likely to put him out for a few weeks.

Two games, no points. The first home match, against Ipswich Town, was a chance to break the duck. Webb and Boyle were still injured, the latter back in Scotland and in plaster after his cartilage operation, and Harris joined the list of absentees, though fortunately Houston was fit to return. Osgood, who despite his claims about training hard had what was to become his customary slow start to the season, was dropped to the bench, Baldwin coming in. Birchenall, out of favour, languished in the reserves at Bristol City.

Osgood, clearly frustrated at being dropped, did what he often did when under pressure and opened his heart to the press, this time to the *Daily Mirror*. He admitted he was 'unable to cope with the massive demands now being made on the fitness and mental attitude of midfield players...I have no real quarrel with the club. I shall have to sort things out with Dave Sexton, and it may be better for me to have another go at settling as a front player....Everyone accepts that teams and players who don't put themselves about aren't going to get anywhere. You have to be hard and aggressive to survive...There's too much I'm not capable of...I just haven't a chance in a midfield role'. A vastly different message from the recent *Evening Standard* interview.

He continued in similar vein to the *Daily Mail*. 'The emphasis is getting more and more on graft. Mr Sexton wants people who can run all day. I am not and never could be, that kind of player. I am disappointed to be dropped but I shall just have to accept the way the game is going'.

To go from being so positive to so negative in a week, after just two matches, demonstrated how fragile Osgood's confidence must have been. He later admitted he was always a slow starter to the season, which possibly demonstrated a lack of enthusiasm for the hard miles demanded in pre-season training, but being dropped at the start of a season he hoped to end starring on the world stage in Mexico was not what he needed, or expected. These comments reinforced the perception that for all his undoubted star quality, Osgood was a high-maintenance player that Sexton and Ron Suart needed to work carefully with to heighten his fragile confidence and get the best out of him.

In a tedious game between two 'mediocre' sides, the disappointing 29,613 crowd was becoming increasingly frustrated, and a slow-handclap started before half-time. Chants of 'Osgood, Osgood' broke out and biggest cheer of the afternoon occurred after 74 goalless minutes when he was sent on for Tommy Baldwin. Seconds later, Hutchinson headed home Cooke's cross to bring two very welcome points. The performance still left a lot to be desired, though, and Ipswich could have equalised late on.

The People waxed lyrical about Hutchinson, again comparing his unstinting effort to that of some teammates. 'His enthusiasm, fortunately for Chelsea, is so far ahead of his short experience that he shames some of his senior colleagues'. Osgood made a difference when he went on, but the defence without Webb and Harris was compared to a 'lace curtain'. They argued the manager was no nearer solving 'how to knot all that talent into a team'. Ipswich captain Bill Baxter felt it was the worst Chelsea team he had ever played against.

With little time to draw breath, Chelsea had four days to recover before a home derby against West Ham. The attendance of 43,346 was nearly 15,000 down on the previous season, probably a reflection of both the team's start to the season and the sheer number of games.

The result was a 0-0 draw, but that score hides 90 minutes of great courage and commitment by a severely depleted Chelsea side, already missing Harris, Webb and Boyle before kick-off. Osgood returned to the starting line-up. Tambling damaged ankle ligaments and had to be replaced by Birchenall early on. Hutchinson then suffered concussion and broke his nose in a collision with Bobby Moore and had to go off after 30 minutes. Hinton had a thigh strapped before half-time and Dempsey required three stitches on a gash on his chin afterwards. Down to ten men, and with Hinton walking-wounded, Chelsea fought magnificently. Birchenall came in for especial praise, the Chelsea programme reporting he had a 'fine game'. The *Daily Telegraph* thought that, after that performance, 'adverse opinions of Chelsea's stamina might need to be revised'.

With just three days before a trip to Southampton, Harry Medhurst perhaps unsurprisingly reckoned it was his worst injury crisis in his 16 years as Chelsea trainer. It had happened at the worst time as with two games a week, injured players missed twice as many appearances. Nine first-team men had been injured in ten days.

Tambling was likely to be out for a while. In fact, though nobody could have guessed it at the time, he was to start just one more Division One game for the club. Boyle, Hutchinson and Harris were also out of the trip to Southampton so the return of Saints old-boy Webb, even if not fully fit, was especially welcome. Chelsea twice fell behind, but Osgood twice equalised with high quality finishes before limping off with bruised and blistered feet. Ron Davies, a real thorn in their side in recent years, was kept quiet by Webb and given the circumstances, a 2-2 draw was a very decent result. The *Kensington Post* thought the 'tough, bruising game against West Ham did wonders for their confidence' and certainly Chelsea stood up for themselves with commendable spirit. The *Daily Mail* was critical of one player, however. 'Things often ended at Cooke, seldom began there. Southampton read him like a book and slammed him shut...Chelsea can only hope that, among their many other problems, Cooke's is merely a temporary...confusion, not a permanent one'.

An unusual incident occurred when referee Gordon Kew blew for half-time after 38 minutes after misreading his watch. The players showed him the clock, he consulted a linesman then played on for the other seven minutes. TV footage of that match demonstrates the excellent away support Chelsea were getting, the noise from the travelling hordes drowning the home supporters.

A tough encounter at Tottenham four days later was not what Sexton's band of wounded brothers needed, but it was what they had to deal with. Young midfield talent Alan Hudson, who the club had such high hopes of, came in for his second first-team game, replacing Baldwin, the only change. Cooke was the victim of a clumsy Martin Chivers tackle and hobbled off in the first-half with a damaged ankle, replaced by Stewart Houston and changing the balance of the team. Webb went up as a striker and headed Chelsea in front just after half-time (a tremendous goal according to Geoff Kimber, who was there), then dropped back, leaving Birchenall up front on his own. Hudson again impressed, the team missed a couple of chances and looked well set for a welcome away win until Jimmy Pearce lashed a 25-yarder past Bonetti ten minutes from time. Given the absences and the very mixed form so far it was a decent result, though dropping a point was a disappointment given the lead and the performance.

The final game of a mixed month was at home to newly-promoted Crystal Palace, only the second League match they had ever played at Stamford Bridge. Harris was back but Tambling, Boyle, Hutchinson and Cooke were not. Hudson retained his place after a solid game at White Hart Lane and Osgood reverted to a striking role. Roger Hoy put Palace ahead against the run of play and though Osgood equalised with a brilliant flicked header from a McCreadie cross, he could have had a hat-trick and was again criticised for his casualness. Palace centre-back John McCormick was unhappy that he heard a 'leave it, John' call to leave the ball, he did so, and Osgood promptly headed home. A lackadaisical Chelsea should have won easily, goalkeeper John Jackson making a series of critical saves to earn a 1-1 draw.

Southampton and Leicester City both made approaches regarding buying Houseman but were turned down by Sexton. Birmingham were the latest club to be interested in buying Birchenall, currently languishing in the reserves. Assistant Ron Suart went to watch highly-rated Blackpool winger Tommy Hutchison and the club were interested in Arsenal midfielder Jon Sammels. Either of those two talented players would have been decent signings, though Hudson's anticipated emergence might have negated the need for Sammels. Harris saw Derek Smethurst, Alan Hudson and Stewart Houston all pushing for first-team places, so maybe the need for new blood was becoming less acute.

The Palace programme contained an interview with Hutchinson detailing how he arrived at Chelsea. Suart and youth coach Frank

Blunstone had gone, on a recommendation, to watch Cambridge United's goalkeeper Keith Barker, and returned singing Hutchinson's praises. Blunstone went back with Sexton, they 'saw something to work with' and paid an initial £2,500 for a player already probably worth over £100,000. Before joining Chelsea, he had gone from Burton Albion to Cambridge United for £2,000.

In the Ipswich programme, chairman Leonard Withey, in a 'The Chairman Writes' column, updated supporters with good news regarding the stadium lease. 'Negotiations between the freeholders and the tenants have been continuous during the past 12 months. I am pleased to say all outstanding matters have been agreed and I expect to sign the new lease within the next few weeks'.

An *Evening Standard* article talked about Chelsea making 'extensive improvements when the motorway goes over the railway at the back in 1971'. The motorway never happened, but this showed that the club were certainly open to ground improvement and redevelopment ideas going forward. The new floodlights were used for the first time against West Ham. They were only 40% effective but still as good as most stadia. Installation was scheduled to be completed by the end of August.

Football Monthly magazine revealed that Palace, somewhat optimistically, wanted to alternate home matches with Chelsea, despite being in different parts of London. A Palace spokesman pointed out there were already a number of Chelsea season-ticket-holders living in the area. 'We can't expect them to give those up right away, but we hope to be able to produce football good enough to tempt them here in perhaps two or three seasons'.

The *Daily Mail*, under a 'Chelsea Are Not Playboys' headline, ran an interview with an angry Sexton. 'People accuse this club of having a playboy element. I know such things have been said behind my back. Playboys, well they must be in a very tiny minority because what we've accomplished in the past few weeks has taken real character. I am proud of them, and they know it'.

One reason the playboy tag might have been used was that earlier in the month Baldwin had been charged with assaulting a policemen. He was a passenger in a car whose driver allegedly failed to supply a breath test or provide a specimen. The reality was that some of the squad, including the most talented players in Osgood and Cooke, were on occasion enjoying a less-than-monastic 'King's Road' lifestyle, something that was going to become more of an issue for Sexton as the years rolled by.

A strange August, and a disappointing one, ended in four successive draws. Just six points from seven games, with one win (against bottom-placed Ipswich Town), meant a depressingly low 15th place. Six goals in seven matches was not good enough, especially when supposed title rivals Liverpool and Everton had scored 18 and 14 respectively. Ten goals conceded was also unacceptable for anyone with title aspirations. Improvement was needed, and quickly. The *Football League Review* correspondent opined that Chelsea were one of the noisiest crowds in the country. It was to be hoped the team gave them more to be noisy about.

In mitigation, the manager praised the spirit of the players, stressing to the *Daily Mail* how the team went to Liverpool lacking Webb, McCreadie and Boyle at the back and held them for an hour. 'Since then we have been hit by injury after injury. Eight of the first-team squad have missed at least one game through injury (after seven games)'.

September 1969

The League Cup was a clear opportunity for silverware, with the added benefit of a Fairs Cup place for the winners, and Chelsea travelled to Coventry City for a Second Round tie. Sexton set up defensively, fielding Marvin Hinton as an extra defender, hoping to catch City on the break. Clearly, he would not have been completely unhappy with a draw, given the fitness issues still plaguing his squad. Ian Hutchinson was fit again, and it was his 50th minute header, from a breakaway cross by Peter Houseman, that put them through to the Third Round.

The *Daily Mail* headline 'Cautious Chelsea Scrape Through' summed up the disparaging press coverage. The *Coventry Evening Telegraph*, perhaps unsurprisingly, was outraged. 'Chelsea unashamedly pulled so many men back in the first-half that it was the nearest thing I have ever seen to the complete negation of football...In the light of their result, it was totally justified from their point of view. Such is the sickness of modern soccer'. Strong words, but Sexton will not have worried a jot, his tactics working perfectly. His target was to qualify for the Third Round and qualify his team did. He was very upbeat after being drawn at League champions Leeds United in the next round. 'Terrific...This is something to get our teeth into. We'll get a result up there'.

Sexton, pleased with the success of his tactics at Coventry, unsurprisingly employed the same team and similar plans at Manchester City three days later. A 0-0 draw showed the effectiveness of the tactics, though the press coverage was again unflattering. *The People's* headline was a classic. 'Chelsea Bores Pinch Point'. They went on 'what a waste...I have never seen such an exaggerated display of defence in depth'. Peter Osgood had a goal disallowed in almost Chelsea's only attack. Alan Birchenall played just outside his own penalty area for much of the afternoon. The ITV television audience must have yawned their way through their Sunday afternoon football.

The *Daily Mirror* reported that City manager Joe Mercer was deeply unimpressed. 'It was a bad match for the crowd, and I only hope Chelsea start to open the game out and give supporters something to look at'. Sexton responded unapologetically. 'We appreciate the fact that this was not an attractive match to watch, but that is what we have to do in this day and age. We came to play defensively. Against a side that prides itself as the best attacking force in the business it is my opinion we won the day' and a point at City was certainly a very decent result. Plenty of teams went to Stamford Bridge and played for a point, and it was up to manager and team to outwit them. The same applied to City that day, and, for all the attacking prowess of Colin Bell, Francis Lee, Mike Summerbee and Co., they were unable to do so.

Mercer, a highly respected figure in the English game, addressed his club's 75th Annual General Meeting later that week. 'We will be adventurous exponents of attacking football no matter how defensive the game becomes. We do not want to be the kind of team Chelsea were here on Saturday because this type of team will never get results'. Sexton will have been delighted by the two clean sheets, evidence that his hard tactical drills with the defence was starting to bear fruit. The next match was at home, against fifth place Wolverhampton, and clearly he would not play nine men back in that one, but it must have been highly reassuring to know that against a forward line as potent as City's his team were able to shut up shop.

Alan Hudson came in for Hinton, a clear statement of intent. Ironically, it was poor defending that prevented Chelsea winning. They went two up through John Dempsey (with his first goal for the club) and Osgood. The latter's goal was lauded by Sexton, 'long used to living with his enigmatic mixture of indolence and brilliance' and not a man prone to hyperbole, as 'I can't recall him scoring a better one'. Chelsea relaxed with ten minutes to go, and Hugh Curran was allowed to score twice, silencing the disbelieving home support and infuriating the manager. To make matters worse, a Dempsey error caused the first, then Bonetti dropped a cross to allow the equaliser. The *Daily Telegraph* was contemptuous of their attitude. 'If Chelsea remember to stay awake during the closing stages of their remaining League games this season, then the point they tossed away on Saturday may yet prove to be well spent…They jogged along contentedly until sleep overtook them'. Ouch.

The sixth successive League draw must have driven Sexton to distraction as, after the notable defensive discipline shown by the whole team in the previous two matches, unforgivable relaxation cost them dear. The phrase had probably yet to be invented, but this was 'game management' at its worst.

The news that Bobby Tambling needed a cartilage operation, and would be out for at least six weeks, was a blow, reducing the number of striking options available. The operation could have taken place earlier, but the problem was initially assessed as a ligament issue. Equally worryingly, it was also reported that Tambling was seriously considering giving up professional football to become a full-time Jehovah's Witness, following in the footsteps of Wolverhampton's Peter Knowles. He made it clear he would let the club know first when he had decided. A perturbed manager clarified that Tambling would make up his mind at the end of the season 'so the less said about it the better'. In the end, he decided not to follow that path.

38,599 watched the capitulation against Wolves and the following Wednesday just 24,790 turned out at Stamford Bridge (which turned to be their lowest home gate of the season) to watch the 14th place draw specialists play Burnley, who had drawn three of their four away matches, including a 3-3 draw at Anfield. Hutchinson, an ever-present so far that season when fit, was dropped for Tommy Baldwin. Sexton explained 'Ian has been doing very well but Tommy gives us something different'. He also pointed out that with two games against Leeds and one against Arsenal coming up in eight days before the end of September, 'obviously Ian will be needed for at least one of those'. The run of six successive League draws ended with a relatively comfortable win. After a tedious first-half, Birchenall headed the first just before the hour and Houseman netted the second in injury-time. The performance was still disappointingly predictable, but the points welcome.

The First Division game at Leeds was to be followed four days later by the League Cup-tie between the two sides. Given the mutual enmity, the chances of all 22 starters from the first match being available for the second were low. And so it proved.

Boyle made his first appearance that season after his cartilage operation, replacing the injured Osgood, and Cooke came in for the unfit Hudson. Leeds won 2-0, through a disputed Johnny Giles penalty and a Peter Lorimer drive. Chelsea defended in depth but were rocked when Harris had to go off with a badly bruised shin, replaced by Houston. Webb badly dislocated a shoulder, so they ended with ten men, and Birchenall limped through most of the 90 minutes after a nasty kick. All three had to go to hospital on their return to London. In addition, Dempsey, Cooke and McCreadie all received injuries sufficient to put them out of the Republic Of Ireland against Scotland clash the following week.

So, apart from the six who picked up injuries at Elland Road, overworked trainer Harry Medhurst also had to deal with the already-unfit Tambling, Hinton, Hutchinson, Hudson and Osgood. Until the casualty count began to mount, Chelsea gave a good account of themselves and were on top for much of the first half-hour. Houseman was 'the best player on the park' according to the *Sunday Mirror*, and he seemed, at last, to have deservedly established himself as a first-team regular.

Medhurst worked miracles, to get Hinton, McCreadie, Dempsey, Birchenall, Osgood and Cooke fit for the cup-tie. 18-year-old centre-forward Alan Cocks was added to the squad and would have played had Birchenall not been fit. To play at Elland Road without Webb and Harris's competitive physicality was a tall order and the team deserved enormous credit for forcing a 1-1 draw. They almost won, a last-minute Paul Madeley equaliser countering Birchenall's superb 71st minute opener.

Bonetti had repelled everything Leeds could throw at him so though the result was a good one, there was obviously disappointment at not hanging on.

Although marginally less violent than the injury-ridden encounter four days earlier, tackles still flew in and Birchenall badly hurt his leg and was replaced by Cooke near the end. The *Daily Mail* was not particularly impressed with Chelsea's approach. The normally even-tempered Houseman was booked when he 'senselessly chose to engage in a personal vendetta with Billy Bremner...(Chelsea) chose to defend in depth, a job they did with skill and commendable understanding...When defence became a matter of desperation for (Chelsea) they almost crossed the narrow line between he-man aggression and a return to undesirable Leeds-London antagonism'. In *Goal* magazine, Ken Jones praised Houseman, highlighting how Sexton used him to hustle Jack Charlton, a tactic that worked well. Jones thought Houseman had blossomed in midfield and was no longer just a touchline-hugger.

As if there was not enough festering acrimony, there then followed a row about the replay date, as Leeds had an immovable European Cup-tie at Lyn Oslo of Norway the following week, though given they were 10-0 up after the first-leg they were hardly under undue pressure. Their boss Don Revie weighed in as vice-chairman Brian Mears criticised the Leeds board for not telling their Chelsea counterparts their intentions in good time. The Football League got involved and the date was put back a week to Monday October 6th to suit Leeds, meaning Chelsea had to move a trip to Ipswich Town. Chelsea accepted this decision, but under protest.

A Chelsea player (possibly Osgood, who regularly aired his views in the *Daily Mirror*) admitted these latest developments would not help feelings. 'There is definitely needle between us. They came out after half-time on Wednesday and gave us a kicking. It was no match for cowards. I can tell you there will be a few scores to settle when we do face them again'.

Hutchinson, seemingly targeted, picked up three separate injuries in a reserve appearance against Southampton the previous weekend. He damaged a hamstring and a tendon but, worse, had to have his knee put in a compression bandage and was likely to be out for a few weeks at least.

There were less than three days for the walking wounded to recover before another likely-to-be-bruising encounter, this time at home to Arsenal, to round off a tough seven-game September. Harris returned and Birchenall was fit to play. It is just as well he was, as he had one of his finest games for the club, scoring twice, having another disallowed, looking particularly sharp in and around the penalty area and leading the much-vaunted Arsenal defence a merry dance. Baldwin chipped in the other in an excellent 3-0 victory, their biggest home win over their North London rivals in 61 years. Brian Moore on *'The Big Match'* was fulsome in his praise and the highlights footage shows a confident, exciting team deserving their comfortable win. *The Observer* bestowed particular praise on Birchenall and Cooke, who 'produced enough of his magic to justify his recall to the side', though it was now 21 months since he had scored a League goal.

Sexton was magnanimous, telling the *Daily Mail* 'people are saying this is the worst Arsenal defeat at Chelsea for 60 years. Statistically they are right, but I thought Arsenal played very well. Chelsea got the breaks and Arsenal didn't'. It was far less physical than recent encounters between the clubs, the *Daily Telegraph* observing 'these keen London rivals proved it is possible to complete an important match without crippling tackles, ill-temper, intimidation or gamesmanship'. They felt Chelsea won…because Hollins, Houseman and Cooke controlled the middle of the pitch'.

Chairman Leonard Withey was taken ill, so vice-chairman Brian Mears took over his position temporarily, Viscount Chelsea becoming temporary vice-chairman. The *Kensington Post* reported that the appointment was made to 'relieve Withey of the worries and problems of Chairmanship during his illness'.

Although Cooke was back in the team, transfer talk resurfaced, and he was linked with a possible swap deal with highly-rated forward Peter Cormack of Hibernian. Barnsley's Terry Fitzgerald and Tranmere's Trevor Storton, both centre-halves, were watched and Reading were thought likely to bid for Marvin Hinton. Not for the first or last time, Chelsea were interested in Fulham's Steve Earle, wasted in Division Three, but their £30,000 bid was rebuffed.

Goal magazine ran an article on Cooke, arguing he and Osgood had 'proved wrong those who said having both in the same forward line was an unaffordable luxury', though there were certainly still afternoons where they were frustratingly ineffective. For all his skill, Cooke had been out of the side until the injury crisis. 'He is occasionally kicked out of games, making him harder to pick'. They thought that maybe he needed to sharpen his wits to avoid the cloggers.

Interviewed by the Kensington Post about football violence, very much that autumn's moral panic across the country, Sexton acknowledged that 'the noise they (Chelsea's young supporters) make during the game is marvellous. It is a spur to the side. The players admire them for that. It is one of the most loyal crowds in the country and one of the most enthusiastic'. His frustration with occasional outbreaks of violence by an element of the support was clear, however. 'I know that the players and myself would like them all the more if they were not violent. They are young and loyal but no one who cares about football cares for their violence'.

Such a comprehensive win over Arsenal was a great way to end a difficult September. Chelsea had moved up to 12th place at month-end, though were already nine points behind leaders Everton, and seven behind Liverpool. After just 12 matches, therefore, the title was therefore almost certainly out of sight. Considerably improved League form and significant progress in both cups, therefore, were critical to a successful season. As an example of the chopping and changing, most of it enforced, Sexton had already chosen six different players in both the No.2 and No.11 shirts, and an astonishing eight in the No.8 shirt, in just 14 games. A significant reduction in injuries, allowing a high level of continuity and stability, was clearly highly desirable.

October 1969

Peter Osgood was chosen for the England Under-23's against Wales at Bristol City, despite his inconsistency thus far that season. It was a key marker for his international future. The *Daily Telegraph* argued it was 'probably his last chance to add application to talent'. England boss Sir Alf Ramsey was unequivocal. 'Osgood can do what is needed, either in midfield or as a striker. We know that. But the future is up to him'. In the event he scored but the *Daily Telegraph* felt it could not be said that he really enhanced his chances of breaking into the senior squad. The *Evening Standard* went further, saying his display 'damaged his reputation'. Their writer Bernard Joy felt he was better in midfield and 'lack the sharpness and robustness to be a striker'. The star clearly had the ability but if Ramsey was uncertain, his hopes of making the plane to Mexico in seven months were diminishing fast.

A couple of off-field issues drew headlines. The club were fined £5 and ruled out of the South-East Counties League Cup for fielding an ineligible player at Reading in September, a strange administrative oversight for a First Division club.

The *Evening Standard*, under a 'Chelsea Ban Harris Book' headline, reported that the board had demanded considerable alterations to the captain's '*Soccer The Hard Way*' book and banned him from publishing it. Ron Harris would 'lose several hundred pounds' according to Donald Copeland, his literary agent. 20 major alterations were demanded, including an entire chapter 'which covered his financial position and the money he had made from the game'. The board had previous form in this area, having censored the draft manuscripts of '*Ossie The Wizard*'.

A rare but welcome seven day gap between matches gave trainer Harry Medhurst a chance to work on player fitness without quite the same pressure a match every three or four days gave. Harris returning after two games out, at the expense of John Boyle, was the only change for the trip to bottom-place Sunderland. Boyle was soon on the field, replacing Tommy Baldwin who went off with a leg injury. Eddie McCreadie and Osgood also picked up knocks in a hard-fought 0-0 draw. A mediocre outfit who were eventually relegated should have been beatable, but Sexton's 'languid' side relied on a series of Peter Bonetti saves to earn a point. *The People* observed that Chelsea 'had the skill but not the fight...Chelsea will continue to slide if some of them do not put in more effort'. Enigmatic duo Osgood and Cooke were both given a 5/10 rating by the paper, so it was clear it was them being criticised.

In addition to the already injured Tambling and Hutchinson, the newly-injured Baldwin, Osgood and McCreadie (who had damaged a hamstring) were all out of the crucial League Cup replay against Leeds United two days later. On the positive side, in addition to the inclusion of Boyle and Alan Hudson, there was the welcome return of David Webb, two weeks earlier than expected, to enthuse the 38,485 crowd. Although on the face of it this was not a massive attendance considering the opposition, it was actually Chelsea's best-ever home League Cup crowd at that point, attendances in that competition generally being considerably lower than for FA Cup or League games.

The Chelsea boss was keen to defuse tensions before the match, insisting to the *Daily Mail*, under a 'Sexton: No Vendetta' headline that 'there was no vendetta, despite two recent highly-physical games and a dispute over the date for this fixture...This is a match I'm sure both sides will approach in the best cup-tie spirit, but there will be nothing more than that between two sets of professionals'. Given in some quarters the clash was seen as 'the third major battle in a private war' this was an optimistic view though, in the event, the manager was proved correct.

On the night, an excellent Chelsea performance produced a comprehensive, exciting, and deserved 2-0 victory. Charlie Cooke scored his first of the season and Alan Birchenall's bullet-like 20-yard volley for the second was one of the very best he scored for the club. It was also his last for the first-team. Praise was widespread for the team's spirit and particularly the endeavours of Birchenall, Webb, Cooke, Hudson, Peter Houseman (playing up front) and John Hollins. The game lacked the malice of recent encounters and Chelsea rose to the occasion with a result that indicated the remainder of the season could be viewed with some optimism after what the *Chelsea News* called one of the finest second-halves seen at Stamford Bridge for a long time. The next round, at Carlisle the following week, certainly seemed eminently winnable.

The *Daily Mirror* echoed a number of comments in arguing that 'Chelsea are firmly established as London's most efficient and threatening team'. The *Daily Telegraph*'s Donald Saunders, not a writer prone to hyperbole, felt that after the interval Chelsea 'suddenly began to play with a purpose and flair I have not seen them produce for many a day'. Hudson was again highly effective, and from that point onwards was a regular selection that season when fit. Chelsea had now not lost to Leeds in five cup-ties, a fine record. The crowd created a tumultuous atmosphere, supporter Brian Gaches calling it 'one of the team's most impressive performances all season'.

In keeping with the season so far, there was more bad news on the fitness front. Baldwin was likely to be out for six weeks with a hairline shin fracture. Given Hutchinson and Tambling were also out, and

Osgood not fully fit, Sexton had to continue to place a lot of faith on Alan Birchenall for the visit of third-placed Derby County on the Saturday. The prospect had excited the support to the extent that all reserved seats were sold out in advance and an exceptional crowd of 51,421, the biggest of the season so far, turned up.

The squad were given two days off after beating Leeds and spent a day at Bisham Abbey preparing for Derby and Carlisle. Sexton reiterated that 'we will have hard training (to make up for the two days off)' but given they had played 16 times in two months, the short break seemed welcome, necessary and deserved.

Chelsea, below their best, twice equalised goals from Kevin Hector and John O'Hare through Houseman's drive and a 30-yarder from Hollins. Osgood, not fully fit, was on the bench but went on when John Dempsey had to be substituted early in the second-half, going up front. Peter Bonetti was Chelsea's best player, saving them from defeat. Supporter Julian Patten felt this was a key match in that era. 'It made a huge impression on the fans and Sexton must have taken note. Here was a team, just promoted, passing us off the field. But also it highlighted Chelsea's strengths of sheer endeavour to get a 2-2 draw'. Certainly, Brian Clough's team were going to be a force in the land, sooner rather than later.

Osgood, despite starting on the bench against Derby, was still selected for the England Under-23's against Russia the following week. He was unsurprisingly pleased, telling the *Daily Mirror* 'it's nice to know Sir Alf Ramsey still sees me as an England player. I have been working very hard in training and playing with a lot more enthusiasm...I have been struggling to shake off one or two knocks, so I haven't been 100% fit. But I've got Mexico very much in mind, and now it looks as if Sir Alf is narrowing down his search for players'.

Carlisle United manager Bob Stokoe had not watched Chelsea play, but acknowledged that all the side were good players. 'Their team-work and method are exceptional, and they have some excellent individuals'. Dempsey was out with an injured ankle, but Osgood returned, playing at centre-forward. The opposition were eighth in Division Two, so it was generally expected that Chelsea would be in the Quarter-Final draw later that week. The reality was somewhat different.

Carlisle won 1-0, full-back Derek Hemstead netting an unlikely 30-yard 75th minute winner. The shock result was not the story in the headlines the following morning, though. The *Daily Mirror* headline was 'Ref Threatens Cup Crowd: I'll Throw You Out' after a lump of slate thrown from the terraces felled Bonetti midway through the first-half. Trainer Harry Medhurst was appalled. 'When I reached Peter he was out cold...I got him going again by slapping his cheeks and using an ammonia phial, but for a while he still did not know where he was'. Other missiles were also thrown. Referee Kevin Howley threatened to clear the ground and play behind closed doors if there was any recurrence of crowd disorder. Bonetti later said he wanted the authorities to fence in pitches to protect goalkeepers and referees. 'If nothing is done, something serious will happen' he said. A couple of weeks later, ludicrously, it was announced that no further action would be taken against Carlisle for the stone throwing.

The missile incident overshadowed a poor Chelsea display, not the first in a cup-tie under Sexton, as a host of chances were missed. Still only 13th in the League, the only chance of silverware was now the FA Cup which did not start for First Division clubs until the New Year. It was essential Chelsea used the intervening matches to pick up as many points as possible to optimise their chance of European football the following year.

The Coventry programme a couple of weeks later contained a letter from Ian Rennie praising the 60 supporters who travelled to Carlisle for the midweek League Cup-tie. Rennie had previously organised a group of 20 die-hards who went to Aachen for the pre-season friendly.

Chelsea's need for more cover at full-back was evident and their interest in Shamrock Rovers defender Paddy Mulligan had been public for a couple of weeks, after a bid of around £80,000 for England left-back Keith Newton of Blackburn Rovers had been rebuffed. Sexton became interested when he saw Mulligan impress for the League Of Ireland against the Football League in September. Chelsea thought their bid of £17,000 had been accepted and the manager was put out, to put it mildly, to hear from the *Daily Mail* correspondent that Everton had supposedly bought him, subject to a medical. 'I can't understand this. If it is right what you say, it is a bit strong'.

Bonetti, as brave as ever, was fit to play on the Saturday, at home to West Bromwich, and was made captain for the day on his 362nd League appearance (equalling Ken Armstrong's club record). McCreadie came in replacing Boyle but sustained another injury as Chelsea won fairly comfortably, 2-0, maintaining their unbeaten home record. Cooke set up the first for Osgood and netted the second just before half-time.

The *Daily Mail* picked up on an emerging star, Alan Hudson, who 'brings a welcome embarrassment to the problem of team selection at Stamford Bridge'. He 'was all things to all men. The crowd loved his instant and insolent control of the ball, and the connoisseurs took to the inside-forward's swift assessment of the play and frequent mastery of it...(He) will be hard to leave out when everyone is fit'. Within a matter of weeks he was getting praise of that type across the spectrum of football.

The Mulligan deal became 'on' again after it became clear he had declined Everton's offered terms. As well as Chelsea, Fulham and Charlton were also interested and all three had met Shamrock Rovers' £17,500 valuation, so it was up to the player. After a bit more toing-and-froing he flew in and signed for Chelsea after four hours of negotiations. A delighted manager commented 'we have signed a very good all-round player'. Mulligan was a commercial representative until he signed for

Chelsea, and also had an interest in a Dublin boutique.

Osgood duly played for the Under-23's against Russia, but although he made a goal for Jimmy Husband he again failed to impress. Chances were surely running out for him to impress Sir Alf Ramsey and book a World Cup squad place.

October ended on a high note, with a hard-won 1-0 victory at Newcastle United. Boyle came in for the injured Birchenall, who had hurt his knee, and his competitive spirit was beneficial at a windswept St. James' Park, their first away League win of the season, Osgood heading the second-half winner. Chelsea's short passing system was praised as just the right tactic in the windy conditions and contrasted with the home side's endless high balls. Rock-steady defence led to a welcome clean sheet and organised, skilful football by Cooke, Osgood, Houseman and Hudson created a number of chances. The *Sunday Mirror* 'Slick Chelsea Put On Style' headline summed up a very encouraging team effort.

Osgood was back as a striker and scoring goals, suddenly clicking and enjoying the chances Hudson created. When Hutchinson was fit, hopefully within a couple of weeks, it seemed likely Sexton would pair them together. What Osgood was not, however, was in the England squad for the game in Holland, unlike Bonetti, expected to play as Gordon Banks was not fit. To add to Osgood's woes, he was also on two bookings already that season, and one more meant likely suspension.

Newcastle enquired after Birchenall but were told nothing doing, though how happy the player would be if frozen out by an Osgood / Hutchinson partnership remained to be seen. Assistant-manager Ron Suart was one of a number of club representatives watching Millwall's goalscoring midfielder/winger Keith Weller. To the usual rumours about interest in Steve Earle of Fulham were added supposed interest in his colleague Jimmy Conway.

The sad news broke that Leonard Withey had died. Chelsea chairman until he was taken ill a month earlier, Withey had been a board member since 1948. New chairman Brian Mears praised his contribution, particularly on financial matters, and the work he had done on the successful negotiation for the new lease for Stamford Bridge.

The *Evening Standard* earlier that month had run a concerning front-page story. Baldwin appeared in court on remand, accused of assaulting a police officer at Old Street police station and 'aiding and abetting a man to drive a car recklessly'. He went into court on crutches as a result of the injury received against Sunderland and was remanded on £20 bail.

The month-end reserve table did not indicate there were many youngsters ready for the step up to first-team football. Just 13 goals in ten matches, with joint leading scorers Derek Smethurst and John Ware netting just three times each. They had also conceded the third most goals in the Football Combination, with only Gillingham and Peterborough United, hardly benchmarks, conceding more.

Chelsea ended October in eighth place, with a game in hand over many of their rivals. They had used 17 players in League games already, and 16 in three League Cup-ties, which showed the size of the squad but also the impact of the string of injuries suffered. 18 goals in 16 First Division matches was the lowest in the Top 12 clubs and more was needed from the front men. The defence was a bit Jekyll and Hyde. Five home League goals conceded was the lowest in the division, but the 11 conceded away was the worse in the top eight.

Everton	p17 30pts
Liverpool	p17 24pts
Leeds United	p16 23pts
Derby County	p17 21pts
Man City	p16 20pts
Wolverhampton	p17 20pts
Coventry City	p17 19pts
Chelsea	**p16 18pts**

November 1969

November's opening day brought a home encounter with Coventry City, faring unexpectedly well and seventh in Division One. A decent 38.899 attendance turned out to watch an unchanged side, with a fit-again Ian Hutchinson on the bench after missing ten games. Coventry exhibited a physical approach in a 'hard, bruising conflict' but managed to hit the woodwork three times, so could probably count themselves unlucky to lose 1-0. Cooke volleyed the only goal, though yet again the Scot did little else. *The People* felt he gave a 'faultless performance as the invisible man of Stamford Bridge for the entire first-half'.

The unlucky John Boyle had to go off at half-time which what looked worryingly like more knee trouble, Hutchinson coming on. Chelsea improved in the second-half as the substitute added his aggression and spirit to the mix, but it was still an uninspiring team effort in a mediocre game which many spectators drifted away from before the end.

Roy Barry, newly signed by Coventry and with a reputation as a hard man, went on as substitute for his debut and almost immediately went down with a suspected broken nose after a clash with Harris, who was booked. The *News Of The World* commented wryly 'if any Chelsea player had to be booked then it was certain to be Harris, whose immunity to pain blinds him to the fact that others are not similarly built'.

Sexton took the opportunity afterwards to praise Webb, who he saw as one of the club's best signings of recent years, highlighting his determination and skill. From a distance of half a century he looks one of Chelsea's best ever signings, not just of that era. The manager also complimented John Hollins, saying he was playing better than he had ever seen him. He later acknowledged Hutchinson made 'a world of difference' when he went on at half-time. 'He's a big fellow and he challenged their big defenders Curtis and Blockley'.

The People reported that Liverpool were very keen on buying Hutchinson. They felt that Shankly 'likes to buy them big, brave and, above all, young' and that Hutchinson 'fits that formula like a glove'. Unsurprisingly, the report ended with the observation that 'Chelsea don't want to sell'. Indeed. Ipswich were also rebuffed. Quite how anyone thought that they were likely to even consider unloading such a promising youngster is hard to fathom.

The day after the Coventry match, the *News Of The World* ran the first part of a three-issue interview with Osgood, based on excepts from his forthcoming '*Ossie The Wizard*' book. Quotes from that interview caused a significant furore at the time and have been widely quoted since. The headline 'Why I Will Never Play For England – I'm Too Lazy For Sir Alf' summed up the theme of the article. Osgood basically seemed to be publicly writing off his World Cup chances. 'My greatest football ambition is to play for England...but I believe it's an ambition I shall never achieve so long as Sir Alf Ramsey is team manager. It's not that I've anything against him. I happen to like the man and respect him as a coach. But my style of play does not fit in with his England requirements. He wants hard work, lots of effort. Players who will run for each other and challenge back for the ball. That's not my game. I'd very much like to play that way...but I can't. I've tried. I know he says I must balance my skill with a high work rate, but I think it's too late to remould my style...I always attempt to do my best. And I envy players like Birchenall, Boyle and Ball who never stop running...Maybe I lack dedication. Maybe my attitude to football is wrong. All I know is that in my view football is primarily a game of skill...I try and let the others do my running for me. It's easier that way...I don't go looking for the ball and frankly my work off it is non-existent...Sometimes I feel I'm just too lazy'.

The star admitted he had upset Ramsey after a series of niggles with Burnley winger Willie Morgan in an Under-23 clash against Scotland. 'Another thing against me is the fact that I hate training...It's widely known at Chelsea that I often need a kick on the backside when my interest fades...I don't think I'll ever be as good as I was before (my leg break)...My pace has gone, and I've lost my shooting power...my right ankle is still sore from the break. I still can't kick a ball properly with that foot because it hurts so much'. He did not think England would win the World Cup. 'The basis of English football is hard work. In the altitude of Mexico that will be impossible'. Sexton, who held great store by effort in training, would not have been too impressed with the comments, though he would already have been all too aware of Osgood's attitude.

It is an astonishingly frank interview, but it is hard to see what Osgood and his advisers were hoping to achieve, apart from sell books. In retrospect it just seems sensationalist and counter-productive. His admission that he was lazy, hated training and wanted others to do his running for him was hardly likely to impress a man like Ramsey who had won the World Cup using selfless, hardworking forwards like Roger Hunt and Geoff Hurst.

The following day's *Daily Mail* reported that Liverpool were interested in signing Osgood. The paper felt his value would have been c£150,000 at the end of the previous season but that would have increased. Osgood commented 'It is marvellous to know that such a fine club and in particular such a great manager as Bill Shankly is interested in me...But I don't think that there is much chance of me leaving Chelsea, because if I was transferred the club would take a lot of stick from the fans, who have always been kind to me and appreciated everything I have tried to do. It's true that I had a disagreement at half-time on Saturday (against Coventry) over a tactical problem in the side, but I don't think that would alter the situation one little bit'. Liverpool chief scout Geoff Twentyman was there, watching Osgood and Hutchinson, but an unequivocal Sexton told Shankly that neither were for sale. 'There is going to be no business concerning either of them'.

Neither story brought much credit on Osgood. Nothing about any loyalty he owed to the club, no denial that he would like to move. What the club, his teammates and the supporters needed was a run of top-quality displays which might, just might, persuade Ramsey he was worth taking a chance on the next summer.

A week later the *Evening Standard* reviewed '*Ossie The Wizard*', referring to 'a young man who readily admits that he is cut out for the life of a country squire'. Osgood continued the theme of recent interviews, arguing that the rarefied Mexico atmosphere would prevent Ramsey's 'recipe of hard work' being successful and admitting he lacked 'the sort of dedication demanded by Ramsey' which would keep him out of the England side.

After his injury against Coventry, Boyle was advised to rest his right knee for a fortnight. It was 50/50 whether he would need the same cartilage operation he had on his left knee in the summer. He would clearly be out for some time and, in fact, did not appear again for the first team until mid-April, desperately bad luck for him and a big problem for a manager who appreciated the Scot's energy, commitment and versatility.

Goalkeeper Peter Bonetti was arguably on as good form as at any time in his Chelsea career, and he did his international prospects no harm with an assured evening's work as England won 1-0 in Holland, against a team including Johann Cruyff, Rudi Krol and Rob Rensenbrink, earning a 'Bonetti Saves England' *Daily Mirror* headline. Had it not been for the brilliance of Gordon Banks it is safe to say Bonetti would have won a lot more than his final total of seven full caps. At the other end of the spectrum, John Dempsey was sent off as Eire lost 4-0 in Budapest against Hungary.

Chelsea's average League gate so far that season was 38,874, an increase of nearly 1,300 on the 1968-69 average, a welcome trend.

Gates tended to vary significantly dependent on the attractiveness of the opposition and with rivals like Everton, Manchester United, Liverpool, Leeds and Tottenham still to visit that season, the average figure was on target to exceed 40,000.

After a week without a match for the non-internationals in the squad came a trip to relegation candidates Sheffield Wednesday, with only three League wins all season. Hutchinson and Dempsey came back for the unfit Boyle and McCreadie. Baldwin and Tambling were still out, though it was hoped the former would be return soon. Sexton seemed fated not to have a full squad to choose from and it was just as well he had good quality cover in most positions. Birchenall had appeared for the reserves the previous week but was not selected for first-team duty. Mulligan, yet to make his debut, was on the bench.

The chosen side was an interesting one:- Bonetti; Webb, Dempsey, Hinton, Harris; Hollins, Hudson; Cooke, Osgood, Hutchinson, Houseman. Sub. Mulligan.

Apart from McCreadie for Hinton, this quickly became the manager's first choice XI. It was the first time that particular midfield and forward line had played together, and it immediately clicked.

Wednesday simply could not cope with the Chelsea forwards. The 'Peerless Osgood' headline in the *Sunday Mirror* described how he was 'peerless as he feinted, body-swerved and pirouetted to cause confusion whenever he had the ball'. Hutchinson netted twice either side of half-time, both created by Houseman, and had a third disallowed. Cooke beat five men and hit the post, Osgood netting the rebound for the third. The only slight blot on an excellent afternoon was conceding a late Mick Prendergast goal, but a 3-1 away win was always welcome, especially when only five away League goals had been scored up to that point. Sexton felt Osgood 'gave us a wonderful 90 minutes' and was delighted with his side.

Considering the fact that Wednesday were a poor side, and were relegated that season, the *Daily Telegraph* made a perceptive observation, arguing 'there was enough in this game to make the neutral onlooker feel that Chelsea now have a team capable of winning something in the next two seasons'. The *Kensington Post* went further, seeing them as 'real title contenders', but though they had risen to seventh place they were 11 points behind runaway leaders Everton, whose visit to Stamford Bridge the following Saturday was eagerly anticipated. Chelsea had won four in a row and gone eight League matches without defeat, but were still 40-1 rank outsiders for the title.

The run up to the Everton match was somewhat disrupted with the shock news that Tommy Baldwin, out injured but a key squad member, was jailed for four months the day before the game, for assaulting a police officer, though he was promptly bailed pending an appeal. He pleaded not guilty, but the magistrate found 'the case proved – beyond any reasonable doubt'. He and another man were arrested after a car chase and the player refused to go into the police station detention room. A police officer admitted punching Baldwin 'to make him let go of my arm'. Sexton told the court the player 'is the most inoffensive person I have ever met' but the *Evening Standard* headline, 'Chelsea Soccer Star Baldwin Sent To Jail' was one the club could well do without.

In bullish pre-match mood, Sexton spoke to the *Daily Mirror*. 'This is an important match for us because I believe that we can come through to challenge for the championship'. He was unworried about the heavy pitch after incessant rain, saying top players could adapt. Ken Jones enthused 'the sudden prospect of a Southern challenge to Northern domination of the Championship is strengthened by the memory of a sparkling…performance by Osgood at Sheffield Wednesday last week'.

McCreadie was still out so Chelsea fielded an unchanged line-up and approached the afternoon filled with confidence, as did the majority of the 49,895 crowd, especially as Everton had won on just one of their last 19 visits to Stamford Bridge. Within five minutes, however, the visitors were ahead through a Jimmy Husband header but rallied as Osgood volleyed a spectacular equaliser. Hudson and Hollins initially found Everton's top-class midfield of Alan Ball, Colin Harvey and Howard Kendall hard to cope with but marked more tightly after half-time and, as time went on, Chelsea became more dominant. They could not manage a second goal, however, so the encounter ended in a creditable 1-1 draw.

Both sides were praised for their contribution to what the *Daily Telegraph* thought the best game staged at Stamford Bridge so far that season, vastly different from their previous, sterile encounter. Osgood was lauded for his effort, Sexton discussing his options up front. 'Strikers have the hardest job on the field because they have to be both robust and skilful. So it is a good idea to share the load between them if possible'. He stressed the benefits of a large squad and striker rotation. Everton was only his second selection of the Osgood / Hutchinson partnership used, so successfully, for most of the rest of that season.

Two good performances and Osgood's mood, as shown in a *Daily Mail* article the Monday after the Everton clash, had changed completely from a fortnight earlier. 'Two weeks ago Peter Osgood said he was too lazy to play for England. Now he is hoping to win a World Cup place in Mexico next year'. He had worked hard in his past two appearances, against Sheffield Wednesday and Everton. When he made those comments, he was 'in the doldrums' but now 'I feel great…I've got my appetite back. I'm looking for the ball, running to get it. I've worked as hard as anyone in the last couple of games'. He had scored some goals and 'the rest of the team is playing so well…things are starting to pop at Chelsea. And it is the World Cup season'. Appearing up front alongside the workaholic Hutchinson clearly suited him and he was lauded elsewhere for his aggression and courage, not adjectives that would have applied a few short weeks earlier.

The *Daily Mirror* joined the Osgood For England press fan club, under a 'Ossie Comes Good – If This Mood Persists He May Yet Play For England' headline. They pointed out that his goal against Everton was 'all sharp reaction and marvellous balance, he (seems) no longer put off by the physical aspects of his profession'.

Osgood enthused 'I may let people down again, but I really feel I have broken through. I can't explain why because I have never been able to explain my attitude to the game...There have been times I have felt like chucking it in...If I have grown up in some people's eyes then it comes from the new feeling which exists at Chelsea...I'm happier playing up front because I am happier when I am scoring goals...There is a tremendous spirit in our side, and we find ourselves attacking teams on their own grounds. We have learned to accept one another's deficiencies and to recognise the strength we have. We no longer hope we can get success. We believe we can get it'.

Looking back, it is a shame Osgood felt it necessary to talk to willing journalists whenever he was off-form or felt at a low, as it did him few favours and cannot have helped his relationship with Sexton. Anything he said was news, and positive comments after playing well were fine, but sweeping statements about his attitude, or international future, probably less so.

The *Kensington Post* joined the happy band of title optimists. 'Chelsea flashed out a message as bright as the new-blue floodlights...we are on the way back and looking for a title'. They felt Chelsea deserved to win but recognised that 'even The Shed seemed satisfied with a draw against a side that is, after all, the best in the country...Sexton's sensations are out for big success'. In a few weeks, a general feeling seemed to have developed that this could be Chelsea's time.

Hutchinson picked up a knock against Everton and was doubtful for the trip to Ipswich three days later. If he had not been passed fit then Baldwin, out on bail pending his appeal but fit again, would have been selected. In the end Sexton could field the same side, with McCreadie fit enough to take his place on the bench.

The *Daily Mirror* 'Osgood Shatters Ipswich – Two Great Goals In A Sizzling Show For Sir Alf' headline said it all. Ramsey, Ipswich manager when they won the League seven years earlier, watched Osgood 'confirm his new appetite for football...played with thriving urgency and complete assurance'. Hutchinson and Hollins also scored in an emphatic 4-1 victory, both their goals made by Hudson, though when Colin Viljoen equalised Hutchinson's opener, it took until the 63rd minute for Chelsea to turn superiority into goals. The impressive run had now stretched to one defeat in 17, with confidence flowing through the side. The manager seemed to have found the line-up, the attitude, the formation and the tactics he wanted and, though Dempsey, Hudson and (no surprise) Hutchinson all picked up knocks, the visit to Nottingham Forest four days later was faced with confidence.

Tambling was fit to play in the reserves alongside Baldwin. Birchenall had suffered a relapse with his knee and there were concerns he may need an operation. Three experienced strikers but none of whom would have got into the first-choice line-up at that point, even if fit. Boyle was working his way back to fitness so Sexton, to the surprise of nobody, kept the same line-up at Forest, McCreadie again substitute as he continued his quest for full match fitness.

Given recent form and results, a 1-1 draw was probably a bit of a disappointment against a side that had not won for 11 games. Cooke scored his fourth in ten matches, equalising Henry Newton's opener. Sexton had to make a change when Hutchinson went off at half-time with, worryingly, another right knee problem. He had only been back three games after missing ten, but had clearly had a transformative effect on the team and, particularly, Osgood. McCreadie came on and Webb was sent up front.

Forest manager Matt Gillies was the latest public recruit to those who thought Chelsea could still win the League. He told the *Daily Mail* 'they looked a team of thoroughbreds, with a ringmaster par excellence in John Hollins...With such quality and such depth they must surely be one of our European title bidders. I know Everton are nine points ahead of them, but there is half a season left and at their present rate Chelsea are going to catch up'. Since the League Cup shock at Carlisle, they had gained 12 points from a possible 14, notable form by any standards.

The home clash against Stoke City scheduled for a week later was postponed because of snow. McCreadie, fully fit and raring to go, would have replaced the unlucky Hinton, who had slotted in very capably after starting just nine times the previous season. 'Now we are getting a fit squad together they will all have to give way from time to time' said Sexton. He told the *Sunday Mirror*, who felt they had arguably the strongest group of players in Division One, 'for the last four games we've been able to field the same forward line. We've started getting the goals'. Playing Cooke further forward and Osgood up front was certainly working.

The *Nottingham Football Post* summed up the wider mood about Chelsea as November drew to a close. 'I haven't seen a team this season to match the organisation, mobility and all-round skill of Chelsea when they choose to put the pressure on. All they need now to challenge for top honours is extra faith in themselves and a bit more ruthlessness in their approach'. They seemed to be the team of the moment and Osgood, as usual, was happy to air his views, telling *Goal* magazine 'Chelsea have been slow starters in the past but this time we've got going early enough to do some damage...It's always easier to play when the team is on song, you want to run into positions because you believe a goal will come.

Hollins had given a series of high-quality performances, without generating the headlines that Cooke and Osgood did. In a *Daily Mail* interview, he complained about being seen as hen-pecked, said his wife was upset by the accusations of dominating him and pointed out a couple of facts. He had missed one England call-up as he was getting married on the Sunday, which Sir Alf Ramsey agreed to. He had turned down another Under-23 call-up as he was house hunting, had already made a dozen appearances for them and, again, Ramsey had said that it was no problem.

Hollins was now back to his best form and hoping to be in the party of 30 for the forthcoming game against Portugal. Sexton was effusive to *Goal* magazine in his praise of the midfield dynamo, feeling he should definitely be in England's World Cup 22. He accepted his chances were getting slimmer but stressed that would only make him try harder. He was, unsurprisingly, enjoying playing in midfield after a spell at right-back the previous season. In the same interview, he also praised Hutchinson's mature attitude, for having coped so easily with his emergence as a first-team star.

David Webb opened a wig shop in London's East End. Comedian Marty Feldman, Cooke, Webb, Osgood, Hinton, Baldwin and Sexton turned out for the opening, which duly received national newspaper coverage, Webb and Feldman hamming it up for the photographers.

With the sad passing of Leonard Withey the vacancy on the club board was filled by film star Richard Attenborough. 'I believe we are potentially a greater team than I can ever remember' Attenborough claimed. His appointment was an astute and popular one by the board, as he had an extremely positive public profile and a genuine love for the club.

Hudson had successfully made the transition from junior to the first-team and the *Evening Standard* ran a feature on 17-year-old wing-half Tony Frewin, who had recently turned professional and was highly thought of within the club. Marvin Hinton tipped him and Hudson as stars of the future.

Defender Ian Delacour (18) signed from Portadown for £4,500. He had already made a couple of reserve appearances and attended pre-season training, but Chelsea had tried to keep him quiet to avoid interest from other clubs. The club were allegedly interested in talented forward Danny Hegan who West Bromwich had only bought from Ipswich Town five months earlier. That, like so many other rumoured moves, went nowhere. The long-time interest in Millwall's Keith Weller ratcheted up a notch when his club indicated he might be sold when they achieved a better position than their current 20th.

Three wins and two draws from five matches that month Chelsea had managed to reduce the gap between them and leaders Everton to nine points. Talk of the League title was surely still wildly optimistic, though, as they were in sixth place, and it seemed unlikely that all those above them would slip up. Both North London rivals were stuck in mid-table, so Chelsea looked good for, at the very least, a Fairs Cup place.

Confidence was high at the halfway point of the League season, and it seemed as though Sexton had found the system, and the team, he wanted. Hudson and Hutchinson had been integrated into the team and were making significant contributions and, despite the injury crisis earlier in the season, he had decent quality cover in most positions. December, despite encounters with both Manchester clubs and fourth placed Wolverhampton Wanderers, could be faced with positivity.

Everton	p21 35pts
Leeds United	p22 32pts
Liverpool	p22 28pts
Wolverhampton	p22 27pts
Manchester City	p21 26pts
Chelsea	**p21 26pts**

December 1969

The announcement of the England party of 30 for the game against Portugal was good news for Peter Bonetti, though hardly a shock after his excellence in Holland. John Hollins was omitted, a disappointment - 'I must admit I was a wee bit confident' - but hardly a massive surprise. The major controversy, though, was that Peter Osgood's name was missing. Maybe his 'I am too lazy for England' comments were counting against him. Speaking to the *Daily Mail* he stresses he had 'not given up hope...I am disappointed – very disappointed. My heart stopped for a moment when I read the names of the 30 in the paper...I hope Sir Alf does realise that I said what I said about England a year ago when I was right down in the dumps. But I suppose he is afraid that my recent form is just a flash in the pan – well, it's up to me to show him different'.

The player implied that the interview was given a year back, for the book, though it only appeared in the paper a month earlier. Why Ramsey should be expected to acknowledge this, when the story ran with great hullabaloo in the *News Of The World*, is not clear. It reinforced a lack of common sense by Osgood and his representatives in allowing the interview to run, though presumably the newspaper publicity was an integral part of the book deal.

Brian James, in the *Daily Mail* piece, felt Ramsey would regret omitting the star. 'Osgood's style, based on an economic and accurate passing ability, on shuffling, deceptive possession and superb acceleration into shooting positions, is precisely what England will need in Mexico'. The five strikers chosen by Ramsey were Jeff Astle, Allan Clarke, Geoff Hurst, Mick Jones and Francis Lee. Osgood offered something different to all of them and there was still time for him to make the plane, but it was fast running out.

In a story that was to impact on Chelsea going forward, The *Daily*

Telegraph reported that the Wembley pitch was in extremely poor condition for the Oxford v Cambridge varsity match. It cut up and the bounce was uneven, and it was highly unlikely to improve for the Portugal international the following week. The blame was put on the long, dry summer after the pitch re-turfing, followed by a recent spell of sustained rain. Denis Follows, FA Secretary, admitted 'it may not be in very good shape for our first full international next week if this weather continues'. The Wembley pitch had been a problem since the FA spectacularly foolishly allowed the 1968 'Horse Of The Year Show' to be held there. There is a recurrent tale that that event was held at Wembley just before the 1970 FA Cup Final, but that was not the case.

The opening December game was at Manchester United, Chelsea's third away match in a row because of the Stoke postponement. Marvin Hinton, John Boyle, Tommy Baldwin and Alan Birchenall had all played in the reserves at Peterborough at the start of the month. The latter three stayed in that side on the Saturday while Hinton travelled with the first-team, taking the substitute's role as Eddie McCreadie returned after missing four games.

United were in ninth place, and though going through a supposed transformation under new coach Wilf McGuinness, fielded eight of the side that had won the 1968 European Cup, including Bobby Charlton and the incomparable George Best. 49,344 turned out, few of them expecting the visitors to dominate the afternoon as completely as they did, winning comfortably 2-0, with only ex-Chelsea goalkeeper Alex Stepney keeping the score respectable. Ian Hutchinson added to his burgeoning reputation with two goals in another barnstorming effort, the first a magnificent header. He and Alan Hudson came in for particular credit, though the whole team deserved praise in what was one of their best performances under Sexton to date. Efficient defence with Best tightly marked and well-covered, skilful and confident ball play and assured finishing were all factors in a polished team effort. They thoroughly deserved their third win at Old Trafford in a row, a record to be proud of.

The title drums beat louder. The *Daily Mail* proclaimed 'Chelsea Proudly Lead London's Title Bid' though as Arsenal and Tottenham were a dozen points behind Everton with 19 matches left that was hardly difficult. The *Daily Mirror* got a bit carried away. 'What Price These Southern Softies Now?', though they were 20-1 for the title before the game. They pointed out that Boyle, Baldwin, Birchenall, Tambling and Mulligan were all on the sidelines, highlighting the squad strength. Bill Shankly had said earlier in the season he could not understand why Chelsea had not won something. David Webb pointed out 'we've got a marvellous blend of hardness and skill' , the manager eulogising 'I've never believed the championship was as good as won. At this moment it's very open...I sincerely believe we're good enough to come out on top'.

Chelsea drew Birmingham at home in the FA Cup Third Round, to be held on January 3rd. The odds had Leeds as 6-1 favourites with Chelsea 8-1, Everton 9-1 and Man City 10-1. The FA Cup was clearly their best chance of silverware that season, so the draw had to be seen as a positive one, though Birmingham had shocked them in the Quarter-Final two years earlier.

The *Kensington Post* pointed out that Sexton had resisted the temptation to splash out large fees and had been rewarded by the marked improvement that bringing Hutchinson and Hudson in caused. They saw Osgood and Cooke as the 'driving force' behind Chelsea's recent run, and their return to top form had without doubt made a huge difference. They also wondered whether England's loss was Chelsea's gain, as if Osgood was not called up, he could rest in international weeks.

Bonetti was retained in the England team that beat Portugal 1-0 on the predicted heavy pitch, despite Gordon Banks being fully fit. Ramsey commented approvingly 'I had been a little worried about his goal-kicking and his distribution from his hands, but tonight he did everything perfectly' and it seemed clear that Bonetti was closing the gap on Banks. Bonetti's quick, accurate throws were a key component of Chelsea's counter-attacking style but in the past there had been occasional reservations about the accuracy and distance of his kicking.

In *Goal* magazine, Everton boss Harry Catterick lauded Chelsea's squad. 'They have the best first-team pool in the country…Against us they played very skilfully. They had a solid all-round side, particularly strong at the back'. This was praise indeed from the manager of the title favourites. There was a slightly contrary view from Sexton's predecessor Tommy Docherty, who reckoned Chelsea were 'not hard enough to overcome the challenge of teams like Leeds, Everton and Liverpool'. This was a surprising opinion as the likes of Harris, Webb and McCreadie could be as physical as anyone in the First Division, though maybe Chelsea did not have the degree of latent nastiness that some teams possessed.

Buoyed by the deserved victory against United, unbeaten in the League for 12 games and with the gap to Everton just seven points, Chelsea travelled to seventh placed Wolverhampton Wanderers in high spirits, despite it being their fourth away match in a row. The visitors had eight corners in the first 20 minutes, attacked constantly for 40 minutes, dominated play, wasted chances, failed to achieve a breakthrough and suddenly found themselves two down before half-time, through winger David Wagstaffe and Hugh Curran. Curran netted a third (his fourth against Chelsea that season) as the away defence struggled to cope with Wagstaffe and the team slumped off at the end after a scarcely believable 3-0 defeat.

The press, so laudatory in recent weeks, turned on the team for being too casual, not turning their first-half dominance into goals and not fighting hard enough when things went against them. *The People's*

'Chelsea Much Too Cocky' headline emphasised the over-confidence. In particular, Osgood, who had a poor afternoon, got some stick, in classic 'build 'em up, knock 'em down' style. The *News Of The World*, which six weeks earlier carried the infamous 'too lazy' interview, opined that 'Osgood's performance justified the wisdom of Sir Alf in leaving him out of the England party. The *Daily Mail* did not pull its punches, either. 'Peter Osgood has thrown more light on his omission from the World Cup squad. His part in Chelsea's 3-0 hammering at Molineux hinted that he goes well only when everything else does…The expected battle cry from Osgood did not come. He was outjumped and outfought by (centre-half) John Holsgrove'. One bad result was not the end of the world, though clearly it gave the title cheerleaders food for thought.

One bit of excellent news was that Baldwin's four-month prison sentence, imposed for assaulting a policeman, was suspended for two years, the appeal finding police evidence seemingly confused. He was fined £75 with £25 costs. The judge commented 'there is no doubt he had too much to drink and behaved in a way which does not reflect much credit on him'. Baldwin's experience, according to Charlie Cooke in '*The Bonnie Prince*', included a night in a police cell.

The next match, at home to fourth-place Manchester City, was a tough one but a real chance to bounce back to form. Previewing the clash in his *Goal* magazine column, Bobby Charlton was positive about Chelsea 'A big, strong, skilful side…top-class…An incredibly strong squad'. He felt both teams were still in with a chance of the title and acknowledged that Chelsea had recovered from a bout of injuries that would shatter most teams. Osgood commented 'we were still in trouble with injuries when we went to Maine Road (earlier in the season), yet we got a point'.

Interviewed by the *Daily Mail* in the run-up to the City encounter, Sexton emphasised he did not like to make predictions but stressed 'Chelsea have the equipment to win the First Division…For the past five or six weeks we've played with the same forward line and played with more rhythm'. He also made the valid point that they had played 13 away games and only ten at home. 'We must keep winning to keep up there with the leaders'. The seemingly unshakable Jekyll-and-Hyde nature of the side, where occasional dire mistakes kept happening, made this aspiration considerably more difficult.

City assistant-manager Malcolm Allison called Hutchinson 'the most promising player in England'. He told the *Daily Mirror* 'I think he is tremendous. I'd like to have him at my club…If he maintains his progress, he could be as exciting a player as George Best'. Praise indeed, though they were completely different types. Allison respected Sexton's team. 'They are a good side, and a difficult one to beat'.

Despite press predictions of a 50,000 attendance, a painfully low 34,791 turned out for one of the most attractive matches of the season. It was a week before Christmas but, given it was the first home match for five weeks, the quality of the opposition and the generally strong form of the team (excluding the final 50 minutes at Wolverhampton) it must have been an unpleasant surprise to those in the board room dreaming of a redeveloped stadium regularly packed with massive crowds.

David Webb was selected as a full-back but contrived to score twice in four first-half minutes. Hutchinson added a third before half-time as Chelsea dominated, an injury-weakened City having no answer to a rampant Blues attack. Mike Summerbee scored a consolation late on, but Chelsea ran out comfortable winners, shaking off the misplaced complacency of Wolverhampton. Hutchinson limped off, again, and Paddy Mulligan came on for his Blues debut. The *Daily Telegraph* felt that, that season, Sexton had 'built Chelsea's most accomplished team for years. Strong at the back, skilful in midfield and inventive up front', though they thought there was still a tendency to be less than clinical in front of goal.

The talented but raw Stan Bowles came in for City and 'began promisingly but was strictly discouraged by the coarse attentions of Harris'. It was not to be the last time in his career that Bowles was robustly marked by the Chelsea captain. City players voted the two-goal Webb man-of-the-match and, slightly oddly, City striker Francis Lee presented him with a set of cufflinks.

The Observer identified Chelsea's orchestrator. 'Hudson, a teenager who cannot fail to play for England unless misfortune intervenes...organised them in midfield with a thoughtful efficiency'. Hudson was justifiably starting to gather regular, fulsome praise. The programme for the Boxing Day clash with Southampton gave the club perspective of his progress. 'Injuries earlier this season thrust Hudson forward perhaps a little sooner than expected, but so well did he grasp the opportunity given him...that he has held his place on merit. And if he maintains the promise, realises all his rich potential, Alan Hudson will provide one of the happiest 'local boy makes good' stories soccer has ever known'. Indeed.

The *Daily Mirror* argued that Chelsea's resultant strength in depth justified having expensive stars who could not get in the team whereas City did not have effective cover for the missing Bell, Lee, Mike Doyle and Glyn Pardoe. They felt 'even a squad player at Chelsea was on a decent wage and less likely to want to leave', though of course this meant the wage bill could be significantly higher that some of their rivals. The *Daily Mirror* thought they approached the second half of the season as 'outstanding contenders' for the title.

Chelsea, like other top clubs, trained over the Christmas period, every day except Christmas Day. They had two winnable games, Southampton home on Boxing Day and Crystal Palace away a day later. Sexton trusted his players. 'They will be sensible, they know they have two tough matches and what they must do to be ready'. Though they had climbed to fourth place, winning both encounters was essential if there was to be any hope of overhauling the nine-point-clear Everton side. The fact that none of Tommy Hughes, Boyle, Hinton, Stewart Houston, Baldwin, Birchenall and Tambling appeared against Manchester City emphasised the strength in depth, which was bound to be useful if form, fitness and suspension took their toll later in the season.

Once Hutchinson was passed fit the announcement of an unchanged line-up against a team with two League wins all season was a formality. 41,489, a decent Boxing Day morning crowd, turned out, though a reported 15,000 only got in after kick-off. Hutchinson scored either side of half-time and Hollins hit a long-range third after running half the pitch, before Mike Channon scored a late consolation. For the second home game running a clean sheet had been thrown away extremely late on, indicating a lack of focus when the pressure was off. 'A match of surging excitement, furious tackling, thrilling open play and superb goals, deservedly won by a dangerous-looking Chelsea'. The 'furious tackling' in a sometimes violent clash from an always-physical Southampton led to Hutchinson finishing at half pace with a damaged knee. The *Kensington Post* reckoned he was the star of the show, and that his 'enormous success must mean that Birchenall will soon leave the club'.

Baldwin, fully fit and frustrated, was ready to take Hutchinson's place if he was unfit for the following day's visit to Crystal Palace, but the indefatigable Hutch played though not fully fit, as he did on so many occasions. The thought remains that if he had been allowed to recover from his various injuries, rather than being patched up, often injected and sent out for another buffeting from tough defenders then his career might well have been a longer one.

A stadium record crowd of 49,498 packed Selhurst Park to see third-from-bottom Palace entertain their London neighbours. A shock looked on the cards when Gerry Queen put the home side ahead with a heavily-deflected shot. Osgood equalised before half-time but with 25 minutes left the score was still 1-1. He then netted another three in an astonishing burst, achieving his first League hat-trick in the process, before Houseman rounded off the 5-1 win with a magnificent diving header. A compelling team performance had the travelling supporters drooling and celebrating so wildly that Geoff Kimber remembers it clearly half a century later.

The other side of Osgood showed itself when, after a goalmouth scramble that ended with Dempsey unconscious, he chased after Palace centre-half John McCormick and had to be led away by teammates. A less lenient referee than John Homewood might have dismissed him, though he contented himself with talking to Harris and Palace captain John Sewell, trying to calm things down. Osgood admitted 'I got a little involved with McCormick and I regret it'. He and Hudson received rave reviews and Webb was praised for his willingness to attack whenever appropriate.

SEXTON FOR GOD

Even the usually-reserved *Daily Telegraph* went to town, calling Sexton's side 'a formidable football machine...Gone are the old moments of abstraction, the almost perverse descents into mediocrity'. All very well, but two weeks earlier they had done exactly that against Wolverhampton. They pointed out that in Hudson and Hutchinson, Chelsea had the twin forward discoveries of 1969, praised Cooke's 'magical performance' and Osgood thought the Scot 'tore their defence to shreds'. *The People* reckoned there was no-one more exciting to watch than Hutchinson and it looked as though, if all went as expected, the young pair could both expect to be full international squad regulars within a couple of years, if not earlier. Hudson reckoned he felt an established team member by that Christmas and certainly his work was of such quality that he was hardly likely to be dropped.

Palace manager Bert Head praised the strength of Sexton's squad. 'Chelsea today had Tambling, Birchenall, Boyle and Hinton on the touchline. If those players were mine, I could build a team around them'.

Osgood's international future continued to be the subject of much debate. A *Daily Telegraph* article by Donald Saunders headlined 'Osgood Must Now Come Into World Cup Reckoning' captured much of the press mood. 'Since being left out of England's squad of 30 for a match against Portugal earlier this month, Osgood has made a determined effort to persuade Sir Alf that he is an enthusiastic worker as well as a gifted craftsman...This, in turn, has allowed Chelsea to produce the finishing power needed to change them from a useful side into a good one'. Sexton received wide praise for bringing the best out of Osgood and Cooke and having the vision to bring Hudson and Hutchinson through into the side.

On a wider issue, Saunders went on '(Chelsea are) in a position...to launch a New Year challenge to the supremacy of Everton and Leeds'. They were six points behind Leeds, seven behind Everton with only 16 games left. Leeds at home on January 10th was clearly going to be a key encounter and a chance for Ramsey to assess Osgood and rival Mick Jones four days before England met Holland.

Hutchinson, very much the man of the moment, was nominated *Evening Standard* 'Footballer Of The Month'. A 'dramatic rise from obscurity to be perhaps the most exciting discovery of 1969', scoring five goals in December. He was rightly praised for his courage. 'It is inevitable I should get a few knocks, but they are worth it to put the ball into the net'. Youth coach Frank Blunstone was effusive in his praise. 'Let's not kid ourselves. It is only once in a generation that you can say that a raw boy of 19 is bound to reach the top'.

Hutchinson discovered his long throw in the reserves when Suart had them all taking throw-ins. He fully realised he had a lot of work to do on his game and praised his teammates. 'I know I've scored a few goals recently, but it would have been a disgrace to miss some of them, so well were they laid on'. Sexton and Suart worked hard with the young forward and, in 'Ossie The Wizard', Osgood thought he initially looked 'clumsy and out of his depth' but soon improved out of all recognition. Their partnership was certainly blossoming and held huge promise for the future.

One reason Osgood was not in the England party might have been the names ahead of him in the First Division top scorers list – Joe Royle, Jeff Astle, Colin Bell, George Best, Hugh Curran, Geoff Hurst, Francis Lee and Bryan Robson made up the top eight. Five of those were in or around the squad so he probably needed to be more prolific if he was going to make a compelling case for a call-up.

Chairman Brian Mears gave a highly positive year-end interview in the *Daily Mail*. 'In the next ten years there is no limit to what we can achieve. So long as we keep this team together. And by team I don't just mean the players. We have a young board, a young squad and a young manager. Dave Sexton has made the side what it is today, and we plan to have him there all the way to the 80s. You don't talk of the future in terms of months, or even a year or two. It is what we can achieve in the next ten years that counts. We are coming up to the greatest period in the club's history and I would like to feel that Dave will stay until the end'.

He went on 'to be a great club everything must be in rhythm. We have got that rhythm now. I think this present team is the finest I have ever seen – and the mind boggles when I think of the great players who are waiting their chance to play. We aim to show them in a new stadium that will have everyone seated, with restaurants, multi-storey car-parks – everything people dream about – and all in the next ten years. These are going to be exciting years'. He may well have been right when talking about the side being the finest in the club's history, though at that stage the reserve and junior sides were hardly packed with 'great' players.

On a related note, the *Evening Standard* ran an article about possible Stamford Bridge redevelopment, under a 'Blueprint For the Sumptuous Seventies – Chelsea Style' headline. They reported plans were in preparation to make Stamford Bridge a 'super stadium' at a cost of at least £500,000. Three alternative architectural blue-prints were being drawn up. A motorway was planned to run over the railway line, a floodlight pylon would need to be demolished and the East Stand could be moved 30 yards. They felt the mentioned £500,000 cost could easily be exceeded if restaurants, car parks and other facilities were included. The East Stand alone could apparently cost £400,000 if it were given the green light. Mears envisaged the day when all spectators would be seated and, eventually, a cover placed over the whole pitch to avoid postponements.

The Birmingham home programme, in the New Year, had more in the same positive vein. 'Just what stage we shall have reached in the club's growth by the end of the Seventies no one can predict, but one thing about which there is no doubt is the sky-high ambition both on and off the field of everyone connected with Chelsea Football Club…Success on the playing front and development off the field are linked hand in glove, and we believe that no club kicks-off into 1970 with richer potential and greater scope than we have at Chelsea. If achievement matches vision - and this is the aim to which we must all be dedicated – both the Club honours list and the appearance of Stamford Bridge will look far different at the end of the new decade from what they do today'.

A new fundraising 'Golden Goals' competition would commence with the Leeds match in January. The new Chelsea Pools Office was open. 'New stands and other major developments cost money – a lot of money – but what other big clubs have done Chelsea aim to do even better'. Every penny of the profits from 'Golden Goals' and other fundraising promotions being considered for 1970 was to go towards the fulfilment of those plans, the club hoping to raise £50,000 a year from the new Chelsea Pools. On that basis, though, it would take over a decade to raise the necessary money, if this fundraising were to be the only extra revenue source. Despite that, any Chelsea supporter reading those articles could only be impressed. The club clearly had vision and ambition, both on and off the pitch.

Top managers Don Revie, Harry Catterick and Bill Shankly agreed with the *Daily Mail* that Chelsea's place among the great winning clubs might come this year. Players like Baldwin, Tambling, Boyle, Birchenall, Hinton, Houston, Hughes and Mulligan were 'tensed on the touchline'. They were showing 'the consistency that erodes even the safest margins'. Osgood enthused 'the lads make so many chances somebody has to get among them. You have to do something special now and then just to keep your place'. Hollins was similarly positive. 'All the work of the past two years is paying off now. The things people admire Chelsea for arise out of habit'. The Mail concluded that 'to Northerners accustomed to easy invasions of the soft south, Stamford Bridge may loom formidably as Soccer movers into the 70s'. Syd Owen, Leeds coach, told *The People* 'Chelsea are a real threat now. They always had loads of individual talent, but Dave Sexton has done a marvellous job in moulding them into a first-rate team'.

One downside about having a large squad was keeping those out of the team happy. Birchenall told the *Daily Mirror* he wanted to talk to Sexton about his future 'after spending the next 14 days getting fit...If I can't get back into the first-team, I don't want to play in the reserves...I understand clubs have been in for me, but Chelsea have turned them down'. Recovering from an injury suffered against Leeds, he strained a thigh in his reserve comeback and had been stuck, hugely frustrated, in the Stamford Bridge treatment room, whereas the fit men trained at Mitcham.

The *Daily Mail*, running Chelsea features on a regular basis, talked to Cooke. A noticeboard chart in the dressing room traced goals back three passes to credit the men who can claim an 'assist' in every score. A gratified manager commented 'Cooke's name, nowadays, leads in a very large proportion of goals', which had not always been the case. The player had a point to make. 'I'd like to shove a copy of that board down the throat of every press man who keeps saying my football is pretty but not productive'. Analysis showed that 16 times against Palace, Cooke got the ball and ran. Nine times he went past the first challenge and passed. Another seven times he beat two men. Only twice did these moves end without advantage to Chelsea. Another 22 times he passed without beating a man. They pointed out that 'no longer does he beat people without advantage to his team'.

In the Manchester United away programme there was an article by Arthur Walmsley. 'There was a languid excellence about Osgood's play – amounting almost to narcissism – which militated against the most effective exploitation of his extraordinary talents. Chelsea compromised by playing him at half-back for a while but this season he has been scoring regularly and the signs are that a more incisive Peter Osgood is emerging...good news not only for Chelsea but also for England'. He was, probably unfairly, less sure about Cooke, who had 'not always satisfied his critics – nor, indeed, his club – that his consummate ability has been integrated into team effectiveness'.

The popular Frank Blunstone ended 17 loyal years as player and coach with the club when moving from his post of youth coach across West London to become Brentford manager, with the best wishes of all at Chelsea and a laudatory programme piece about his 'wonderful service'.

Reserve goalkeeper Tommy Hughes gave a brilliant display for Scotland Under-23's that month and had been tipped to become Scotland's first choice goalkeeper, but wanted to leave Chelsea and had submitted a written transfer request. He was unhappy he did not get bonus payments that others, also out of the side, did. The club argument was that they did not penalise those who lost their place through injury.

It was a relatively quiet month for transfer speculation, though Ron Suart watched promising Ayr right-back Dick Malone. 15-year-old wing-half Gary Locke signed as an apprentice.

Everton	p26 41pts
Leeds United	p27 40pts
Chelsea	**p26 34pts**
Liverpool	p25 32pts
Derby County	p27 31pts
Stoke City	p26 31pts

The defeat at Wolverhampton notwithstanding, December was another good month for Sexton and his team. He deservedly won the December 'Manager Of The Month' award and Chelsea ended the year in third place, their highest League position since Autumn 1966. They were playing exciting football, though they had only kept one clean sheet in nine games. He had a settled line-up which, if they remained fit, had every chance of a decent FA Cup run and continued League progress, though winning the title was still highly unlikely. All they could do was keep consistently picking up points, hope that Everton, Leeds and Liverpool dropped them and when they met one of their close rivals, ensure they won.

January 1970

Bobby Tambling, out of the side since September, recovered from a knee injury and desperate for first-team action, went on a month's loan to Crystal Palace, potentially involving three League games, though Sexton did not want him cup-tied. 'There is no question of our making the transfer permanent...He has only played three Combination matches since August 28th, so we get him match-fit and help someone at the same time'. It is fair to say that Palace's relegation rivals were less than impressed at this unusual act of generosity.

After the defeat of Manchester City, *The People* ran a 'Chelsea For the Cup?' headline. David Webb was clear about a key target. 'When we develop the killer instinct more strongly, we'll take some stopping in the cup'. Supporter Barry Holmes reckons that winning the FA Cup had become an obsession at the club, similar to winning the Champions League in the Abramovich era. Holmes thought there was a feeling among the support that the Seventies could be Chelsea's decade, and the FA Cup would be a good place to start.

Birmingham coach Joe Mallett felt that 'youngsters Alan Hudson and Ian Hutchinson have matured so rapidly. They know what it is all about...They are a better side than when we played them in Cup competition in each of the last two seasons. Those early season injuries may have done Sexton a service by allowing this side to come good together'. An interesting point, and it is certainly unlikely Hutchinson or Hudson would have become key first-team members before Christmas if vacancies had not appeared due to the swathe of fitness issues.

Chelsea were clear favourites to beat Birmingham City, and so it proved. A 3-0 win in front of 45,088 supporters, paying £16,022, looked on the face of it extremely comfortable. Things could have been more interesting, though, if ex-Chelsea winger Bert Murray, still good friends with some long-serving squad members, had not missed two good chances. Osgood scored the opener, Hutchinson the other two, as the much-discussed partnership laid waste to the 'dour' visiting defence, the latter's long throws causing chaos. Chelsea were in control, though they could only become comfortable once Hutchinson scored the second after 75 minutes.

The *News Of The World* pointed out that 'Chelsea have always possessed efficiency and the determination to run the extra yard. To these virtues they now add Osgood's renewed appetite for the fray up front and the subtle, perceptive skills of Hudson'. They also identified that Hutchinson's development had been as rapid and remarkable as Hudson's. From a big, raw forward primarily recognised as the man with the longest throw in the League, he had become 'a robust, coveted striker'. Hutchinson was the guest on ITV's *The Big Match*' the following day, a sign of his quickly-growing profile.

Tony Hateley, a £100,000 Tommy Docherty signing three years earlier who had never really come off at the club, had an ineffective afternoon and was jeered by home supporters. Birmingham boss Stan Cullis thought Chelsea, who he tipped to win the trophy, were 'far better than two years earlier when Birmingham knocked them out of the cup...Hutchinson and Hudson have made a huge difference'.

Burnley at home was considered a very winnable Fourth Round draw, and Chelsea were promptly installed as 6-1 second favourites, behind clear 7-2 favourites Leeds United, drawn at Hillingdon or Sutton United. There was talk of that Leeds tie taking place at Fulham, which upset Chelsea chairman Brian Mears who could see part of his potential gate revenue disappearing down the Fulham Road to Craven Cottage, but that fear came to nothing.

Osgood, not for the first time, was hugely frustrated when not chosen for the England party of 30 to play Holland the following week. Brian James, in the *Daily Mail,* spoke for a lot of supporters when he complained 'I am still struck by the oddity of Osgood's absence, especially as the form that gave him such a strong claim has been maintained since, with a four-goal game at Crystal Palace to give it drama'. Time was clearly running out for a man who was in great form but could not even get in the 30, let alone the team and seemingly had at least five strikers (Jeff Astle, Allan Clarke, Geoff Hurst, Mick Jones and Francis Lee) ahead of him in the queue for the plane to Mexico.

A couple of weeks earlier Sexton had identified the home League clash with Leeds as critical to Chelsea's title hopes, a must-win encounter. If they won, they would be four points behind Leeds, who would have the added distraction of the European Cup later in the season. *Goal* magazine carried a preview of the Leeds clash. They described David Webb as the 'teak-tough Chelsea full-back with the steel-trap tackle'. He described the encounter at Leeds in September, where a number of players were hurt, as 'a hard game...but it certainly wasn't a dirty one', which may have been pushing it a bit. He felt the League Cup replay win over Leeds was a turning point that season. They talked to Cooke, who commented that when Sexton arrived, he thought the manager 'saw running and fitness as the be all and end all of football' but now realised that was not the case. In their Leeds preview the *Kensington Post* reflected the general mood. 'Chelsea are playing their football fast, slick, neat and powerful...Leeds are really going to have to pull all the stops out to get both points'.

Two seasonal factors in the build-up meant the Leeds game might be in doubt. The pitch was frozen, though Chelsea Secretary John Battersby was always confident the match would go ahead after the ice was removed, assuming the temperature rose. Luckily, there was a rapid thaw and though soaking wet, with ice underneath, it was on unless there was heavy rain.

More controversially, the *Evening Standard* reported that, after an outbreak of flu at the club, Chelsea were highly optimistically asking the Football League for a postponement. Peter Bonetti had flu and his deputy Tommy Hughes had been sent home with a heavy cold and sore throat, so if it went ahead, 17-year-old rookie Alan Dovey, with just a handful of reserve appearances behind him, might have to be thrust into action against Division One's leading scorers. The manager made a plea via the *Evening Standard*. 'In view of our predicament, we have asked the League to consider a postponement and have asked for an early decision in the hope of preventing Leeds from travelling'. League Secretary Alan Hardaker, who had to answer Chelsea's request, was himself in bed with flu. To the surprise of nobody, the request was summarily turned down. Sexton explained 'they told me that so long as we had a goalkeeper, no matter how inexperienced, the game would have to take place'.

Dovey woke up to a shoal of back-page headlines on matchday about himself but, in the event, Hughes was able to play. The gates closed on the largest Stamford Bridge attendance so far that season, as 57,221 crammed into the ground with huge anticipation, which deepened when Chelsea took a 2-1 lead at half-time. Clarke put the visitors in front, but Hollins and Osgood responded. At the interval, all looked well, the hosts on top and playing really well. Clarke went off injured and Billy Bremner was moved up front. The combative Scot was not a natural striker, but the change caused utter chaos in the home rearguard, and Chelsea contrived to concede four goals in 17 catastrophic minutes, through Terry Cooper, a Johnny Giles penalty, Peter Lorimer and Mick Jones as a ruthless Leeds made hay.

The myth is that Hughes, whose transfer request was being considered by the board the following week, had a calamitous game, the goals totally his fault. If you watch the *Match Of The Day* footage you realise that although the unwell Hughes was at fault for one of the goals, and demonstrating a degree of nervousness, much of the blame for the 5-2 embarrassment must fall on the defence, who crumbled and ended in disarray.

Sexton told the *Daily Mail* 'I know he (Hughes) was well under the weather, but I don't think the goals were his fault'. Bonetti later said he was angry with the criticism Hughes received. 'It was so unjustified. On the day, Leeds could have scored five whoever was in goal'. He felt his side had lost their composure. Hughes later admitted the club dosed him up on antibiotics and a swig of brandy. Supporter Geoff Kimber blamed 'calamitous' defending, rather than the goalkeeper.

The whole defence - Webb, Dempsey, McCreadie and Harris - looked nervous and the sense of panic became all-pervading. Inevitably, Chelsea players picked up knocks. Charlton clattered Osgood and Hunter 'twice assaulted Hutchinson with a cruelty that called for more than a simple reprimand from the referee' as *The Observer* put it.

This was a critical challenge in Chelsea's season, and they came up woefully short. *The Observer* commented 'Chelsea's delusions of grandeur disintegrated abruptly at Stamford Bridge yesterday' as their unbeaten home record crumbled into dust. Now nine points behind Everton and eight behind Leeds, any title hopes had surely gone. It was clear, too, that they were not yet a top-class side. *'The Unforgiven'*, written from a Leeds perspective, called the result a rout and thought the hosts were humiliated. It was hard to argue with this analysis.

That week Chelsea accepted a £100,000 bid from Ipswich for Birchenall, who had lost his place to Hutchinson and seemed to have little prospect of getting it back. Sexton told the *Evening Standard* 'Alan has asked for a couple of days to think over the offer. He has not yet arranged to go to Ipswich to discuss terms...The first-team hit their winning streak at the beginning of November, and he has not been able to get back'. He had not played in the first-team since damaging his ankle against West Bromwich on October 18th, though he had made three reserve appearances. Birchenall, understandably, was not happy with reserve football, Chelsea seemed happy to release him and would expect to get their £100,000 investment back. He commented 'Ipswich's interest is a complete shock to me...I'm keen to get back, but if I accept there would be a lot of upheaval like moving home'. He would get 5% of the fee as he had not asked for a move. Chelsea had repeatedly been linked with Millwall's Keith Weller and the money raised from selling Birchenall could be spent on him.

The following day Birchenall turned down the move as the terms were not acceptable. He told the *Daily Telegraph* 'Ipswich couldn't match the financial terms I wanted. It's nothing to do with their low League position...I desperately want first-team football and when I do get back, I mean to stay in. I was unfortunate to lose my place through injury, but Chelsea are doing well and the competition for places is intense'. Ipswich manager Bobby Robson did not lose hope, saying it was still up to the player, but in reality, the deal was dead.

A shell-shocked Chelsea had a week to recover from their humiliation before a visit to Highbury to meet an underachieving Arsenal outfit, in 12th place with just three home League wins. Their hosts had lost an FA Cup replay at Blackpool two days beforehand, having beaten Rouen in the Fairs Cup two days before that, so this was their fourth match in a week. Chelsea had lost just once in ten years at Highbury, scoring 25 goals against 10. Tommy Baldwin came in for Cooke, who had an operation on an abscess, his first League appearance in three months and the first outfield change in the team for eight matches.

Bonetti returned, which was just as well, as Hughes had still not fully recovered from the virus which caused him to miss another Scotland Under-23 cap.

As they recovered from the Wolverhampton defeat by beating Manchester City, so Chelsea put the Leeds hammering behind them by thrashing Arsenal 3-0, a scoreline that was actually kind to the hapless North Londoners, only the heroics of goalkeeper Bob Wilson keeping the score remotely respectable and preventing Osgood scoring a hat-trick. Hollins scored before half-time with a cross that went straight in, and Hutchinson and Baldwin netted in the last ten minutes. The *Sunday Mirror* picked out Hudson, majestic despite the heavy pitch, for especial praise. 'This fop-haired 18-year-old whose delicacy is made all the more remarkable by the bulk of his build, and whose calm maturity is more normally a veteran quality, wrested control of the engine room, the midfield'. Wilson called him 'the find of the season'. Hudson saw it as his best Chelsea display so far.

Sexton told *The People* 'I was tremendously pleased with the way it went after that Leeds result. The lads worked hard and showed a lot of fight' and it looked as though that debacle had caused no permanent impact on confidence. They had a week to prepare for the FA Cup-tie against Burnley. Cooke was not selected as he had not fully recovered from his abscess, so Baldwin retained his place in an unchanged side. Under a *Daily Mail* 'Chelsea's Target Is Still The Double' headline, the manager was defiant. 'It may seem to people outside that we did our chances when we lost to Leeds, but we don't see it that way at all...We want the cup and the League'.

A large crowd was expected for the Burnley cup-tie, so the recorded 42,282 attendance, nearly 3,000 less than the Birmingham tie, must have been a massive disappointment to a club hierarchy already thinking about the money needed for ground redevelopment. Those that turned up watched a tight first-half, with Burnley's Brian O'Neil and Ralph Coates dominating midfield, but when Hollins, with a trademark run and shot, and Osgood put Chelsea two ahead after 69 minutes it seemed as though earlier missed chances would be irrelevant as the Fifth Round beckoned. The inability to keep clean sheets came back to haunt them, however. For Hugh Curran six weeks earlier, read Martin Dobson. The midfielder scored twice in the last ten minutes, taking advantage of shoddy defending, to earn Burnley an unexpected replay three days later. A hugely frustrated Sexton complained 'we paid the price for non-vigilance. It was careless'.

The *Daily Telegraph* felt the result 'revived the perennial question of Chelsea's ability to win honours...In the past they have been thwarted by immaturity and an absence of professional aplomb'. This was hardly a new criticism. They noticed that Osgood's spirits slumped visibly as he 'missed a string of chances'. The replay programme thought the first tie was a 'fascinating and thrilling spectacle...a feast of football excitement and skills' and that Burnley deserved the draw. Supporter Barry Holmes, who was there, felt it quickly 'went from comfortable to sweaty desperation'.

Hutchinson's long throws as usual caused chaos but were twice called foul throws as referee Jack Taylor and his linesmen paid close attention to him. The player blamed it on 'rigorous scrutiny by television' on *The Big Match* six days earlier (after the Arsenal clash), which pointed out that sometimes he seemed to be illegally lifting his foot.

The winners of the replay were drawn at Tottenham or Crystal Palace. Chelsea were 9-1 fourth favourites despite the difficult replay they were about to face. Osgood, who had hit the bar in the first minute, damaged his ankle and had to miss the replay. Hutchinson suffered a groin strain, McCreadie hurt his shoulder and Baldwin spent Sunday in bed with concussion, but all three were declared fit. Cooke's craft and ability to slow things down had been missed, so it was fortunate that he was fit to replace Osgood.

32,000 crowded into Turf Moor, including a large contingent from Chelsea, with thousands more locked out. Supporter Bob Ruthven remembers travelling up on one of two special trains. Paul McParlan remembers chaotic scenes outside the ground with so many trying to get in. He reckoned there were well over 3,000 visitors there, excellent for a midweek away trip up North. He remembers that Hutchinson's throws were greeted with 'Ooh it's a corner' chants from the visiting support.

Chelsea making their commitment very clear, conceded 11 fouls in the first 25 minutes. McParlan, in a piece for the *These Football Times* website, recalled that this, perhaps unsurprisingly, antagonised the home support, which in turn inspired their favourites. Coates, again top class, scored before half-time and ran things until Harris and McCreadie slowed him by fouling him harshly enough for both to be booked.

In the second-half Chelsea started to seize the initiative but, as McParlan recalls, Burnley closed down threat after threat. With 18 minutes left Chelsea were 1-0 down and looked to be going out of the cup, their quest for honours that season seemingly over. Houseman, given a free role, then scored a truly magnificent equaliser, running thirty yards with the ball before curling a glorious left-foot drive past Peter Mellor from outside the box. The importance of that goal cannot be over-stated. The season turned on the equaliser, one of the great Chelsea 'Sliding Door' moments.

Hutchinson hit the bar as Burnley began to wilt, but the tie went to extra-time where Chelsea's superior fitness told, and the home team were left chasing shadows. Baldwin gave Chelsea a 94th minute lead and Houseman, the hero of the night, sealed the crucial win. Bob Ruthven recalls 'What I remember most was the supporters singing a very slow "Chelsea, Chelsea" with each wave merging into one and not quickening up so completely drowning out anything else'.

A totally-committed 3-1 victory led to a grudging 'Beefy Chelsea

Muscle Through' *Daily Mail* headline in what they saw as 'a grim and graceless game'. Sexton, unsurprisingly, was delighted, especially considering the talismanic Osgood was missing. 'I couldn't be more pleased with the way they played'. The Chelsea programme called Houseman's opener 'the most important goal he ever scored' as he bagged the first pair of his career. Houseman, not a crowd favourite, won some supporters over that night, according to McParlan. He remembers that some loyal travellers had to get a local train to Preston to get the midnight train back to London.

In '*The Working Man's Ballet*' Alan Hudson felt 'the fans lifted us' when they were 1-0 down. That night he felt 'we showed a combination of the will to win and resilience that was to weld us into a very tough unit'. The boost to the side's confidence was commented on by Dempsey, who saw the win as a turning point. The importance of winning that night cannot be overstated, as if Chelsea had been eliminated from the FA Cup, the next few years would have looked vastly different, on and off the pitch.

The FA Cup was significantly condensed that season, with the Final 3-4 weeks earlier than usual on April 11th, to allow it to end early, hopefully giving the England squad adequate time to work together before the World Cup started on May 31st. The Fifth Round was therefore just 11 days after the replay. To general surprise, Crystal Palace beat Tottenham in their replay and therefore Chelsea had to travel to Selhurst Park.

Before that, Chelsea had a home match against perennial relegation strugglers Sunderland on the final day of January. Osgood was fit so Baldwin, despite his efforts and goal at Turf Moor, was demoted to substitute. His recall was fully justified when he scored twice in the first 22 minutes. Joe Baker, who four years earlier almost signed for Chelsea, pulled one back but Osgood completed his sharp and skilfully taken hat-trick to round off a fairly straightforward win, the hugely popular star serenaded by The Shed with 'Osgood for England' chants. Harris had to go off at half-time with a pulled leg muscle. Sunderland put in a number of bruising tackles and Osgood, Cooke, Hutchinson and Hudson all had to use ice packs on injuries post-match, Webb suffering a cut mouth.

The *Daily Telegraph* saw Chelsea as ranking alongside Manchester United, Leeds and Everton in the box-office ratings and without doubt the addition of Hutchinson and Hudson to the team had increased the attractiveness of the fare on offer. The board hoping this would be reflected in increased home crowds.

Hollins was given a guest column in the *Nottingham Football Post*. At the end of August when Chelsea were in the bottom half with one win from their first seven matches, he took a bet they would finish in the top six, 'in the knowledge that I was in the best team I have known during my six years as a professional with the club'. The previous season they had found it difficult to utilise the 'tremendous individual flair' to be in the best interests of the team, but he felt that the emergence of Hudson and Hutchinson had forced 'the more established stars to produce a 100% effort to get back into the team', the improvement of Cooke and Osgood in recent months 'another vital factor in our success'. He confirmed that Cooke 'has worked tirelessly' to improve his passing and linking with other players, as opposed to trying to beat the opposition on his own. Osgood was now fighting for the ball rather than waiting for it. In a feature on Hollins in *Goal* magazine, he admitted he had had a poor 1968-69 but was fed up with those blaming poor form on his marriage. He was now back to his best and knocking hard on the England door.

The *Daily Mirror* ran a 'Must England Leave Osgood Behind?' article. Will 'a history of doubtful temperament ...influence the immediate international future of a very talented footballer...Chelsea have hinted that Osgood does not take kindly to the sun...I put this to Osgood last night, suggesting that he does not enter footballing top gear until the cooler September days, and he would be below his best at high-noon Mexico'. He retorted 'I don't think it affects my play as much as people have said'. He said he had played in Australia and Mozambique and had been OK. 'But surely every player would feel some sort of effect. Why should it trouble me more than anybody else? People have said I don't start playing until the autumn, but that is more likely to be because I am a slow starter'. Exactly why he was a 'slow starter', and why he just accepted this fact, was not explored. Strikers Osgood, Joe Royle and Jeff Astle were not in Ramsey's side but were all scoring goals regularly, so would certainly be in Ramsey's deliberations.

In his *News Of The World* column, Jimmy Hill felt Osgood was 'a moody player but doesn't lack courage...It was suggested Osgood may have ruined his (England) chances by publicly proclaiming lack of interest in being chosen for the England team...We have seen an amazing transformation in Osgood recently. He has added fire to his undoubted flair. And what a difference that has made to Chelsea'. Hill felt Ramsey would take a close look, but that it was up to the player to convince the manager. Time was certainly running out.

The influential Hugh McIlvanney column in *The Observer* highlighted three very promising youngsters – Manchester United's Brian Kidd, Burnley's Ralph Coates and Hudson. 'Players with the capacity to be great are rare phenomena'. The point was made that Coates had made his Burnley debut in 1964 and Kidd had already won the European Cup, so Hudson was certainly the new kid on the block. He saw all as outstanding prospects but 'Hudson impresses me most...At 18 he is already, in terms of performance not promise, one of the most influential midfield players in the country. He was praised by John Boyle as 'marvellously sure of himself'. McIlvanney praised his 'splendid control and the ability to delay his move until precisely the most devastating moment'. Described as naturally polite and self-deprecating, McIlvanney concluded that 'only some kind of accident can prevent Alan Hudson from being one of the greatest players in Britain in the 1970s'.

Unsurprisingly, the board turned down Tommy Hughes' transfer request. Despite his travails against Leeds he was a good goalkeeper and ideal cover for Bonetti, and the club would have been foolish to let him go. Sheffield Wednesday and Crystal Palace, both fighting to stay up, were interested in Tommy Baldwin but, though not a first-team regular at that point, again he was a key squad member.

The Ipswich deal having fallen through, Liverpool made a firm bid for Birchenall and Newcastle United were also interested. He was watched in two reserve games and manager Joe Harvey was 'keeping a watching brief...we want to be sure he has fully recovered from injury'. Alan Cocks, 18-year-old centre-forward, went to Brentford on a month's loan, linking up with Frank Blunstone.

Bobby Tambling was recalled from his controversial loan period at Crystal Palace. Sexton commented 'we would have liked to extend the loan for a further period, but it is a question of ethics as far as other clubs are concerned. When you lend a player of that calibre, he can have a considerable influence on League positions. At the time when we lent him, they (Palace) were very hard pressed by injuries'.

After the Burnley replay, McCreadie had three bookings that season, Harris and Osgood two. If that pair were cautioned again, they would join McCreadie in the queue for a disciplinary hearing. If the Scot's appeal against his Burnley booking failed, he would get a suspension. Despite the size and quality of the squad, the manager could ill afford to losing players to suspension, especially those three.

Chairman Brian Mears, following in the footsteps of his father Joe, became a member of the FA Council, increasing Chelsea's influence in the corridors of power.

Goal magazine ran a feature on the new Chelsea Pools operation, to be set up and run by Pat Abel, who had previously run the highly-successful Sky Blue Pools for Coventry City which had 130,000 members and £2,000 weekly prize money. She had turned down the Chelsea job once as she did not think she was ready and was fully aware some considered it tough as 'Chelsea supporters are so far-flung'. She was keen to sign up members who supported other clubs.

To aid the Chelsea Pools operation, the club carried out market research to identify where their support lived, which turned out to be from London down to the South Coast, with large pockets in Slough and several South Coast towns. The pool was scheduled to start in August 1970, though the new one shilling Golden Goal ticket competition had just gone on sale. The target was 50,000 members for when the pool started on August 15th. Full-time representatives equipped with royal blue Chelsea vans would have the job of selling the pool to the public, a computerised system showing whether a member had paid that week. There was clearly a concerted effort to run the pool on a highly professional basis, and it was to be hoped that effort would pay off in terms of significant revenue.

Chelsea ended January in the Fifth Round of the FA Cup and third in Division One. The Leeds defeat, though, clearly ended any realistic chance of the title, despite Sexton's protestations. The team was garnering significant amounts of positive publicity - particularly Cooke, Hudson, Hutchinson and Osgood - and the club really seemed on the up, possibly more than at any time since early 1965, when Tommy Docherty's side were competing seriously for the treble. Crystal Palace, who had been beaten 5-1 weeks earlier, were certainly beatable in the FA Cup the following Saturday and arguably only Derby County, Leeds, Liverpool and Manchester United of the teams remaining in the competition could hope to cope with an on-form Chelsea.

Leeds United	p30 45pts
Everton	p29 44pts
Chelsea	**p28 36pts**
Liverpool	p27 35pts
Wolverhampton	p29 35pts
Derby County	p29 33pts
Stoke City	p28 33pts

February 1970

The FA Cup-tie at Crystal Palace loomed large. 1,000 supporters had gained admission to their Tottenham replay using forgeries. Fears of fake tickets meant all 48,500 Chelsea tickets had to be overprinted with an image of midfielder Steve Kember to try and beat counterfeiters. The visitors comfortably sold out their 12,000 allocation the Sunday beforehand and plenty of other Blues bought theirs directly from Selhurst Park where they were still on open sale. The benefit of a decent cup run could be seen from the fact that Palace's new stand cost £150,000 but after the Chelsea tie they had already recouped nearly £50,000 of that money from FA Cup revenue. As their manager Bert Head enthused, 'the cup means money'.

Anticipation was high, especially after the resounding defeat inflicted on Palace over Christmas. Ron Harris pleaded with Sexton to wait until his fitness test before picking their cup team. 'I refuse to be ruled out before Thursday. I'd say I have an even chance of playing' as he and Charlie Cooke were receiving intensive treatment. Key midfielder John Hollins was sent home with a head cold but in the end was passed fit. In the end, Tommy Baldwin came in for Cooke who did not recover from the ankle problem suffered at Sunderland, and the ultra-tough Harris played.

In front of 48,479 spectators, paying Palace record receipts of £22,250, Peter Osgood gave Chelsea a first-half lead, the visitors struggling to break down a packed home midfield. Roger Hoy equalised soon after the interval, but the visitors rallied and John Dempsey, Peter Houseman and Ian Hutchinson saw them comfortably home. On a heavily muddy pitch, all four goals came from set pieces, proof of the diligent planning involved in Sexton's training sessions, though Head thought the first and last should have been disallowed for pushing at corners. Head also felt **Chelsea were 'now full of the qualities Leeds had about 18 months to two years ago – all efficiency and professionalism'.** The *Daily Mail* claimed 'If (Chelsea) can win the FA Cup that success could carry Osgood, Hollins and even 18-year-old Alan Hudson into England's World Cup squad'. Unquestionably, it would do no harm.

An excellent result, building FA Cup momentum nicely. The Quarter-Final draw produced a visit 12 days later to near neighbours Queens Park Rangers, which ratcheted cup fever up a few more notches. Rangers were in Division Two, having been relegated the previous season, their first ever in the top-flight. The draw caught the public imagination - as soon as the draw was made, crowds turned up at Loftus Road optimistically looking for tickets. The match was all-ticket, with a record attendance (the current record was 31,138 but the capacity now 33,000) and record receipts confidently expected. Leeds United were 9-4 FA Cup favourites, Chelsea joint second-favourites with Manchester United at 3-1.

There were five ex-Chelsea men at Queens Park Rangers – Terry Venables, Barry Bridges, Ian Watson, Alan Wilks and Alan Harris – to give the clash a further edge, and Sexton enthused 'they play an attacking game like ourselves'. Chelsea had won 4-0 at Loftus Road in the League the previous season, easing up, so were clear favourites for arguably the biggest match ever played at Loftus Road. Chelsea received 8,000 tickets but those would all be allocated to season-ticket-holders, officials, players and staff, leaving none for general sale, according to Secretary John Battersby. In the end, surprisingly, around 1,000 Chelsea season-ticket-holders did not take up their option, so those tickets were sold at short notice on open sale at Stamford Bridge. Brian Gaches 'went home sick' from school to spend the day queuing for one of those last 1,000 tickets. Bob Ruthven got there early enough that the queue had yet to develop and also acquired a precious ticket.

Touts were already asking five times the face value for a game that could have filled the 33,000 capacity at least twice over. **Ludicrously, there were no half-price children's tickets, according to the** *Acton Gazette*, 'following a request from Chelsea who never have half-prices (so) this might have caused administrative difficulties'.

Jarvis Astaire head of Viewsport, the leading sporting closed-circuit TVG company, was keen to show the match in cinemas. FA Secretary Denis Follows, head in the sand as usual, refused, citing concerns about the impact on other attendances. This excuse was a total nonsense as the screenings could just be made locally and tickets only put on sale at

Stamford Bridge.

With all the cup excitement, it was easy to forget that there were two tricky Division One games to negotiate, a midweek trip to Derby followed by a home encounter with Liverpool. Mulligan made his full League debut at Derby alongside Hinton, as both Harris and Dempsey were out with injuries picked up at Crystal Palace. Osgood gave Chelsea the lead just before half-time when a Hutchinson long throw caused chaos and, when Hudson made it 2-0 from outside the penalty area with 13 minutes left, they appeared safe. Yet again, though, a lead was somehow thrown away as Alan Durban and Kevin Hector scored in the next four minutes to make the final score 2-2, not a bad result but yet another point needlessly jettisoned.

Worse from Chelsea's perspective, Osgood received his third booking of the season for putting the ball in the net after the referee Gerry Jones had blown for offside and was in line for a suspension, a real concern with a crucial FA Cup-tie looming. Managers Matt Gillies of Nottingham Forest, Bill McGarry of Wolverhampton Wanderers and Tony Waddington of Stoke City all saw the booking, and were each very graciously prepared to help him, an indication that the booking was indeed a harsh one. There were concerns that the two players with three bookings, Osgood and McCreadie, could miss a Semi-Final should Chelsea get there. Harris had two with Houseman, Baldwin and Hutchinson having one each. Harris and McCreadie were appealing against the FA Cup bookings at Burnley.

The *Evening Standard* reported that Baldwin's legal issues were not yet over. Under a 'Footballer For Trial' small front-page headline, they reported that he was to be charged with aiding and abetting a man to drive a car recklessly. He was given £50 bail.

A frozen pitch caused the Liverpool home League game to be postponed, meaning that as Queens Park Rangers were at home that day, there were sudden concerns about a phalanx of Chelsea supporters heading to Loftus Road to buy tickets. This was made theoretically more difficult as Rangers were supposedly only selling tickets to supporters who had a programme from the previous round against Derby County.

The extra break gave the squad the chance to try and reach full fitness before the short journey across West London. In the end everyone, except Tambling, was available so Sexton could field his preferred team. The *Daily Mirror* reported that Chelsea were scaling Hudson's training down to prevent him doing too much. Trainer Harry Medhurst explained 'Alan is growing quickly, and we don't want him to lose his edge' so he missed a 'demanding' PT session at the National Recreation Centre. He was also recovering from a stomach upset and a bug.

The *Daily Telegraph* carried an interview with Sexton in the Cup-tie build up. He was not worried about his side's marking of Rangers talisman Rodney Marsh as his defence had had to deal with George

Best. He said he had changed his philosophy 'from a side hard to beat into a side hard to prevent from winning…Winning the ball is then not an end in itself, but the point at which the side comes alive. It's human nature to want to do enough and no more. The manager's job is to try and get more than 'enough'…They say…that it's not what you know, but what to do with what you know…I can only hold their (the players) respect if what I tell them is shown, by their own experience, to be correct more often than it is incorrect'. The players prepared for their sixth FA Cup Quarter-Final in consecutive seasons, the first club to achieve that since Sheffield Wednesday the previous century.

The *Daily Mail* ran a feature on Houseman, under a 'The Unsung Star - Houseman Fights Chelsea Apathy' headline, complaining 'the best he can hope for is a lull in the barracking'. He was fulsomely praised by manager and colleagues. Webb pointed out 'it's fantastic the work he does for us off the ball' and Hutchinson approvingly noted 'I should think he has made 50% or 60% of my goals. You know if you go for a ball from him, your running is going to be worthwhile'. In another piece *Goal* magazine pointed out that Houseman used to play better away because of the Stamford Bridge boo-boys. Sexton complained 'the job he does for us is more widely appreciated (but) he has only to make one mistake to start them off again'. He was without doubt appreciated by teammates and those in the game, having moved from midfield back to the wing since emergence of Hudson. Despite his two crucial goals at Burnley, the manager reckoned he needed to improve his finishing.

There was a lot of talk about Osgood and Marsh in the press and their clash was the subject of huge anticipation. Supporter Barry Holmes remembers that 'Rod Is God' was a common piece of graffiti on the walls of Putney and Hammersmith, 'a direct challenge against the Chelsea chant of 'Osgood is Good''. That anticipation was proved correct, as the 33,572 spectators were treated to a thrilling encounter. A clear majority of spectators in the packed ground were supporting the visitors, despite the efforts of the Rangers hierarchy to prevent that happening. Supporter Geoff Kimber remembers that, again, Chelsea supporters seemed to fill 75% of Loftus Road.

In a match of fiery tempers and harsh tacking on a very heavy pitch, Chelsea's skill dominated, and they ran out 4-2 winners. Cooke made goals for Webb (a great volley) and Osgood in the first eight minutes, causing a surge at the Chelsea end, resulting in a crush and spectators spilling onto the pitch. Terry Venables pulled one back with a twice-taken penalty against his old club after McCreadie had brought down another ex-teammate, Barry Bridges. Chelsea, rattled, lost their cool and Osgood was booked for a vicious tackle on Dave Clement. Then fortune favoured the visitors. Rangers goalkeeper Mike Kelly failed to hold a Hollins shot and Osgood flicked the ball into the net. Osgood completed his hat-trick with his sixth FA Cup goal of the season before Bridges pulled another back, scant consolation in a 4-2 defeat. Marsh was largely anonymous, unable to escape Harris's close attentions.

The *Daily Mirror*'s Ken Jones eulogised 'Hudson the Great'. 'Peter Osgood's Cup hat-trick may not prove as significant as the mature football played by his 18-year-old teammate Alan Hudson. Osgood's goals, taken with the certainty of a man in peak form, will amplify the clamour for his inclusion in England's team. But Hudson, after only 26 senior appearances, might well be closer to selection when Sir Alf Ramsey announces the names of those who will travel to Mexico'. Ramsey famously commented that weekend 'there is no end to what this boy could achieve. He could become one of the greats'. Jones agreed with the England boss. 'His game carries the marks of extraordinary wisdom for one so young. He is quick, combative, intuitive and skilful…He has all the qualities Ramsey looks for in a player and seems to be blessed with an unshakable temperament'. Ramsey had insisted there was time and room for young talent to come through and there was speculation Hudson could be given Under-23 and Football League appearances to prove himself.

Hudson later reckoned Osgood booked his ticket to Mexico that afternoon. Battling Jeff Astle at the top of the goalscoring charts, he knew he was being watched by Ramsey, who had seen him score seven goals in four games. 'It is not for me to say whether I have shown enough. All I know is that time is flying by, matches are flying by, and time is running out for me'. In an interview in the Palace programme with his agent Greg Tesser, Osgood commented 'I truly believe Chelsea are the best team in the country right now'. He saw the visit by Everton as the turning point. 'Everything seemed to click for me. All my old shooting ability and ball-skills returned'. Without doubt, his form was worthy of an international chance. George Best added to the clamour, making it clear he thought Ramsey had erred by leaving out Osgood.

The other Semi-Finalists were Leeds United, Middlesbrough or Manchester United, who needed to replay, and Watford. All over the country, schoolkids with surreptitiously-carried transistors tuned into Radio 2 to hear the midday draw. Whoever drew Watford, shock conquerors of Liverpool, would seem to have a strong chance of reaching Wembley. In the event, Chelsea were the lucky side, and were immediately installed as 11-8 favourites with Leeds at 13-8, United 7-2, Watford 25-1 and Middlesbrough 66-1.

The FA decided in their infinite wisdom to play the Semi-Final on one of the few pitches in the country worse than Wembley, Tottenham's notorious farmyard of a pitch, White Hart Lane. The FA rightly wanted a London venue to minimise supporter travelling but Arsenal were at home to Liverpool that day so Highbury could not be used. The tie was to kick-off at 14.45 and Arsenal's at 15.30 to try and minimise North London traffic congestion. An optimistic move.

Though the draw was exciting for Chelsea supporters, even that was overshadowed for many by the news the same day that Osgood had been given a late call-up for the England party to play in Belgium two days later, as Bobby Charlton was involved in the FA Cup replay and Colin Bell was unfit. Chelsea happily agreed to play their home game against Newcastle the same day without him. Press speculation was that Osgood was likely to start, either up front or in Charlton's midfield role, and he would be under real pressure to perform after the clamour for his inclusion.

The *Daily Mail* headline 'Osgood In By Public Choice' summed up the position. 'Peter Osgood, the people's choice but ignored by Sir Alf Ramsey, was hauled without previous hint or hope into the squad...to play Belgium on Wednesday'. If picked he needed to perform extremely well to allay Ramsey's 'mistrust'. 'This is a breakthrough for me, but it has proved nothing yet...Even if I don't play in this team, I can accept that at least I have a real chance and it hasn't all been just talk'. In '*Back Home*', on England's 1970 World Cup campaign, author Jeff Dawson felt Osgood had had a cracking season and it was generally recognised that he deserved his chance. The player, selected for his debut alongside both Geoff Hurst and Francis Lee, said pre-match 'I realise that I'm on a hiding to nothing tonight in view of the publicity I've had recently. I know it's going to be tough'.

Osgood did have impressive game, Ramsey commenting 'I was pleased with Osgood, he had an extremely good match in difficult conditions' as England won 3-1 on a mud bath. He was also selected for the Under-23's the following week, as Ramsey clearly wanted to see as much of him as possible. The manager had opened the door in Brussels because Charlton and Bell were unavailable. Now it was up to Osgood to storm through it.

Hudson and Hutchinson were also in that Under-23 squad while reserve keeper Tommy Hughes was called up by Scotland. Hudson, whose star was definitely in the ascendency, beamed 'I'm delighted to be picked for the Under-23 party but dare not think about Mexico and the real thing. Just say I'm hoping, quietly'.

With Osgood and Bonetti in Brussels, and Hutchinson out injured, Hughes came in against Newcastle and two near-forgotten strikers started front, Baldwin and Alan Birchenall. A 0-0 draw, in front of a very decent 35,341 midweek crowd, hardly did either any favours, though the desperately unlucky Birchenall had worse things to worry about on his first first-team appearance in four months. A collision with Newcastle goalkeeper Iam McFaul caused a gaping wound below his left knee which required eight stitches and a few days in hospital. Trainer Harry Medhurst revealed 'Alan will be out for four to six weeks. He has a terrible gash, and we must take our time with him'.

It looked as though his season could be over and an understandably despondent Birchenall told the *Daily Mail* 'I'm feeling lousy, sick. Sorry for myself. Worst of all I feel beaten'. He made it clear it was an accident but was bitterly disappointed to have had such a fragmented season, what with the knee trouble in October. He was happy to be back against Newcastle, and at half-time he felt he would get his old sharpness back, then the gash happened. 'The Cup's out. So Is Mexico' he bemoaned, though to be frank his chance of the latter was slim indeed.

Sustained brilliance from Hudson was the only bright spot of the evening, as not even sending David Webb up front could produce a goal. Osgood and Hutchinson were clearly badly missed. Keeping Hutchinson fit and Osgood away from suspension was clearly critical if hopes of winning the cup were to be realised.

February ended with a trip to Coventry City, flying high in fourth place, just two points behind Chelsea. McCreadie was missing with a groin problem, replaced by Mulligan, and Baldwin kept his place as Hutchinson still had a back problem.

In a preview in the *Daily Mail*, Harris 'known affectionately at Chelsea as Chopper and acknowledged throughout football as one of its toughest defenders' claimed, 'I am a reformed man...I've only been suspended once in my career'. In the Coventry side would be Roy Barry, who had his nose broken by Harris (who claimed it was 'an accident') on his debut four months earlier. Barry commented 'I do not bear grudges. Harris is a professional and it was just something that happened in the heat of the moment'.

A comfortable 3-0 win at Coventry, who aspired to be a top team and had conceded just seven goals in 11 matches whilst gaining 18 points, was an excellent result that impressed everyone present. Baldwin, Webb and Hudson scored, Hudson's after a 65-yard run which the scorer regretted was not on television. The visitors were strong and self-assured so despite 'a barrage of intimidatory tackling' by their opponents they failed to kick Chelsea into submission. Defeated City manager Noel Cantwell told the *News Of The World* 'Dave Sexton has taken all his great individuals and created a team. They're capable of anything'.

The *Coventry Evening Telegraph*, under a 'Superb Chelsea' headline, opined that they ranked alongside Leeds as one of the best sides in the country with 'a superb display of controlled, aggressive, top-grade skills such as few sides in Europe are capable of giving'. Leeds boss Don Revie told the *Daily Mirror* 'we were half-convinced we had knocked the stuffing out of them (by beating them 5-2). But, if anything, Chelsea seem to have improved. They have got tremendous strength in depth and a tremendous amount of skill. If we get to meet them in the Cup Final, it will be a great game'. The *Kensington Post* rued their spluttering start. 'Chelsea look better every week and come the end of the season, that bad start to the campaign will be the only thing that separates them from the title'.

Ronnie Hallstroem, Sweden's first choice goalkeeper, spent five weeks training with Chelsea and watching Bonetti. West Germany wanted to meet Chelsea in a friendly on April 8th but were turned down by Secretary John Battersby as the club hoped to be at Wembley three days later.

Chelsea ended February very much on the up, in third place and with a seemingly eminently winnable FA Cup Semi-Final to look forward to. Osgood, Hutchinson and Hudson were getting international recognition and if the first choice line-up could stay fit and avoid suspension, they had little to fear, and much to look forward to, for the rest of the season. As supporter Barry Holmes recalls, Chelsea were in a unique phase, genuinely exciting to watch with a classic mixture of skill and steel, an innovative coach, a club with ambition. Yet there was always the inconsistency, that foreboding threat that the supporters took with them to every game which made supporting them during that period 'an incorrigible habit'.

Leeds United	p34 51pts
Everton	p33 49pts
Chelsea	**p32 42pts**
Derby County	p34 39pts
Wolverhampton	p34 38pts
Manchester U	p33 38pts
Coventry City	p31 37pts

March 1970

Goal Magazine clearly saw Osgood as second only to George Best in the celebrity football stakes, with a front cover plus a laudatory feature. 'A born showman. It is in his blood, his manner and the way he plays football...(At) Chelsea, where the team is the only thing that matters, he has been able to curb that youthful tendency of over-elaboration to become one of the star products of the age...In this self-discipline he has developed into a far better player...A cocky, self-assured 17-year-old (who) glorified in the publicity and the acclaim (has matured)...He wears the number nine shirt and plays almost everywhere...The petulance remains but so does his ability. He has been able to blend his own individualism with the team wishes of Sexton. It has been a key factor in their shaping'. Certainly, both manager and player deserved enormous credit for so effectively marrying Osgood's huge talents to the needs of the team.

Chelsea's other glamourous figure, Alan Hudson, was the subject of a feature in *The Observer*. They thought he looked more 'like a King's Road stroller than an athlete, dressed in fur-lined suede, discreet bell-bottoms and patent-leather shoes'. One of the few footballers to have grown up within the sound of the roar of Stamford Bridge, who started training at the club aged 12, they talked about his rocketing reputation. Certainly in the past few months his ascendency to star status had been meteoric. The *Evening Standard* describing him as modest and dedicated with 'precocious judgement'.

The following week a two-page Hudson piece by Ken Jones in the *Daily Mirror* was headlined 'Alan Hudson Seems To Have Everything That Sir Alf Ramsey Is looking For In A Player'. Jones thought he had been 'outstanding' at Loftus Road and 'consistently impressive' all season. He was making a late move towards the World Cup squad and Jones saw him as 'skilful, competitive, supremely fit, determined and intelligent - mature beyond his years on the pitch'. He felt Osgood, Hudson and Burnley's Ralph Coates were under consideration for a late seat on the plane to Mexico.

Chelsea's first game in March was Nottingham Forest at home but before that, in midweek, Osgood scored twice for England Under-23's before the match was abandoned after an hour because of heavy snow, with England 3-1 up against Scotland. He went off after 57 minutes, having been asked by Ramsey to play 'on a little longer (after half-time), in the hope he might score another goal' (he did). He had suffered a calf strain at Coventry, but it was not felt to be serious. Hudson, on his Under-23 debut, took time to settle but was coming more into things when it was called off and Hughes did much to restore a reputation damaged by the Leeds defeat. Hutchinson was unfit and the focus was on him getting fit for the Watford Semi-Final.

Osgood told the *Daily Mirror* that 'conditions were impossible, but I still enjoyed the game. I was delighted with the two goals, but it was a pity to put them past my Chelsea mate, Tommy Hughes'. The paper thought Hudson 'was obviously feeling his way...but he did enough to confirm Sir Alf's opinion that he will be the big star of the future'.

That Saturday, man-of-the-moment Osgood was awarded *Evening Standard* 'Footballer Of The Month', presented by chairman Brian Mears, and Bernard Joy wrote a laudatory piece to mark the occasion. He saw the switch to striker as pivotal, coming on for Baldwin against Ipswich and feeling 'at home right away'. He admitted that in his first two appearances, in midfield, 'there was nothing there. No inspiration, nothing to offer'. He pointed out that in midfield, you had to worry about an opponent, whereas as striker the opposition needed to worry about you. 'When things were going badly for me at the beginning of the season, I told myself I had to be more responsible or finish as a nobody'. He mentioned that there were reports of interest from Liverpool but was clear that 'there was only one club for me'. Ramsey had told Sexton in mid-January he was ready to try Osgood in the full international side, and he had an 'outstanding game' on his debut.

Osgood was seen as easy going, a good mixer and liked a practical joke. 'I used to need a gee-up every now and again to get me back on the rails but that's not so necessary these days. I've grown up a lot'. He had not found it easy to adjust to the fame and the increase in money from £10-a-week as a bricklayer. Joy concluded that 'the evidence is that the playboy is being left behind and he is dedicating his immense ability to becoming a match winner for both Chelsea and England'. His wonderful talents were certainly being used to good effect, but that playboy image occasionally resurfaced.

Hutchinson was fit but not chosen against Nottingham Forest despite being recovered from his back problem, to ensure his fitness for Watford the following week. A fit-again John Boyle returned to the matchday squad having been absent for four months. In all the excitement about the looming Semi-Final, it seemed as though the League had taken a back seat, and so it proved as Jimmy McCaffrey equalised Baldwin's early opener with ten minutes to go, as Chelsea threw away yet another lead, Osgood failing to convert two straightforward chances. They played attractive football but 'sleepwalked' through the second-half, casually assuming they would retain control and the equaliser was a shock to them, their angry manager and the 38,280 present.

Hollins' brother Dave, in goal for Forest, made a magnificent string of saves fulsomely praised by Sexton, who refused to comment on whether some of his players were saving themselves for Watford. Baldwin impressed and must have assumed he was in with a chance of retaining his place for the Semi-Final the following Saturday, in preference to Hutchinson.

McCreadie needed a groin operation, but trainer Harry Medhurst revealed 'the injury is not serious and cannot get worse, but the only cure is surgery, though the operation could wait until the end of the season'. He had missed the last two matches and Medhurst explained 'we will push him in training this week, and then it is up to him and the manager whether he plays'.

Watford tickets were put on general sale on the Sunday morning, six days before the Semi-Final, after season-ticket-holders had been taken care of. Supporter **Peter Gray** remembers a station announcement telling ticket purchasers to get out at Earls Court Station as the queue started past West Brompton. He queued for well over two hours. The ludicrous practise continued whereby the host club and FA between them got a third of Semi-Final tickets, meaning Tottenham sold thousands, many of which went straight onto the black market.

The looming threat of possible suspensions occupied a few minds that week. Osgood had a Disciplinary Committee hearing on Monday March 9th, having received three bookings. Any suspension would not take effect until after the Semi-Final the following weekend, and there should easily be enough matches scheduled for him to have finished the suspension before Wembley. McCreadie had been due to appeal against his booking against Burnley in Manchester, but his train was cancelled because of snow, giving rise to concern that a delayed sentence could possibly affect his availability for the Cup Final.

Osgood's hearing went better than expected, with a 14 day

suspended sentence and £50 fine. He left the hearing grinning broadly at the leniency shown. The FA stressed that his good record saved him from heavier punishment. If he had been suspended, he would have missed the chance to appear for the Football League against the Scottish League the following week and, potentially, ended his chances of going to Mexico. He also contested his booking for kicking the ball in the net at Derby after being given offside. Nottingham Forest manager Matt Gillies gave evidence on his behalf and the player claimed he did not hear the whistle, but the appeal was rejected.

McCreadie was less fortunate, was suspended for 14 days from March 17th (two days after the Semi-Final), and fined £75, after three bookings. His appeal against the last was turned down and he elected to be dealt with immediately. He would miss four League appearances but not the Semi-Final (though would be suspended for any replay) and would be available for the Final if Chelsea made it. The break would also enable him to rest his troublesome groin. Harris failed in his appeal against his Burnley booking.

In the build-up to the big match, Watford manager Ken Furphy bullishly (and possibly foolishly) told the *Evening Standard* 'Chelsea have some brilliant individuals, but they are not as good as they are made out to be. Opponents have been brainwashed into believing they are better than what they are. As a result, teams have gone on to play tight, have surrendered the initiative and got beaten. There will be nothing negative about us and we are going to attack them'. Fighting talk.

Unusually, Sexton went on the attack himself, retorting 'I think they lack fight in their attack, like we did before Osgood and Hutchinson moved forward'. He thought 'it would be strange, indeed, if such ability and experience (as his side had) were now to fail'. He told the *Daily Mirror* 'I think we have reached the point where we need only concern ourselves with what WE do and not what the opposition are planning. We have the players and the confidence…The game is there to be won and we have got to go and win it'. He pointed out Chelsea had scored 16 goals in five FA Cup matches.

Goal magazine's preview talked to an impressed Stoke City manager Tony Waddington who felt 'they are all potential goalscorers and Alan Hudson is the greatest find for years'. Equally laudatory was Birmingham boss Stan Cullis, who purred 'the introduction of Hudson and Hutchinson has meant a great deal to the side this season while Osgood has now reached his real potential as a striker'.

The *Daily Mail* ran a concerning 'Play-In-Pain Secret Of Hudson - Agony Of A Young Star Bidding For The Cup' headline. Injury to his right knee had meant he missed nearly a year as a youth player, and he had damaged left knee ligaments at Carlisle in October. 'I have had to play through the pain barrier because I knew I could not drop out of the side. The thought of that other injury business made me determined not to give up my place'. He had had to miss training on occasions, had rested his knee a little and felt it was improving. A fully-fit Hudson was such an asset that the thought of his playing while not 100% fit was worrying.

Hutchinson and McCreadie were declared fully fit, Osgood recovered from a bad head cold and, to the surprise of nobody but to the understandably massive disappointment of Baldwin, the manager chose the strongest side, that had got them to the Semi-Final, including Hutchinson. Not for the only time in his career, Baldwin immediately asked for an interview with Sexton, who commented 'Tommy is disappointed – naturally. It is only human, players who have done well and are left out want to know why. But nothing will come of the talk yet - he did not ask for a transfer'.

The Semi-Final did not lack incident, as the 55,209 spectators and viewers of *The Big Match* appreciated. David Webb scored after three minutes but Terry Garbutt equalised nine minutes later with a long-range shot which hit a bump and beat Bonetti. Watford stayed in the tie and put pressure on Chelsea for the rest of the half but tired badly after the interval in the mud, as superior fitness told. Osgood, who had scored in every round of the competition, netted in the 55th minute, his seventh of the competition, swinging from the net in celebration. Houseman scored twice in the last 15 minutes, sandwiching Hutchinson's goal and in the end, Chelsea reached Wembley comfortably despite the appalling, glutinous, sand-laden pitch. Watford had no answer to Cooke, Houseman and Hudson and Chelsea racked up the biggest FA Cup Semi-Final win, 5-1, since World War Two. The *Daily Telegraph* felt that in the second-half, after a pointed managerial team-talk, Chelsea gave 'the most convincing performance I have seen in a Semi-Final since West Ham beat Manchester United in 1964'.

Of 21 goals Chelsea had scored in the FA Cup, 15 came in the second-half and 11 in the last half-hour. Sexton enthused 'that is how we play – flat out, and then we suddenly go harder still. It's hunger for goals that does it'. Captain Harris concurred. 'It's not just a fitness thing. It is more a mental thing, it's a ruthlessness'. They had reached Wembley without being drawn outside London and, though they had been fortunate with the draws, it was still a wonderful achievement. Manchester United and Leeds United drew the other Semi-Final, so it was unclear who their opponents would be on Saturday April 11th.

Baldwin, understandably unhappy about being dropped against Watford, had refused to join his teammates at their pre-match hotel and opened his heart to *The People*. 'I told him (Sexton) I wanted to leave because reserve football is no good for me. He said he wouldn't let me go and that I'd have to put in a request in writing if I insisted. So I am. It's ridiculous. If he doesn't want me in the team, why shouldn't he let me move'. This interpretation of the discussion contradicted Sexton's but whatever was said it was clear that, with the trip to Wembley imminent, Baldwin was hardly likely to be allowed to leave. Deep down he must have known the manager was hardly likely to omit a fit Hutchinson for the biggest match of the season so far, but this cannot have diminished the upset. John Boyle, out through injury in November and unable to get his place back, was clearly more philosophical than Baldwin, working hard and using reserve football as a platform to hopefully win a place in the side.

Osgood, who thought it had been the worst pitch he had ever played on, was suffering a cold and went to bed to try and ensure he was fit to play for the Football League in midweek. Unfortunately, it worsened, so he had to drop out. 'I feel miserable. I am very disappointed because this was my last chance before the World Cup 40 are named'.

Three days after the high of the Semi-Final victory came a relatively mundane rearranged home match against Stoke City, though points were still crucial as, if the FA Cup Final ended in defeat, a strong position was essential to clinch a European place. Marvin Hinton replaced the suspended McCreadie. Only 28,996, their second-lowest home League crowd of the season, turned out to watch a dull and disappointing affair, and had indulged in a spell of slow-handclapping before Cooke netted a magnificent 89th minute volley for the only goal. Tambling, preferred to the discontented Baldwin in his first Chelsea League appearance since August, had a quiet match on what turned out to be his last start for the club.

Attention turned to the visit by Manchester United the following Saturday, a potential Wembley rehearsal. Osgood had recovered from illness so returned in place of Tambling. With the exception of Hinton ('one of the good reserves Chelsea have in store' according to ITV commentator Brian Moore) replacing the suspended McCreadie, a full-strength Chelsea side turned out.

George Best told the *Daily Mail* he was looking forward to playing at Stamford Bridge 'A visit to take on Chelsea has usually meant a good game for me'. Harris had a different perspective. 'George Best used to score goals against Chelsea until I started marking him'. The Mail felt the captain had 'this season shown himself without equal in the destructive art of tight marking, sharp tackling and defensive covering'. Harris explained his approach. 'My game is based on doing to other players the sort of things I never like having done to myself...I shall spend the game getting as close to him as possible to stop him turning with the ball to face me and dictating the game to me'.

As usual, the game was not all-ticket and there was already a 100 yard queue outside at 09.00. A remarkable 61,479 squeezed in and another 15,000 were locked out when the gates were closed at 14.15. The numbers outside were so vast, United's team coach could not enter the concourse behind The Shed.

Hutchinson scored twice early on, the second a high-quality header from a Houseman cross in a brilliant counter-attack, and though Willie Morgan pulled one back towards the end, Chelsea, who had three goals disallowed by referee Maurice Fussey, held on for a win against opponents who had not lost in 18 matches. That victory made European qualification through the Fairs Cup highly likely, should they lose the FA Cup Final. Watching the highlights 50 years on, the languid control and effortless passing of Osgood stands out.

The People reported that Baldwin had made his peace. In the end he did not write a transfer request as Sexton told him it was a waste of time, as he would not sell him. He must have realised that only injury or suspension could give him a starting place at Wembley, however, as the first choice team were so strong and effective. The two United's fought out another draw, so a second replay was needed.

Osgood came third in the football writers 'Footballer Of The Year' award behind Billy Bremner and Gordon Banks, due recognition of his impact that season, and maybe a last nudge to Ramsey regarding World Cup selection. Birchenall kicked a ball for the first time in a month and targeted being fit for the FA Cup Final, in case he was required, beaming 'I didn't think I'd be fit again until next season'. This was good news for Sexton as it gave him extra cover up front, and, with seven League games still to come, more opportunity to rest his first-choice strikers.

The initial England World Cup squad of 28, plus 12 reserves, was due to be announced that Wednesday March 25th, the day of the visit of Sheffield Wednesday. The *Daily Mail* ran an article pondering whether Hudson would be in that 28. despite only being a first-team regular for five months. They analysed his 'superb' performance against Manchester United and the statistics were impressive. 21 out of his 23 passes reached teammates. He dribbled past 11 opponents and was only stopped three times. He lost only three out of 11 tackles. Sexton called him a 'great competitor'. The only question, as the paper saw it, was whether his age, 18, would count against him.

In the event, Bonetti and Osgood made the 28 (and later the final 22), Hudson and Hollins the reserve 12. For Hollins this was the second World Cup in a row he had made the 40 but got no further, bitterly disappointing news. Osgood had been in the 40 in 1966 so this was a step further, and a deserved one, and Bonetti had made the 22 for the second tournament in a row. Osgood's rise to prominence was impressive, as before Christmas he appeared to have no chance of making the trip. Hudson commented on his selection as a reserve 'that's not bad' given that, all being well, he had a long international career to look forward to. He was the youngest player in the 40, goalkeeper Peter Shilton the only other teenager.

Bonetti, Webb (both hurt against Manchester United) and McCreadie were all missing so Hughes and Mulligan came in against Sheffield Wednesday who were comfortably beaten 3-1. Hudson celebrated his call-up to the World Cup 40 with one of the best solo goals scored anywhere that season. He beat five men and slid the ball under Peter Grummitt, receiving a standing ovation from the 29,590 Stamford Bridge crowd. Jackie Sinclair had put Wednesday ahead early on, but

Hutchinson and an Osgood penalty (amazingly, Chelsea's first of the season) gave them the lead before Hudson's 'wonderful' goal, clearly remembered by supporter Tony Foss half a century later.

The victory was overshadowed, however, when Harris was taken off on a stretcher after an hour, after pulling his left hamstring, the third such injury of his career. Sexton was optimistic. 'Ron is a quick healer and I still think he could make the Final' but he was clearly genuinely concerned. Supporter David Gray remembers the shock as Harris was carried off, with immediate fears as to whether he would make Wembley.

Two more games remained in March, a Saturday visit to leaders Everton, followed two days later by a visit to West Bromwich Albion. That still left four League matches to play in April, three of them after the FA Cup Final, usually the climax of the season. Leeds prevailed in the second replay, so Sexton now knew his opponents at Wembley, the side that had thrashed Chelsea 5-2 in January.

Playing the leaders without Bonetti, McCreadie and Harris was never going to be easy, especially in front of 57,828 fervent Evertonians scenting the title. 16 seconds after kick-off Howard Kendall opened the scoring and that set the theme for the afternoon. Alan Ball scored a second four minutes later, Joe Royle a third before half-time. The dazed visitors were 5-0 down at one stage, Alan Whittle and Royle adding two more, before Everton eased up and allowed Dempsey and Osgood to claw back some respectability in a 5-2 defeat. Sexton was desperate to have his full-strength defence fit for Wembley in a fortnight's time as without Harris's bite, the Everton midfield were allowed to roam free, deputy captain Hollins simply over-run. Hughes' nervous 90 minutes was less of an issue as Bonetti's fitness for Wembley was not in doubt.

The Chelsea allocation of 16,000 FA Cup Final tickets were being sold to supporters, once season-ticket-holders had theirs, on the basis of having collected a full set of home programme vouchers that season, probably the fairest method at the time. As ticket fever intensified, *The People* ran a story about forged Chelsea programme vouchers. The club had been tipped off and ran checks. For some applications, all 20 vouchers were fakes. Some others were a mix of genuine and fake. Staff and volunteers were working to sort it out. Chairman Brian Mears commented 'we don't know how big the problem is yet' and Hammersmith CID were involved. A club official admitted 'there is little doubt that we would not have discovered the fakes if we had not been warned'. 100 forgeries were found in the first 5,000 applications checked, 20,000 applications were received in total.

Meanwhile, supporters outside the ground were desperately trying to swap presumably genuine vouchers to complete their sets. In the end many of those die-hards who had the full set of vouchers queued up on a Sunday morning to purchase their precious tickets, others trusted theirs to the post. Bob Barlow's brother posted off their families three complete voucher forms to Chelsea but as he only included a normal stamped addressed envelope, not a registered one as was mandated by the club, they did not receive their tickets, an issue that unsurprisingly stays with Bob 50 years later.

The *News Of The World* contained a feature on the captain, Harris stressing his confidence that he would be fit for Wembley. He had damaged the same hamstring against Sunderland in January but was fit for the Palace game a week later. He felt the fact that Baldwin, Birchenall, Boyle, Hinton, Mulligan and Tambling could not get in the starting line-up emphasised the squad strength. Eulogising about the impact of Hudson, he stressed 'we all knew Alan was hot stuff, but I don't think any of us expected him to prove such an instant success'. Harris called him very fit, 'a quiet lad off the field, he has tremendous self-confidence...(He is) a little bewildered at his own success story'. He praised Hutchinson's bravery and his 'priceless' long throws.

March ended with a trip to the Hawthorns, against a West Bromwich side with little to play for. McCreadie was back but Sexton resisted the temptation to rest any of his stars 12 days before the Final with just one more match, against Tottenham, before Wembley. After a 3-1 defeat, Hutchinson heading Chelsea's consolation goal, the manager must have wished he had fielded his reserves. Hudson damaged ankle ligaments in a challenge, though it was hard to immediately tell how badly, and was substituted by Tambling who pulled a hamstring. Hutchinson bruised his hip and kidneys but could not go off as the substitute had already been used, so played on in agony. Bonetti hurt himself in a collision with Jeff Astle, who scored his 28th goal of the season, putting him level with Osgood. Meanwhile Leeds, who had in effect given up on the League to focus on the European Cup and FA Cup, fielded 11 reserves at Derby, losing 4-1 but not having to worry about injuries 48 hours before their European tie against Celtic.

Hudson was the major worry, having an x-ray and his ankle put in plaster. He was clearly a serious doubt for the Final. Harry Medhurst was more hopeful about Hutchinson, though clearly he should have been taken off, regardless of whether that meant playing with ten men. Bonetti was expected to be fit for Wembley. Tambling was out for the season, though his chance of a Final appearance was minimal anyway. Reserve defender Stewart Houston, who had made seven appearances that season, had a cartilage operation and was out for the rest of the season.

Clearly the West Bromwich game was a disaster for Sexton, in all likelihood significantly weakening the Wembley line-up and depriving Hudson of the chance to prove himself on the biggest stage. The player harshly blamed himself, though surely it was just one of those things. 'It was not on for me to go into the tackle and if I had kept out of it nothing would have happened'.

Transfer stories were few, though two hardy perennials appeared. Chelsea had a £40,000 bid for Fulham's Steve Earle turned down and were one of a number of clubs still watching Keith Weller of Millwall.

They were also interested in promising young inside-forward Alan Glover of West Bromwich. Secretary John Battersby, an essential cog in the Chelsea machine, received a Football League long-service medal for 21 years with the club.

A month that was going so well ended with two defeats and, worse, an injury to the most promising midfield player in the country, whose skills were desperately needed against Leeds. Chelsea were down to fourth, though with games in hand on Derby above them. Despite the fitness worries, the sense of anticipation was building. They had badly under-performed in the FA Cup Final three years earlier, but they now had the chance to make history and win the trophy for the first time.

Everton	p40 63pts
Leeds United	p38 54pts
Derby County	p40 50pts
Chelsea	**p38 49pts**
Liverpool	p39 47pts
Coventry City	p38 45pts
Newcastle United	p40 43pts

April 1970

The forthcoming League game against Tottenham was almost an irrelevance when compared with the fitness chickens that had come home to roost at the Hawthorns. The two main concerns were Alan Hudson and Ron Harris, with Wembley just 11 days away. The former had to wait to see how the torn ligaments in his left ankle were when the plaster was removed on the Friday – the x-ray showed no bone damage. Trainer Harry Medhurst said 'he had a similar knock last season and was over it in under three weeks'. He felt Harris had a reasonable chance of being fit, though the captain was still getting pain from his hamstring injury when he attempted ultra-light training. It was a bitter irony that the Final was often in early May, when Hudson would almost certainly have been fit to play, but the FA bringing it forward three weeks, to its earliest date since 1897, severely reduced his chances.

The *Daily Mail* carried a picture of Hudson with his girl-friend Maureen, him in bed with his leg in plaster, ten days before Wembley. 'The World Cup reserve for England in his first season of League football was put in plaster yesterday after an x-ray on his injured ankle... (he) must be rated as doubtful'. He was clearly upset, but defiant. 'I don't know what my chances of playing at Wembley are, but I shall be there if I have to go on crutches. If you ask me now, then I'll say I'm going to make it'.

Leeds played West Ham just 24 hours after their European Cup Semi-Final first-leg defeat at home against Celtic. Tragedy struck for their full-back Paul Reaney who broke his leg, thereby missing both the

SEXTON FOR GOD

FA Cup Final and the World Cup.

Osgood was interviewed by Brian James in the *Daily Mail*. He felt Celtic would beat Leeds because they were not scared, and felt Leeds made a mistake by playing reserves and losing their title chance. He admitted that the pressure of Sir Alf Ramsey watching him 'bucks me up'. He was fully aware that a suspended sentence from the FA Disciplinary Committee meant opposition players and referees were watching him. He caught Watford's Walter Lees in the Semi-Final. 'I admit it. It was a damned silly thing to do. But he had been giving me the odd hammer. When he went down, rolling about and moaning, I felt sick. Not for him. For myself. I thought 'Gawd. Ossie, you've done it this time'. I could hardly bear to turn round and look at the referee. Luckily (the referee) was Gordon Hill, one of the good 'uns. He KNEW'. Lucky indeed.

For the Tottenham home encounter, Alan Birchenall was likely to be fit after five weeks out with a badly gashed knee, his second comeback in an unhappy season. If Hudson missed out, Birchenall could have a chance of starting or being on the bench at Wembley. He told the *Daily Mirror* 'The Cup Final? I've heard rumours but that would be a miracle for me' and was absolutely delighted to be facing their London rivals. Bonetti was fit, Hinton was in for Harris, Birchenall for Hutchinson and Baldwin for Hudson. There was no direct replacement for Hudson in terms of his talents and what he added to the side. If he missed out then Baldwin, so unhappy before the Semi-Final, was the most likely beneficiary.

Against Tottenham, Houseman started in midfield but prospered when he moved wide. Baldwin it was who scored the only goal of a scrappy, mediocre affair, capitalising on a Phil Beal error to volley home. He and Birchenall put in unstinting effort, determined to show Sexton what they could do, as Chelsea picked up two deserved points and, critically, no new fitness concerns. There was little tough tackling, which suited a home side now guaranteed European football the following season through their League place if they lost at Wembley.

The message coming out to the press was that Hutchinson and Harris would be fit for Wembley, but Hudson was touch-and-go, to the extent that daily updates were given in most sports pages. After the Tottenham game he talked to the *Daily Mail*, under a 'Hudson's Chances Sinking' headline. 'The finest discovery of the season has been virtually ruled out by Chelsea'. Watching on crutches, he commented 'I know it will take a miracle to get me to Wembley...I don't have to tell you how sick I am about this, or how depressed all the family are'. It is impossible to overstate just how distraught the player must have been - in brilliant form, with every prospect of playing a key role in the biggest match of the season.

The *Evening Standard* ran a similar piece. Under a 'Baldwin Will Not Fail Us – Hudson', the star 'who has virtually considered himself out' of the FA Cup Final', said of his 'deputy' 'he would surely have played anyway – he had a great game against Spurs'. The reality is that Baldwin would almost certainly not have started as Sexton was hardly likely to change his winning side, and the tactics, to accommodate him. If Harris was unfit, Hinton would come in, if Hutchinson had a relapse, Birchenall was the likely replacement. A week before Wembley, the manager was clear in terms of tactics. 'I will change nothing unless I have to'. Hudson felt he 'would be in the running again' if the Cup Final went to a replay.

In a *News Of The World* interview Harris admitted 'Leeds are such a tremendous team that it would be a crying shame if they failed to collect a single honour this season...I know Leeds will start favourites...but favourites have a habit of coming unstuck at Wembley'. He praised the 'introverted' Sexton, who would 'usually...criticise a player in private, rather than in front of the team'. Leeds had only conceded one goal en route to Wembley and were likely to have Norman Hunter, who had missed a number of games in recent weeks, fit along with centre-forward Mick Jones.

The Cup Final build-up was dominated by Hudson's fight for fitness. He made optimistic statements and used 'an American wonder machine', an ultrasonic box, in a last ditch attempt to strengthen his ankle. There were concerns that, though he was no longer on crutches, he could seriously damage ankle ligaments long-term if he played.

Cooke strained a muscle in training but got the all-clear. Intensive treatment sorted out Harris, who did a cross-country run to help prove his fitness. In the end, he survived 'two shuddering tackles' by assistant-manager Ron Suart on the Friday in a final, definitive, test. Hutchinson was raring to go. McCreadie was managing his groin and sensibly spared heavy training. The only doubt was Hudson. In the end the club had to bow to the inevitable and accept he would not be fit. The fact that the pitch was in such poor condition that it was having to have 100 tons of sand poured on it to prevent waterlogging would not have helped his chances. He had decided to go to Wembley to watch. 'I'll have a couple of drinks before I go to make it bearable'. Presumably not too many drinks, as he was signed up by ITV to give his views on events.

The inevitable ticket touting stories appeared as demand once again seriously exceeded supply. Tickets were on sale outside Stamford Bridge at £7 for a 12/6 (62.5p) terrace ticket and £15 for a 25/- (£1.25p) seat. Embarrassingly for Leeds, two of them were stamped 'Leeds United AFC', the *Daily Mirror* found out and went to town. Jim Manning of the *Evening Standard* identified players as a significant source of tickets, an accusation made every year and clearly not without foundation.

A selection of the wide range of squad interviews and match previews make interesting reading and give some perspective of the respect Sexton and his team were held in at that time.

Hollins, interviewed by the *Daily Mirror*, was understandably extremely disappointed to be only a World Cup reserve, explaining 'I'm desperately keen to do well in front of Sir Alf'. He had wanted to leave at the time of the 1967 Final, having a contract dispute with the club. 'Now I cannot visualise myself as anything but a Chelsea player. Dave Sexton deserves the credit for that. He's made us into a team in every sense of the word...a team that is going to get even better. A team to challenge for every honour in the game...I reckon it was the Burnley tie that really put us on the right road'.

McCreadie gave the Daily Mail an insight into his boss's approach. 'His final words will be 'good luck my bonny lads'. Afterwards he may say 'well done my bonny lads'. 'He's not a guy who throws compliments around. He only needs to say those words and we'll all feel that he's given us a million pounds'. The players saw him as strict but fair. He didn't talk much about opposing teams. "Let them worry about us' is his attitude...As a man he's straight. As a coach he's bloody marvellous'.

Bernard Joy's *Evening Standard* preview was extremely positive. 'Early season injuries and the bold bid for honours have put Chelsea under heavy pressure, yet their skill has poured through...Their assurance and aggression should see them through and bring them the prized trophy in their third Final after 65 years of trying'. Like others, he saw Cooke, Osgood and 'the courage and speed of Hutchinson' as critical.

Sexton told the *Daily Mail* that he obviously wanted to play his best team 'and that would have included Hudson...Houseman has had a great season, and his two best matches have been in deep midfield against Billy Bremner...Chelsea started this season with a horrible crop of injuries. Overcoming those injuries is exactly the thing that has put the present character into this team...Leeds? They are the best team in Europe. (but) we shall win'. Honest and positive, just what would be expected of a man and manager of his calibre.

He told *Goal* magazine 'I'm delighted with (Hudson's) progress this season. Alan's a player who creates for other people with his hard running and intelligent use of the ball'. Hutchinson 'explodes like a grenade around the penalty box. His lively running and deadly finishing have taken a lot of pressure off Osgood this season and make him a perfect foil for the skilled Chelsea leader...Most of his goals come from perfectly timed headers...he must rate as the biggest bargain in Chelsea's history'. Houseman was a 'skilled creator (and) ball artist'...(the crowd) now...recognise the job he is doing for us, and this has had an obvious effect on his confidence this season'. The winger was also praised by Leeds boss Don Revie. 'He is determined and skilful and his running can disturb the best teams'. Harris was praised for driving 'others beyond the boundaries of effort'.

Goal magazine ran a series of features on Chelsea personalities. Their piece confirmed the manager believed in artistry and self-expression, that all top teams must have outstanding individuals. He felt 'we have the players, the confidence and the ability' to win the cup. Houseman, transformed under Sexton, was unsurprisingly laudatory.

'Things started to happen when Dave took over. Up to then, nothing seemed to go right for me. In the old days it had been individuals playing under the name of Chelsea. Dave changed all that. Now we are a team, and he has helped my game enormously'.

Osgood, inevitably, received much of the attention as the most glamorous player on either side. The *Evening Standard* carried a full page interview with renowned screenplay writer Ray Connolly on the big day. He admitted he 'had a bad image when I first came up. Really, I was just growing up and I thought I could get away with pranks and being silly, but I couldn't. Docherty fined me about £500 in six months. I was getting fined every week'. He blamed the leg break and the resultant 'subconscious fear about his leg' as the reason his play was inconsistent for a time after he got back into the team. 'It's really taken me three years to get over it'.

Connolly pointed out that Osgood was generating lots of commercial activity – a national newspaper column, posters, a tie-up with a sportswear firm, possibly an advertising agency. He had a deal with Fords where he got a basic salary as an area sales manager – he did not work but his name was used in advertisements. He would like 'to own a nice boutique, with trendy gear like they have in Cecil Gee...Really, George Best has had it too good up to now. There's been nobody to challenge him. I will – although I've got a different image from him.' Connolly pointed out 'his image is, in fact, almost the complete opposite to that of Best. There's no narcissism about Osgood. He doesn't like those long-haired types, he says...He's open and garrulous and honest to the point of naivete". Connolly did point out that Rosemary Osgood 'gets lonely sitting in by herself, and she doesn't like it when Peter goes out at night. He likes to go to the clubs for dinner and a cabaret'.

'Quite simply, his one ambition is to be a rich man'. He wanted to make enough money and have enough business interests during the next six years or so to make sure he never had to get a full-time job after getting out of football. He wanted 'to be able to sit back and enjoy himself. To be a playboy. Well, a married playboy'. He never wanted to have to worry about money again. From football he earned around £200 a week. Ex-manager Tommy Docherty arranged for Chelsea to buy him the house in Windsor for £7,000 – in two years he would have paid back the full cost. He was hoping to earn at least £5,000 from the World Cup pool, which 'isn't bad money for seven weeks, is it?'.

Peter Osgood Ltd was set up to promote his off-the-field activities. Birchenall signed a similar agreement with the company and Hudson was thinking about it. That month, Osgood's agent and business partner Greg Tesser enthused 'I believe he has just as much potential as George Best...I think he can earn more money outside the game than inside, with all the firms who want to use his name and project his image. Peter's interest in Peter Osgood Ltd will be looked after by other people, and he will be totally free to concentrate on the game. He is insistent that nothing shall detract him from his football ambitions, particularly making the World Cup team...The experts will take care of it for him. The sky's the limit for him'. Osgood's goals, and performances, for Chelsea that season merited a World Cup place, which could only increase his profile and hence earning potential.

In '*Ossie - King Of Stamford Bridge*' Osgood details that he was later called in by the bank manager to discover that Peter Osgood Ltd had run up debts of £1,500 when it should have been in a healthy surplus, and, as he put it, he'd been 'had'. Sadly, therefore, his aspirations to make a significant sum from off-pitch activities through the company were thwarted. Tesser eulogises about Osgood, Hudson and Cooke in '*Chelsea FC In The Swinging '60s*', but unsurprisingly without reference to the company losses or his break-up with Osgood.

The main front-page story on matchday in the *Daily Mail* was about money, under a 'Big Bonus For Cup - £5,000 For Each Man' headline. This was, though, an optimistic figure including European bonuses the following season. The Chelsea Cup Final pool was likely to earn £400-£600 a man for the 19 first-team squad members, with bonuses from the club giving another £700-£1000 each.

Both managers were unsurprisingly critical of the state of the pitch, especially as two newly turfed areas were firmer than the rest of the sand-laden mess. Leeds were 8-11 to win the cup, Chelsea 11-10 and most journalists tipped the Yorkshire club to prevail. Eric Jennings was refereeing his last match before retirement.

McCreadie felt the team were 'quietly confident', with 'none of the nervousness we felt before the 1967 Final'. The team spent Friday night at home and lunched at noon at a Gloucester Road hotel, having their normal pre-match meal of beef fillets, toast, rice pudding and tea, before travelling up to Wembley.

The teams lined up as expected :-

Leeds United:- Sprake; Madeley, Charlton, Hunter, Cooper; Bremner (Capt.), Giles; Lorimer, Clarke, Jones, Gray. Sub Bates.

Chelsea:- Bonetti; Webb, Dempsey, Harris (Capt.), McCreadie; Cooke, Hollins, Houseman; Baldwin, Osgood, Hutchinson. Sub Hinton.

The 2-2 draw was as exciting as anyone in Wembley or watching on television could have hoped. In '*100 Years Of the FA Cup*', Tony Pawson felt the Wembley clash was the pick of the post-war FA Cup Finals at that point, though the football was always not of the highest quality, three of the four goals coming from defensive or goalkeeping errors. Jack Charlton's 21st minute header trickled towards the goal but both Harris and McCreadie contrived to misread the bounce and on it trickled, over the line. Houseman's equaliser, five minutes from half-time was a run-of-the-mill shot that a diving Gary Sprake should have easily saved but did not. Shortly after Mick Jones had put Leeds ahead with six minutes left, Charlton gave away an unnecessary free kick. In a rehearsed set-piece move, Harris played it to Hollins whose cross was converted by

Hutchinson, who moved as the defence stood still. Tony Pawson recounts how the Leeds team were 'lost in a heady euphoria', they celebrated too soon, and their concentration lapsed. The players were exhausted in extra-time, so a replay, the first since 1912, was not a surprise. The teams, rightly, did a joint lap of honour.

Leeds were the better team, hit the woodwork three times and deserved to win. As Harris said decades later 'we were fortunate to get away with a draw that day'. Chelsea, though, despite missing Hudson's creativity and ability to run with the ball, showed enormous depths of strength, tenacity, doggedness and character. David Webb was famously given the run around by man-of-the-match Eddie Gray. Webb admitted to the *Daily Mail* that Gray gave him a torrid time. 'I have never played against Gray before, but I knew he could play a bit...The pitch didn't help...I was sick at the end, really down and depressed, until Dave Sexton came over and thanked me. Not for playing a great match – he doesn't talk nonsense – but for sticking to my guns'. The *Daily Mail* made the point that if Harris had been fully fit, he would have taken Gray and Webb would have marked Allan Clarke, a switch Sexton would doubtless have in mind for the replay.

Hollins and Houseman unsurprisingly found competing with Billy Bremner and Johnny Giles tough, though stuck diligently at their task. Luckily, Bonetti was on excellent form. Harris, whose appearance was described by Pawson as 'a minor triumph for medical science', was replaced by Marvin Hinton for extra-time, in pain with a lump on his leg. In '*The Bonnie Prince*', Cooke stressed how disappointed the team were with their performance and how they saw the replay as a chance to redeem themselves.

The pitch, frankly, was a disgrace and was the subject of much post-match controversy, sapping energy from legs and preventing any attempt at flowing football. The decision to hold the 1968 'Horse Of The Year Show' there was the subject of much anger. As McCreadie put it 'you didn't need football boots to play on it, you needed hooves'. The FA were very unhappy about it, an official talking about the 'appalling' way in which it has deteriorated. Revie reckoned Leeds would have played Chelsea to death on the old, lush pitch. Like everyone else, Osgood hated it. 'Stamina's not my strong point – it made it hard to run and hard for a touch player'. He felt an improved pitch could only help his side in the replay as 'our game is to break quickly from the back'. A £20,000 pitch overhaul was promised for the following season. Too little, too late. It was to the credit of both teams that the afternoon was such an entertaining one.

Osgood, interviewed post-match by the *Daily Mail*, acknowledged Leeds had hit the bar a couple of times but pointed out Chelsea had a couple of efforts cleared off the line. He was disappointed with his own display. 'I was back to how I felt at the beginning of the season – awful'. He thought Chelsea stood up to Leeds. 'They got in front and started dishing out the stick. But Chelsea are no longer a side to be intimidated. Now we're as hard as they are and a lot more honest. You saw what they were handing out, but you didn't hear any of our lads squealing out the way they did when we got stuck into them'. Hunter, Giles, Charlton, Bremner and the rest of the Leeds hard men can only have been further fired up for the replay.

The old animosity between the two sides had been held in check at Wembley. It might not at Old Trafford. The astute Frank Butler, in the *News Of The World*, felt the replay would be much tougher, as Old Trafford would not have the Wembley decorum with the Royal Family. He saw the replay as 'a Cup Final for the real fans'. Ken Jones in the *Daily Mirror* had a similar prediction. 'It will not be a pretty match...I expect it to be hard, intimidatory, perhaps bitter, possibly violent and there will not be an easy winner'.

Osgood thought a fit Hudson would improve their replay chances. 'Alan and I have a good understanding and a lot of my goals come from him'. *Goal* magazine criticised his lethargy and also thought Harris needed to make 'a more emphatic contribution' though the latter comment seemed highly unfair as he was far from fully fit.

The replay, the first in an FA Cup Final since 1912, was not until Wednesday April 29th, over two weeks hence, at Old Trafford. Each club would get 20,000 tickets, the remaining 22,000 being split between Manchester United and the FA, a situation perfect for touts looking for a decent source of supply. The *Evening Standard* reported that the FA were insisting that the two clubs take the name and address of anyone buying a ticket. A Chelsea spokesman advised 'we are thinking of using the programme voucher system'. The FA threatened 'immediate disciplinary action' against 'anyone under their jurisdiction' selling tickets at inflated prices. Touts, utterly unperturbed by this threat, had got £11 for 12/6d (62.5p) terrace tickets and £40 for £4 stand tickets outside Wembley and were licking their lips at anticipated similar replay profits.

Hudson, clearly in with a chance of being fit for Old Trafford, admitted hoping Wembley would be a draw. Trainer Harry Medhurst told the *Daily Mirror* 'we are going to get him (Hudson) off his feet for a few days and really get to work. He's determined to make the replay...and we're making every effort to get him there'. He spent five days in the Princess Beatrice hospital receiving intensive treatment on his ankle.

There was initially a fear that the sides may need to use the toss of a coin, or share the cup, if the replay was drawn. The FA were worried because of time constraints caused by World Cup preparation. In the end, a second replay, were it required, would be at Coventry's City's Highfield Road on May 2nd.

There was an immediate impact on the Home International Championship, both teams unsurprisingly withdrawing their players. Cooper, Charlton, Hunter, Clarke, Bonetti and Osgood of England were affected as were Bremner, Lorimer, Gray, McCreadie and Cooke for

Scotland and Sprake and Yorath for Wales. This was no help to Osgood's hopes of making the final 22, though presumably a more effective replay display would do him no harm.

50 hours after trudging exhausted off the Wembley pitch Chelsea had to visit eighth-place Stoke City. Hughes, Mulligan and Hinton came in for Bonetti, McCreadie and Harris who were all receiving treatment. Stoke, with the physically imposing likes of Alan Bloor, Eric Skeels, Dennis Smith and John Ritchie in their side, were unlikely to give the visitors an easy ride, so it was a surprise when the visitors went 2-0 up in 20 minutes through Hutchinson and a Skeels own-goal from a Cooke cross. Though Willie Stevenson pulled one back, they held on for a 2-1 win, highly commendable under the circumstances.

The ludicrous schedule of four games in eight days, including an FA Cup Final, continued two days later with a visit to Burnley, safe in 16th place. Hughes continued as Bonetti was still in light plaster after hurting his knee, though he was expected to be fit for Old Trafford in a fortnight. Hinton continued in place of Harris. McCreadie returned and Boyle and Birchenall made rare appearances, in for the rested Osgood and Hutchinson.

The crowd, a woeful 12,030 for Burnley's last home match of the season, saw Hughes drop a Steve Kindon cross, allowing Martin Dobson, who netted twice in the FA Cup at Stamford Bridge, to score. Kindon made it two, but Hollins pulled one back with a 25-yarder. Chelsea unsurprisingly looked tired and once Kindon made the score 3-1, there was no way back.

In the *Evening Standard*, Sexton angrily dismissed stories that Hutchinson could miss the replay because of mysterious 'headaches' possibly caused by sinus trouble. 'There is no danger of Hutchinson not being available for the replay' he stormed. The paper contained a letter from supporter Colin Brinton praising the man he thought should be 'Manager Of The Year'. 'His transformation of Chelsea from a team of excellence to a team of disciplined excellence in the elite class, and his unassuming manner, deserve immense praise'. A pithy and accurate description of the transformation he had driven.

One more League game, at home to Liverpool on the Saturday, then a blessed eleven days before the replay, a chance for tired legs to recover and those needing rest or treatment to receive it. The Liverpool clash was originally going to be two days before the replay, but common sense prevailed, and it was brought forward nine days.

Bonetti, Osgood and Hutchinson returned so only Harris and Hudson from the preferred line-up were missing. Heavy rain could not prevent Chelsea finishing their League season on a high, a 2-1 win ensuring they finished ahead of the visitors in the table in third place, though both were guaranteed European football. Osgood tormented Liverpool, scoring twice, once from the penalty spot. Sexton was delighted there were no further injuries, and the squad were given four days off before resuming pre-replay training. England, meanwhile, were drawing 1-1 in Wales.

Chelsea included a replay ticket application form in the Liverpool programme. Supporters needed to queue up and hand in a completed form (detailing name and address) the following day, with one ticket per form and only two forms per person. Chelsea had around 6,000 season-ticket-holders whereas Leeds had 12,000, so would have far more tickets going on general sale. Chelsea booked an initial ten special trains to Manchester, taking over 5,000 up, the obvious way for many to travel.

All 12,000 general sale tickets initially put on sale were, unsurprisingly, sold on the Sunday morning. The *Daily Mail* reported that touts bought as many Liverpool programmes, with ticket application forms, as they could. 40,000 programmes were sold to the 36,521 present. They observed that boys queued up on behalf of touts, got the tickets, got a small commission and joined the back of the queue again with fresh forms. Programmes containing forms were being sold for 5/- (25p). No checks were made on names and addresses, and fake details could be used, so the FA anti-tout initiative was, almost inevitably, a farcical waste of time. The remaining 1,000 15/- (75p) terrace and 300 £4 stand replay tickets were sold the following Saturday morning. After the hiatus of his Wembley tickets, Bob Barlow and his family were at Stamford Bridge at 5am on the Sunday to ensure they got tickets. Leeds, bizarrely, initially only sold 4,000 of the 7,000 they put on general sale, despite being located considerably closer to Manchester.

Osgood gave a bullish interview to the *Daily Mail*. He hoped elimination by Celtic in the European Cup Semi-Final would demoralise Leeds, but was disappointed to be missing the Home International tournament with the World Cup coming up. Asked 'apart from getting busy, are you also getting a bit rich?' the honest reply was 'yes, the money side is great. We can earn a bomb in the next year – something to put away for my old age. Yet, you know the one thing I never think about these days is money. Success is the thing, doing something big in football, being somebody. Money is part of this...cars, clothes, good meals and all that. But it is the success that counts, all the rest just follows'. He was buying a 'big' house in Epsom when he returned from Mexico. 'It will cost a stack, but I don't think of the money, just the lovely big house. Once I helped build places like that for the nobs. Now I'm buying one'.

'When I stopped being a £10-a-week building labourer and became a £150-a-week footballer I went a bit potty – right off the rails. People started calling me a playboy, and they were right. But how could it be any other way...it was like...a pools win every week'. Like the other players he got 13 standing tickets and 12 seats for Wembley, but he claimed players were not the ones who sold big match tickets to touts.

Hudson left hospital that weekend and the papers who spent the Wembley build-up giving daily fitness bulletins on the young star did exactly the same in the build-up to Old Trafford. Two days after the Liverpool win Hudson told the *Evening Standard* 'everything seems to be going OK. The five days in hospital seem to have done my ankle some good'. He had lost half-an-inch off his calf muscle, but reckoned he needed six days training to be full fit for the replay. If he was fit, the papers reckoned it would be Cooke or Baldwin who missed out but, given Sexton praised Cooke for 'three very good games' in Hudson's absence, it would almost certainly have been Baldwin.

The *Evening Standard*, unsurprisingly, ran several replay stories a day. In an interview with Harry Medhurst, the trainer explained 'this is my busiest season at Stamford Bridge. We have had three bad spells. In August we had nine first-team men receiving treatment. Hudson, Harris, McCreadie, Tambling and Houston are all currently receiving treatment. Hudson is the doubt in terms of those in Cup Final consideration'. Hutchinson had seen a sinus specialist and been given the all-clear regarding his headaches.

Goal magazine, in their replay preview, calculated that Leeds expected to make about £75,000 from their three Semi-Finals and two Finals. Chelsea would earn around £58,000 from one Semi-Final and two Finals. Manchester United would get around £33,000 from three Semi-Finals and a third place play-off. The FA would make around £90,000 from those six matches, the Challenge Cup pool, which was shared between all competing clubs, getting the same.

After a host of 'Decision Day for Hudson' style headlines, and much optimistic talk, it was announced the day before the replay that he would not be fit. He could run but could not kick a ball. It was a bitter, bitter blow for the youngster. Chelsea were to ask the FA for a special medal but that would be tiny consolation. Sexton named the same side, Hinton remaining as substitute. Whether Harris and Webb swapped positions would remain to be seen. The other injury concerns post-Wembley (Harris, Bonetti and Hutchinson) were declared fully fit.

The day before the replay the *Daily Mail* ran another Osgood interview. His agent and business partner Greg Tesser was certainly working extremely hard on profile raising. 'If we can win this replay it will confirm the belief we have in Dave Sexton and ourselves...I know the way people talk about us – that we're playboys who aren't dedicated to the game, that we would rather be drinking than training'. This was indeed quite a widely-held opinion. He pointed out that Hudson was fighting to be fit rather than giving up and relaxing. He felt that for a long time the crowd 'hoped we would win something but made it clear they thought we wouldn't...There's nothing worse than getting stick off your own supporters. You expect it away but some of our players were taking a terrible hammering at Stamford Bridge...It's really bugging me that after looking forward to the Final I played so badly. I am grateful personally for the chance to put that right...Physically it will be bloody hard, and Leeds must be desperate after blowing out in the League and the European

Cup. But they've never frightened us'.

The day before Old Trafford, Arsenal were crowned Fairs Cup winners and as Chelsea faced Leeds, Manchester City were beating Gornik Zabrze to win the Cup-Winner's Cup. There was no doubt which was the biggest match, though. The TV audience for a rare live midweek match was expected to be large. What nobody anticipated, however, was how large. A truly astonishing 28,490,000 viewers across BBC and ITV, more than half the population of England, watched the replay, the largest ever UK TV audience for a club football match They were as gripped as the 62,078 packed into Old Trafford, at least 25,000 of them Chelsea supporters, most packed into the Stretford End. Touts caught a cold when few ticketless hopefuls turned up outside, so were selling below face value, but were still stuck with some unsold ones.

Chelsea fielded the same side. As anticipated Webb and Harris swapped positions, Cooke went into midfield with Houseman wide on the left. Leeds replaced the injured Gary Sprake with David Harvey. The pitch was, as predicted, considerably better than the Wembley one, giving every opportunity for a feast of football. What was actually served up was without doubt exciting but was also possibly one of the most violent high-profile clashes in the history of English domestic football.

First, the football. Leeds took the lead after 36 minutes through Jones, beating Bonetti who he had earlier recklessly clattered and partially immobilised, though his shot was such that a fully-fit Bonetti would have struggled to stop it. He had his knee strapped at the interval and Dempsey had to take goal kicks. Bonetti's knee was twice its usual size at half-time, and Webb was extremely happy afterwards that he did not have to go in goal as replacement. Osgood equalised with a glorious diving header from Cooke's cross with 12 minutes to go, a wonderful counter-attacking move forcing extra-time. In '*The Bonnie Prince*' Cooke emphasised how happy with his cross for the equaliser he was. 'It seemed to loop and float just perfectly...it was a beautiful cross, a great finish and a great moment'.

Webb won the cup in the 105th minute, famously forcing the ball home after a Hutchinson long throw was inadvertently headed on by Jack Charlton. Osgood was forced off in the second-half of extra-time with a calf problem, but Hinton came on and shored up the defence, so it was a beneficial move anyway. Leeds rallied but could not equalise and Hutchinson had a goal dubiously disallowed for offside before Chelsea, gloriously, showing astonishing spirit, had won the FA Cup for the first time in their history.

What is often better remembered by neutrals, half a century later, is the violence between the two sides and the utter ineffectuality of referee Eric Jennings. The number of free-kicks, the constant whistling for minor offences and the lunging tackles and foot-over-the-top tackles that went unpunished were all down to bad refereeing. Leeds were awarded the first eight free-kicks. In the first-half Leeds were awarded 11, Chelsea 3.

In the second-half Leeds were awarded 13, Chelsea 6. In the first-half of extra-time Leeds were awarded 3, Chelsea 1. It was only in the second-half of extra-time that Leeds gave more fouls away, 3, to Chelsea's 1. In total Leeds were awarded 28, Chelsea 13. These figures starkly give a lie to the theory that only Leeds could dish it out. Chelsea stood up and fought, as they had at Wembley. The *Daily Telegraph* rightly thought there were feuds lingering from Wembley and that Jennings 'apparent desire for a pacific match had the perverse effect of bringing it to the verge of going out of control'. Harris set the tone early on, committing 'a frightening foul' on Gray whose mobility was severely restricted for the rest of the evening.

The *Daily Mirror* match report captures the flavour of what went on. 'A game spoilt by ugliness and spite. The fouls came in a flow to halt and hamper the football. Partly I blame Chelsea, for their self-disgust in again not achieving anything like their best was expressed in a frenzy. Less, I blame Leeds, though these are no mugs at the mean stuff and met every provocation with equal fire. But mostly I blame the referee, Eric Jennings. This was to be his last big occasion and he seemed to want peace at any cost. His casual license allowed the hacking and the tripping, the thrashing of arms and the swinging of feet to go largely unchecked. The bookings of Hutchinson and Bremner came late and merely as a gesture. Bonetti was laid out by Jones...Cooke and Clarke were involved in a kicking match. Charlton was floored by Osgood and got up and ran three paces before knocking him flat. Osgood tangled with Bremner and the Scot hacked at the other. Hutchinson rushed up and knocked him flat'. That analysis excluded the karate kick McCreadie executed on Bremner. In 1997 referee David Elleray reviewed the match and concluded that the sides would have received six red cards and twenty yellow cards between them, in the modern era of football. That figure would only have increased in the intervening 24 years. As Kenneth Wolstenholme observed in his BBC TV commentary, the replay 'was no place for boys'.

On '*Kicking And Screaming*' a 1995 BBC TV documentary about the history of football, two Chelsea players who starred at Old Trafford were interviewed. Their comments are revealing. Hutchinson's view was 'they hated us and we hated them', Baldwin adding 'they kicked us and we kicked them'.

In '*Ossie The Wizard*' the striker praised Harris for playing at Wembley with a cortisone injection. 'He lifted us all and held us together when it looked like we might crumble'. He beamed that 'scoring in every round was something special'. Indeed it was. At the time of writing, nobody has done it since.

Webb, who played like 'a man inspired' according to Cooke, observed that 'Leeds thrived for a long time on intimidation, but we were too brave for them'. He also pointed out that 'these Northern geezers have got to get used to the idea that the Soccer scene is moving to London'. Harris reiterated what was pretty obvious to observers. 'You've got to be ruthless to be a good side...we have to keep going up to the final whistle'. Cooke continued in a similar vein. 'Let's not mince words. We all know the reputation Leeds have for being hard men. In all the heat of the match, when all you can think about is winning, it lifted me to see the way some of them were turning away and appealing to the ref'.

Supporter Julian Patten recalls reading that Sexton and the squad held a meeting between Wembley and Old Trafford where the manager agreed to a team request to use a more 'earn the right to play' attitude. They certainly did that. Although it is easy to criticise manager and players for such a robust approach to the replay, it is quite simple. If they had not competed like that, against that side, they would almost certainly have lost. It may have been a cynical approach but, on the day and given the occasion, it was the right one. Chelsea were not there to entertain, though the replay certainly had plenty of excitement. What they went to Manchester for was to bring home the cup. In that they succeeded. As anti-hero Arthur Seaton says in the film '*Saturday Night And Sunday Morning*', 'everything else is just propaganda'.

In '*The Chelsea Football Book*' Sexton felt his men had been very nervous in the first-half at both Wembley and Old Trafford. 'If we're not playing well, we hang on and hang on. That's the quality of our football, and it's paid off. That's why we're a good side...We have set a standard we do not want to fall below...You've got to be ruthless for 90 minutes'. He had instilled a competitive spirit and never-say-die attitude that, at its best, had few equals.

To his credit a bitterly disappointed Revie, who had seen hopes of a treble shrivel to dust, was magnanimous in defeat, calling his rival 'a great manager' and Chelsea 'a great team with great fighters'. Webb told the *Daily Mirror* 'I have never scored such an important goal in my life'. The Mirror observed that 'Chelsea delivered a final crushing blow in a season of ultimate despair for Leeds'. They called it 'a triumph of spirit and determination, a glowing example of what a team can achieve when it refuses to quit' and praised their 'stamina and sustained effort' since the turn of the year. The *Daily Mail* lauded 'Chelsea's infinite and amazing capacity to survive last night gained them the FA Cup in a Final that made history for its length and for its injustice' under a 'Pity Leeds' headline. Injustice? Pity? Plenty of journalists had clearly wanted Leeds to win and maybe they deserved to win at Wembley but indominatable spirit, exemplified by Webb, won the day. They simply would not give up, would not believe they were defeated. Leeds went behind once and could not recover. 'Soft Southerners', a jibe used by Revie in the past, no longer.

The contrast afterwards was telling, if unsurprising. The dejected Leeds players ran straight to their dressing room at the final whistle, where they were later presented with their medals. The *Daily Mirror* reported, under a 'Losers Leeds Snub Lord Mayor's Party' front-page headline, that they ducked out of the Lord Mayor's champagne party and did not meet their supporters. Revie had accepted the invite three weeks earlier 'win or lose' but changed his mind. Alderman John Rafferty complained 'This is rude and chicken-hearted...They look like bad losers'. The Leeds faithful booed Harris long and loud when he picked up the trophy, but that will not have exactly worried the victorious captain either. Chelsea had the trophy, the glory, and the winners' medals. A number of Chelsea celebrants wore Leeds shirts when picking up their medals and, as supporter Neil Fitzsimon recalls in *'Rhapsody In Blue'*, an FA blazer attempted to stop the white-shirted Hutchinson collecting his medal until Derby manager Brian Clough intervened.

The reaction in the winning dressing room was somewhat different. Collecting the cup, the lap of honour, the dressing room celebrations, the party, the train journey back to London the following morning all passed by in a blur for the victorious Chelsea party. The FA Cup-winning team received bonuses of £2,000 a man, with £500 for other squad members.

Wildly celebrating supporters, watching on television, filled the streets near Stamford Bridge. The *Daily Telegraph*, somewhat exaggerating, ran a 'Chelsea Fans Run Riot' headline. 'Crowds of singing dancing fans' forced police to block off King's Road in the small hours. Traffic was diverted, a man knocked down and a No.11 bus taken over. Three were arrested. They were later fined £1 each for being drunk and disorderly. The judge, Sir John Aubrey-Fletcher commented 'They had a very good reason to, didn't they?', commendably understanding attitude.

Most newspapers carried pictures of Harris with the cup on their front-pages. The *Evening Standard* headline 'London: It's Your Cup' said it all. The following lunchtime there were chants of 'Chelsea, Chelsea...We won the Cup' at Euston as the team returned. The *Daily Telegraph* reported that Osgood 'had to run the gauntlet of backslapping fans to be first into the teams' victory carriage – an open-top coach'. The loudest cheers came as Harris held the Cup aloft.

The open-top bus parade with the cup was utterly chaotic, as large chunks of South West London took the afternoon off work or school to greet their heroes as the bus, preceded by a lorry crammed with 100 young supporters, arrived at Fulham Town Hall for the civic reception. The original plan was that the open top parade would not include the World's End, a Chelsea hotbed. Local supporters complained and the route was changed. The *Daily Mail* interviewed Harry Pemberton, one of Chelsea's original ball-boys, who enthused 'I've waited 65 years for this moment'. They enthused that 'skinheads and hippies stood shoulder to shoulder singing supporters' songs and war cries'.

Supporter Terry Cassley returned from Manchester in the small hours and was at Euston to see the team emerge with the cup before 'scooting back to the World's End to see them again as they came through. It seemed every man and his dog had come out to celebrate'.

Brian Gaches was also there. 'Another day where it was necessary to have a 24 hour stomach bug to miss school to see the parade. Like many others I made my way to Euston which was packed with Chelsea fans waiting for the lunchtime train arriving back from Manchester carrying the team. The songs echoed around the old station, especially on the slopes to the platform where the train would arrive. It was as jammed as being in The Shed in a full house at the Bridge. I always remember the team eventually made their way through the masses to their open top bus waiting nearby in a warehouse at the back of the station, but it didn't stop the bus being surrounded by thousands of Chelsea fans. As soon as the bus made its way out of the station there was a stampede to Euston underground station to get the tube to Fulham Broadway. The first train was jam-packed with singing Chelsea fans, and this was around lunchtime on a Thursday – the look on the faces of commuters and shoppers on the train was a picture! The crowds from Euston including myself arrived at Fulham Broadway before the open top bus, making it all worthwhile!'.

After the dust had settled, *The Observer's* Hugh McIlvanney shared some illuminating thoughts. 'The match was too gladiatorial for many tastes (with) its grimly physical tone and sequence of bitter personal confrontations'. Cooke, a personal friend of the writer, felt 'It was no harder than we expected. Did people expect us to fanny about? Nobody was going to do you any favours out there'. The writer felt the Scot's 'combative and tireless contributions in midfield surely gave a permanent answer to those who have dismissed him as no more than an erratic fringe influence in the modern game'. McIlvanney's most scathing, and famous, comment was reserved for the hapless referee. 'At times it appeared that Mr Jennings would give a free kick only on production of a death certificate'.

The Observer made a telling point. 'Chelsea used to be a club with more than its share of half-boiled supporters who thought it quite jolly to sit in the stand at Stamford Bridge with a tartan travelling rug over their knees and chat later in a pub on the King's Road about the capers of the chaps. They paid their money and were entitled to enjoy the matches any way they pleased. But the Chelsea players were obviously delighted to find themselves backed by less genteel followers in Manchester on Wednesday...David Webb and others were...paying mildly stunned tributes to the numbers and noisy enthusiasm of their followers'. The support had been superb. Osgood, in '*Ossie The Wizard*' praised the supporters for endlessly chanting 'Chelsea, Chelsea' from his equaliser until the final whistle.

Skipper Harris also praised the support at Wembley and Old Trafford. 'We've never had support like it. Anyone can cheer a team when they are in front. Our lot did it non-stop and pulled us back from the edge of defeat'. Peter Gray was there and remembers 'the atmosphere at the ground was terrific, even more so in extra-time when the Chelsea fans seemed to up a gear with their support'. A letter was sent to Brian

Mears by British Rail praising the behaviour of the thousands of Blues who travelled on the special trains.

Sexton, to whom so much credit was due, looked forward. 'When you win something like this you begin to build up pace. We have set a standard at Chelsea we do not want to fall below'. He told *Goal* magazine 'this is only the beginning. This team will bring a lot more honours to Stamford Bridge – and our magnificent supporters'.

For chairman Brian Mears this was an unbelievably proud moment. 'The FA Cup is only the beginning. We are going to bring many more trophies back to Stamford Bridge'. He talked to the *Kensington Post* about the emergence of a new Chelsea 'a team with the ability and potential to become not only the most exciting and successful side ever to wear the Chelsea blue, but one that is poised to challenge the best in Europe'.

Mears told the *Evening Standard* 'The club's waited 65 years for this. It's just wonderful'. He stressed 'we have to build a ground worthy of the players, and the present team is the best we have ever had. We are seeing our architects next month and there is no reason alterations cannot be started during the season, as Everton and Burnley are doing, instead of cramming a rush job into the summer months'.

Season Summary

Everton	p42 66pts
Leeds United	p42 57pts
Chelsea	**p42 55pts**
Derby County	p42 53pts
Liverpool	p42 51pts
Coventry City	p42 49pts
Newcastle United	p42 47pts

And so ended one of the most tumultuous, memorable, and triumphant seasons in the club's history. As Rob Steen in '*The Mavericks*' put it '1969-70 was unquestionably the maddest, gladdest, grooviest in the history of Chelsea FC'. Sexton's team had physicality, persistence, a wonderful will-to-win and tremendous skill. Add that to supreme managerial tactical nous and there was every reason to hope that further honours would be in the offing.

To develop and bring through Alan Hudson and Ian Hutchinson in as regulars deserved great credit. To adapt the style of play after Hudson's desperately unlucky injury spoke volumes about the man's tactical ability.

The regular team, in terms of most League appearances made, was:- Bonetti; Harris, Dempsey, Hinton, Webb, McCreadie; Hudson, Hollins; Cooke, Osgood, Houseman. Sub. Hutchinson.

Hudson was without doubt the discovery of that season and the most promising teenager in Britain. Respected journalists talked about him in revered terms. Given he was not fit for the replay 18 days later, it is hard to see how the positive prognoses on his fitness for Wembley were more than the height of wishful thinking and can only have added to the mental agony when he was finally diagnosed unfit a couple of days beforehand. Missing both finals hit Hudson extremely hard, as he made clear in 'The Working Man's Ballet', and some of his later behaviour and actions maybe need to be seen in that context.

The Chelsea Supporters Club members voted John Hollins their 'Player Of The Year', due reward for a season of diligence and total commitment. He may not have attracted the headlines others did, but he was crucial to the team's success. Osgood finished second, Hudson third.

The final League table showed Everton won at a canter, though it helped that Leeds concentrated on the cups at the very end of the season. Given their poor start, third position was probably the best Chelsea could have hoped for, producing their best placing for five years. Six points from the first seven games and a mediocre 12th place at the end of September made a realistic title challenge difficult, despite Sexton's brave words in mid-season. Two League defeats in six months from September showed the quality and potential in the side, and it was to their credit that they bounced back from the heavy home defeat by Leeds. Chances were missed up front but the reversion of Osgood up front, and his pairing with Hutchinson, led to him getting 31 goals in 48 games, Hutchinson netting 22 in 36. Hutchinson's striking partnership with Peter Osgood is remembered, half a century later, as one of the greatest in the club's history. Osgood ended the season tie second with Everton's Joe Royle on 23 League goals, two behind West Bromwich's Jeff Astle in the Division One scoring chart. Hutchinson's bravery was without doubt but if he continued to attract such close attention from defenders his injury record was unlikely to improve.

Again the defence leaked too many League goals. 50 conceded in 42 matches was worse than any other side in the top seven, champions Everton conceding just 34, and a real challenge to Sexton to tighten it up.

Chelsea's average 1969-70 League attendance increased to 40,342, up 2,746. More success in the years to come would surely mean that figure would expand further, increasing gate revenue and thereby aiding the club's ground expansion plans.

However, that was for the future. In the now, with a major trophy in the cabinet, European football again beckoning, a strong squad, an ambitious board publicly talking about stadium improvement and some money available to the manager for further strengthening (probably necessary if a concerned challenge for the title was going to happen), there was every reason for a real sense of optimism as the players dispersed after a lively celebration back in London. Chelsea were installed as 5-1 third favourites for the title the following season, behind Leeds and Everton.

Season Overview 1969-70

League Appearances (inc sub) (top 11 players) – Hollins 42, Houseman 42, Osgood 38, Dempsey 37, Bonetti 36, Cooke 35, Webb 35, Harris 30, McCreadie 30, Hudson 29, Hinton 2

League Goals (5+) – Osgood 23, Hutchinson 16, Hollins 6, Baldwin 5
League Clean Sheets – 15
Biggest League Win – 5-1 v Crystal Palace (A) 27/12/69
Worst League Defeat – 2-5 v Leeds United (H) 10/01/70, 2-5 v Everton (A) 28/03/70

Final League position – 3rd
League Record –
Home W13 D7 L1 F36 A18. *Away* W8 D6 L7 F34 A32. Pts 55

Hat-Tricks – Osgood (4) v Crystal Palace (A) Division One 27/12/69 Osgood (3) v Sunderland (H) Division One 31/01/70 Osgood (3) v Queens Park Rangers (A) FA Cup Quarter-Final 21/02/70

Sending Offs – None

Biggest Home League Crowd – 61,479 v Manchester United 21/03/70
Smallest Home League Crowd – 24,904 v Burnley 17/09/69
Average Home League Crowd – 40,342

Cup Performances –
FA Cup – Winners
League Cup – 4th Round
Europe – n/a

Chelsea League Debuts – Paddy Mulligan
Player Of The Year – John Hollins

Close Season

Chelsea took a strong squad to Cambridge United as part of the Hutchinson deal, 48 hours after winning the cup. The hosts hoped it would help their application for a Football League place. 14,000 turned up to watch the FA Cup winners, and the gates were closed 30 minutes before kick-off, giving the hosts welcome receipts of £3,000. Peter Bonetti, Eddie McCreadie and Peter Osgood were the only names missing from the cup winning heroes, young keeper Alan Dovey, Marvin Hinton and Alan Birchenall coming in. Chelsea, perhaps paying the price of over-indulgence, lost 4-3. Ten Chelsea reserves substituted for the Cambridge players in the second-half as the hosts had a critical game two days later. Joe Cruickshank, Derek Smethurst, Richard Gomes and John Boyle scored for Cambridge. Baldwin scored twice, Birchenall the other. Cambridge United were duly voted into the League that summer and, hard though it would have been to believe at the time, a decade later met Chelsea in Division Two.

Sexton had talked about not standing still and was true to his word. A week after winning the cup he signed long-time target Keith Weller from Millwall for £100,000. He envisaged using Weller, who could play wide or in midfield, as a striker and was not signing him as cover, which put immediate pressure on a number of the Cup Final side. It seemed a very sensible piece of business, Weller, understandably delighted, joined his new teammates on tour.

After that signing, the *Daily Mail* reckoned the club had £1 million worth of forward power. Osgood £175,000, Hudson £150,000, Cooke £120,000, Hutchinson £110,000, Birchenall and Weller £100,000 each, Baldwin and Houseman £80,000 each, Boyle £60,000, Tambling £40,000. Total value £1,015,000. Hutchinson's valuation was probably an under-estimate given the interest shown by Liverpool boss Bill Shankly. Whether Sexton needed all that firepower was arguable and the likes of Birchenall, Tambling and maybe Baldwin could theoretically be considered surplus to requirements at some point in the not-too-distant future.

After the Old Trafford replay Bonetti, Osgood and Jack Charlton all needed treatment before meeting up with the England squad in preparation for Mexico, though none were prevented from doing so. The Chelsea party flew out to Venezuela for a 16-day post-season tour also including Barbados. Sexton missed the trip, taking a well-deserved family holiday before heading off to the World Cup. As well as the two World Cup hopefuls, Eddie McCreadie stayed behind, finally having his delayed groin operation. Chelsea lost to Vitoria Setubal 2-0 and Santos 1-0 in Venezuela but beat a Barbados XI 4-0 and 4-1.

The unlucky Hudson, his ankle still not fully recovered, was sent home from the tour without playing, suffering a fever. He told *The People* he wanted a pay rise. He claimed he was on reserves money and wanted parity with the likes of Osgood, Hollins and Weller. Happily, at the end of May it was reported in the *Daily Mirror* that the young star had been given a new deal after talks between Sexton, him and his father Bill. 'We were happy with the terms offered and he will be getting only a little less than Chelsea's big name stars'. He was still suffering from his ankle injury and was keeping in trim with runs on the King's Road. Chelsea thought he would be fit to start pre-season training at the end of July. In *'The Working Man's Ballet'* Hudson reckoned he put on weight that summer as he could not train properly, and in photographs from the time he does look less sleek than the previous season.

The tour ended and the transfer speculation, bubbling away since Weller arrived at the club, intensified. At the start of June Crystal Palace, long interested in Baldwin, bid £140,000 for forward pair Alan Birchenall and Bobby Tambling, the younger man valued at £100,000. Chelsea accepted the bids, the players found the terms favourable, and they were gone. Both were entitled to 5% of the fee as they had not asked to go, and the ultra-loyal Tambling was generously given a bonus on top.

Tambling had given the club phenomenal service, was their record goalscorer and went with the best wishes of everyone at the club. '*The Chelsea Experience*' recounts how Tambling hoped Sexton would try and talk him into staying but he did not 'so I moved on (to Palace)...I was heartbroken that I had to leave Chelsea'.

In *'Bring Back The Birch'* Birchenall highlighted the money he was on at Palace, a very decent £100 plus £60 a point. Birchenall, a supporter favourite, had been unlucky with injury in the season just finished, compounded by the irresistible rise of Ian Hutchinson. He commented 'I feel I am better suited to playing just behind the main strikers. That is something I have never been able to do at Chelsea'. His wish for regular first-team football was entirely understandable.

There was speculation in *The People* that some combination of Cooke, Baldwin and Boyle could be next to leave. Champions Everton were long-time admirers of Boyle who 'would do a good job for any First Division club' and Sheffield Wednesday had also shown interest. Newcastle had made a bid for Baldwin, but Chelsea turned them down. Cooke, seen as the likely victim with Weller's arrival, was hardly likely to be sold until Sexton was convinced Hudson was fully fit. Anyway, he was unlikely to want to further reduce squad numbers without bringing others in. He was £40,000 up on the Weller, Birchenall and Tambling deals, the FA Cup had generated pots of money and the club had European football to look forward to. He would need as strong a group as possible to compete on all fronts, as he fully intended to do the coming season.

Young full-back Michael Maskell joined Brentford on a free transfer, linking up with ex-youth coach Frank Blunstone. Alan Cocks, recently on loan at Brentford, was also freed and ended up at Southport. Manchester United boss Sir Matt Busby, a long-time admirer of Hollins, denied he was interested in signing him but, anyway, it was extremely hard to see

Sexton letting his midfield lynchpin leave. Forward Peter Feely signed professional terms after winning the Amateur Cup Final with Enfield, the hope presumably being that he could replicate the roaring success Chelsea had enjoyed in signing Ian Hutchinson from non-League. His trainer at Enfield, Laurie Churchill, had a month's trial but the interest in him was not progressed.

The World Cup was a disappointment for the team (and nation) as a whole and for Osgood and Bonetti as individuals. Osgood made two inconsequential substitute appearances in group matches but was not given the chance to start a match. Bonetti came in for the ill Gordon Banks in the Quarter-Final against West Germany and, 50 years on, is still blamed by some for England's 3-2 defeat. He was responsible for one goal and arguably another, though a dispassionate view would be that he should by no means be alone in taking responsibility for a 2-0 lead becoming a crushing 3-2 defeat. Whatever, it was his last appearance for his country and Osgood was not to win his fourth and last cap until late 1973 after England, crushingly, had failed to qualify for the 1974 World Cup.

The *Daily Mail* looked at Chelsea's finances. They made a £97,000 profit in the previous financial year. Coventry City were the most profitable First Division club, making over £100,000, but seven of the 22 clubs lost money. Arsenal made an £8,000 loss before transfers.

Chelsea were putting admission prices up the next season. At a time when inflation was running at 6%, terrace admission was increasing 20% from 5/- (25p) to 6/- (30p) and there were similar increases in seat prices and season-tickets. The highly popular executive boxes were unsurprisingly going up from £500 to £650, an increase of 30%. Secretary John Battersby was unrepentant about the increases. 'British football is probably the cheapest form of entertainment in the world. We have undersold the game for far too long. We pay 40% of our gate money to players. Some of our top men are on anything up to £9,000 a year. For us that is not too high. For other clubs it is crippling. At Chelsea I say good luck to the players...They deserve all they can get within the limits of the industry employing them. But other clubs are less fortunate, they wouldn't survive without pools and other sidelines...Football is a business providing entertainment at poor man's prices and based on economics gone mad'.

Chelsea's police bill in 1968-69 was around £20,000 according to Battersby. In 1950-51 it was just £5,000, worth £10,200 in 1970, so costs had almost doubled. There were 70 police constables on duty for a crowd of 45,000 or more, the minimum ratio for Football League clubs being one per 1,000 spectators.

That July the club produced a positive, forward-thinking pamphlet called '*Blueprint for the Seventies*', talking about ambitious stadium development. Chairman Brian Mears was clear that 'this season we have seen the emergence of a new Chelsea, a team...that is poised to challenge the best in Europe...The most fascinating phase in Chelsea's history'. Analysis of the stadium redevelopment plans, and what actually happened when the work started, are covered in detail in *Stamford Bridge Is Falling Down*'.

CHAPTER FOUR
1970-71
European Conquest

Pre-Season

In his foreword to the first '*The Chelsea Football Book*', written after the FA Cup win, Sexton stressed the importance of not standing still, aiming to become a force in Europe and pushing for the League title, in a season containing so much promise. In the '*Blueprint*' pamphlet he praised his squad, commenting 'I would not swap our players for any squad in the world'.

The squad reassembled for pre-season training on July 13th. New signing Keith Weller, clearly extremely happy to be at a top club, enjoyed his first day of training - a cross-country run, a game of tennis and, after lunch, some five-a-sides. 'Chelsea are so professional, so well-organised. It's easy to see why they are one of the top teams in the country'. A few days earlier it was announced that after 16 weeks, Alan Hudson had been given all-clear to start training. A mightily relieved youngster commented 'it won't be anything strenuous at first, because I can still feel a twinge from the damaged ligaments...This is a load off my mind'.

On the second day of training the *Daily Mail*, under a 'Hudson: Three Career Doubts' headline, ran a concerning article. He admitted 'the ankle is still painful...It's 17 weeks since I played last. I still get twinges of pain in the ankle'. Though he had resumed training, the *Daily Mail* asked three questions :- Was he injury-prone? Would he be fit for the start of the new season? Was his career in jeopardy? The last question seemed ridiculously harsh, and cannot have helped the mental state of a young man still getting over the bitter disappointment of missing the FA Cup Final. He had just completed two weeks private training with assistant-manager Ron Suart and was hopeful he would be recovered sufficiently to cope with full training. Later in the week, Sexton advised that for the second day of training, 'Hudson had worked well without any strapping on his ankle, and it stood up to everything'.

A *Football Monthly* magazine piece on promising youngsters saw Hudson as having made the biggest impact the previous season. 'He has added skill, steel and determination to the team's attack'. Sexton enthused 'I am delighted with Alan's progress. He is a positive player and a fine organiser in midfield. He creates chances for others with his hard-running and intelligent use of the ball. He is also quick to seize on an opportunity to have a go at goal himself'. All that was needed now was him to become, and remain, fully fit.

A summer break would not be complete without a Chelsea star opening out to a journalist about a contract dispute with the club. Ian Hutchinson was on lower wages than his colleagues, as he had only been a professional a year. Under a *The People* 'Chelsea Pay Row' headline, Hutchinson explained he was unhappy that his basic wage increased but appearance money reduced. 'I can see no improvement on my present earning power'. The club, unsurprisingly, took up a 12-month option on his contract. John Dempsey was also unhappy with the higher basic / lower appearance money policy. The club argument was that the player had greater certainty and more money if he was out of the team.

Chelsea had drawn Aris Salonika in the First Round of the European Cup-Winner's Cup, the first-leg being in Greece on September 16th. This was considered a highly-winnable tie, the *Daily Mail* labelling it a 'European Stroll'.

Three pre-season friendlies had been arranged in Holland between July 26th and August 1st, including an intriguing encounter with rising European force Ajax of Amsterdam. A low-key friendly at Sutton United followed, before the Charity Shield at Stamford Bridge on August 8th against Champions Everton. League games began a week later with the visit of Derby County, a tough start indeed.

What Sexton did not need was a list of injuries comparable with 12 months earlier, but that is what he got. Eddie McCreadie damaged knee ligaments in a training ground challenge with Osgood so missed the trip to Holland, and it was doubtful whether he would be fit for the Derby game. McCreadie explained 'there's no telling how long it will be before I'm fit...It's all very depressing'. Marvin Hinton and Paddy Mulligan also stayed behind with pulled muscles, Tommy Baldwin with a tendon problem. Stewart Houston was also out, recovering from his summer cartilage operation. 16 players travelled to Holland, including Peter Feely and Hudson, who complained 'I had to miss a day's training this week with stomach trouble, but I'm fit now. The ankle injury is completely gone, and Dave Sexton says I'll definitely make my comeback in Holland'.

The day of the first friendly, against Ajax, *The People* ran a front-page story 'Why I Left Home - By Chelsea's Wonder Boy'. Hudson had moved out of his parents prefab because his mum did not want him to get engaged to Maureen. He had moved in with relatives while looking for a flat in the King's Road. 'I moved out a month ago - and I've not spoken to the family since'. Why this deserved to be on the front-page of a national newspaper is unclear, but showed how Hudson had emerged in terms of profile over the past year.

A 1-1 draw was a very decent result against a team which ended the season winning the European Cup. Cooke and Bonetti had good games, but many players appeared to treat it as merely a pre-season stroll-around. Hudson played a half with no reaction to his ankle problem. Johann Cruyff gave Ajax a first-half lead, Hutchinson equalised late on.

A fit-again Hinton flew out to replace Dempsey, who had hurt his ankle. Tommy Hughes came in for the second friendly, against NAC Breda, and sadly broke his leg, and though luckily doctors told him it was a straight break, it was to be his last ever first-team appearance for the club. Hollins and Osgood scored in a 3-2 defeat, Breda winning with a last-minute penalty.

The Dutch tour ended with a 2-0 defeat to PSV Eindhoven. The results were immaterial, what was important was that the players worked towards match fitness. Crucially, Hudson played in two and a half of the three matches and John Boyle in all three, having missed much of the previous season. New boy Weller, who the *Evening Standard* pointed out was the first genuine outside-right Sexton had been able to use, did the same. Youngsters Peter Feely and Derek Smethurst made substitute appearances.

With the Charity Shield a week away Chelsea had one more friendly, a charity friendly at Sutton United in aid of the Bud Flanagan Leukaemia Fund, remembering triallist Tommy Sinclair who had sadly died of the disease two years earlier. Chelsea won 3-0, Hutchinson with two goals, Osgood the other. The concern was Cooke, who went off with an achilles injury and was doubtful for the Charity Shield and, possibly, the start of the League season.

After a disappointing World Cup, Osgood was interviewed by the *Daily Mail*. He thought 'Individualists are a dying breed' and saw too big a focus on tactics. 'Too many clubs overdo it. When that happens, all you get is boring football'. He praised Rodney Marsh, George Best and Francis Lee, and complained that of all the sides in Mexico, England 'were the one with least flair'. Of Chelsea he had nothing but praise. 'Dave Sexton has his priorities right. He is a brilliant tactician, but we still have plenty of flair players'. It was later revealed that the England World Cup pool paid just £2,300 a man, the anticipated lucrative commercial contracts not materialising. This will have disappointed Osgood as it did his international colleagues.

Football Monthly magazine's season preview predicted Chelsea would be in the reckoning 'and if maintaining form will make a strong bid for European honours…The speed and bite of…Weller…should make for an even livelier attack'. There was a general feeling that Chelsea were well placed to pressurise Leeds and Everton in the League, as well as make a strong European challenge. The *Evening Standard* reckoned they would be the main rivals to Everton and felt that the size and strength of his squad would be a real asset, and certainly the pre-season injuries meant it would be fully utilised.

A *Daily Mirror* interview with Harris found the captain bullish about prospects. 'Pre-season tours? If you judged Chelsea year after year on them, we'd be a disaster...It doesn't seem to affect us though. Come the end of next month, and we've won a few games, it won't even be a memory...I think we proved that Chelsea under Dave Sexton have really arrived, and that Southern teams are every bit as good as those in the North'. He saw the League as the main thing to win. 'It's harder to win, I'll admit that. You've got to be consistent throughout the year. That's what we want to be'. He was confident 'that Chelsea will be up there' and talked about 'tremendous ability...a happy club...the rewards for us to do well are big...We're in Europe too, and that's an incentive in itself'. He thought Weller might need a little time to adjust 'but he's going to be a terrific asset for us'.

'*Rothmans Football Yearbook*' reported that Chelsea had sold out seat season-tickets and banked £142,000 in season-ticket sales, a club record and evidence of the strong sense of anticipation that existed regarding the season ahead. Success would mean every prospect of another financially successful season.

August 1970

Sexton's Charity Shield plans were disrupted by the injuries to Eddie McCreadie, Charlie Cooke, John Dempsey and Tommy Baldwin. McCreadie was the most worrying. In an interview with the *Daily Mail* he admitted the problem had got him down and he was spending long periods on the treatment table. He had recovered from his groin trouble, returned to training a week early but tore ligaments in training. Cooke's leg, Dempsey's ankle and Baldwin's achilles strain were also concerns, added to which John Boyle, impressive in pre-season, had hurt his knee.

It was not clear where new signing Keith Weller would play, though there was speculation the manager was mightily impressed by Jairzinho's performances for Brazil at the World Cup and wanted to use him in a similar role, as a speedy, direct, goal-scoring winger. The player told the *Daily Express* 'Sexton has made me see the game in a completely different light...He is a fantastic coach'.

21-year-old South African amateur forward Derek Smethurst was called up for the Charity Shield squad, and likely to be on the bench. Sexton praised him, saying he had scored some remarkable goals for the reserves.

Everton's public approach to the Charity Shield was made clear by their manager Harry Catterick. 'The match is just another pre-season friendly and is of little consequence....the result is unimportant'. That didn't stop him picking a full-strength team, including the 'holy trinity' midfield of Alan Ball, Colin Harvey and Howard Kendall. Alan Hudson, so unfortunate to miss both Wembley and Old Trafford, was back in the team as the manager fielded his strongest possible side, in front of a decent 43,547 attendance. Peter Bonetti; Paddy Mulligan, David Webb, Marvin Hinton, Ron Harris; John Hollins, Alan Hudson, Peter Houseman;

Keith Weller, Peter Osgood, Ian Hutchinson.

Chelsea cranked up the pre-match atmosphere nicely by parading the FA Cup round the ground. Beforehand Osgood was also presented with *Striker* magazine 'Striker Of The Year' award by Radio One DJ Ed Stewart, ironically an Everton supporter. The award was hardly a surprise, as in his book '*Chelsea FC In The Swinging '60s*', Osgood's agent and business partner, Greg Tesser, admitted that he was good friends with editor Tony Power.

Sadly that was as good as it got, as Everton deservedly ground out a 2-1 win in a physical encounter, belying Catterick's pre-match musings. Weller, kicked throughout, was praised for his part in some 'fine, attacking, football' and quickly won the crowd over. Harris countered with some persistent physicality on Alan Whittle. Hutchinson headed a consolation goal from Weller's cross after Whittle and Kendall had put Everton two goals ahead.

The afternoon's aftermath was interesting. Peter Osgood had been substituted, Sexton thinking he 'looked disheartened', and Hudson did not look fully fit. Two days later the *Daily Express* reported, under a 'Sexton Cracks Down' headline, that Osgood, Hutchinson, Webb, Hinton and Mulligan had been ordered in for extra training after a 'pedestrian performance'. The manager, unhappy with the defence, complained 'we gave it to Everton on a plate'.

The imposition of extra training seemed a strong reaction to what was basically a glorified friendly, showing the manager took that game very seriously, and also wanted to impress on his squad that he was going to be ruthless in demanding 100% from every man in every appearance. The *Daily Express* also revealed that on the recent tour of Holland several players had been fined for breaking a late-night curfew, hardly a unique occurrence in Chelsea's history. *The People* reported Sexton's denial that Baldwin, picked for the reserves, had asked for a transfer after a midweek training flare-up. Clearly the Chelsea ship was a less happy one than might be expected, so soon after winning a major trophy.

The club was forced to apologise in the programme for the late sending out of season-tickets and Charity Shield tickets 'due to circumstances beyond our control'. Exactly who else's fault it might be was hard for disgruntled supporters to work out.

The *Sunday Mirror*'s interview with Osgood was interesting in terms of the target he set himself. He had been the leading marksman in England with 31 goals, 23 in Division One and 8 in the FA Cup. He felt a successful striker should be getting 20 to 25 goals a season. 'I'm going to be more than a little disappointed if I don't get around that number...(We know we should) do well in the League, the Cups and Europe'. He claimed he and Sexton had been working on ways to counter tight marking. The paper felt he had 'a maturity (that) will make for an even greater player than before'.

The same day, in *The Observer* Hugh McIlvanney talked to Hudson. He had the coincidentally-named 'Osgood-Schlatter disease', a weakness of the leg, as a schoolboy. Now 19, he could have the disease till 21, and put it down to playing too much football, though his right leg was not affected. He had soldiered on with knee ligament trouble for three months, before the ankle injury that ended his season. 'I've always been one-footed and never found it a big handicap'. He felt he did well over the summer while training at Stamford Bridge but the rock-hard pitches on the Holland tour made him 'disturbingly aware' of his ankle.

Hard things were apparently said to Hudson by unnamed teammates during those games and he did not hide the fact that hurt him. 'I...think about...how somebody called me a stupid **** and I feel like crying. It really chokes me'. Strangely, McIlvanney spoke to other players whose 'respect was so great that several were not embarrassed to call it love'. McIlvanney pointed out that supporters needed to remember Hudson, still a teenager, had left his parents' home with some acrimony recently. 'In the football sense, too, he is some way from home. But he will get there'. The midfielder was concerned that the hard pitches at the start of the season would impact on the troublesome ankle.

Match reports on the Charity Shield bemoaned the physicality on display, from Harris and Everton's Keith Newton in particular, seeing it as very different from the majestic football played by Brazil and designed to kick wingers out of the game. Fair enough, though there were not many Carlos Alberto, Gerson, Jairzinho, Rivelino or Pele clones starring in Division One.

Desmond Hackett, reactionary but legendary *Daily Express* correspondent, found a different stick to beat the Chelsea players by. Their hair. Under a 'For Soccer's Sake Get A Haircut, Chelsea' headline, he ranted. 'The image is bad. It almost encourages the opposite and vicious end product, the skinheads. Chelsea look like throw-outs from a hippie outing...I can't see them winning anything if they persist in being bearded weirdies. They should look at Sexton and Harris and follow their example'. Brian Mears, presumably biting his lip to stop laughing, observed 'this is trendy and so long as the chaps can play football how can we protest?'. The *Daily Mail* reckoned the Chelsea players, presumably the first-team squad, earned an average £180-£200 a week the previous season, so maybe Hackett felt they could afford a short-back-and-sides.

Weller and Birchenall were the biggest English transfers that summer. Chelsea's next deal was not as large, £30,000, but it was a potentially important one. Tommy Hughes had never really convinced as cover for Bonetti, and his leg break created a worrying lack of back-up in a key position, so Sexton was pleased to be able to pick up highly-rated young Welsh goalkeeper John Phillips from Aston Villa at a reasonable price. Tommy Docherty had bought Phillips for Aston Villa from Shrewsbury, but he was dropped for fellow ex-Blue John Dunn when Vic

Crowe took over as manager. Sexton discussed keepers with Docherty at the World Cup in Mexico. The Doc raved about Phillips, so when Tommy Hughes broke his leg, he followed up with Crowe and bought the player.

As the opening League match approached, it was generally acknowledged that Chelsea were the best Southern bet for the title. There was much interest in Sexton's team selection, and it did contain a couple of surprises in addition to the omissions of McCreadie and Boyle through injury. Webb, so fundamental to the team's success the previous season was dropped for Hinton, seen as a better reader of the game and passer of the ball, as the manager introduced a zonal marking defensive strategy, where players marked space rather than man-to-man.

Cooke, often architect of so much that was positive about Chelsea, was left on the bench as the team lined up:- Bonetti; Mulligan, Dempsey, Hinton, Harris; Hollins, Hudson, Houseman; Weller, Osgood, Hutchinson.

Webb, to his credit, did not complain when he, along with Baldwin, was selected for the reserves. 'I knew I played poorly against Everton...It's nobody's fault but mine that I'm out and it's up to me alone to get my place back'. A slightly different perspective to some of his teammates finding themselves in similar circumstances.

Derby, who had won the Watney Cup the previous week, beating Manchester United 4-1 in the Final, took the lead at Stamford Bridge through John O'Hare after defensive uncertainty, but two headed goals from the indefatigable Hutchinson in the last 20 minutes won the points for Chelsea. The loudest cheer of the afternoon was when supporter favourite Cooke warmed up, his name bellowed for ten minutes before he came on for an out-of-sorts Osgood. Sexton explained 'I felt Ossie was a little bit disheartened, as goalscorers can become when they are not scoring. There's no question of him losing his first-team place or anything like that'. League debutant Weller would have been cheered by the positive supporter reaction to his efforts.

Osgood admitted 'The manager was right...When goals don't go in you get a bit frustrated'. Brian James in the *Daily Mail* suspected it was a matter of discipline as much as strategy. 'When you have as many good players unemployed as Chelsea currently have - it was the volatile Cooke who scurried on in his place - it is never too soon to remind the incumbents that depression is a luxury they indulge in at their own expense'. Sir Alf Ramsey was there to watch. The reserves lost 3-0 at West Ham. Webb felt he did OK and with 'more spirit' and vowed that once he got back in the side he would stay there.

The Derby programme detailed the launch of Chelsea FC Pools Association. It cost a shilling (5p) to join, and a shilling a week to enter. 'The entire profits will go towards ground redevelopment. If some of you are wondering why new stands, electronic scoreboards etc. have not shot up since you last saw League football here four months ago, may we say that planning is now at an advanced stage with the architects.

SEXTON FOR GOD

We intend to have a first-class job done rather than regret a little more time was not taken in perfecting it, and when the whole vast project is completed you will not be disappointed, we can assure you'. The Golden Goals competition continued, the profits from the previous season were used to carry out renovations on all existing toilets. Quite why money generated through fundraising was used to renovate toilets, which surely fell under the heading of routine maintenance as opposed to redevelopment, was unclear.

A midweek visit to Manchester United followed. Proving that idiotic behaviour is not a totally modern phenomenon, two anonymous phone calls to the *Daily Mirror* were made the day before the game, threatening to shoot Osgood when he appeared at Old Trafford the following night. To his credit, he played regardless.

Chelsea fielded an unchanged side, though Hutchinson collided heads with Dempsey in training and was a doubt. All the headlines after a tedious 0-0 draw were about the 'superb' Bonetti, with four late saves as they clung onto a point, though Alex Stepney also made decent saves as the visitors dominated early on. Hollins and Hudson dominated a United midfield including the aggressive pairing of Nobby Stiles and John Fitzpatrick, pleasing Sexton.

As ever, the early part of the season was a relentless schedule of two games a week, every week, a glut heightened by two European ties in September. For the Saturday trip across London to West Ham, an unchanged team was again fielded. A genuinely thrilling encounter ended in a 2-2 draw, but that does not tell the whole tale. Chelsea were 2-0 down at half-time through goals by Bobby Howe and Geoff Hurst when Weller, who later admitted he felt he had been trying too hard to justify his fee, stepped up to the mark, scoring two near-identical volleyed goals from Hudson crosses headed down by Osgood. Referee Ricky Nicholson enthused it was 'just about the best match I've been in', the *Daily Telegraph* thought it 'a majestic example of how fine English Football can be' and it was fine entertainment for viewers of *The Big Match*. Osgood gave his best performance of the season so far and Weller made his £100,000 fee look a bargain.

Despite the team's fighting comeback, it was clear that defensive lapses were costing goals and as well as Dempsey and Mulligan, midfielders Hudson and Cooke also volunteered for extra training. The team were on a £10-a-man bonus every time they scored three goals and won, but maybe a clean sheet bonus should have been introduced.

Up next, a chance to get revenge for the Charity Shield defeat as Everton visited Stamford Bridge. A 48,195 crowd was excellent for midweek in August. An unchanged team, still missing substitute Cooke, current reserves Webb and Baldwin and the injured Boyle and McCreadie, twice went behind to Jimmy Husband and Joe Royle goals but twice drew level, through goals by Dempsey and Weller. Everton, as they had in the Charity Shield, placed more emphasis on physicality than skill, Chelsea happily reciprocated, and a spate of blatant fouling dominated affairs.

Chelsea had not scored first in any match that season, including friendlies, apart from the Sutton United friendly and had just earned their third draw in four games, probably not title-winning form. Though coming from behind showed laudable spirit, the fact it had to be done highlighted weakness at the back. Dempsey had struggled against Joe Royle. Whether the zonal marking strategy, that led to Hinton replacing Webb, was working effectively was arguable, but with Arsenal visiting on the Saturday, it needed to.

Spending a reported £362,000 in his three years in the job, Sexton had recovered a reported £348,000 by selling ten players. Chairman Mears reiterated 'Dave has all the help we can give him in building up his squad. If the money's there we believe it should be spent and he is so good at knowing when we must recover some of our expenditure. We like to let our actions speak louder than our words and, from our transfer dealings and what we are prepared to invest in ground improvements, it must be clear that our intentions are to be established at the very forefront of football'.

The manager had long been interested in Sheffield Wednesday right-back Wilf Smith. The day before the visit of Arsenal the back-pages (and the *Evening Standard* front-page) were full of the story that Smith was to join Chelsea for £100,000, with £60,000-valued John Boyle going the other way, a deal that would allow Harris to return to centre-back. The *Daily Mail* 'Chelsea Snatch Smith' headline was typical. Terms were agreed between manager and player after two hours, and Smith went home to talk to his wife, Sexton commenting that he did not visualise any snags. Boyle visited Hillsborough and Wednesday manager Danny Williams had initially hoped to play him on the Saturday, but was still hopeful the deal would go through.

The following day, the *Daily Mail* reported that Boyle had turned down Wednesday's offered terms, so it looked like the whole deal was off. 'I wasn't happy with the terms, and I told Dave that it wasn't really in my interests to go'. Smith, who had fallen out with Williams, had still to make his mind up, asking for the weekend to discuss it with his wife. Sexton must have been surprised by this, given the step up from Division Two that Smith would take.

In the end, early the following week Smith turned down the move, as a salary of £100 a week would apparently not allow him to live comfortably in London. He pointed out that Chelsea did not have club houses. 'I could have finished my playing career in eight years' time with a beautiful house and nothing else'. Coventry, still interested, would pay him less but with 'European incentive bonuses'. He signed for Coventry, who promptly went out of Europe in the Second Round, so that may not have worked very well financially. It was felt possible the Boyle deal could be revived if an accommodation over terms could be reached but that never happened. He later revealed that the clubs had agreed terms, he went up there but the talks broke down and he had a change of heart. 'I was happy at the Bridge and deep down knew I didn't want to go. I had been at the club since I was 15 and it would have been a terrific wrench to leave'.

Sexton side against Arsenal was unchanged, for the fifth time in a row. The game was a strange mix of thuggery and high-quality football. A series of fouls by a variety of Arsenal defenders was aimed at stopping Hudson and Hutchinson by any means necessary. Hutchinson was so badly hurt that he had to go off, his right side heavily strapped, to be replaced by Cooke. Arsenal picked four full-backs and two centre-halves, making their intentions pretty clear. Osgood was booked for a scuffle with old adversary Frank McLintock. 'I'm really sick about this because I've been making an effort to curb myself' he complained. With two inevitably physical encounters at Burnley and Leeds coming up, he knew that, with his suspended sentence from the previous season still in operation and now with his second booking since the disciplinary hearing, one more booking could lead to a long suspension.

On the other hand, two memorable Chelsea goals stayed long in the memory and were enjoyed by millions of *The Big Match* viewers. Hollins ran from midfield, controlled Harris's pass, hit the bar, pounced on the rebound with his back to goal, turned and shot home magnificently. This touch of magic gave Chelsea the lead and earned him the ITV '*Goal Of The Season*' the following spring. The Chelsea programme wondered whether it was the greatest goal ever seen at Stamford Bridge and it was a fair question. Hollins certainly thinks it the finest he ever scored.

After Eddie Kelly's equaliser, again caused by defensive confusion, Mulligan brilliantly hit an 85th minute winner from Osgood's superb pass. The crowd had slow-handclapped just before the goal, apparently fed up with the ongoing savagery. The *Kensington Post* felt the zonal marking system kept breaking down. Osgood and Weller were again praised, as was Harris.

Brazil manager Mario Zagallo watched the game and did not enjoy it. 'No, it was too defensive, it was just too hard. How can players perform as they should in such an atmosphere?' and questioned how they could enjoy it. He praised Hudson and Arsenal's George Graham for having good technique but blamed referee Dennis Smith for being too lenient and thought Osgood and McLintock should have been sent off. He also commented 'you will never produce a Pele while you play like that'. Indeed.

Webb held a 'clarify my position' talk with the manager. 'I deserved to be dropped. Now I am happy to fight for my place. My contract has two years to run, and I aim to fulfil it'.

The Derby programme had listed more of the young players who had left that summer and where they had ended up. Joe Larkin had gone to Shamrock Rovers, Tim Haydon to Bournemouth and Roger Hawkins to Oxford. Apprentices Laurie Craker and Charlie Morrison signed full professional terms. Among the apprentices on the books were Steve Sherwood, Tony Potrac, Gary Locke, Ian Britton, and Garry Stanley. Transfer speculation was low, the only name mentioned as a possible target (apart from Wilf Smith) was Mansfield striker Malcolm Partridge.

Peter Bonetti had, slightly surprisingly, been voted 'the most exciting player in English football' by Shoot readers the previous season. He was presented with the award by Bobby Moore before the Charity Shield.

It was estimated that the plans to redevelop Stamford Bridge may cost in the region of £1,000,000. At the start of the season Chelsea Pools had 30,000 members, over 700 agents and prize money of £500 a week. Even if the Pools brought in £50,000 a year, it would still take around 20 years to pay for the redevelopment, so other sources of finance were clearly needed, including, hopefully, increased gate revenues from increased attendances and the proceeds of domestic and European cup runs.

Chelsea's quest for the League Cup would begin at Second Division outfit Sheffield Wednesday in September. The Aris Salonika trip on September 16th was switched to the Olympic Stadium, ending fears that they could have been playing on a cinder pitch. Sexton had spent 18 months in Salonika on National Service 20 years earlier.

Chelsea ended August in 6th place, undefeated but with a worrying tendency to concede goals.

Leeds United	p5	10pts
Man City	p5	8pts
Liverpool	p5	7pts
Derby County	p5	7pts
Nottingham F	p5	7pts
Chelsea	**p5**	**7pts**
Arsenal	p5	6pts

September 1970

Burnley had lost three times at home already, so Chelsea travelled there in midweek in the hope and expectation of two points. Ian Hutchinson's treatment by the Arsenal defenders three days earlier meant he was unfit, so young Derek Smethurst made his League debut, Sexton's first change that season. What the volatile Tommy Baldwin's view on the untried Smethurst being chosen in preference to him can be imagined. Baldwin, John Boyle, David Webb and fit-again Stewart Houston were all in the reserves playing at Norwich City the following day, together with new signing John Phillips.

Though on top for much of the evening, Chelsea had to settle for a 0-0 draw, as Burnley picked up their first home point that season in front of just 14,543 spectators. Worse, the visitors were hanging on at the end.

Still undefeated but with two wins and four draws, a clean sheet little consolation as another point was wasted, against a side that in the end lost nine home games that season and were relegated. Hinton, though not substituted, suffered concussion. The Chelsea programme noted that debutant Smethurst 'fitted in neatly'.

Charlie Cooke, yet to start a match that season, was the reflective subject of 'Talking In Person' with Brian James in the *Daily Mail*. Displaced because of Weller's 'impressive start', he had to be content with brief substitute appearances but was 'still the darling of the terraces'. Cooke was philosophical, describing being substitute as 'like being named in the team. Almost, but not quite'. He still felt nervous before games. 'I always try to dribble off with a ball. That way, I don't have the problem of where to put my eyes' and described the 'conflict of interest' when a player went down. 'When you go on, you usually go a bit daft' trying to impress. He hated the support 'trying to get you on by shouting your name. I cringe...It embarrassed me to hell' as happened during the Derby and Arsenal matches. Cooke was certainly a lot more interesting in interview than the majority of footballers of the era (or, indeed, any era) and his comments certainly revealed the complexities of an intelligent, likeable man.

Hutchinson was fit to come back for the trip to Leeds United four days later, their first encounter since the brutal replay in April. Hinton was out because he had not fully recovered from concussion, so Webb made his first League appearance of the season after five reserve appearances. Osgood kept his place despite failing to score in six First Division appearances so far. That barren run continued as Chelsea lost 1-0 to an Allan Clarke goal. Weller performed well but missed a glorious chance to equalise. *The News Of The World* felt Hudson 'whose hairstyle makes George Best look like a skinhead, faded after a promising start'.

Leeds boss Don Revie observed 'Chelsea obviously came for a draw and made it difficult for us to play open football'. The visitors had now lost their last six League visits to Elland Road, scoring just once. It was their first League defeat of the season, and though they defended and competed well, it was hard to argue about the result. Leeds had 13 points from a possible 14 and were already five points ahead of the visitors.

Eddie McCreadie played in the reserves against Bristol Rovers on his comeback but had to go off. An x-ray showed a damaged ankle bone, meaning a month out for the increasingly unlucky Scot.

For the League Cup-tie at Sheffield Wednesday, Cooke made his first start of the season, replacing Hudson who was substitute. Webb retained his place. Wednesday were in the lower half of Division Two, with just one win all season, but hopes of an easy 90 minutes were dashed as the home side competed hard. Even when Osgood finally hit his first of the season after half-time, a casual Chelsea could not hold on and it was no surprise when Jackie Sinclair equalised. A replay was the last thing Sexton needed, especially with the Athens trip just a week away.

A home match against lowly Wolverhampton Wanderers seemed a perfect way to end a run of just one win in seven, so it was a shock to team, manager and the 34,889 spectators when the visitors took a two-goal lead in at half-time through debutant Kenny Hibbitt and old-boy Jim McCalliog, who always seemed to turn it on against a club that sold him cheaply five years earlier. A heavy storm just before kick-off had left masses of surface water on the pitch but that could be no excuse. Harris pulled one back when an attempted cross went straight in, his first goal since May 1966, and Hutchinson headed an equaliser, but it was another patchy effort and another point dropped. It could have been worse as Derek Dougan had two goals disallowed, though against that Chelsea hit the woodwork three times. Hudson, returning for the injured Peter Houseman, failed to impress and neither did Cooke, an unusually uncertain Peter Bonetti or Osgood, still without a League goal.

Erratic form, key stars under-performing and Houseman out with a swollen elbow. All less than ideal preparation for the trip to Greece. The situation was exacerbated when Hutchinson needed hospital treatment for leg and knee problems, though in the end he was fit to travel and play. As *The People* observed, he was 'seemingly forever bruised'. Weller was also doubtful with a swollen knee and Webb and Mulligan travelled with knocks.

In the end, all except Houseman and McCreadie were fit to play as a squad of 16, excluding Baldwin who Sexton felt would benefit from a run-out in the reserves, flew out. The manager commented 'we don't know that much about them, but they are sure to give us a difficult game'. Harris made it clear that the team needed to remember the DWS disappointment two years earlier and not take their opponents lightly. Aris were offering their semi-professional players bonuses of up to £200 depending on their result on a new pitch. A hostile capacity crowd of 60,000 was anticipated.

A dreadful pitch had only been planted ten days earlier, was rutted and in places resembled a paddy field. Against a committed opposition, Chelsea played with commendable spirit and persistence and looked in control. They were awarded a penalty when Mulligan was fouled, incensing the hosts particularly Angelos Spyridon who argued, kicked the ball away and did all he could to put Osgood off. It worked, as his shot was saved by Christidis. Worse, five minutes before half-time John Dempsey was controversially sent off. He reacted when Papaioannou took a flying kick at Bonetti, threw himself at the offender and was immediately dismissed. Backed up by Bonetti and Mulligan, he was insistent he had not touched the Greek player but to no avail.

Alexiadis put Aris ahead early in the second-half and the visitors deserved praise for keeping their cool. Their reward came when Hutchinson volleyed home an Osgood pass with 15 minutes left. 'The

SEXTON FOR GOD

Daily Mail reported that 'a thin but noisy crowd of Chelsea fans' celebrated the equaliser. Hutchinson worked like a trojan, successfully occupying defenders so they could not move forward.

The Chelsea party flew home happy enough with the result, especially given the state of the pitch, and Sexton was pleased that his side did not react to provocation but pointed out that 'if you don't play (in Europe), you don't learn'. Osgood was spat at and repeatedly grabbed at set-pieces, and it was to his great credit that he did not lash out at Spyridon. In *'Rhapsody In Blue'* he recounted 'Aris Salonika. Horrible they were. Spitting at you, touching you up' and it is clear that the behaviour of some home players was completely unacceptable, appalling both the Chelsea party and the accompanying journalists.

The *Daily Mail* reported that Chelsea were undecided whether to ask for a personal hearing for Dempsey. Chairman Brian Mears commented 'from what I could see, Dempsey was harshly dealt with, but I think it would be wise to say no more until we have a chance to discuss the incident at our next board meeting'. Sexton was 'pleased with the way our players responded to the physical challenge without losing their heads'. Cooke, booked for retaliation, complained that 'if you got by them, they had no hesitation in putting you down'.

There was no time to recuperate from the journey, let alone the physical attentions of the hosts, as a trip to Coventry followed. The home team were buoyant after a notable 4-1 win at Bulgarian side AFD Trakia Plovdiv.

Chelsea fielded an unchanged side, played fluid football, and deserved their 1-0 win, earned through a Hollins shot just after half-time that squeezed under goalkeeper Bill Glazier's body. Bonetti and Webb were towers of strength, the latter back to his form of the previous season. The downside of their first away win was two potentially bad injuries. Late on, Weller was nastily clattered by Geoff Strong and was taken off on a stretcher. There were fears he had broken his leg but luckily it was a bad thigh bruise. Chelsea were down to ten men as Cooke had suffered an ankle problem and been replaced by Houseman.

The two-games a week treadmill, in place since the start of the season, continued with the home League Cup replay against Sheffield Wednesday. Baldwin, who had not made a competitive first-team appearance since the FA Cup Final, came in for Weller, Houseman for Cooke, and Smethurst for Hutchinson, all three omitted players unfit.

Steve Downes put Wednesday ahead after three minutes, countered by an Osgood penalty and a 23rd minute Webb header. Chelsea were in complete charge most of the time, and Peter Grummitt made a series of fine saves, but only a quality late save by Bonetti from Mick Prendergast stopped the tie going to extra-time. A 2-1 win meant a home tie against Middlesbrough in a fortnight's time, and a very decent League Cup run looked on the cards.

Webb, back to his best, was featured in the *Daily Mail*, who felt he had 'carved a new career for himself as a destroyer in the middle of the defence (since) battling his way back into Chelsea's first-team', though he and Dempsey were still part of a zonal marking system. A content player enthused 'I knew that once I was in, I wasn't going to make it easy for anyone to get me out again'. Certainly, the Webb and Dempsey partnership looked very solid. Mulligan and Harris were a decent fullback pairing, but the return of McCreadie, hopeful of a reserve try-out in the next couple of weeks, would be welcomed. Whether Harris would swap to right-back and displace Mulligan at that point remained to be seen.

The following match, against Ipswich Town, is remembered half a century later for an incident that attracted huge publicity at the time, the worst of a number of controversial refereeing decisions that afternoon. Cooke and Hutchinson were fit, Baldwin and Smethurst making way, but Weller was still out. Frank Clarke put the visitors ahead, though whether he actually touched a Jimmy Robertson indirect free-kick was arguable, and argue the Chelsea players did, but to no avail. Hutchinson and Houseman created a magnificent headed goal for Osgood who happily acknowledged the huge ovation from The Shed for his first League goal of the season. Referee Roy Capey missed a bad challenge by Webb on Trevor Whymark and gave a free-kick for a foul by Webb on Robertson when it seemed a clear penalty.

Things got a lot more fraught three minutes later when Hudson shot. Nearly everyone in the ground apart from Capey and his linesman seemed to realise it had hit the outside of the net and spun back onto the pitch via the stanchion, though David Gray, sitting in the North Stand which was the end Hudson 'scored' at, could not see what the resultant fuss was about, because of the angle.

Hudson and his teammates did not celebrate until the goal was given. Ipswich keeper David Best had placed the ball for a goal-kick. Capey consulted the linesman, who agreed with his decision. After Hudson's goal 'the Chelsea lot stood around looking sheepish' at 'a massively incompetent decision'. The Ipswich players were aghast and then, rightly, furious. Some supporters were unsure of the final result after Hutchinson netted only for the final whistle to have gone just before the ball entered the net.

The post-mortem was a lively one. Hudson commented 'I've been told to say nothing...but I'll say this. The referee said it went in and that is what counts. Let's say it makes up for a couple I scored that were disallowed last season'. Sexton told his friend, Ipswich manager Bobby Robson, 'we all know it wasn't a goal, but he has given it, hasn't he? I'm as amazed as you are'. As the supporter next to Geoff Kimber in The Shed said, 'I like to see us win, but I like to see them go in'. Brian Gaches, also in The Shed that day, remembers that the crowd 'showed what we thought of it a few minutes later when another shot hit the side netting and we started celebrating a 'goal!''. Chief Inspector Harry Porter, in charge of policing Stamford Bridge that day was pleased the decision was not against Chelsea as 'we would have had a riot to deal with'.

Capey, in full ostrich mode, said afterwards 'I was amazed that they queried it'. Brief highlights were shown on BBC2 News that evening (fortunately they had filmed the match, though not for *Match Of The Day* coverage), and it was immediately evident that a major injustice had occurred. Robson wanted it replayed, commenting that Capey had consulted the wrong linesman, but that was never going to happen. *The Observer* headline '**Goal Farce At The Bridge**' headline said it all. They reported that 'a refereeing performance by Mr Roy Capey, which bordered on the bizarre, destroyed what had been...a game of sometimes refreshing movement and attack'.

The *Daily Mail* ran a remarkable 'Don't Forget Poor Ossie' headline. Osgood in full-on 'it's all about me' mode, complained 'that's just marvellous. I score a good goal at last, and no one will talk about it because of all this trouble about all the other goals in the game. The way my luck is, they will make us replay the match and wipe my goal off the records'.

The People ran a fairly predictable 'Baldwin: I've Had Enough' headline. In an 'exclusive', they reported he would ask for a transfer after being dropped against Ipswich. 'I am sick and fed up'. He was still in the team at lunch 'but an hour later Mr Sexton told me he was moving me to substitute'. The player thought the best thing to do was 'part company with Chelsea...I don't think Mr Sexton has been fair to me'. He was fully recovered from injury, and had all his inoculations for Greece but was then left off the trip and told it would be better if he had another couple of reserve run-outs. 'I've had enough'. Given the promising form shown by Smethurst, Sexton could have seen a possible opportunity to cash in on an occasional malcontent, but made it clear he would not be allowed to leave.

The final game of a busy nine-match month was the return tie against Aris Salonika. 40,425, an excellent crowd, turned out, hopeful that revenge would be extracted for the unpleasantness a fortnight earlier. Cooke was dropped for the fit-again Weller and Hinton replaced the suspended Dempsey. Sexton pointed out 'we talk to our players of the need for care. We make no exception for European matches'.

In the event, Chelsea won comfortably, 5-1, as class told. Hollins and Hutchinson scored twice each, Hinton the other as they eased through in an encounter notable for none of the nastiness of the first match. Alexiadis's late goal was little consolation. Aris had no answer to the dynamic Hollins, who was everywhere in addition to his goals, scored from 20 and 35 yards. He enthused '**I don't think I have played a better game**'. Goalkeeper Christidis's heroic efforts stopped at least five more goals. Osgood had to go off late on with a thigh problem, replaced by Baldwin.

The *Daily Mail* report was extremely forceful, referencing the behaviour of the Greeks in the first-leg. 'Chelsea last night kept the promise they made to themselves two weeks ago – when they stood wiping the spittle from their faces in Salonika and swore that the Greeks would pay with goals...rivals who had heaped obscene indignities upon the London club in the first-leg...Hollins 'perhaps significantly the Chelsea man most sickened by the unpleasant passages of the first game...strode the pitch...like some avenging figure from a Greek legend'.

The *Evening Standard* eulogising under a 'Power-Packed Chelsea The Best In The Land' headline, thought it the team's best performance of the season so far. 'I doubt there is a more powerful first-team squad in the country'. Talking about the challenges of having such a strong group, Sexton observed 'as I see it, the problem is not so much to keep them all happy but to do the right thing in picking the right team for the occasion'. Keeping the whole squad happy would be impossible, anyway.

The Ipswich non-goal fallout continued. Alan Hardaker, Football League Secretary, complained that the Chelsea players should have pointed it out to referee Capey. Ron Harris rightly argued that teams were endlessly told to accept the referee's decision, and Hudson added that, pre-match, Capey had specifically told them not to dispute any decision. Hardaker, always happy to voice his opinion on any hot topic, also claimed players should not talk to the press after controversial incidents, though Professional Footballers Association chairman Derek Dougan unsurprisingly disagreed.

Ron Suart went to watch Nottingham Forest to discuss a possible exchange deal involving Baldwin. Chelsea also watched promising young Aldershot full-back Joe Jopling and prolific Cardiff centre-forward John Toshack.

Leeds United	p10 16pts
Man City	p9 14pts
Tottenham H.	p10 13pts
Arsenal	p10 13pts
Chelsea	**p10 13pts**
Liverpool	p9 11pts
Southampton	p10 11pts

A positive month with progress in two cups and a climb to fifth place, just three points behind leaders Leeds United, though with areas of concern. Until the Aris thrashing, Chelsea had conceded first in eight of their 14 matches so far that season (another two were goalless draws) and had not scored more than twice in one game. Their 23 goals had been shared among ten players, which took the pressure off the misfiring Osgood. There was much to look forward to in October, including the League Cup-tie against Middlesbrough and a potentially difficult first-leg of the Cup-Winners' Cup Second Round tie in Sofia against CSKA.

October 1970

October brought another seven matches, or eight if Middlesbrough were overcome in the League Cup. The first was arguably the trickiest, a trip to Anfield to play a Liverpool side in transition, as Bill Shankly eased out 1960s icons like Tommy Lawrence, Ron Yeats and Ian St John, but still tough opponents.

John Dempsey returned after his European suspension and Peter Osgood's thigh injury meant Tommy Baldwin started, presumably slightly mollifying the unsettled player. Liverpool won 1-0 through a 21st minute Alun Evans goal. Without Osgood and Charlie Cooke, Ian Hutchinson's long throws were Chelsea's main threat, which spoke volumes. Alan Hudson, again, failed to have much impact. Unfortunately, Baldwin, desperate to impress, missed a last-minute sitter, their only real chance, as the *Sunday Mirror* 'Baldwin Fluffs Chelsea Last-Gasp Saver' headline made all too clear. John Hollins was again exemplary, covering at the back and 'trying desperately to prompt a sluggish attack'.

Chelsea mixed it physically. The *Liverpool Echo* euphemistically called them 'robust', the *Daily Telegraph* remarking that they caused 'a rampage of crash-tackling that would have disconcerted even the London Welsh Rugby Team' but they were always second best, despite home forward Bobby Graham sadly breaking his ankle. Keith Weller was repeatedly punched by home hard-man Tommy Smith, who was trying to move him out of Liverpool's defensive wall, an action seen by millions on *Match Of The Day* but not referee Ray Johnson. Weller, to his credit, made light of it. 'It probably looked a lot worse than it was…I certainly wasn't hurt'.

The *Daily Mail* ran a back-page feature on Hutchinson, under a 'Is Hutch Soccer's Bravest?' headline. He had a bruised back, stud marks on one leg and a calf problem with the other after Liverpool, not an untypical post-match tally for the fearless striker, but hoped to be fit for Middlesbrough. Osgood opined 'he has got to be the bravest forward I've ever seen'. He was also praised by Larry Lloyd, who had marked him at Anfield, and Arsenal's John Roberts.

Alan Hudson was selected for the Under-23's against West Germany in 11 days' time despite variable form and concerns about his fitness. The *Daily Mirror* pointed out that Sir Alf Ramsey was 'clearly not influenced by Hudson's indifferent start to the season'. Hudson thought he was left with a mental barrier after his ankle trouble. 'Now I can feel myself getting better with every match and this selection is just what I needed'. In the end he missed out on an Under-23 cap through injury, but selection must have given him a fillip.

After the bruising Liverpool clash, Hudson, Hutchinson, Osgood, Dempsey and Paddy Mulligan were all fighting to be fit for the Middlesbrough League Cup-tie. In the end, John Boyle came in for Mulligan, Marvin Hinton for Dempsey and Charlie Cooke for Hudson.

Baldwin kept his place as Osgood was still unfit.

One up after 12 seconds, three up after 14 minutes and in the end hanging on at 3-2. A strange cup-tie, but Chelsea went through to Round Four. Keith Weller scored almost immediately, intercepting a back-pass, a goal that remains Chelsea's quickest ever. Baldwin and Hutchinson put them 3-0 ahead and the 28,597 crowd waited in vain for the floodgates to open. Opportunities were squandered, casualness crept in and John Hickton and Gordon Jones scored in the last three minutes. This over-confidence and over-elaboration when comfortably ahead was something Sexton needed to eradicate or one day it would surely cost them dear. Hutchinson was forced to go off and was replaced by reserve defender Stewart Houston, who was making what turned out to be his last competitive first-team appearance for the club. The Fourth Round draw had supporters excited, a trip to Manchester United in three weeks.

Sexton made a big call at home to Manchester City, dropping Dempsey, who had expressed to the manager his dissatisfaction with the zonal marking system. He told the *Daily Mirror* 'I much prefer man-to-man marking, and I feel I was playing much better last season this way than I have done this season. I don't like it and I have told Dave so. We had a few words about it. I'm not worried about being left out, but I shan't want to play in the reserves for too long. That's not the place to get your form back'. The manager was clearly convinced zonal marking was the system he was going to use, an added benefit being that Hinton was also an excellent passer of the ball. He partnered Webb at centre-back, Mulligan returning at right-back for Boyle. Hudson and Osgood returned, Hutchinson not recovering from his knee injury, and Cooke dropping to the bench.

Showing Chelsea's crowd potential, and the appetite for big matches, 51,903 poured through the turnstiles for City's visit, despite it being the sixth Stamford Bridge game in under a month. An entertaining 1-1 draw was enjoyed by the nation's football supporters on *Match Of The Day*. Colin Bell put City ahead with a cracker as Chelsea conceded the first goal for the ninth time that season, but a brilliant Weller volley from Osgood's header equalised. Chelsea had two goals controversially disallowed for offside and probably deserved to win but City goalkeeper Joe Corrigan was in superb form. Hollins gave another prodigious display but Hudson, again, was worryingly subdued.

In that City game, there was an absence of the persistent fouling and roughhouse play that were a feature of so many matches that season. The papers had been highlighting what a regular physical battering the likes of Osgood, Hutchinson and other top strikers were taking every time they took to the field, calling for more protection from the illegal attention of their markers.

The *Kensington Post* match report summed up how positive things were at the club at that time. 'Under the calm, calculated and confidence-inspiring team management of Dave Sexton, Chelsea have now assembled a first-team squad that makes them envied by almost every opponent: their recent cup win has made them feared and respected by all'. Weller had hit the ground running and quickly made himself an integral part of the team, an excellent signing who was strong, quick, direct, brave and had an eye for goal.

A deeply frustrated McCreadie was recovering from an ankle operation following groin and knee problems. He had only played one reserve game since the FA Cup Final replay, against Bristol Rovers, and his ankle had given way.

Joe Mercer, Manchester City manager, made no secret of his relief at the absence of Hutchinson, who he rated so highly. Worryingly, it became clear that Hutchinson's damaged knee picked up against Middlesbrough was a potentially serious problem, likely to keep him out for a while. Baldwin and Smethurst could cover for him but clearly the side would miss him. Don Revie's column in the *Sports Argus* also praised the player, pointing out 'he has to have courage to keep going in the face of the robust tackling meted out to him every week'. Courage was not a quality Hutchinson lacked.

The first free midweek of the season gave those carrying knocks, particularly Hudson and Weller, a chance to rest and receive treatment, before the trip to Derby County. A strong team won 2-0 at Fulham in Stan Brown's testimonial, 11,024 paying £3,458. Smethurst and Osgood netted and youngsters Alan Dovey and Gary Locke made substitute appearances.

Sexton could field an unchanged team at the Baseball Ground, and they responded with one of their best and most determined 90 minutes of the season so far. Chelsea went behind to a John O'Hare goal but, playing some top-class football and showing real desire, fought back to win the points with two goals from the in-form Weller either side of half-time. The pairing of Osgood and Weller was praised as, inevitably, were Bonetti and Hollins.

Hinton was applauded for an effective marking job on O'Hare and it was clear that Dempsey had been frozen out of the first-team picture, at least temporarily. The Irishman was unsurprisingly less than happy. 'I know Hinton has been playing well, but I think I am playing well enough to get my place back'.

Weller was the man of the moment, and the *Daily Mail* ran a feature, under a 'Practise Makes Weller Goals' headline. Chelsea's leading scorer so far that season had spent hours perfecting the art of a new breed of goalscoring winger. 'I once told Dave Sexton I didn't think I could do the job'. At **Tottenham** and Millwall he was a midfielder who scored a few goals. The manager told him how to do it, then 'worked and worked' on him to make it happen. This diligence was certainly paying dividends.

There was uproar when Dempsey was banned from the two ties against CSKA Sofia, in addition to the home encounter with Aris

Salonika. A concerned chairman Brian Mears admitted 'it is very distressing'. There was no recourse to appeal or listening to the player's side of the argument, but Chelsea planned to urgently talk to the FA. The *Daily Mirror*, on Chelsea's side, argued that 'justice was not seen to be done' adding that the FA 'must pursue the matter with vigour'.

The FA gave players the right to a personal hearing, UEFA did not, which made the governing body judge, jury and executioner. Chelsea were deeply unhappy as they wanted a personal hearing but were not notified until the ban had been imposed. Sexton was rightly furious and Dempsey absolutely adamant that he did not push the player. UEFA's excuse was that they would find any appeals process hard, because of the complications in getting witnesses from different countries, an utterly feeble argument as written statements could surely have been gathered. At the end of October, to the surprise of nobody, **the appeal against Dempsey's ban was duly rejected by UEFA.** A spokesman commented 'we considered Dempsey's action as particularly grave and felt we would not grant him a pardon as Chelsea had requested'. Another example of a kangaroo court operating in top-level football.

Bulgarian opponents CSKA Sofia were a team Sexton admitted he knew little about. The first-leg was bound to be tough, but prospects seemed bright for a Quarter-Final place. Chelsea flew out to Sofia, where **CSKA had not lost a European tie in 30 matches,** without the suspended Dempsey and the injured Hutchinson. Promising 19-year-old defender Derek Vaughan travelled as cover. Smethurst had scored twice for the reserves, but Baldwin was the favourite to replace Hutchinson. The *Daily Mail* emphasised the size of the task under a 'Man-Sized Task For Sexton's Swingers' headline. The manager watched film of CSKA in action before flying out, and was impressed by a 'fine, strong, attacking side' who were promised 'huge' bonuses to beat Chelsea. The trendy stars – the King's Road's own Alan Hudson in particular – arrived in Sofia to 'curious stares at their long hair and colourful clothing'. The manager was clear that this would be a tough evening, insisted his side would attack and, unsurprisingly, went with the team that won so well at Derby.

A 1-0 victory in front of 45,000 spectators was a superb result against a particularly good side, the *Daily Mail* going as far as to call it one of the finest performances in the club's history. Just before half-time Baldwin, with his second goal of the season rounding off a typically gutsy effort, netted Weller's cross and Chelsea resisted all the Bulgarians could throw at them after the interval as the defence performed impressively well. Webb, outstanding, was booked, as was the excellent Osgood, for a stupid backheel on goalkeeper Filipov. Petar Jekov was European Golden Boot winner the previous season but Chelsea 'crowded him out', according to Sexton. The supporters sportingly clapped the victors off, reserving the jeers for their own players.

The *Evening Standard's* Bernard Joy, a well-renowned writer not prone to hyperbole, under a 'Osgood Ready To Replace Charlton' headline felt he was ready to take over from Bobby Charlton in the England team, praising his mature displays as 'among the top rank of the world's creative forwards'. Osgood felt he was a bit stale after Mexico and 'in any case, I never play well in the first few weeks of the season when it is still hot'.

Two cautions in Europe meant automatic suspension from the next European tie, but the *Daily Telegraph* reported that Osgood thought his Sofia booking did not count domestically, as Cooke's booking against Salonika had not been the subject of any action. Unfortunately, and absurdly, it turned out the FA Disciplinary Committee considered reports from the European Football Association about bookings received, then decided whether they should be recorded depending on the severity of the referee's report. This latest example of bureaucratic confusion and incompetence at the top echelons of English football was duly confirmed by FA Secretary Denis Follows.

Baldwin, so impressive in Sofia, retained his place for the trip to Blackpool despite Hutchinson being passed fit for selection. Sexton kept the same side, apart from giving John Phillips his debut as Bonetti had a groin problem. Ron Suart told the *Daily Mirror* 'there are no problems with his nerves. He is very quick, a safe handler and an excellent kicker. He's not as agile as Bonetti - but who is? I'm sure he will do well'.

After one of the Chelsea defence's best displays in years in Sofia, they somehow contrived to be 3-0 down at half-time to an outfit who had scored just eight goals in 12 matches and were languishing in 21st place. Old adversary Fred Pickering, twice, and Alan Suddick gave the hosts a seemingly unassailable lead but after 65 minutes, in a rare unforced substitution, Sexton replaced Baldwin with Cooke, pushed Webb up front, moved Houseman to full-back and the game was immediately transformed. Veteran Jimmy Armfield was roasted by Cooke and Chelsea scored three in nine minutes through a brace from Weller and the equaliser by Webb. With just seconds left a Houseman cross was horribly sliced into his own net by an unchallenged Dave Hatton to give the visitors a truly remarkable win. As the *Kensington Post* said, this was another Blues Houdini act.

Although buoyed by the remarkable success of his tactical change, defensive frailty and inconsistency were ongoing problems. Debutant Phillips could not be blamed for the goals, though it was clearly a chastening first-half for him. Tommy Hughes, recovered from his broken leg, came through a reserve match so Sexton had to decide who was back-up goalkeeper to Bonetti and whether the other one should be sold. Hutchinson scored for the reserves with no effect on his recent knee injury.

Supporter David Gray was not at Bloomfield Road but remembers events well. 'With the first-team at lowly Blackpool I went along to watch the reserves play at home to Southampton, sitting in the old East Stand.

In a late change to that team, Alan Dovey was in goal as John Phillips had been called up to make his first-team debut in place of the injured Peter Bonetti. All seemed well until, at half-time, we heard that the team were 0-3 down! Most people, I suppose naturally, wondered if Phillips was having a nightmare and the atmosphere was pretty subdued (even for a reserve match) in the second-half as the score remained the same up to the 70th minute. We then heard, via someone's radio, that Chelsea pulled one, then two, then three goals back and was delighted for us to get a point after trailing so badly. At the end of the match (won 4-1), our radio source had disappeared, so we walked over to the old ivy clad offices to get the final score from Blackpool. We couldn't believe it when a beaming official emerged to tell the small crowd gathered that we had won 4-3'.

The League Cup-tie at Manchester United was a real opportunity to reach the Quarter-Finals, against a side languishing in 14th place in Division One. Hudson was out with sore shins and back in hospital for an X-ray. The player unsurprisingly complained 'I'm really fed up. I've had the trouble for some weeks and a kick against Manchester City three weeks ago aggravated it'. Cooke replaced him. Bonetti and Hutchinson returned to the side. The number of games Hutchinson had missed through injury, and those he bravely started when less than fully fit, were causing concern at the club. The best thing to do would clearly have been to have rested him but the match schedule, and his irreplaceability in terms of the current squad alternatives, made this difficult.

Bobby Charlton scored one of his 30-yard thunderbolt specials, but Hollins equalised with an equally spectacular volley before half-time. Hutchinson hit the bar and unluckily had a goal disallowed but United went through after a famously brilliant televised goal by George Best, beating a string of defenders, including a flying Ron Harris, going round Bonetti and slotting it home. Weller hit the bar late on Chelsea gave it a go, and they probably deserved at least a draw, but it was a case of one down, three to go as far as trophies were concerned.

Hudson was told to rest completely from football for three to four weeks, amidst wild rumours that his career was in jeopardy, but he confirmed there was no bone damage. 'The trouble is bone fatigue and has come from a combination of my age - I am still growing - and the hard grounds we have had this season'. Eddie McCreadie, too, was highly frustrated, ordered to rest his ankle for another fortnight.

Osgood was fully aware that a booking against Southampton, who made physical challenge a central part of their play, on the Saturday would probably bring him a four week ban. He explained 'sometimes you just cannot help but retaliate, but now I think I have curbed myself well...I've held myself back a lot more than last season'. Hutchinson added 'If I'm in trouble Ossie tends to look after me with the referee, and I try to do the same for him'.

A pleasing crowd of 44,843 turned out to watch their unchanged heroes take on a side with a deserved reputation as the hardest in Division One. After a desperately, brutally physical display, Southampton escaped with a 2--2 draw, Mick Channon twice put the visitors ahead, Hollins and Webb both equalising but the hosts unable to turn dominance into further goals. Channon broke the net with his first, Chelsea choosing to use orange nylon nets that looked the part but failed to do their job.

The away side, according to an angry *News Of The World*, faced the charge that their physical prowess vastly outstripped their technical ability. Brian O'Neil was booked for 'an appalling lunge' on Cooke. Goalkeeper Eric Martin even ran to the touchline to take out Hollins. To their credit Chelsea's hard men 'could not be roused to retribution'. Hutchinson who 'took more punishment than (boxer) Jerry Quarry, battled alone and ineffectively up front' and twisted his knee after a blatant retaliatory John McGrath kick. Osgood had an ineffective afternoon. Referee Tony Morrissey failed to crack down on Ted Bates' team who had previously been dismissively described by Liverpool boss Bill Shankly as 'animals' playing 'alehouse football'. Bates denied they were dirty, but few agreed with him, and his players were again booed off the Stamford Bridge pitch.

A Jim Manning article in the *Evening Standard* the following week criticised Bates' men for pushing, shoving, tripping and hacking and reinforced the praise deserved by Sexton's men for showing great discipline in the face of such provocation.

The People ran a headline that had been used before. 'Chelsea All Set To Sell Baldwin'. Dropped for the Southampton clash, he again asked to leave and again used the press to make his dissatisfaction clear. Sexton apparently relented and said he could go at the end of the season. Newcastle were interested in getting him earlier. Chelsea were supposedly interested in their winger Alan Foggon, so a swap deal was possible, with Chelsea also getting a fee. As an alternative destination, the *Daily Mail* ran a 'Forest Ready To Buy Baldwin' headline. Matt Gillies, Forest manager, apparently had money to spend after the £150,000 sale of Henry Newton to Derby and needed a striker. '(The) £90,000 striker is unsettled by his failure to win a regular first-team place'. If Sexton agreed to let him go, they felt Forest would be first in with a bid. Nothing came of either deal, but it seemed that at that point the manager might be ready to sell, if the right deal could be struck.

Since the arrival of Weller, Cooke could not be sure of a regular first-team place and it was reported that Bill Nicholson of Tottenham could offer him first-team football. Micky Droy, a giant centre-half, was signed on amateur forms from Slough Town, but would not sign professional terms while they were still in the Amateur Cup, signing the professional contract later that month. Promising youngsters John Sparrow, Steve Wicks and Ray Wilkins signed on Associate Schoolboy forms. Sexton watched Tranmere striker Jimmy Hince and was again reported to be looking at full-back Dick Malone, now with Sunderland. Centre-forwards John Toshack of Cardiff City and, less obviously, Bill Coulson of Consett Town were also reported to be under review.

In a *Daily Mail* interview, Leeds captain Billy Bremner praised Chelsea's 'established sound principles like attacking and defending in strength. They have powerful forwards, competitive midfielders and one of the most underrated men in the business...Peter Houseman'. He felt that if the winger had a bit more pace he would have played for England.

The *Daily Mirror* reported that 'Weller Sets His Sights On Chelsea Record'. He was chasing Bert Murray's club record of 17 from the wing and already had nine. His power from the right wing had added an extra dimension to the attack. 'I can't believe it has gone so well. Frankly, I had a few doubts about settling in at Stamford Bridge....I was a little nervous at first'.

In the middle of the month there was considerable publicity about plans to redevelop Stamford Bridge, to include a new East Stand, training facilities, restaurant, supporters' social centre, scoreboard, medical rehabilitation centre and new club offices. It was announced at the club Annual General Meeting that Chelsea FC were to buy the freehold for £475,000. Mears explained it was the signal to go ahead and finalise plans for redevelopment and confirmed they were in consultation with architects. 'On the field we have shown we have one of the finest teams in Europe. We intend to match that by developing Stamford Bridge into one of the finest club centres in the game'. There were also plans to move the pitch nearer to the 'new' West Stand so supporters would be closer to the action. Promisingly, Chelsea were one of only six First Division clubs with increased League crowds so far that season. Gates overall were down and blamed in the press on too much football.

The club response to a letter in the Manchester City programme on the state of the ground highlighted the need for redevelopment and basically told supporters, in the short term, to put up or shut up. 'The very complex problem of redevelopment is high on the agenda at every board meeting. But during this tiding-over period, while plans are being finalised, it would be neither common sense nor good housekeeping to spend substantial sums of money refurbishing property which is to be pulled down in the foreseeable future'. The programme also reported that the roll out of new computerised ticket system was delayed due to 'technical difficulties'. This became an ongoing saga, and it took weeks to sort out all the bugs. Tickets were sold for the forthcoming Tottenham home derby using their new system, including on the reverse of the ticket the message 'the theatre management reserve the right to refuse latecomers admission to the auditorium until a convenient break'.

The *Daily Mail* carried a main back-page story 'Chelsea Shock – Battersby Quits After 'Personal Differences' With Club'. 'John Battersby, one of the most powerful men in football, has resigned from Chelsea.

This decision by the Stamford Bridge Secretary will shock fans'. A key figure in Chelsea's transformation from the old music-hall image, the widely-respected official had a significant impact on club policy for many years. He left because of differences of opinion with club officials. He clarified that there had been no flare-up with Sexton and that he was resigning on a matter of principle. In *Chelsea: The Official Biography*, Chelsea Official Historian Rick Glanvill interviewed Battersby, who pointed out that 'they excluded me from the new stadium completely. It was one of the reasons I resigned'.

The *Daily Mail* also reported that a row had broken out between the club and ITV. Under a 'Players Fight ITV Blackout' headline, it detailed how Chelsea had banned ITV cameras in a row about money – the club wanted £250 a televised match towards the cost of their £30,000 floodlights. Chelsea had not been on *The Big Match* since mid-August. John Bromley of London Weekend Television said that some stars had been in touch with him, and 'I think they intend to have a go at the club if the dispute is not sorted out. They feel they miss the exposure that television gives them and that other London players are stealing a march on them'.

A total of £200,000 (or £3.2 million in 2020 money) was paid to clubs by BBC and ITV for League highlights. ITV paid £90,000 a year of that, plus the special fees paid for midweek matches. They also paid a £100 'disturbance fee' to the home club for every televised game. Chelsea asked for £350 a time then reduced this to £250. BBC settled on the figure, but they covered the whole country and got up to 11 million viewers, whereas LWT just covered the London region, though other regions could show very brief highlights. The *Daily Mail's* Brian James commented 'Chelsea's action is grasping and a symptom of British Soccer's attitude to all mediums of publicity'. Asking for an extra £150 a time, the most additional revenue they could hope to generate was probably around £1,200 a year (assuming eight home matches were shown on *The Big Match*). Mears, on the back foot, argued that Chelsea were not 'graspers' and claimed that the TV companies had recommended the purchase of expensive floodlights for colour TV transmission and therefore felt they should contribute.

The People started a New Paul Trevillion strip cartoon *'Ian Hutchinson - An Expert Looks At The Stars'* where Hutchinson made comments about, and analysis on, star First Division players. This was an early flexing of his commercial muscles, with every hope that as his career progressed, his off-field earnings would do likewise.

Ending October in fifth place, with two defeats in 14 and progress in Europe likely, was tempered by elimination from the League Cup. The squad's strength in depth was already paying dividends. Only five matches were scheduled in November and it was fervently hoped that Hudson would quickly regain fitness and Hutchinson remain fit.

Leeds United	p15 24pts
Arsenal	p15 22pts
Tottenham H.	p15 21pts
Man City	p14 19pts
Chelsea	**p15 19pts**
Crystal Palace	p15 18pts
Wolves	p15 18pts

November 1970

In the build-up to the Sofia home tie the *Daily Telegraph* reported that Tommy Baldwin was to stay with the club, Sexton reiterating that he was a key squad member despite stories linking him with Nottingham Forest, Liverpool and Newcastle United. He made other headlines the same day when the *Daily Mirror* reported he had been in court, charged with aiding and abetting a motorist to drive recklessly during a 70 mph police chase. A passenger in a car driven by a man he met at a party, he threw a half-filled vodka bottle out of the car. The prosecution claimed it was thrown into the path of a pursuing police car, but Baldwin claimed he threw it to get it out of the way and the jury cleared him. Charlie Cooke had recently been fined £60 and banned from driving for a year for drink-driving. These were headlines the club could well do without.

 The Sofia second-leg was a crucial test. Play well, concentrate, avoid defensive errors and an over-physical approach and progress to the Quarter-Finals in the New Year. Relax, make mistakes or lose their heads, and in all likelihood get beaten by a technically strong team. Ian Hutchinson was receiving intensive treatment on his knee but was passed fit to start, despite still having a number of nasty bruises.

 41,613, paying £18,718, turned out to see an unchanged team produce another highly efficient 1-0 victory, David Webb scoring just before half-time. Paddy Mulligan had to go off with a torn hamstring, John Boyle came on, tackled Boris Stankov, was punched for his pains and the CSKA player was promptly sent off. Bulgarian defenders continually clattered into Osgood and Hutchinson, who their manager Manol Manolov thought were the roughest of a 'very rough side'. The creativity of Hudson was again missed, making the efficiency and hard work of Hollins even more critical. Bonetti made what he considered to be the finest save of his career from a swerving Asparuh Nikodimov shot, Webb and Hinton snuffed out any threat from the CSKA strikers and, in the end, it was a relatively comfortable progression to the last eight. The side could concentrate solely on the League for two months, as the FA Cup was not until January, and Europe did not resume till March.

 The CSKA tie may have come too early for Hutchinson, as he had to miss the trip to promoted Huddersfield Town three days later. Ken Jones in the *Daily Mirror* noted that Hutchinson at times that season 'seems to have been limping from match to match, disturbing defences with his aggressive courage but paying for it in the days that followed'. Mulligan, who hurt his hamstring against CSKA, was also missing. Baldwin and Boyle came in. The excellent Cooke set up Baldwin for a late counter-attacking winner in an exciting encounter where visiting artistry was pitched against the fervent enthusiasm of the home team. Bonetti, not for the first time, made a series of quality saves to ensure both points went back to London.

So far that season Chelsea's League goal count for the strikers was an embarrassment. Hutchinson had 3 from 11 matches, Baldwin 1 from 5, Osgood a concerning 1 from 15. Sexton had said he was not worried as long as someone scored, and he was sure goals would come, but the lack of spark from his strikers must have given him food for thought. Weller was doing his job, with 8 from 15 appearances, Hollins had chipped in 3, Webb 2.

In the build-up to the Tottenham home game, their manager Bill Nicholson, under pressure from journalists wanting to know why on earth he had sold Weller, made it clear Chelsea's new star left the club because his contract was ending and he wanted to go, not because they wanted to lose him. The visitors were third, two points ahead of Chelsea, and having their best League season for some time. Sexton claimed his opponents were 'the hottest team in the country' and fielded an unchanged side. Hudson and McCreadie had started light training but were by no means ready to return.

Weller was captain for the day against his old club. He was forced to have a late fitness test after a Harris tackle in training damaged his thigh. 'No Grudge, Says Harris' ran a *Daily Mirror* headline. 'Some people are suggesting I have a grudge against Keith. But that is ridiculous. We normally have a five-a-side match on the forecourt and people sometimes get injured'. In '*Ossie The Wizard*' Osgood reckoned Harris put Weller out for a month after he called Harris's wife 'a taxi' as she picked him up after training, but though there were certainly rumours about ill-feeling, Weller was not out for a month after that training incident.

The match was played in a downpour so heavy that in the first-half, referee Pat Partridge offered abandonment to the two captains, but Harris and Alan Mullery wanted to soldier on, as did the majority of the enormous, sodden, 61,277 crowd, who produced record receipts for a Chelsea home League match of £24,500. Cooke was highly impressive in appalling conditions, his best for months. Tottenham held on under severe pressure, though, and eventually broke through. Their injury-time goals, from Mullery and Jimmy Pearce, were so late Chelsea could not mount one of their famous comebacks. Chelsea had some chances, Baldwin missing the two best, and Pat Jennings made some excellent saves (including one from Baldwin that supporter Geoff Kimber puts on a par with the famous Gordon Banks save in Mexico earlier that year), but, again, sharpness up front was missing. Hinton was carried off with a bruised ankle, giving John Dempsey a rare first-team appearance as substitute.

Hollins was back in England's squad of 22 against East Germany, having largely been out in the cold since his only cap, against Spain in May 1967. He admitted to the *Daily Mirror* that he owed it to Sexton. 'He has stopped me rushing about the field too much and wasting energy. And he has given me the confidence to go forward and get goals...Dave is the best coach I've ever known'. Osgood was also chosen for the party, but Bonetti again excluded.

In the Cup-Winners' Cup Quarter-Final draw, made by **French singer Mireille Mathieu**, Chelsea were paired with Club Brugge (Bruges), the first-leg in Belgium on March 10th. The other ties were Real Madrid v Cardiff, Gornik Zabrze v Manchester City and PSV Eindhoven v SFC Vorwaerts of East Germany. Bruges were second in the Belgian League, with one defeat in ten games. Harris commented that they knew all about their opponents reputation, but always went into these sort of matches with optimism.

Another midweek off, another unchanged team with Hutchinson as unused substitute, this time for the visit of Stoke City, who had just three points from nine away trips. In what was Bonetti's 400th League appearance he was not busy but had to watch a pretty dreadful match unfold in front of him. He rightly thought it was one of his side's worst performances that season. Osgood headed Chelsea in front from a Harris cross, his first for nearly two months and only the fourth of an unproductive season to date. Terry Smith equalised on his debut, but Cooke beat four men and his attempted pass to Baldwin was turned into his own net by Mike Bernard. There were no further goals and little good football, with many among the 36,227 present leaving early. Sexton thought his team performed better the previous week and lost. Weller came in for criticism for a poor afternoon's work, his form having slipped since his ultra-impressive start to his Chelsea career.

Hollins was fit for England duty despite a boil on his instep but neither he or Osgood were in the side, or on the bench, against East Germany. Hudson, after a month out with shin-bone fatigue, played in the reserves at Crystal Palace. Both he and Hutchinson, despite their fitness issues, were chosen for the Under-23's in Wales the following week. The unlucky **McCreadie** was hopefully close to full fitness. He played against a college team in midweek and was scheduled for another try-out the following week. At that point he had only made one competitive appearance - in the reserves - that season after a litany of injuries.

For the following week's trip to West Bromwich, Sexton resisted the temptation to bring back Hudson and dropped Baldwin to the bench, replaced by the supposedly fit-again Hutchinson. Baldwin, predictably, had something to say on the subject, telling the *Daily Mail* 'Of course I'm sick. No one likes to be dropped and I thought I'd been playing well'. One goal in seven League matches was hardly a compelling rate of return and, anyway, the manager understandably wanted to pair Osgood and Hutchinson whenever possible. Dempsey, too, was unhappy at his continued exile from the team and, again not for the first time, wanted to talk to the manager, who commented 'I am just picking the team that I think is right for Chelsea'.

A 2-2 draw at West Bromwich should have been a better result, both home goals, by Colin Suggett and Jeff Astle, being the result of defensive errors. Weller had equalised with his ninth League goal of the season and Cooke, with his first, had given the visitors the lead. Again Chelsea looked casual when ahead, a trait an exasperated manager still could not eradicate.

The headlines, though, were not about the football. A *Daily Mirror* headline 'I'm Guilty, says Osgood', was not what player, manager or club needed. He went on 'the referee would have sent me off if he'd seen me kick John Kaye'. Osgood explained 'I retaliated because I was fed up with being kicked from behind by Kaye'. He got up from his tackle and ran five yards to kick him above the right knee, though he reckoned he was kicked four times before retaliating, having had no protection from the referee. Arthur Jones, who did not see the incident, only spoke to him because of the stud marks causing a six-inch gash above Kaye's knee.

Kaye fumed 'it's ridiculous for players to go over the top like that. We are all in this business together and it's our livelihood. I know everyone wants to win, but to win at all costs is ridiculous'. His colleagues were furious, and the home support spent the remaining 80 minutes on Osgood's back. After the incident, the striker was ineffective, leaving the ever-eager Hutchinson to soldier on, largely alone. This sort of headline-attracting behaviour (the *Daily Mail* led with 'Osgood: I Kicked Kaye, He Asked For It') did him few favours, as if and when he had to attend an FA Disciplinary Committee, the members would be fully aware of this contretemps. Sir Alf Ramsey would also have been singularly unimpressed.

Hudson, in the reserves against Birmingham City, was fit for Under-23 duty against Wales. Sexton hoped Hughes (suffering with a thigh strain), Mulligan (torn hamstring) and McCreadie could make a comeback in a midweek reserve trip to Reading, so maybe he was not far from having a full squad to choose from.

The *Daily Mail* ran an article on the tackle from behind, talking to, among others, Hutchinson and Osgood. Hutchinson reckoned he had already missed eight matches that season because of it. Osgood complained 'he (Hutch) gets defenders kicking straight through him to get the ball. It's the biggest curse in the game. He comes off every match with the backs of his legs black, blue and cut to pieces'. Hutchinson agreed that something needed to be done. Osgood blamed it for the lack of goals from him, Hutchinson and Baldwin – 'the trouble is they know about us and they're trying to kick us out of it'. The problem with that argument is that the top strikers at every club were getting kicked, hard, but the likes of Tottenham's Martin Chivers, Allan Clarke of Leeds, Southampton's Ron Davies and Jeff Astle of West Bromwich were still scoring goals whilst taking the same battering as Osgood and his forward colleagues.

Programme sales were at an extremely healthy average of 84% of attendances, with a figure of over 90% v Arsenal, continued testament to the quality of Albert Sewell's publication, which was heavily praised in *Football League Review* magazine. Over 55,000 programmes were sold against Tottenham, producing revenue of over £2,750, more than some League clubs took at the gate.

Chelsea and ITV reached agreement on the fee for showing League matches. A Stamford Bridge match had not been shown on *The Big Match* since August, but common sense prevailed, and a deal was done. Hutchinson was chosen for a BBC Sport competition to find the longest thrower of a ball. Seven rivals included Malcolm MacDonald, Martin Chivers and Tommy Taylor.

A quiet month for transfer speculation, apart from Chris Garland of Bristol City and the usual links with Steve Earle and Les Barrett of Fulham. South African forward Derek Smethurst, having almost completed the two-year residential qualification, would soon be allowed to sign professional terms.

Chelsea ended November in fourth place, though with almost half the season gone were nine points behind leaders Leeds United. It seemed, once again, that carelessly wasted points would cost them a genuine tilt at the title.

Leeds United	p20 33pts
Arsenal	p19 29pts
Tottenham H.	p19 26pts
Chelsea	**p19 24pts**
Man City	p18 22pts
Wolves	p19 22pts
Liverpool	p18 21pts

December 1970

The day before the Under-23 match in Wrexham, Hudson was interviewed by Brian James of the *Daily Mail*, under an 'It's Been A Drag But Now I'm Really Buzzing Again' headline. With reference to Sir Alf Ramsey and Dave Sexton, he commented 'I don't care so much whether I impress them – I am more concerned about pleasing myself'. He had been out of the side since mid-October but claimed he had not really enjoyed a game since the Watford Semi-Final the previous March and had not felt right earlier that season. 'I was under the weather. I don't know what it was. Lack of confidence I suppose'. The coaches asked him what was wrong and eventually he told assistant trainer Norman Medhurst 'That's it. I am not playing any more with this injury. Leave me out. Let me get my form back', and he felt that the long spell off had worked. James saw Hudson, Hutchinson, Larry Lloyd, Dave Thomas and Alan Whittle as among the young England hopefuls being assessed for the 1974 World Cup in West Germany, which everyone assumed England would qualify for.

Ian Hutchinson made his Under-23 debut in a 0-0 draw and though he had a quiet match, there seemed every prospect he could join the top pantheon of English strikers before 1974. This cap entitled Cambridge United to another £2,500 transfer fee (making £7,500 to date), with another £2,500 to follow if he won a full cap. Hudson was the pick of England's side, which would have pleased the watching Sexton. The midfielder enjoyed his 'exciting' Under-23 appearance but feared (correctly) that he would be in the reserves at Gillingham on the Saturday. 'This was my first real game of the season...(My legs) hurt so much as they did before I had this month off to rest the shins. Who cares about the pain if you can turn it on a bit?'. Ramsey suggested salt tablets might help solve the problem.

Eddie McCreadie was finally back in training with the first-team and played for the reserves that Saturday. The period since the FA Cup Final had been a torment of injury, operation, pain and struggle so he was desperate to get back.

Hudson was indeed back in the reserves, as an unchanged first-team beat Newcastle United 1-0 in front of 39,413, attendances holding up well despite only four wins in nine home League games. Weller's wonderful, volleyed winner, from a delightful Osgood chipped pass, was enjoyed by *Match Of The Day* viewers. Weller was pleased he was scoring because, as he told the *Daily Mail*, 'I'd have been struggling without those goals. I've had a couple of bad patches. I'm still settling into playing on the wing and I'm not taking full-backs on, and cutting in and making chances, the way I should do'.

Another bruising encounter, another fuss about Osgood's fouling and retaliation. This time he reacted when fouled by Tommy Gibb, which meant he was subsequently targeted by Gibb's colleagues. He then got in a row with full-back Frank Clark, who accused him of 'going over the top' and complained it happened regularly. 'Something snapped. I chased Osgood and had about four goes at him'.

A week later, McCreadie and Mulligan joined an unhappy Hudson in the reserves against Ipswich Town. Sexton told the *Daily Mail* 'Alan had proved he is ready. Charlie Cooke had to be patient when waiting for his chance and his great form at the moment gives us the chance to hold Alan back until he is 100% in fitness and form'.

The first-team match at Nottingham Forest kicked off at 2.30pm to allow it to finish while light was still good, as floodlights were banned, a national industrial dispute involving electricians causing power cuts. The result was a 1-1 draw, a Weller volley put the visitors ahead, but slack marking and a cross missed by Peter Bonetti allowed Ian Moore to equalise before half-time. It was a disappointing result against a team just outside the relegation places, another point thrown away. Supporter Geoff Kimber remembers that the travelling support were enraged by one of the linesmen giving offside so often that the flow of the game was completely broken.

Once again, though, it was foul play and retaliation that caught the headlines, with a series of incidents in the last 20 minutes. Hutchinson broke his arm clouting Bob Chapman, a defender with a reputation, in retaliation for a foul. Chapman was concussed and booked, Hutchinson was booked for the third time that season and had to be substituted by Dempsey, leaving the ground with his arm in plaster, a badly cut nose and missing a tooth, the latter two as a result of the attentions of the Forest defence.

Referee Iorwerth Jones explained that 'Osgood was booked for kicking a man on the back of the leg...things got a bit out of hand, and I had to take a firm line'. Of greatest concern was the fact that this was his third caution of the season and given he was under a suspended sentence, he could expect no leniency at the disciplinary hearing.

The FA Cup draw meant another visit to Crystal Palace, following the 4-1 victory there earlier that year. There were complaints that with 8,000 Chelsea season-ticket-holders and only 2,250 seats allocated, putting them on sale after the forthcoming visit of West Ham meant any supporter wanting one would have to miss much of that match. The Selhurst Park terraces were not all-ticket. Chelsea were 14-1 to retain the trophy, Leeds United were 6-1 favourites.

Chelsea planned a four-day mid-winter break to play Santos in Kingston, Jamaica on February 2nd. Chairman Brian Mears explained 'the trip has come out of the blue. The Cavaliers Club of Jamaica said they wanted to stage a match between two of the world's leading clubs, and we are honoured that they should have come to us'.

Baldwin was selected for the West Ham match as Hutchinson was missing with his broken arm, a steel plate having been inserted, with the expectation he could be out for a month. Baldwin had come in six times for Hutchinson and once for Osgood that season and could well have another run, if Osgood was suspended, the thinking being he might get a ban of four or so games. Baldwin explained that what he really wanted to do was establish himself, such that it was impossible for him to be dropped, an entirely understandable desire. Hudson was only on the bench against the Hammers, increasing his frustration.

Osgood was interviewed by the *Daily Mail* about Geoff Hurst's absence for the London derby, with his back in a plastic cast to try and repair the damage caused by continuous crashing tackles. 'This is nothing to gloat over. It's a victory for the cloggers...With the hammering he takes, I'm not surprised'. He admitted the rough treatment niggled him, whereas Hurst ignored it.

Under threat of a significant suspension and without his preferred striking partner, Osgood put in a sustained effort, scoring two excellent goals as Chelsea won 2-1, also hitting the bar and having a goal disallowed. His first, moving onto the ball after a robust block tackle by Harris on Johnny Ayris and casually flicking the ball home after rounding goalkeeper Bobby Ferguson, had the crowd in raptures. 2-0 up and cruising, casualness again crept in. Frank Lampard pulled one back from 30 yards before half-time, but Chelsea held on for a welcome and deserved two points to take into the Christmas period. It turned out to be Jimmy Greaves' final appearance at Stamford Bridge after a stellar Blues career from 1957 to 1961.

Weller went off with a troublesome ankle that had been worrying him for a while, Hudson coming on for the last 20 minutes. The main sports story on the Monday was Hudson's unhappiness at being on the bench. The *Daily Mail* article was typical. 'I don't really want to say anything much about this. What I have to say to Dave is private. But there is no question of me asking for a transfer or any of that nonsense. You don't talk to Dave like that…This uncertainty is getting me down…(I want to know) where I stand… This substitute lark is no good. You can't get the pace of the game in a few minutes'. Brian James felt Hudson was depressed rather than a 'ranting rebel'. The obvious reason he was not selected was the consistently excellent form Cooke had shown since replacing him in October, and Sexton was not going to drop the Scot just because Hudson was upset.

Chairman Brian Mears described Hudson's frustration as 'a storm in a teacup'. He pointed out that you were bound to get some of the squad frustrated if they were not in the side. Providing 100% backing, he emphasised that, at Chelsea, Sexton was completely in charge of the playing side. 'We listen to what he has to say. He can handle a situation like this'.

The Boxing Day match at Crystal Palace was postponed because of a snow-laden pitch, so in the end the squad, who had played a sapping 31 games already that season, had the chance to rest and recover before their next match, at Palace in the FA Cup in the New Year.

Just before the New Year it was announced that Tony Green had been appointed Chelsea Secretary after only 14 months in top-class football administration, replacing John Battersby, widely recognised as one of the best secretaries in the League. Green had joined the club as Assistant Secretary in November 1969, expecting a five-year apprenticeship. Mears, who had advertised the position in the press, was happy that the appointment had been kept within the Chelsea family.

Hollins and Osgood were named in a 26-man England training party to meet at Roehampton on January 11th. Bonetti was not selected, and it was assumed his international career had ended with the defeat by West Germany.

Hutchinson withdrew from the BBC's long-throw competition. 'I don't like the idea of a long-throw competition, it's ridiculous' said Hutchinson. His agent, Ken Johnson, said the BBC would probably only pay £50. 'We'd probably be interested if, say, £1,000 was involved' he stated, rather undermining the striker's argument.

Youngsters Tony Frewin and Joe Cruickshank were given free transfers, both moving to Highlands Park FC in South Africa. Young, fourth-choice, goalkeeper Alan Dovey went on loan to non-League Folkestone. Hughes and Phillips would apparently alternate in the reserve side. Chelsea were keen to offer John Fraser of Scottish non-League side Largs Thistle, scorer of three recent hat-tricks, private trials.

It was strongly rumoured that the one-city, one-club rule was to be abolished in the Fairs Cup, which might be helpful if Chelsea finished below Arsenal or Tottenham in the table. If so, this move was not before time.

Santos, including Pele and Carlos Alberto were lined up to appear at Stamford Bridge on April 19th in Bonetti's testimonial, though that was later called off and a fixture against Standard Liege in early May arranged instead.

Osgood was chosen for a World XI for a Mario Coluna testimonial in Lisbon with Moore and Hurst. He was moving into a £16,000 four-bedroomed house near Epsom, ten minutes from the Mitcham training ground. He enthused about it to the *Daily Mail*. 'Winning the FA Cup last season was the breakthrough for Chelsea as a club and for a lot of the players financially...Now we've grown accustomed to the status of being Cup holders and for nearly a year we've all enjoyed the celebrations and being feted by everyone and everything that goes with it...This house we're getting shows how good the game is being to me...The beauty of it is that we've got a team young enough to enjoy it for at least another five years. Other clubs like Manchester United and even Leeds are starting to go over the top or getting near the day it will happen. Not us'. Clearly Osgood and his teammates enjoyed the money success brought in, but they needed continued success to earn the bonuses that were the icing on the financial cake. In the New Year Osgood advised he would probably buy a racehorse. 'I have always admired the country squire way of life ever since seeing them pop into my local in Windsor. Now I am going to join them, and I can't wait'.

The season had been an uneven one, with too many low spots. The club were unlucky that neither Hudson nor Hutchinson really maintained their promise in late 1970, mainly due to injuries, which also affected other key squad members. The *Kensington Post* wondered whether the adulation had gone to Hudson's head. Hutchinson, especially for one so young, missed a lot of appearances as a direct result of his own astonishing bravery and the calculated thuggery of opposition defenders. Osgood's inability to shrug off fouls, and his tendency to get drawn into highly-publicised retaliation, was likely to cost him, and the club, severely when his case was reviewed by the FA Disciplinary Committee in January. It was hoped Hutchinson, lacking Osgood's disciplinary history, would receive leniency.

Too many home matches were drawn, too many goals conceded. Ten points off the lead, albeit with two games in hand, meant that the chance of the title, yet again, was a remote one. Chelsea were good enough to be top of the table but were inconsistent, too casual on occasion and seemingly unable to effectively close up shop in the way that Leeds or Arsenal could. There was, however, still much to play for.

Leeds United	p24 39pts
Arsenal	p23 36pts
Chelsea	**p22 29pts**
Tottenham H.	p22 28pts
Man City	p22 27pts
Wolves	p23 27pts
Liverpool	p22 26pts

January 1971

Before the Crystal Palace FA Cup-tie, Chelsea had concerns about flu, with Eddie McCreadie, Alan Hudson, Charlie Cooke and Keith Weller all missing training, though trainer Harry Medhurst insisted there was not an epidemic at the club. Paddy Mulligan was back in the squad after eight weeks out but, in the end, Sexton fielded an unchanged side. Still no Hudson, still no John Dempsey, no Ian Hutchinson, no McCreadie. Old boy Bobby Tambling missed out with a hamstring problem. Each member of the Cup-winning team was presented with a personally inscribed photograph album, reminding them how the cup was won the previous season.

Goal magazine interviewed captain Ron Harris and he was pictured on the front cover, with a 'We'll Hang On To It Says Ron Harris' headline. 'Despite what some people say, we won the cup on merit and we are determined to hang onto it...Let's be fair, we haven't shown consistent form in the League. We've thrown away silly points at home, but our away record is still second to none over the past three years'. Chelsea definitely had the ability and the spirit to retain the trophy and Harris was right to focus on League inconsistency.

The tie only went ahead after a 10am pitch inspection, the ground staff having cleared the pitch of snow though Hollins felt 'it had a bit of everything - frozen hard with ice, a thawed skin on a bone-hard surface and thick mud in the goalmouths'. Cooke took advantage of the dreadful surface, which meant defenders had trouble turning, to put in a truly masterful exhibition of running with the ball in a highly entertaining game. John Boyle, too, mastered the conditions without trouble. Osgood headed the visitors into an early lead, but defensive frailties allowed

Palace captain John McCormick to score with an overhead kick and ex-Blue Alan Birchenall to put Palace ahead two minutes later. Tommy Baldwin equalised in the second-half. Chelsea probably deserved to win but given the pitch, were happy enough to have a replay the following Wednesday.

An 18ft crash barrier collapsed at Selhurst Park and nearly 200 children tumbled onto the pitch. Police had to form a human chain. Fortunately no-one was hurt but as supporters travelled home, they heard the appalling news about the Ibrox Stadium disaster, where 66 died when a barrier collapsed on an exit stairway at the end of the Rangers v Celtic match. Stamford Bridge had experienced a few barrier collapses over the years, though fortunately they were far less serious, and injuries were few. Rightly, with big attendances likely in forthcoming weeks, Chelsea's engineers checked all 100 safety barriers and, according to new Secretary Tony Green, were satisfied the barriers were in good order. He pointed out many of the barriers had been replaced in the past couple of years and that the architects had sent a signed safety certificate to the FA. Sports Minister Eldon Griffiths went to the Palace replay to see first-hand how crowds reacted at big matches.

If Chelsea beat Palace in the replay, they would host Manchester City, an encounter that would surely fill Stamford Bridge and attract enormous interest, the FA Cup holders against the Cup-Winner's Cup holders. Leeds were 9-2 favourites to lift the trophy, Chelsea 12-1. Harris commented 'it's still our trophy and we intend to keep it'.

On a pitch that had gone from frozen to sodden, Chelsea, in particularly good form throughout the side, comfortably won 2-0. Cooke was watched by Scotland manager Bobby Brown but could not recreate his Selhurst Park majesty. Baldwin, with an excellent lobbed goal, and Peter Houseman scored in the first-half, his first since the FA Cup Final. Both goals were made by Weller. Manchester City managerial duo Joe Mercer and Malcolm Allison, present, were impressed by Chelsea. The huge attendance of 55,074, paying £23,220, showed the interest in the FA Cup and the revenue that could be earned from a good cup run.

The team only had three days to recover from a hard cup-tie on a wet pitch before facing Manchester United at home. Osgood (thigh), Weller (back) and Hutchinson, the first choice forward line, were all injured so Hudson made his first start since October, Derek Smethurst made his second League appearance and Baldwin kept his place. George Best made front-page headlines as he missed training and the train to London, so was not selected.

The gates were locked at 14.30 with just 53,482 inside, as clubs focused more on crowd safety in the aftermath of Ibrox and a joint decision was made between club and police to close the gates. Thousands were locked out. There was no turnstile-recording apparatus, so it was impossible to know accurately how many spectators were in the ground when considering shutting the gates.

SEXTON FOR GOD

Hudson played on the right wing, scored a stunning volley after an error by Bobby Charlton, and also hit the bar. Chelsea were well below par, however, and offered little up front. Willie Morgan equalised with a disputed penalty with 12 minutes left and Alan Gowling ran half the pitch before scoring United's winner.

Webb needed eight stitches over a cut eye and would have to miss the rearranged League visit to Crystal Palace in midweek. Dempsey, omitted from the starting line-up since early October, came in for Webb at Selhurst Park, Osgood returned for Smethurst but, after two exciting cup-ties between the sides, this was a dull 0-0 draw. John Boyle and John Hollins were booked in a clash with 45 fouls, 28 committed by the hosts.

The fifth game in a fortnight for a team that looked weary at Selhurst Park was at champions Everton, who were having a strange season, languishing in mid-table. Webb was still out, and a fit-again Weller was only substitute as Dempsey and Hudson continued in the side. Osgood had a day to forget. Chelsea lost 3-0, he missed a penalty and, with impeccably bad timing, was booked for fouling Alan Ball, just days before his disciplinary hearing. It was his eighth booking in two seasons, a statistic unlikely to help his pleas for leniency because of provocation. To Ball's credit, he asked referee Harold Davey not to book the player. Jimmy Husband, Henry Newton and Joe Royle netted for a dominant Everton.

Chelsea had a week to dust themselves off before the crucial Manchester City FA Cup-tie. The week's headlines regarding Chelsea were much less positive though, after Osgood was given a brutally severe eight week suspension, to come into effect after the City clash, and fined £160. The FA Disciplinary Committee took the unprecedented step of ordering his records to be forwarded to the Senior International Committee. Vernon Stokes, committee chair, explained 'we are not asking for Osgood to be dropped. But this is a warning to him and to any other player likely to be selected for England'. Perhaps fortunately, his bookings in Sofia and at Everton were not considered when considering sentence. He would not be available until the Bruges home second-leg and might well not be match-fit for that. He would still be paid but could not pick up bonuses. Hutchinson was, as hoped, shown leniency with a two-week suspended sentence and a £25 fine for being cautioned three times inside a year.

The fact that Osgood, like George Best, was clattered by cynical defenders week in and week out was not considered. It seemed that mercurial personalities were treated in a draconian manner whereas the dour hatchet-men were not. There was also the issue that the disciplinary committee members were directors or officials at other clubs, a clear potential conflict of interest. A grim-faced player told the *Daily Mail* 'I am not very pleased but there is nothing I can say. Chairman Mears added 'We all have our reactions and feelings. I think it is better that we keep them to ourselves'. The *Daily Mail's* Jeff Powell captured the thought of many. 'Though the flamboyant Osgood's record looks bad, I believe him to be desperately unlucky to suffer this sort of punishment'. He pointed out that he had never been sent off.

In *'Ossie - King Of Stamford Bridge'* Osgood recounted how Mears told him they would appeal what was originally a six-week ban. 'The FA owe a great deal to my father. We'll rattle a few cages'. They duly appealed and the FA promptly added two weeks to the ban. The player wryly observed in his book that 'Brian certainly rattled a few cages'. Joe Mercer, Manchester City manager, told *Football Monthly* magazine 'the flaw in his (Osgood's) play is the flaw in his make-up. It is something of a tragedy. You can talk Osgood off his game. He can be kidded into doing stupid things. Such players are bad risks'.

Goal magazine carried a pre-City interview with John Boyle, unsurprisingly happy to be back in the side. He had come in at right-back when Mulligan was injured against CSKA in early November and kept his place. Bitterly disappointed at missing out on the FA Cup Final, he was praised by Webb for his hard work. Boyle thanked McCreadie and Sexton for their help and support and felt his confidence had improved significantly since being back in the side.

Hutchinson came through a reserve appearance with no ill-effects so was back in the first-team after six matches out, wearing a lightweight gauntlet to protect his arm. Weller and Webb were also fit, Baldwin injured and Hudson omitted. In *'Kings Of The King's Road'* Hudson expressed his upset at being omitted for that crucial match. Webb partnered Hinton, with Dempsey relegated to the bench. Bonetti had been doubtful for the game after hurting his shoulder playing for a Rangers/Celtic XI to raise money for the Ibrox Disaster Fund but was passed fit.

City boss Joe Mercer made it clear his team would attack, despite the absence of Francis Lee, so it promised to be a cracking cup-tie. A surprisingly low attendance of 50,176, almost 5,000 less than the midweek Palace replay, turned up, despite publicity about getting there early to ensure getting in, and the use of crowd packers to fit more supporters on the terraces.

Chelsea regularly attacked in the first-half and looked well-placed at the interval. After half-time, however, some defensive chickens came home to roost. Hinton let Bell go past him and score. Shortly afterwards the same defender, normally assured, suffered an expensive aberration, absurdly leaving a cross under no pressure and allowing Bell to net a second. On *'The Big Match'* the hapless Hinton was described as 'a sad and sorry figure'. Heads dropped among the team, and many of the bewildered home support had departed before Ian Bowyer scored a late third after a shambolic goalmouth scramble. The exultant City supporters accurately bellowed 'easy, easy'.

Frustratingly ineffective in his last match for two months, Osgood suffered the indignity of being substituted for Dempsey late on. Chelsea had chances but missed them. City did not. Bonetti, in his 500th first-team appearance, could do little about the goals. Only Hollins stood out in a woeful team effort that shocked and deeply disappointed Sexton, who pointed out they were starting to take charge until the mistakes that killed them. With the title again out of reach, the clashes with Bruges took on even greater importance if a trophy was to be salvaged from a season that promised so much. Supporter Brian Gaches remembers that the feeling of throwing the cup away after all the highs of the previous season was a mighty blow at the time.

ITV showed the City highlights on *The Big Match* but BBC News showed two minutes, including all three goals, on their Saturday night news bulletin. They also had Bell and Mercer on *Match Of The Day*. ITV was very unhappy. The ever-pompous Jimmy Hill, London Weekend TV Head Of Sport, complained 'this was downright sabotage. It cost us £3,000 for the right to screen the Chelsea game. The BBC could only have paid £300 for a news film unit...It was a very dirty trick'. It also meant that Chelsea supporters had more opportunities to suffer.

Clearly Sexton needed to act after the second-half embarrassment against City that had attracted so much unwelcome press comment. For the visit of West Bromwich a week later he dropped John Boyle, bringing back Eddie McCreadie for his first first-team game of the season. Hinton, perhaps unsurprisingly, was replaced by Dempsey. Cooke, more surprisingly, was relegated to the bench, replaced by Hudson. Osgood's place was taken by Derek Smethurst. The team reverted to a 4-3-3 system, with Houseman, Hollins and Hudson in midfield. Boyle, unlucky to be dropped, thought he had been playing well. 'I'm a bit sick about it all...My future with Chelsea? Well, let's just wait and see'.

Hollins scored twice, Hutchinson another and, after missing chances Smethurst netted his first League goal. Jeff Astle netted a consolation goal, but Chelsea won comfortably, 4-1, and it should have been more. Sexton was delighted with Smethurst and with McCreadie's sorties up the wing. The players were on a bonus of £10 a man when they scored three or more goals in a match they won, which they collected for the first time at home that season. The attendance, though, was just 26,874, an indication of how flat things felt after the FA Cup elimination.

Football Monthly magazine, in an article headlined "Olly' Driving Force At The Bridge', explained how Hollins enjoyed his non-stop midfield dynamo role, attacking and defending. His long-range shooting had improved after he had worked at it - he had scored eight goals already that season, compared with seven the whole of the previous one. Sexton felt he deserved another cap but stressed he was still only 24 so time was on his side. The magazine also ran a feature on reserve goalkeeper John Phillips. He had enjoyed the season, except for his debut where he let in three at Blackpool, even though Chelsea won.

Ian Delacour, the young Irish defender bought from Portadown the previous season, was released to join South African club Johannesburg Jewish Guild club in South Africa. Forward Richard Gomes returned to South Africa after 30 reserve appearances in 14 months, re-joining Durban City. When Dempsey was languishing in the reserves, West Bromwich Albion expressed interest in signing him and Blackpool made an unsuccessful bid for young defender Stewart Houston.

Stories appeared regarding a number of players unsure of a first-team place. Crystal Palace, looking for a full-back, were supposedly interested in Boyle, who did well against them in the FA Cup. Queens Park Rangers could apparently come in for the often-unsettled Baldwin 'with an offer too big for Chelsea to refuse'. Blackpool were interested in goalkeeper Tommy Hughes, third in line after Bonetti and Phillips, but the move did not progress. It was clear, though, that Chelsea did not need all three goalkeepers. They were reportedly watching promising Orient full-back Dennis Rofe, 16-year-old Mansfield wing-half Godfrey Briggs and Portsmouth full-back George Ley.

Cooke was interviewed by well-known *Daily Mail* feature writer Lynda Lee-Potter, showing his appeal outside football. 'I'm just a guy doing a job'. He had no idea what he would be doing in ten years and had not quite come to terms with money and glory. He had opened a DIY shop in New Malden.

The *Daily Telegraph* ran a feature on 'Chelsea – A Younger And Wiser Club', with one of the youngest boards in the Football League. Chairman Brian Mears was just 39, Leslie Mears 41, Viscount Chelsea 36, George Thomson 55 and Richard Attenborough 48. Sexton was just 39 and 'completing the 'with-it' image' new Secretary Tony Green was just 30. The departing Battersby gave him 'considerable assistance by staying on for a couple of months'. The West Bromwich programme had a picture of Battersby being presented with a decanter before the City tie by Sexton. Tony Green is in the picture but, strangely, no Chelsea directors feature.

In the Manchester City programme, chairman Mears, in 'The Chairman Writes...', informed supporters that architects Darbourne and Darke had appointed to handle the stadium development. 'The day is not too far away when dreams become realities'. The club had agreed to buy the ground for £475,000 from the JT Mears Trustees, three years ahead of schedule. They estimated redevelopment could cost £100,000 for each of the next ten years and the programme also revealed that Chelsea Pools membership was up to 50,000, an encouraging start to a scheme less than six months old. Stamford Bridge was clearly in need of improvement. After an *Evening Standard* expose of the state of a small part of The Shed terracing, an inspection was carried out and it had been duly closed.

A letter appeared in the Crystal Palace programme from the Shah of Persia's PR spokesman, advising that the Shah was a Chelsea supporter and had ordered 24 sets of Chelsea kit from Lilywhites for a match played in Persia on his birthday. Sadly, that result is not recorded.

A 4-1 win may have been a good way to end the month, but January had been full of disappointment. Defeats by Manchester United and Everton, magnified by painful, emphatic FA Cup elimination, meant there was much to reflect on. The even-more-critical trip to Bruges was still six weeks away but 700 supporters had already booked flights to Bruges, in addition to coach trips. Chelsea had a 2,500 ticket allocation for that crucial game.

Leeds United	p27 43pts
Arsenal	p26 38pts
Tottenham H.	p25 32pts
Chelsea	**p26 32pts**
Wolves	p26 32pts
Southampton	p26 31pts
Man City	p26 31pts

February 1971

Chelsea's friendly in Kingston, Jamaica was a chance for the squad to have a break from both the incessant pressure of competitive matches and the English winter. Derek Smethurst was included in the 14-man party, Sexton had been delighted by his performance against West Bromwich when he scored and missed other chances. It seemed he had a good chance of keeping his first-team place for the duration of Osgood's suspension. Hudson enthused 'he could be the best player to come out of South Africa for a long time'. Bonetti flew out with the party, despite his shoulder still being sore after the Ibrox Disaster Fund game, and played against Santos.

The team were hoping for a relaxed encounter with a side that included the incomparable Pele in front of Jamaica's largest ever attendance, 33,000. What they got were headlines like 'Chelsea Fail In A Riot'. Spectators invaded the pitch after Douglas scored for Santos, the only goal of the game, and play was held up for six minutes while the police used batons to clear the pitch, the crowd hurling bottles at them in retaliation. A baffled Keith Weller told the *Daily Mail* 'everyone seemed to go potty the moment Santos scored. It was ten minutes before we could carry on. Even then the pitch was like a public thoroughfare'. He told the *Evening Standard* that Pele had intervened to protect a fan who was being batoned by the police.

Bonetti aggravated his damaged shoulder and had to miss the trip to Newcastle on the Saturday, a rather different experience climate-wise to Jamaica. Chelsea did not look tired after their midweek jaunt. Phillips came in and looked assured as the visitors won 1-0 through a very clever Hudson goal, audaciously side-footing the ball in from an acute angle after deceiving goalkeeper Iam McFaul into thinking he was going to pass it. Webb and Dempsey provided a solid partnership, Cooke and Hudson ran the midfield and the team looked comfortable playing 4-3-3. Phillips made three second-half saves and Harris's *Evening Standard* column praised him in what was only his second Chelsea first-team appearance. Hollins praised the team and, two weeks too late for the FA Cup, despite the absence of Osgood it looked as though Sexton had identified a system that worked.

The *Kensington News* looked at Hudson, who put the writer in mind of George Best, and had a warning for the fledgling star. 'He is taking well to the niche of soccer's new breed of superstar...But an image of this kind can really only be sustained by constant performances of note on the field. If they do not come, the chances are that all will fail before the public gaze'.

Another Sunday, another 'unhappy Baldwin' story, This time he told *The People* he had been dropped from the 'lucrative' first-team pool and had been accused by Sexton of not trying hard enough. 'I'm the one he always seems to leave out. I shall just wait till the end of the season to see if he'll let me go'. The *Chelsea News* reignited talk of a swap with Newcastle United winger Alan Foggon.

Managerial frustration with Hinton's mistakes against Manchester City was clear when 6ft. 4ins 19-year-old Micky Droy was called up for the Wolverhampton away trip the following week to replace the injured Harris, the match moved from April as both sides were out of the FA Cup. Droy had made just 13 reserve appearances. It was a tough debut, up against experienced strikers Hugh Curran and Derek Dougan, but he acquitted himself well and Phillips again demonstrated solidity. A spectacular Ken Hibbitt goal gave Wolverhampton all three points, Sexton again bemoaning missed chances.

Baldwin's spell in the reserves ended, for a while at least, when he broke his toe and was expected to be out for a month. This frustrated Tottenham assistant-manager Eddie Baily, who had gone to watch him. Even more frustrated was Newcastle manager Joe Harvey, who went to watch him in the first-team at Wolverhampton, unaware that he was not in the side. Hudson and Hutchinson were both selected for the Under-23 squad in Glasgow the following week.

In midweek came a home match against Nottingham Forest, who had won their last three games but were still in danger of relegation. Weller was demoted to the bench to allow Smethurst to start and a fit-again Harris replaced Droy. Driving rain, erratic recent form, unattractive opposition and a midweek evening kick-off combined to reduce those present to just 19,339, the lowest home gate of the season at that point. Liam O'Kane's own-goal gave Chelsea the lead, but they spluttered enough for the slow handclap to start before Hollins wrapped up the 2-0 lead late on. Weller went on for Hudson, who suffered a concerning recurrence of his shin problem.

Bonetti had recovered from his shoulder injury but caught flu which, nastily, turned into pneumonia so he was likely to be out for a while. Sexton saw the suspension of Osgood and absence of Bonetti as opportunities to give Smethurst and Phillips, as well as Droy, a chance. On Smethurst he made it clear that though a lot of attention had been paid to the chances he had missed, the manager preferred to focus on the fact that he got into the positions.

Weller came in for the injured Houseman at mid-table Stoke City, unbeaten at home for 19 games. Terry Conroy gave Stoke the lead just after half-time but, against expectations, Chelsea stepped up, Hutchinson equalised and Smethurst touched home Harris's cross for the winner. Another solid Phillips effort made it clear that Chelsea had got a bargain. Sexton praised his team and stated he would be satisfied with that form 'any day of the week'. Stoke manager Tony Waddington lauded Chelsea's sophistication and intelligence.

Hudson and Hutchinson duly played for England Under-23's in a 2-2 draw in Glasgow, but though Hutchinson's long throws caused problems and Hudson's corner led to a goal for Larry Lloyd, neither stood out.

A trip to Southampton to play the outfit that Liverpool boss Bill Shankly labelled 'animals' was always a test of resilience and courage, and this last game in February was to be no different. It was to have a significant impact on the career of one of Chelsea's star players and begged the question, again, on how the hosts were regularly allowed to get away with blatant fouling and sometimes outright brutality. The result, a 0-0 draw, was almost an afterthought, though Chelsea dominated for long spells and could have won. The visiting supporters made it clear what they thought, channelling their inner Shankly and chanting 'animals, animals'.

A collision with Mike Channon left Hutchinson rolling in agony and he was stretchered off. Absurdly bravely, he came back on but collapsed five minutes later and was carried off again, replaced by Boyle. He was diagnosed with a twisted knee, a serious injury that it was immediately feared might need a cartilage operation and keep him out for the rest of the season. Harris, kicked by Ron Davies, spent the rest of the match limping on the wing and suffered ligament damage.

The *Sunday Mirror*, under a 'Chelsea's Battle Of Saints and Sinners' headline, was appalled. 'Private feuds, kicks, punch-ups and injuries - this grim battle was a disgrace to soccer. There was needle on both sides as Chelsea collided with a stone-wall defence that gave nothing away'. They lost count of how many times Blues trainer Harry Medhurst had to go on the pitch to treat hurt players. Only two men were booked by referee Peter Walters, Davies and McCreadie.

Sexton commented afterwards that it was difficult for any side to go to Southampton and stay out of some sort of trouble and, extremely optimistically, felt Chelsea were still in the title race. The home side's Jimmy Gabriel retorted that since Shankly's comments, teams went to Southampton thinking they had got to be hard. He argued that 'Saturday was a 50-50 business'. If ever a team deserved to be punished as an entity, that team would surely be early 1970s Southampton.

Before their next home match, against West Bromwich, FA Disciplinary Committee chairman Vernon Stokes went into the dressing rooms at The Dell for an unprecedented visit to warn the players he expected a clean game with the referee's decisions accepted without question. Too little, too late. In the Ford Motor Company Sporting League, five points were deducted for a booking, ten for a sending off. To the surprise of nobody, at that stage Southampton had more points deducted (95) than any other First Division side. By comparison, Chelsea, seen as a pretty physical side, had 45 deducted, Leeds United 40.

The unlucky Paddy Mulligan had been out for 12 weeks with hamstring trouble but, after a couple of reserve appearances, he was now back on the treatment table so was in no position to replace the injured Harris. Hutchinson's injury and Osgood's suspension were good news for Baldwin, recovering from his broken toe. Newcastle had expressed definite interest in him, and it was thought he might fancy a return to his native North East, but there was no way Sexton could let him go with his two main strikers out. Queens Park Rangers were also interested.

Boyle was strongly linked with moves to both Crystal Palace and Tottenham but with Mulligan out was the obvious replacement for Harris so, as with Baldwin, there was no way he could be allowed to go. Brighton enquired about taking Tommy Hughes on loan, though with Bonetti's illness, he was required as cover for Phillips. Chelsea had watched centre-back Peter Allen, who Sexton had signed for Orient, as well as Aberdeen forward Davie Robb and 18-year-old Distillery midfielder Martin O'Neill.

Leeds United	p31 49pts
Arsenal	p30 44pts
Chelsea	**p31 39pts**
Wolves	p31 38pts
Liverpool	p30 35pts
Tottenham H.	p28 33pts
Southampton	p30 33pts

Seven points from five League games was a decent return, and third position was an improvement, but the title seemed out of reach. Tottenham beat Aston Villa 2-0 in the League Cup Final so unless the Fairs Cup one-city, one-club rule was finally abolished, as had been strongly rumoured, Chelsea's one route into Europe would be to win the Cup-Winners' Cup. March would bring the two legs of the Cup-Winner's Cup Quarter-Final against Bruges, crucial matches both.

March 1971

A welcome week off before a visit by bottom-placed Blackpool gave a chance to take stock of a deeply concerning fitness situation, exacerbated by the hugely challenging trip to Bruges the following Wednesday. Hutchinson was definitely out for a while, though it was not yet clear if he needed a cartilage operation, he was to see a specialist in a couple of weeks. Harris, in plaster with badly strained knee ligaments, might be back for the Bruges second-leg on March 24th, when Osgood would be free to return from suspension. Bonetti was convalescing from pneumonia in Portugal. As Sexton told the *Evening Standard* "It just goes to show that you can't have too many first-team players'.

Tommy Baldwin made a midweek comeback in the reserves and was immediately picked against Blackpool, Smethurst making his fourth appearance in a row alongside him. Boyle came in for Harris. After a first-half where Chelsea were lucky not to fall behind, Sexton gave the team a rocket and they were significantly better after the interval. Hudson inspired the improvement, which led to a 2-0 win through a Webb header and a Baldwin glanced header after a 'move of sheer soccer poetry' involving Hudson, Smethurst and Weller. There were concerns that Baldwin might have aggravated his toe problem but, fortunately, all those who played were fit for the Bruges trip.

Sexton still claimed that mathematically his team could still win the Championship, with only two of their last ten games outside London. It did not seem a convincing argument, given they were in third place but ten points behind Leeds, with just ten matches left, and three behind Arsenal who had two in hand. Leeds had imploded the previous season but that did not mean that would recur, and Arsenal were on excellent form.

Of all the stories Chelsea did not need that week, rumours in a number of papers about Sexton filling the vacant managerial post at Manchester United was right up there. Sir Matt Busby, in temporary charge at United after Wilf McGuinness's dismissal, denied the story, as did Chelsea chairman Brian Mears. It was an unwanted distraction but also a reminder about how highly Sexton was respected. He complained to the *Evening Standard* 'The rumour came at an unfortunate time as I am trying to achieve so much at Chelsea'. He also reiterated that 'Tommy (Baldwin) has never been available for transfer. There is no question of him leaving. We need him even if everyone is fit'.

Osgood used a guest column in the *Nottingham Football Post* to ponder his career going forward, under a 'Life Is Going To Be Tough' headline. 'I will be at the crossroads of my career when I play again. I am certain to be a marked man...It has never been easy avoiding the attention of certain defenders who provoke forwards in the hope of retaliation'. He admitted he had a fiery nature but was regularly kicked in the back of the legs or elbowed in the spine. Reiterating a point he had made elsewhere, he felt that the tackle from behind should be banned in Britain, as in the rest of the world. He was also concerned that players were forced to take the law into their own hands because they were not given adequate protection by referees. He was indeed a marked man, but he had an extremely valid point.

A *Sunday Mirror* Bruges preview, under a 'Don't Dismiss Chelsea Yet' headline, pointed out they were travelling to meet 'the muscular men of Bruges' while missing Bonetti, Osgood, Hutchinson, Houseman and captain Harris, still concerned he may not be fit for the second-leg. Luckily, they had 'one of the most powerful squads in Europe'. Hudson admitted the season had not been as good as expected. 'There have been signs in the last few weeks that we are beginning to click...We'll be in the Semi-Final, don't worry' was his confident analysis. He seemed to have finally shrugged off the constant run of injuries. 'In the last few weeks I've felt my confidence come flooding back...I (now) feel almost at peak form'. The *Evening Standard* reported that 51-year-old ground staff member Arthur Pitman was apparently chosen to be baggage man for the trip as he had seen Chelsea drop fewer away points than any of his colleagues.

The *Daily Telegraph* reiterated the hostility Chelsea were likely to face, on and off the pitch, against a side that had not lost at home in three years. The Klokke stadium 'has earned itself the reputation as one of the noisiest and most daunting in Europe'. Two years earlier Bruges supporters invaded the pitch against West Bromwich after their goalkeeper was charged. Jeff Astle was kicked by both players and supporters and had to be taken to hospital. Sexton, who had faith in his depleted team's spirit, was pleased with the way Smethurst had stood in for Osgood. He and Phillips were making their European debuts.

The match lived down to expectations, as 'Brawl As Chelsea Go Down' and 'Deplorable Scenes As Chelsea Crash In Bruges' headlines graphically showed. Raoul Lambert gave Bruges an early lead, Gilbert Marmenout netting a second before half-time. Baldwin hit the bar and missed other chances but was probably rushed back too quickly from his broken toe. The final whistle brought Bruges supporters spilling onto the pitch, some of the 1,700 travelling support reacting by brawling with them.

Chelsea were outclassed, well beaten and did not play well but returned home convinced that, with their injured and suspended stars back, they could claw back two goals in the second-leg against a team that had lost all six of its away ties in Europe. McCreadie warned that things would be quite different in London.

Phillips' assurance again impressed, to the extent that there was no guarantee Bonetti would get his place back once fully recovered.

Three days later, and still missing the four stars, a derby at Tottenham beckoned. Houseman was recalled after four games out, replacing Smethurst who had a difficult night in Bruges. Chelsea dominated the first-half and Weller enjoyed putting the visitors in front against his old club after half-time but late goals by Martin Peters and Martin Chivers meant they had done the double over Chelsea. Another example of lost concentration when leading. Weller's nose collided with Cyril Knowles's arm, but luckily without serious damage.

Hollins, a late call-up, played for the Football League against Scotland, showing he had not been forgotten by Sir Alf Ramsey. There was a stroke of luck for the club when Hollins and Boyle had their bookings against Crystal Palace wiped off after referee Keith Walker admitted he had mixed up the reports on their two respective incidents. Walker felt that, given this 'it is only right that…the players should have the benefit of the doubt'.

Osgood had lost five pounds in weight while suspended, telling the *Daily Mail* 'I have never worked harder in my life'. He was raring to go in the second-leg, two days after his suspension ended, but agreed 'I'm not sure whether they will risk me…maybe they'll want to throw me in for 30 minutes if things look desperate'. He again made the point that he knew he needed to stop retaliating but 'it is easy to say now that I won't retaliate…until it happens and I get hit again…I won't know until I'm involved…I need to prove I'm man enough to accept it. Otherwise I'm only damaging my career and my club. I've been out long enough'. The problem was, he had said all this before and, under severe provocation, lapsed. Actions would speak louder than words. After just four goals in 23 League games, he had a lot of catching up to do in a personally underwhelming season.

There was potentially good news a week before the Bruges return, as Ian Hutchinson was cleared by specialists to play again. The thinking was that he would not need a cartilage operation as originally feared. Training has gone well, he was expected to play in the reserves at Plymouth and, if there was no reaction, could be at least a substitute against Bruges. The club were delighted with his progress, though the thought he might be rushed back too quickly seemed to have been discounted.

Hudson recovered from gastroenteritis and was fit to start against lowly Huddersfield Town. Only 28,207 turned up, hoping for a form boost before the challenge of the following Wednesday night. What they got was a tedious 0-0 draw, slow handclapping, booing, jeering, and cries of rubbish. The team lacked heart and direction, causing concern not just about Bruges but the visit of table-topping Leeds the following Saturday. 'Chelsea had about as much rhythm as a busted drum' as the *Daily Telegraph* put it. The only bonus was that, apart from a bruised thigh for Webb, the players came through unscathed in terms of fitness. Weller, though, went down with flu and was doubtful for the big match.

Hutchinson started for the reserves at Plymouth, which was clearly a risk, and the worst thing that could have happened promptly did. He broke down, had to go off, would definitely miss Bruges and was probably out for the season. It is easy to be wise in retrospect, but the reality is that, because he was so brave, so willing and so important to the side, he was rushed back when what may have been most beneficial in the long-term would have been rest, treatment and proper recuperation.

The *Daily Telegraph* Bruges preview focused, as so often, on Osgood. 'Chelsea's wayward genius will bounce straight back to the centre of the stage'. He had spent much of the previous eight weeks training with the reserves and running on Epsom Downs. 'If the suspension has done anything, it has made me hungrier for goals'. He was clearly not match fit, but with Hutchinson ruled out he was desperately needed. Quickly pressing Harris back after four matches out with knee trouble was clearly a risk. Phillips retained his place, having done well in the last nine games, even though Bonetti had recovered from his bout of pneumonia. Webb was fit but leading scorer Weller had not recovered from flu, a worry as Chelsea needed to score at least twice and could not afford to concede as away goals counted double. If a play-off tie were needed, it would be at Stamford Bridge. Harris asked for the supporters to 'really let it rip' like at Old Trafford and the *Kensington News* felt 'the West London skinhead answer to the Vienna Boys choir must be in good voice'. They were in excellent voice.

45,558 paid £20,323, though there are those there that night who think the attendance, and hence the receipts, were somewhat higher. The Shed was absolutely rammed. In a raucous atmosphere Chelsea attacked from the off. Houseman scored after 20 minutes but, despite wave after wave of attacks the equaliser would not come. Dempsey had to go off with concussion and a cut-head at half-time, replaced by Boyle. As so often happened when goals were urgently needed, the piratical, never-say-die Webb was sent up front. The crowd bayed, the team pressed and pressed, and sent in high ball after high ball but, though chances were created, the critical goal would not come.

But then cometh the 81st minute, cometh the King. Substitute Boyle, constantly looking to overlap, pounded forward, his long cross was flicked on by Charlie Cooke and Osgood stabbed it home. Cue absolute bedlam. Bruges, clearly wilting, held on to force extra-time. Baldwin, in another Stakhanovite performance, hit the bar but Chelsea were resisted and a play-off the following week loomed. Home stamina began to tell and, finally, after 114 minutes, Chelsea went ahead. Hudson, in one of his greatest games, crossed for the irrepressible Osgood to put Chelsea ahead for the first time in the tie. Cue further absolute bedlam. Three minutes later Baldwin finished off a Hudson-Cooke move to cement a Semi-Final place. Amidst utter euphoria, hundreds invaded the pitch at the end as the support wildly celebrated inside, then outside, the ground.

Hudson in '*Working Man's Ballet*', Osgood in '*King Of Stamford Bridge*' and Albert Sewell in '*Chelsea Football Book No.2*' all eulogise in glowing terms about the supporters that night. Sexton, not a man prone to hyperbole, called them 'marvellous'. After the third goal Osgood 'jumped the dog track and fell to my knees and saluted the human cauldron that was The Shed. In that moment, the fans and I were one, united in euphoria. It was a special moment in my life'. It was also, arguably, his greatest moment at Stamford Bridge. His teammates, feeling he has been so harshly treated in terms of his suspension, shared his wild celebrations. Hudson reckoned 'the Chelsea crowd never gave us more fantastic support' than that night.

Supporters who have been watching the team for 50+ years still remember that night and the noise the crowd made. Here is a selection of their comments. 'Fantastic atmosphere'. 'Electric night, up there with the very best'. 'The best game I've ever been to'. 'Magnificent'. 'I was 11 years old and remember lying in bed in Battersea and heard the roar'. 'This was THE night at the Bridge'. 'It was the first time they were chanting in the stands. Fantastic'. 'In my 50+ years at the Bridge, the one that sticks with me for atmosphere'. Geoff Kimber, a matchgoing supporter for over half a century, thinks it one of the top five matches he has ever seen, certainly in terms of atmosphere and excitement. Fellow supporter Brian Gaches recalls the 'astonishing' support and reckons 'anyone who was there will never forget it – it remains in my top five best ever games seen at Stamford Bridge'. A fantastic result, a magnificent exhibition of spirit and talent and a place in the Semi-Final. The risks taken on the fitness of Osgood and Harris had gloriously come off. The Leeds programme felt, rightly, that that night 'belonged among the great occasions in the history of football played at Stamford Bridge'. 50 years later, many supporters think it still is. Sadly, no TV footage of the tie seems to exist.

The Semi-Final opposition was not decided, as Chelsea were drawn against the winners of a play-off between holders Manchester City or Polish side Gornik Zabrze, the first-leg being at Stamford Bridge in three weeks' time after three away first-legs. City won 3-1, meaning an all-English Semi-Final. A tough draw, but a chance to revenge the embarrassing January FA Cup defeat.

After the breathless excitement of the Wednesday night, Sexton's men had less than 72 hours to recover from 120 minutes high-tempo football before facing table-topping title favourites Leeds United. Interest was immense, 58,452 squeezing into the ground. It was to the enormous credit of an unchanged side, Dempsey having recovered, that they comprehensively won 3-1, opening up the title race for second placed Arsenal, who Chelsea had to visit a week later.

Houseman, on top form, scored after six minutes, again benefitting from a Gary Sprake error. Osgood, who was on superb form, danced round Sprake for the second and set up Houseman, who played brilliantly, for the third. Terry Cooper's goal was no consolation for Leeds, who knew this defeat could have serious ramifications in terms of their title aspirations. A delighted crowd gave the team a standing ovation at the end. Leeds, particularly in the first-half, were outclassed. Phillips again impressed, he had the supporters on his side, and it was hard to see how Bonetti, in the reserves, was going to replace him.

Cooke was probably the most intellectual and erudite Football League star at the time. He sufficiently intrigued *Vogue*, doyen of the fashion magazines, for Osgood's agent Greg Tesser, who did some work for Cooke as well, to liaise with the Scot on a short article, with photo, that appeared in the March 1971 edition. The piece covers the period in the dressing room before kick-off and Cooke was open about the nerves and tension he and other players felt. He also talked about the guilt and day of reckoning for the times you worked less hard than you might in training.

Young goalkeeper Alan Dovey, previously on loan at Folkestone, was loaned to Brighton for the rest of the season. Apprentice midfielder Garry Stanley signed as a full professional. Wimbledon of the Southern League were ambitiously thinking about Marvin Hinton, out of the first-team picture but clearly still of a high standard, as a possible player-manager. Sexton and Suart watched Fulham's Steve Earle against Bristol Rovers, not for the first time. Tottenham were reported to be interested in Boyle, though that, like so many paper transfer rumours, went nowhere.

Chairman Mears made a presentation of an inscribed silver salver to ex-Secretary John Battersby at the Bruges tie. Battersby became a sub-postmaster in Devon, which given his almost-unrivalled experience and knowledge of top-flight football, seemed a waste.

A tempestuous, eventful March ended on two euphoric highs. When the team clicked, they could beat almost anybody. When they didn't, as against Huddersfield, they were pretty hopeless. The inconsistency had still not been eradicated. What mattered most, though, was that they were in a European Semi-Final and also in third place in the League.

Leeds United	p35 54pts
Arsenal	p32 48pts
Chelsea	**p35 44pts**
Wolves	p34 43pts
Liverpool	p33 39pts
Southampton	p34 39pts
Tottenham H.	p32 38pts

April 1971

Double contenders Arsenal had a superb home League record, conceding just six goals all season, scoring 35, and dropping just three points. The trip to North London was clearly going to be tough, very tough, even if Sexton's unchanged side were at their best. The gates closed 30 minutes before kick-off on 62,087 spectators, Arsenal's biggest attendance in three years. Eddie McCreadie made his 350th first-team appearance for Chelsea. They lost 2-0 and were lucky it was not more as they were outplayed and outclassed. Peter Osgood's ongoing feud with Frank McLintock continued, Osgood barging the Arsenal captain to the ground. There were briefly fears the Scot had broken his arm, a nightmare with the FA Cup Final looming, but luckily for him it was just a damaged nerve.

Jimmy Hill, on *The Big Match*, criticised Ron Harris and Osgood for robust challenges, but failed to comment on similar physicality from Peter Storey and Charlie George. Maybe his composition of Arsenal's execrable '*Good Old Arsenal*' FA Cup song had affected his impartiality.

Chelsea and Manchester City were both rightly furious when they both had League games arranged on the Saturday and the Monday before the Cup-Winners' Cup Semi-Final first-leg on Wednesday April 14th. Chelsea had home encounters with Crystal Palace and Liverpool and given their bad luck with injuries that season, Sexton was rightly worried that he was going to lose key players. Why the Football League could not postpone the relevant Easter Monday games by a week was never explained.

Peter Bonetti was determined to win his first-team place back from John Phillips and denied he sought a move, after reports appeared that Leeds United were interested in signing him. He had been out of the first-team since January 30th but was now fully fit. He felt he and other England stars had suffered a reaction after returning from the World Cup.

Osgood and John Hollins were selected for the full England squad for the European Nations Cup-tie against Greece on April 21st. The FA International Committee made a statement that Osgood had been sufficiently punished, and should not be debarred from England call-ups, which was only fair, but a massive relief to the player all the same.

Unluckily, the fear that injury would strike before the Semi-Final was realised when Osgood damaged ankle ligaments early on against Palace and had to be replaced by Keith Weller. He watched the rest of the 1-1 draw with his foot in plaster. As the first-leg was just four days off, his chance of recovery was limited. Webb was sent up front and equalised Jim Scott's goal. The team did not play well, the absence of both Osgood and Ian Hutchinson severely limiting the striking potency. Eddie McCreadie was unfit, John Boyle coming in. Ex-Blue Bobby **Tambling, playing up front for the visitors, was presented with an illuminated address by chairman Brian Mears to mark his 202 Chelsea goals.**

For the unwanted Liverpool game two days later, Webb went up front and Micky Droy came in for his home debut. Derek Smethurst replaced Osgood, Weller remaining on the bench. Bonetti made his first appearance for ten weeks, but Sexton made it clear Phillips would start against Manchester City. Smethurst justified his selection with the only goal of a boring match, though it was credited in some quarters as an

Alec Lindsay own-goal. Of most managerial concern, however, was Hudson limping off with a badly bruised knee with ten minutes left. City had a number of injury troubles of their own, including Colin Bell, Mike Summerbee and Mike Doyle, so the ludicrous fixture congestion adversely affected both sides. The dismal parochialism of Football League Secretary Alan Hardaker and his blazered sidekicks certainly did English clubs competing in Europe no favours.

Webb was happy to start as a striker in the first-leg against City, telling the *Daily Mail* 'give me the job and I'll run myself into the ground for the goals...I'll play anywhere in this game'. He thought it is 'bound to be a classic game'. Harris asked 'what we want is plenty of encouragement to help us to a two-goal lead for the next leg. The crowd pushed us through against Bruges and can do so again'. Kick-off was moved back to 19.45 to allow more time for the post-work/school crowd to get in, the match not being all-ticket, and the gates opened at 17.45 to facilitate this.

The absence of Osgood and Hutchinson meant Webb duly wore the No.9 shirt. Baldwin and Weller were on the bench, Smethurst started. Droy came in alongside Dempsey and had seemingly moved ahead of Marvin Hinton in the centre-back pecking order.

A makeshift side lined up: **Phillips; Boyle, Dempsey, Droy, Harris; Cooke, Hollins, Hudson; Smethurst, Webb, Houseman.**

Bizarrely, only 45,595 turned up (16,000 below the season high against Tottenham and 6,000 below the League crowd against City). Receipts were £33,995, a ground record, but it was still a massive surprise that Stamford Bridge was not packed for as big a match as the stadium had hosted in years. Increased ticket prices may well have affected the attendance, terrace admission being increased from 30p to 50p and seat prices proportionately higher. It is hard to blame the club for trying to cash in on such a big night, but a 66% increase was always likely to deter some regulars. Though the players achieved £180 a head bonus on the basis of £4 per thousand supporters, they must have been hoping for £40 a head more.

Chelsea attacked but a weakened City team defended well, and goalkeeper Joe Corrigan demonstrated exactly why he was so highly-rated. City made seven passes back to Corrigan in the first six minutes, so their intentions were pretty clear. Weller made a difference when he went on for Cooke at half-time, immediately working with Webb to set up Smethurst to score a potentially crucial goal. City held on and were probably the happier with Chelsea's 1-0 win at the end. Supporter Bob Barlow remembers how good Chelsea were that night and how they deserved a bigger lead.

It was touch-and-go whether 1-0 was sufficient, though Sexton was happy with the clean sheet and with the display of Droy. Chelsea had grossed over £90,000 from their four home European ties, even more incentive for the club to achieve European qualification the following season.

A quirk of the fixture list had Chelsea visiting City three days later for a League encounter. Webb played up front again. McCreadie, Baldwin and Weller returned, the latter scoring an unusual 55th minute goal, shooting the ball into the net and his boot over the bar at the same time. He contrived to hurt his heel doing this and was replaced by Droy. Lee scored a controversial equaliser ten minutes from the end. A scrappy match, but Chelsea would have won but for another strong Corrigan display and a string of missed chances by Smethurst and Baldwin.

Another clear midweek, followed by two home games, Coventry on the Saturday and Burnley two days later, then the second-leg on at City on the Wednesday. This schedule meant both League games were likely to involve reserves in an attempt to minimise the risk of further injuries.

Osgood was passed fit to join Hollins in the England squad for the Greece match that week, though neither played nor was anything approaching first choice for Sir Alf Ramsey. The fit-again Bonetti's international career seemed to have ended as Peter Shilton was chosen as cover to Gordon Banks.

One piece of bad but inevitable news was that Hutchinson needed a cartilage operation on the knee he damaged against Southampton seven weeks earlier. He was clearly out for the season and the challenge now was to ensure his full fitness for the start of the following one. He also had the steel plate removed from his right arm, inserted after he broke it against Nottingham Forest.

Baldwin injured his ankle in training, and it needed to be put in plaster, making him doubtful for Maine Road. Osgood was still out with his own ankle problem so 21-year-old reserve Peter Feely was chosen up front alongside Smethurst against Coventry, in as inexperienced a front two as Chelsea had picked for some years. Feely had scored nine goals in 21 reserve appearances but there were basically few other options. He had cracked an ankle bone in August but had fully recovered.

Phillips had hurt his back, so Bonetti returned. Under the circumstances a 2-1 win was not a bad result, Smethurst and debutant Feely scoring in two second-half minutes, the latter's goal going in off his back, as Chelsea retained third place. Very worryingly, Hollins hurt his knee before the interval. He bravely carried on but had to go off after half-time and was diagnosed with damaged ligaments. His energy and drive would be extremely hard to replace if he was unfit for Athens. Boyle was the obvious cover, though he had been performing solidly at full-back. Hollins was substituted by McCreadie, himself still struggling for full fitness.

Sexton had a growing set of fitness issues he could do well do without. No Hutchinson until the following season. Osgood still unfit. Baldwin in plaster. Hollins with damaged knee ligaments. Phillips with a bad back. Weller played in pain against Coventry and had possible achilles trouble.

The Burnley home game usually attracted one of the lowest crowds of the season and this was no exception, but 14,356 was not a great send-off to the team two days before the second-leg, though to be fair it was the last, and arguably least attractive, of five matches in 16 days at Stamford Bridge. McCreadie, Droy, Phillips and Osgood came in. Chelsea, perhaps understandably, seemed distracted and lost 1-0, Steve Kindon scoring after the interval, following a misjudged back-pass by Droy, for an already-relegated visiting side. Osgood disconsolately limped off with 15 minutes left, replaced by Mulligan. McCreadie, so desperately unlucky that season, got another knock and was doubtful for Manchester, as was Droy.

If a play-off were necessary, it would be at Villa Park the following week, but Sexton was confident his team could prevail. Seven special trains and a host of coaches helped transport an estimated 10,000 Chelsea supporters to Manchester. In the end, a patchwork side, missing McCreadie, Hollins, Osgood, Hutchinson and Baldwin, faced an equally patchwork outfit missing Joe Corrigan, Bell, Glyn Pardoe, Alan Oakes and Tommy Booth. Mulligan made his first start for almost six months and Weller was passed fit.

Chelsea lined up: Phillips; Mulligan, Dempsey, Webb, Harris; Cooke, Boyle, Hudson; Weller, Smethurst, Houseman.

To their great credit, Chelsea coped with the absence of star players far better and dominated proceedings, forcing seven first-half corners to one. Smethurst had a goal disallowed for offside before the visitors scored the only goal of the night just before half-time, when reserve City goalkeeper Ron Healey fumbled a Weller indirect free-kick into his own net – if he had left the ball, it would not have counted. City, without Bell, had little inspiration and Chelsea won comfortably. The team had run themselves into the ground and Houseman was so exhausted, his face was blue in the dressing room afterwards and he would have been given oxygen if any were available. Harris told the *Fulham Chronicle* it was their best away performance of the season.

A superb result, and one Sexton and the travelling supporters had every right to be hugely proud of. Apart from a trip to Ipswich on the Saturday the manager had three weeks to rest his fit squad members and hope the medical staff could work their magic on the unfit ones. The Final was in Athens on Wednesday May 19th, the opponents the mighty Real Madrid, the most famous club in the world. Though a comparative shadow of the team that won the first five European Cups in the late 1950s, they still had Francisco Gento from that side and a world-class forward in Amancio.

Queens Park Rangers were the latest club to express interest in Bonetti, should Chelsea or the player feel Phillips had supplanted him as first choice. He could hardly be blamed for not wanting to play second fiddle. Much would depend on who played in Athens. Chelsea were keeping an eye on highly-rated young Hartlepool centre-half Bill Green, Partick Thistle midfielder Charlie Smith, and Hearts full-back Dave Clunie. Sexton went to watch Fulham play Rochdale, checking on Rochdale's Norman Whitehead, but left impressed with a man he had seen plenty of times - Steve Earle.

Ticket prices for the following season were unchanged, a generous gesture by the board considering inflation was running at around 9%. The Chelsea Pool was already the third largest English football club competition, which boded well for fundraising for the redevelopment of Stamford Bridge.

The FA announced, nearly a year after the event, that Hudson would receive 'a' medal but not 'the' medal after missing the 1970 FA Cup Final through injury. Sexton was disappointed, rightly feeling that anyone who had played two or three FA Cup-ties in the run to Wembley deserved one. Consolation for Hudson was that he was finally back to his pre-injury form, perfectly timed for the forthcoming Athens trip.

So an exhausting, if triumphant, April came to an end. Eight matches, five at home. Four wins, two draws, two defeats. Crucially, though, there were wins in the two games that mattered most, which meant the club, and the more intrepid or wealthy of its supporters, could look forward to a mid-May trip to Athens. Third place would a decent final position, though retaining it depended on beating Ipswich Town away in the last League encounter of the season and Tottenham not winning their games in hand. The title race was going to the final day, Arsenal having gradually clawed back Leeds' lead.

Leeds United	p41 62pts
Arsenal	p40 61pts
Chelsea	**p41 50pts**
Wolves	p41 50pts
Liverpool	p41 49pts
Tottenham H.	p39 48pts
Southampton	p41 44pts

May 1971

A tedious 0-0 draw with six first-teamers missing against an Ipswich side with nothing to play for, having already avoided relegation, meant Chelsea finished sixth in the final table, their worst position for four months and a disappointment given they had spent much of the season in the top four. It also meant that the only way to achieve European football the following season was to win in Athens. Real were knocked out of the Spanish Cup by Deportivo La Corunna so they, too, needed to win to qualify for Europe.

An insipid performance was perhaps understandable given the importance of avoiding injury and the fact that six regulars were missing.

The Real Madrid manager and directors attended but they would not have learned very much. Peter Bonetti came back in for John Phillips, hoping to impress Sexton before Athens, and made a series of important saves. The goalkeeping decision was a genuinely tough one.

Osgood missed the Ipswich trip, but came in for Bonetti's testimonial against Standard Liege four days later. A decent 18,363 turned out to watch a strong Chelsea line-up lose 2-1 to the Belgian side, raising over £10,000 for Bonetti in the process. Supporters from 'The Shed' presented him with a pair of gold cufflinks. What mattered to Sexton, though, was his players remaining fit so he must have been sickened when Osgood limped off before half-time with a damaged ankle, replaced by a fit-again Tommy Baldwin, though trainer Harry Medhurst was hopeful that their most high-profile star would be fit for the biggest occasion of his career in a fortnight's time.

Hollins and Osgood were called into the England squad for the game against Malta, a week before Athens, followed by the three Home Internationals but, given their fitness struggles, there was no chance of them meeting up with Ramsey's party, let alone playing.

The squad were given time off to rest and recuperate from nine matches in 29 days before reconvening to prepare for the biggest club occasion of any of their careers to date. With 58 games played already that season, a litany of injuries to key players, some temporary losses of form (for example Webb, Hudson, Osgood and Cooke) and Osgood's lengthy suspension, it had been a long, draining nine months. Sexton's task was to raise his men such that they were physically and mentally fresh for the challenges Real Madrid would bring. He watched their opponents beat St Johnstone 3-1 in a friendly and predicted Chelsea would beat them 2-1.

The uncertainty as to whether Osgood and Hollins, who was swimming every day, would be fit meant the manager could not finalise his line-up or his tactics. There were also doubts about Dempsey, though he was passed fully fit. Sexton also needed to decide on his goalkeeper. The incredibly unfortunate McCreadie broke his nose in training and was unavailable for selection. Five substitutes could be named and two used.

The team's flight out the day before the game was delayed an hour after a passenger checked bags in but did not turn up, the crew fearing Chelsea might be the target of a terrorist act. It was hoped locals, who would make up the majority of the crowd, would support Chelsea, looking, perhaps optimistically, for reciprocity when Panathinaikos faced Ajax in the European Cup Final at Wembley in a fortnight's time.

In the end, after fitness tests, both Hollins and Osgood were declared fit though there were concerns about whether the former, particularly, could last 90 minutes and the latter needed a cortisone injection to be able to play. Bonetti was chosen ahead of Phillips, to the huge frustration of the Welshman, who had let nobody down in his 18 appearances that season and had gained the confidence of his teammates. Reg Drury in the *News Of The World* felt that Bonetti's experience was the clincher, together with maybe a feeling that Phillips' time for honours would come.

Real's average age was over 30, four years older than Chelsea, and it was hoped that stamina might become an issue as the match progressed. Sexton had told his team the pitch was in poor condition to pleasantly surprise them when they saw it was a decent one.

Chelsea took 6,000 tickets, Real just 2,000 and the *Kensington Post* estimated that up to 5,000 Blues supporters travelled to Greece. 2,000 were flown out from London by 4S, the biggest sports tour operator. The cost for their two night stay plus flights was £39, flying out on the Tuesday and home on the Thursday. The *Daily Mail* featured 14-year-old paper boy Piers Fletcher, who saved his money to pay his own fare. Others booked a longer trip, not flying home until the weekend. Some devotees hitch-hiked there and back from London.

The FA, predictably, had refused to allow the Final to be shown on television in the UK as England were facing Wales the same evening, so the only place to follow the whole game live was on BBC Radio London, with commentary by Chelsea programme editor Albert Sewell and Michael Field. A request to allow CCTV screenings in cinemas was also, inevitably, refused for the same reason.

The team lined up:- Bonetti; Boyle, Dempsey, Webb, Harris; Hollins, Hudson, Cooke; Weller, Osgood, Houseman. Phillips, Mulligan, Hinton, Baldwin and Smethurst were the five substitutes, of whom two could be used.

It fairly quickly became clear that the skills of Amancio, Velazquez, Zoco and Gento were causing problems and that Hollins and Osgood were affected by the injuries they were carrying. Only Cooke stood out for Chelsea in an attacking sense, so it was a slight surprise when Osgood put the English side ahead after 56 minutes, brilliantly hooking home Boyle's cross and celebrating with a somersault.

Harris was booked for a foul, Chelsea were hanging on and with two minutes remaining the struggling Osgood was replaced by Baldwin. A minute later Dempsey mis-kicked, allowing Zoco to equalise, just as the guard of honour was starting to line up for the presentation ceremony. The final whistle went before a shattered Chelsea could restart the game. Seconds away from glory, they had to hang on in extra-time, Webb clearing off the line twice. Hollins, clearly struggling, was replaced by Mulligan at half-time in extra-time. Sexton praised the heroic Webb for saving the situation in extra-time and was extremely bullish about the replay 48 hours later. 'We will do them in the replay. We have survived their great moment and we are going to win the cup'.

The biggest cheer at the England v Wales game at Wembley was when the scoreboard flashed up that Chelsea were ahead. The Greek spectators did indeed support Chelsea, but it became clear that most of the supporters who had flown out from London were booked on charter flights the following day that could not be amended and would therefore miss the replay, despite desperate pleas to the travel agents. Aviation regulations meant that charter flights could not be rescheduled. Only around 400 supporters were booked on flights that went back at the weekend, though plenty of others deliberately missed their flight, slept on the beach and worried later about how to get home.

The team relaxed on the Thursday. Some went shopping, some met their wives, Baldwin, Cooke and Osgood drank by the pool, but the team got the events of the previous evening out of their minds and systems and Sexton managed to turn the squad's inevitable bitter disappointment into a hungry desire to finish the job.

Hinton stood by as Dempsey had a troublesome ankle but, in the end, he, Osgood, Weller, Houseman and Hudson, all of whom required treatment, were passed fit to play. Once it became clear Hollins was not going to be fit, despite a pain-killing injection, Sexton had a choice. Bring in Mulligan at full-back and field Boyle in midfield or draft in Baldwin. In the end he chose the latter, Osgood dropping back into midfield. Pirri played in plaster after sustaining a broken hand in a collision with Bonetti who, with Webb and Boyle, was praised for his heroics in extra-time.

The replay was to be shown on BBC 1, depriving millions of the delights of '*Me Mammy*' with Milo O'Shea. Hollins was hired to provide a Chelsea perspective to the TV viewers. It was announced that if the tie was level after extra-time, the winners would be decided on penalties. Only 24,000 attended the replay, compared with the 45,000 who had been there on the Wednesday. Amancio opined before the replay 'If we stop Cooke, we will win', forgetting that Chelsea had more than one star.

Chelsea dominated much of the replay and thoroughly deserved to win, taking a 2-0 lead before half-time. Dempsey volleyed the first from a punch by goalkeeper Borja after Cooke's corner, only his fifth goal in 105 appearances for the club and, obviously, by far the most important. Osgood kept up his happy knack of scoring in finals with the second from 20 yards after sending three defenders the wrong way, but had to go off late on, replaced by Smethurst. They conceded after 75 minutes through Sebastian Fleitas but held on for a 2-1 win thanks largely to two inspired saves by the recalled Bonetti.

The tactical change of Osgood playing in midfield worked but it was the competitiveness, courage, fitness and desire of Sexton's men that won them the trophy, wearing down their Spanish rivals. Talking to the *Daily Mail*, an exultant manager called it 'a triumph that makes me even happier than winning the FA Cup...This means we go straight into Europe again...We set out to attack, took the initiative and here we are with a European trophy'. Real coach Miguel Munoz blamed the referee who turned down a penalty appeal when Harris floored Amancio, but the victorious captain rightly argued 'we deserved the victory. We were much better tonight than in Wednesday's match'.

Webb, Cooke and Boyle came in for especial praise and Osgood singled out Bonetti and Hudson for their performances. The *Sunday Mirror* argued that Boyle's efforts against the legendary Francisco Gento, last survivor of the great 1950s side, showed he must have a permanent future at the club. At the final whistle, Boyle managed to swap shirts with the great man. The pictures of the exultant players parading the trophy round the Karaiskakis Stadium make clear the sheer joy the victorious team were experiencing.

The team celebrated late and loud, drinking Cuba Libre's in the Athens Hilton. At home, there were wild scenes in the Kings' Road and Fulham Road, with traffic brought to a complete halt. The team flew home to another victory parade in an open top bus, chairman Brian Mears telling the mayor 'this is the second time in 12 months you have honoured us - and I think we ought to make this an annual fixture'.

As so often, Hugh McIlvanney, in *The Observer*, caught the underlying mood so well. He listened to the team praise Webb and Cooke in 'a persistent stream of emotionally sincere tributes'. They were quite different sorts of players. His friend Cooke 'a man to whom the highest skills of the game are as basic as his blood...(His problem is) forcing himself to accept the responsibility that goes with such a talent'.

Webb argued his game was '80% physical'. McIlvanney saw this as a gross exaggeration. 'What he has in unsurpassed abundance are heart and will and honesty...(His) alertness, self-sacrificing mobility and absolute rejection of defeat warded off an unjust defeat', particularly in extra-time of the first match and the second-half of the replay. Webb did most to save it, Cooke most to win it...A team that as a whole had done so well by British football'. Osgood was laudatory in his praise of Cooke. McIlvanney pointed out that 'Chelsea reminded us in Athens that the highest rewards can be won by flair and grace and boldness'.

He pointed out one issue of concern to every Chelsea board member, player, employee and supporter. 'The assumption that Dave Sexton is on his way to Old Trafford becomes more widespread every day'. He did point out, though, that 'if the qualities available to him at Stamford Bridge continue to cover the gamut from those of Webb to those of Cooke, he should not be in any rush to change his colours'.

In one final piece of transfer business that season, third-choice goalkeeper Tommy Hughes moved to Aston Villa for £12,500. A friendly at Slough Town three days after the replay, part of the Micky Droy deal, involved a strong Chelsea side containing most of the Athens heroes playing out a 2-2 draw. The squad then had a week to recuperate and/or celebrate before a close season tour to El Salvador and Trinidad, where they played Southampton twice, but unlike recent League encounters with the Saints managed to avoid serious injury, and both national sides.

The squad of 18 received £1,500 a man (before tax) for winning the Cup-Winners' Cup. Originally their contracts had only stipulated £200 a man. A delighted Mears reckoned the club would clear £115,000 from the run and beamed Sexton is 'the best manager Chelsea ever had'. The manager, rightly, saw it as a greater achievement than FA Cup glory as it put Chelsea firmly on the European map, beating such diverse opponents en route to picking up the trophy. He used 19 players in the successful cup run, demonstrating again the importance of a large squad. He proclaimed that 'our ambition is to win the Football League championship'. Indeed.

Season Summary

Arsenal	p42 65pts
Leeds United	p42 64pts
Tottenham H.	p42 52pts
Wolves	p42 52pts
Liverpool	p42 51pts
Chelsea	**p42 51pts**
Southampton	p42 46pts

A season that started on August 8th with Charity Shield defeat and ended an exhausting 60 matches and 41 weeks later on May 21st with European triumph was clearly no ordinary one. Given the run of injuries and illness that deprived Sexton, at various times, of most of the squad, some for extended periods, the benefit of his strategy of a large group of experienced players was clear. Add in Osgood's two-month suspension and it seems clear that if Chelsea only had a small, tight squad they simply could not have won the Cup-Winners' Cup. It also helped that the likes of David Webb, Ron Harris, John Boyle, John Hollins, Peter Osgood, Peter Houseman, Keith Weller and Charlie Cooke could play in more than one position.

The win in Athens was the pinnacle of the Chelsea careers of the 14 men who took part in one or both of the matches. It happened because a group of exceptionally good players were extremely well coached and possessed the never-say-die spirit needed when backs were against the wall, as exemplified by Webb, Harris and Boyle. Add in the sheer quality of football the likes of Hudson, Osgood and Cooke could produce and the consistency of Bonetti, Hollins, Weller and Houseman and you had a heck of a team. In reality, they under-achieved in the League and the FA Cup and, arguably, the League Cup though the relentless two-games-a-week schedule that did for Leeds the previous season meant it was almost impossible to compete on three fronts, and they did bounce back well from the trauma of the Manchester City cup defeat. Arsenal, however, did the next best thing that year, winning the League and FA Cup double, an achievement that set the benchmark for Sexton and his peers.

John Hollins easily won the 'Player Of The Year' award from Chelsea Supporters Club, for the second year running, with Weller runner-up and Hutchinson third, deserved reward for consistency over a long season.

There were still flaws. Up front, Osgood scored just 5 League goals, Hutchinson 3, Baldwin 2. Weller, a resounding success, scored 13 and the ultra-reliable Hollins 6, including Goal Of The Season. 52 League goals was a mediocre total, comparing unfavourably with Arsenal and Leeds, both of whom scored over 70. 14 First Division players scored more League goals than any Chelsea striker, certainly food for thought for Sexton.

42 goals conceded may have been Chelsea's best record in the top flight since World War Two, but was probably too many for a side to make a serious tilt at the title, especially when compounded with the comparative lack of goals. Sexton persisted with Hinton and zonal marking but, after City dumped them out of the cup, left him out for the rest of the season.

The regular team, in terms of most League appearances, was:- Bonetti; Webb, Dempsey, Hinton, Harris; Hudson, Hollins, Houseman; Cooke, Osgood, Weller. Sub. Hutchinson.

The fact that Hutchinson, in a hospital bed after his cartilage operation when Harris picked up the trophy, was only fit to start half the League games was a growing worry. He was crucial to the team's play, working so effectively with Osgood and it was to be fervently hoped that a summer's recovery would enable him to start the next season afresh. Osgood had problems of his own, seemingly a marked man for opponents who would systematically wind him up with persistent fouling and niggling, knowing how short his fuse could be. It was essential he learned to turn the other cheek, no matter how unpalatable this was, to avoid more suspensions like the massive one he, and the club, had to endure in the New Year.

The gap in points to Leeds and Arsenal was still significant and by slipping from third to sixth place was arguably getting bigger. The tail-off in League form towards the season end was understandable given injuries and the focus on Europe, but still Chelsea seemed to have the spirit to win cup-ties but not the grinding persistence to win sufficient matches to make a serious run for the title that lasted to the business end of the season.

Supporter Brian Gaches remembers that The European Cup-Winner's Cup saved the season, albeit gloriously. Winning a trophy glossed over the fact that results and performances in the League and domestic cups were mixed at best, and short of the high expectations supporters had at the start of the season. The average League attendance was down 800, a disappointment, and the club slipped to fifth in the attendance table. Arsenal's average increased by 8,000 in a clear indication of the potential impact of success on gates.

Sexton had brought a European trophy to the club, the first man to do so. He had won two major trophies in two seasons, doubling the club's all-time tally. The challenge now was to continue to gather trophies whilst at the same time make a consistent, long-term challenge for the title. He told the *News Of The World Football Annual* that 'surely winning (the League) is not beyond us'. He also told them that he saw Phillips, Smethurst and Hudson as possessing the quality he looked for in young players, and that there was also a good-looking crop of apprentices and young professionals working their way through the junior system.

The future indeed appeared bright. Appearances, though, could be very deceptive.

Season Overview 1970-71

League Appearances (inc sub) (top 11 players) – Hollins 40, Harris 38, Houseman 37, Weller 36, Hudson 34, Webb 34, Cooke 31, Dempsey 31, Bonetti 28, Osgood 27, Boyle 20, Hinton 20, Hutchinson 20

League Goals (5+) – Weller 13, Hollins 6, Hutchinson 5, Osgood 5
League Clean Sheets – 11
Biggest League Win – 4-1 v West Bromwich Albion (H) 30/01/71
Worst League Defeat – 0-3 v Everton (A) 16/01/71

Final League position – 6th
League Record –
Home W12 D6 L3 F34 A21. *Away* W6 D9 L6 F18 A21. Pts 51

Hat-Tricks – None

Sending Offs – Dempsey v Aris Salonika (A), Cup-Winner's Cup First Round, first-leg 16/09/70

Biggest Home League Crowd – 61,277 v Tottenham Hotspur 14/11/70
Smallest Home League Crowd – 14,356 v Burnley 26/04/71
Average Home League Crowd – 39,545

Cup Performances –
FA Cup – 4th Round
League Cup – 4th Round
Europe (European Cup-Winners' Cup) – Winners

Chelsea League Debuts – Micky Droy, Peter Feely, John Phillips, Derek Smethurst, Keith Weller

Player Of The Year – John Hollins

CHAPTER FIVE
In Hindsight

Dave Sexton

Dave Sexton seems underappreciated when discussions take place about great Chelsea managers. He did not possess a high public profile in the way that contemporaries like Bill Shankly and Matt Busby did or the likes of Tommy Docherty, Jose Mourinho or Frank Lampard have had at Stamford Bridge. He was a thoughtful, reserved, intelligent man who, crucially, was a brilliant coach and master tactician. The man management aspects of the job probably appealed less, especially given the occasionally wayward behaviour of several squad members, but he loved coaching, improving players and working on tactical plans, practising drills until they became second nature.

Those he inherited from Docherty were full of praise for Sexton's technical expertise. In *'The Chelsea Experience'* Peter Bonetti called him 'the best manager he played under', a great tactician and a great coach. Ron Harris praised him for sending players on coaching courses. In *'The Special Ones'* Peter Osgood, later to fall out spectacularly with him, admitted 'Dave was the best coach I ever worked under, an absolute genius as a coach'. Charlie Cooke pointed out in *'The Bonnie Prince'* that the squad was delighted by his appointment and John Boyle felt he was a very decent man and a wonderful tactician.

Harris, in *'Soccer The Hard Way'* (published in 1970) reiterated that Sexton was big on practising and repeating set pieces. He did a lot more tactical work than Docherty, drilling and coaching, so training was not as physically hard as under The Doc. 'I think everyone likes and respects Dave Sexton' he reflected. 'Dave Sexton wasn't happy in the spotlight' according to programme editor Albert Sewell, in *'Chelsea - The Official Biography'*. 'He was happy with the players, in the dressing rooms, but once he came out of the dressing room, he found it hard work'.

'Kings Of the King's Road' details how Sexton had a sign on his office wall pointing out that 'When the going gets tough, the tough get tougher'. He later said that he chose a method of playing that suited his squad. His approach was to work to toughen the skilful players and make the tough guys better footballers. He knew that the skills of Osgood, Alan Hudson and Cooke were not enough, on their own, to win trophies. *'Rhapsody In Blue'* made the point that 'Dave Sexton, in his monastic, methodical way, was intent on bringing the club the serious success it craved'.

SEXTON FOR GOD

In *'Chelsea Football Club - The Official History In Pictures'* Sexton reminisced about the trophy-winning side. 'I don't think I have ever been suspicious of glamorous or good players...Basically we all went there, we rolled our sleeves up and we had a go and it worked very well. We had enough skill to give pleasure and we had enough hard work in us to fight for things. So it worked out ok'. In *'The Chelsea Football Book'*, chairman Brian Mears enthused 'Dave is a strong character with a lot of depth to him...and brought in the players that...would stiffen the team up and make us better'. He had worked with Webb and Dempsey before, and trusted them, so there was less risk. He liked playing wingers, so Houseman became a regular within a year of his arrival.

It should never be forgotten that without massive surgery on a squad that was rudderless and underachieving when he arrived, he built a formidable side that doubled the amount of major silverware in the Stamford Bridge trophy cabinet. The League title was beyond him, which in theory was a blot on his copybook, but the money he had available to spend was less than his peers were able to speculate. Crucially, he brought through Hudson and Ian Hutchinson, whose performances had a significant impact on the two cup runs in 1970 and 1971, despite serious injury.

Supporter Brian Gaches has fond memories of Sexton 'with the glory of the two cup wins...I always liked him. He was popular with The Shed, always giving us a wave pre-match from his viewing seat high up in the roof of the East Stand when we chanted his name'. Though not as demonstrative and exuberant as Docherty, he had the respect of most supporters and, even now, those who watched his teams in the golden 1969-71 period speak so fondly of him.

Supporter Bob Barlow felt Sexton was 'a guy happy with a clipboard or creating set pieces at training. He went on to do well but he's almost the perfect assistant'. This seems a little unfair, as although he was the polar opposite of Docherty, for the first four years of his reign he certainly had the respect of the players, even the more wayward ones.

His peers were in the late 1960s were probably Sir Matt Busby, Don Revie, Harry Catterick, Bill Shankly, Joe Mercer / Malcolm Allison, Bill Nicholson and Bertie Mee. These were managers at clubs who were expected to collect silverware every couple of years. That is a formidable list and Sexton's record against them stands up pretty well, especially given the funds most of them had available.

Given the disarray when he arrived at the club and the paucity of money to spend, to win the two trophies he did must ensure his place in the highest rank of Chelsea managers. Supporters from that era are eternally grateful for that. Things did turn sour later in his reign but at his 1967-71 Chelsea peak he did a remarkable job.

The League

Chelsea finished 6th, 5th, 3rd and 6th between 1967-68 and 1970-71, demonstrating that they were consistently among the leading English clubs without ever breaking through. The table below shows that during the period under review, among the nine leading First Division clubs, Chelsea scored the 4th most goals, and, in terms of aggregate points, were only beaten by Leeds United, Liverpool and Everton. Given the problems Sexton inherited, this was indeed laudable.

Total Goals And Points Of Leading Clubs
(From 23/10/67 to end of 1970-71 Season)

	Played	Goals For	Goals Against	Points	Position
Arsenal	156	218	139	192	5
Chelsea	156	**242**	**181**	**195**	**4**
Everton	156	252	157	200	3
Leeds United	157	276	136	228	1
Liverpool	156	220	122	201	2
Man City	155	227	172	167	8
Man Utd	157	258	224	170	7
Tottenham H	156	216	177	171	6
Wolves	156	205	218	152	9

With the talent at his disposal Sexton should arguably have had a more effective tilt at the League title. His side were 10, 17, 11 and 14 points behind the champions in those four seasons which, in the days of two points for a win, was a chasm. Slow season starts, the inconsistency of key creative players, silly goals conceded and an inability to close games out were all ongoing problems and contributory factors to the 'close, but no cigar' scenario. In the table above they had the third worst defensive record, reinforcing the point that further strengthening at the back was probably required to mount a strong title challenge.

Against that, it can certainly be argued that Sexton regularly got the most out of what he had. It seems likely that if he had sacrificed flair and talent for greater consistency and professionalism, attempting to build teams like Everton, Leeds United or Liverpool, Chelsea would almost certainly have suffered in cup competition as a result, as well as being less attractive to watch.

Cup Competitions

No other club in England in 1970 had three players in their side with the intuitive talent and flair of Charlie Cooke, Alan Hudson and Peter Osgood. Not Leeds United, Manchester City or Manchester United. Not Liverpool or Everton. Not Tottenham or Arsenal. With this creativity and match-turning ability came inconsistency which, as argued above, did not help in the quest for League titles. Where it proved invaluable, though, was in cups.

Osgood, then, now and always the 'King Of Stamford Bridge', is as fondly remembered as any star in the club's history, as his statue outside the West Stand demonstrates. His goal in every round of the FA Cup in 1970, his remarkable pair against Bruges after being out suspended for two months, and his goals in both Athens encounters will never be forgotten by supporters from those days. Cooke and Hudson, too, could often shine brightly on big occasions but not every week. The whole club seemed lifted by cup competition and in knock-out matches feared nobody. Sexton could provide his players with coherent plans for all-out attack and for counter-attacking, for taking the initiative and for taking time, though recklessness was not in his nature.

Against that, of course, were the unexpected FA Cup Quarter-Final defeats against Birmingham and West Bromwich, the 1971 home capitulation against Manchester City and the inability to put together a decent League Cup run. Worst of all was the inept, unimaginative 1968 Fairs Cup struggle against DWS Amsterdam, in a tournament eventually won by a Newcastle United side who could only finish ninth in the League.

Some of the displays on the way to the 1970 and 1971 trophies (the Burnley replay, the two finals against Leeds, Sofia away, Bruges at home, the two winning Semi-Final legs against Manchester City and the two Athens encounters) rank very highly in the very greatest performances in the history of the club. It is the two cups that that team won that they are most fondly remembered for, trophies still celebrated and appreciated today by supporters old enough to remember them.

The Board

The arrival of Brian Mears in the chair was a game-changer for Chelsea Football Club. Charles Pratt was arguably out of his depth, though he certainly deserved praise for the appointment of Sexton, and Leonard Withey sadly never really had a chance to make his mark. Mears, though, was ambitious for the club, both on and off the field. He wanted success and wanted a stadium the club could be proud of. He wanted both, and he wanted them quickly. He was young, energetic and a welcome change from some of his peers at top clubs. Autocrats like Bob Lord at Burnley. Aristocrats like Denis Hill-Wood at Arsenal. Ruthless businessmen like Manchester United's Louis Edwards.

His boardroom colleagues Viscount Chelsea, Leslie Mears, George Thomson and Richard Attenborough clearly loved the club, but if one criticism could be levelled at the board in those days it is that they never gave Sexton the money to buy really top quality players. He bought well, and possessed a strong squad, but more genuine quality might have led to a concerted title challenge, and quality cost money, then as now. To keep the club running effectively, to build a stronger team and redevelop Stamford Bridge it was clear that alternative sources of income were needed, above and beyond matchday income and the fundraising activity, and maybe inviting outside investment would have provided a significant extra funding stream.

The Team

In October 1967 Sexton inherited a team that had arguably underachieved for the previous 12 months, ever since Peter Osgood broke his leg at Blackpool in early October 1966. The majority of the players he inherited were still on the books 43 months later at the time of the Athens triumph, but he made some crucial additions. The squad was a strong one but, as argued earlier, probably not a title-winning one, especially as creative stars were sometimes prone to inconsistency and spells of poor form.

Three players - Harris, Hollins and McCreadie - were almost always only out of the side in the period under review if they were injured, which sadly in the case of the latter was an increasing amount. Webb was in the same category after his arrival from Southampton apart from a spell early in 1970-71 and Bonetti later that season. Osgood was dropped briefly before his move to midfield in Autumn 1968. Cooke and Hudson were both left out on occasion when fit. Dempsey spent a few months out in the cold when the zonal marking system was used in late 1970. Houseman was pretty much guaranteed a place after Autumn 1968. Others - Boyle, Baldwin, Hinton - were in and out of the side.

A composite side over all those four seasons, based on appearances, would look like this:- Bonetti; Harris, Dempsey, Webb, McCreadie; Boyle, Hollins; Cooke, Baldwin, Osgood, Houseman. Sub. Hinton.

Sexton rarely made substitutions except in cases of injury, preferring to use the chosen players for the whole 90 minutes in the belief that they, and the chosen tactical system, would deliver. He made just 50 substitutions in the 156 League matches under review.

Incredibly, largely through Hutchinson's appalling luck with injury, the classic Cooke, Hudson, Osgood, Hutchinson, Houseman front five only ever played together just 18 times. Had they been able to continue as a unit for 2-3 more years it is likely the club's 1971-75 history would have looked pretty different.

This table shows that there were few seasons when continuity in terms of the players wearing any single shirt lasted for most of a season. This clearly demonstrates the impact injuries, but also loss of form, had across the squad and across the period.

Number of players wearing each shirt (League and Cups)											
Shirt	1	2	3	4	5	6	7	8	9	10	11
1967-68 (from 23/10/67)	2	7	2	3	5	4	3	3	1	3	4
1968-69	2	6	3	6	2	4	7	8	4	7	4
1969-70	2	7	6	2	3	6	4	9	5	7	7
1970-71	2	4	2	3	4	3	5	5	6	8	4

The squad developed organically, rather than as a huge splurge of transfer activity, hoping some of it stuck. Few young players came through the system into regular first-team places, compared to the days of Ted Drake and Tommy Docherty in the early 1960s. Alan Hudson was the resounding success. Stewart Houston and Barry Lloyd had a few chances but never really broke through at Chelsea. Peter Feely and Micky Droy had made first-team appearances in the latter part of the 1970-71 season and there were real hopes that they and Derek Smethurst might become regulars, but they had not come through the youth system. Frankly, the cupboard in terms of emerging young talent ready to seriously challenge for a first-team spot was pretty bare, with few, if any, of the reserve or youth team regulars looking likely short-term candidates for a regular place. There was a trend for reserve regulars to be given free transfers having never made a first-team appearance, Tony Frewin and Joe Cruickshank being the latest examples.

In terms of the squad as a whole, social change possibly impacted on Chelsea players more than those at other English clubs, because of their fashionable location and the congregation of a number of glamorous stars at one club. George Best outdid everyone for glamour but his Manchester United colleagues arguably less so. '*Chelsea - The 100 Year History*' makes the point that Chelsea were 'the first players to dress like pop stars' and even the Leeds-centric '*The Unforgiven*' describes Chelsea as the 'Emperors of urbane King's Road cool'. Osgood had an extremely high profile and was understandably keen to cash in on it. Hudson was certainly developing an image and looked the epitome of a trendy young man-about-town.

As Charlie Cooke argued in '*The Bonnie Prince*', when Chelsea were on form they provided as much entertainment and exciting football as almost any team in the country, one reason they are remembered so fondly. As John Dempsey told *ChelseaFC.Com* in 2021, 'it was a great moment to be living. Football has always been about characters, and we had them in that team'. Indeed they did.

Goalkeepers

Peter Bonetti was well-respected by the football world and revered by Chelsea supporters. It is unfortunate that many non-Chelsea supporters primarily remember him for the World Cup Quarter-Final against West Germany and the goals by Franz Beckenbauer and Uwe Seeler.

He was brave, agile, a great shot stopper, had an unerring throw and undoubtedly played a key part in the almost immediate improvement under Sexton. He let in a dismal 32 goals in 12 League games at the start of the 1967-68 season, undermined by woeful defending in front of him, but the new manager quickly stabilised things and he only let in another 29 goals in his remaining 28 League matches.

The Chelsea Experience' detailed how Bonetti liked playing behind Harris, Webb, Dempsey and McCreadie, the first choice defence for much of 1969-71, who were all strong, tough tacklers. He was confident behind a decent defence, and his ability gave them confidence. Bonetti's courage in the FA Cup Final replay after he was clattered by Mick Jones spoke volumes about the character of the man. He rose to the big occasion for the club, as he was also on top form in both Athens finals a year later.

Tommy Hughes was a decent goalkeeper but let in 21 goals in 9 matches under Sexton, so it is entirely understandable why he bought John Phillips as replacement cover in Summer 1970. Phillips developed into a keeper of real quality and stood in extremely competently for the injured/ill Bonetti in the second half of the 1970-71 season, playing a big part in the run to Athens, especially in both Bruges ties. Supporter Brian Gaches has always thought Phillips was unlucky not to be selected in the Final against Real Madrid as his form was consistently top-class, but as he says, Sexton went for the fit-again Bonetti and this proved the right call given his performances.

Full Backs

When Sexton took over he had no shortage of full-backs, but few were of the desired quality. By the end of the season he had sold three. Geoff Butler, signed by Docherty a couple of weeks before his departure, was not happy and did not earn a regular first-team place. Moving him on, to Sunderland, made sense. Two other full-backs, Jim Thomson and Joe Kirkup, were allowed to leave. Though decent players, neither won a regular spot under Sexton so selling one of them was logical, though losing both left the squad noticeably light on full-backs until Paddy Mulligan arrived a year later.

Eddie McCreadie was a high-quality tough-tackling left-back, one of the first over-lapping full-backs in English football, in tandem with Ken

Shellito, but there was no clear candidate for right-back. This meant John Boyle, John Hollins and Marvin Hinton all had to do stints in a position that was not their natural one. David Webb and Ron Harris both played there, but Sexton never resolved who was the better bet until after Webb got roasted by Eddie Gray in the 1970 FA Cup Final. Harris could play on either side, especially useful when McCreadie was injured, as he was for much of the 1970-71 season.

When the £100,000 Wilf Smith deal fell down at the start of 1970-71, there was clearly money available, and Sexton should probably have gone for a top-class full-back at that point. Peter Rodrigues moved from Leicester City to Sheffield Wednesday for £50,000 in October 1970. A player Tommy Docherty was interested in five years earlier, he was an experienced international right-back and would have been a particularly useful signing. Keith Newton was the England left-back in the 1970 World Cup and he went from Blackburn Rovers to Everton for £80,000 in late 1969, after Sexton had a bid rebuffed that autumn. Within 18 months he had asked for a transfer and could potentially have been picked up for a bargain price, but no interest was expressed, despite McCreadie's growing list of injuries.

The arrival of Mulligan was timely, and an astute purchase. He was a popular, quality player comfortable going forward. He probably deserved more than six League starts in 1969-70 and 16 the following season, though he was affected by injury in the latter. Supporter Geoff Kimber thought very highly of him. 'I thought he was the best full-back I saw until the arrival of Dan Petrescu'.

Chelsea fielded no less than 16 different full-back partnerships in the four years under review, with 11 different players appearing in one, or both, positions. This lack of continuity cannot have helped with defensive solidity, where a consistent line-up heightens understanding. A high-quality regular partner for McCreadie could only have improved the team. It would have caused selection issues once Webb and Dempsey arrived, but Sexton would have coped with that.

Centre Backs

When Sexton arrived Chelsea had a clear weakness in the air at the back. Colin Waldron's deal to move to Burnley was already in train when the new man took over and he was sold a day later. The move from Bury that summer did not work out, Ron Suart did not pick him for either of his two games in charge, Sexton made no obvious move to keep him, and it suited all parties to move him on.

This left Hinton and Harris as the main centre-back partnership in late 1967. Harris was tough, a great competitor and natural leader of the team, though his distribution on occasions was lacking. His 'Chopper' nickname was deserved, as some of his tackling was brutal. Supporter **Brian Gaches argues that every team of the 1970s needed a Ron Harris** because of the highly physical nature of English football. He was not a truly top-class player either at full-back or centre-back, and there was an argument that for Chelsea to be a genuinely top outfit he would maybe need to be replaced, but he provided the backbone and leadership that any side needed, especially in an era where opponents regularly set out to intimidate. Nobody intimidated Ron Harris.

Hinton was a good reader of the game and supporter Geoff Kimber remembers his as 'probably the most underrated player I ever saw. He had a level of skill more associated with an inside-forward than a defender'. After his error-strewn performance against Manchester City in the FA Cup, however, he was never first choice for an extended period again.

The problem was, neither Harris or Hinton were strong in the air, in an era when the likes of Jeff Astle, Ron Davies, Wyn Davies and Joe Royle were centre-forwards so dominant in aerial challenges. Sexton astutely plugged this weakness by buying Webb and, a year later, Dempsey.

Webb's attitude, spirit and commitment shone through from day one and he remains one of the most important signings in the history of the club. The ultimate utility player, he wore every shirt including goalkeeper in his time at the club, and quickly became a huge crowd favourite. It was fitting that he should score the winning goal at Old Trafford. Supporter Barry Holmes recalls 'Webb was one of the great 'characters'...a Desperate Dan of a man who, lamentably, would not be allowed in today's game'.

Supporter Bob Barlow recalls Webb as 'the backbone of our team. Maybe one of our best signings ever. Playing in goal over Christmas (as he was to do in December 1971), and scoring the Cup Final winner makes him a legend. As good as that was, his 120 minutes of torture against Eddie Gray at Wembley may rank as one of the worst embarrassments that a Chelsea player has faced... Webby was a character, the fans loved him and vice versa'.

Dempsey was bought when Sexton was desperate for a tall centre-half. As Brian Gaches says, he was a quiet, commanding, reliable player who generally did his job without fuss, was well-respected by his colleagues and contributed significantly to both cup winning teams in 1970 and 1971.

The fact that Sexton had to field 16 different centre-back partnerships involving 12 different players in the four seasons under review, indicates a lack of consistency and it was noticeable that it was the latter two when a regular Dempsey / Harris partnership, followed by a Dempsey/Webb pairing, came to the fore, that success was achieved.

Midfield / Wingers

Sexton inherited a midfield where he had two hard-working, ultra-reliable midfielders in John Hollins and John Boyle, augmented on occasions by the sometimes unpredictable Charlie Cooke. His preference was always to include at least one wide man in his side, often two, though on occasions wingers Cooke or Peter Houseman would play in midfield, rather than hug the touchline.

Hollins was 'the heartbeat of the side', as supporter Brian Gaches observes, for a decade. A super-energetic, positive, disciplined and committed box-to-box midfielder, his tireless efforts allowed the more creative members of the midfield to apply their skills, safe in the knowledge that Hollins would be covering for them. He was arguably the most consistent team member from 1967-71, along with Bonetti, and his efforts are probably underappreciated half a century later because, unlike some of his more extrovert colleagues, he led a quiet life, was undemonstrative by nature and was rarely the subject of newspaper features. He was very unlucky not to win more than one England cap, given he performed at a consistently high level for so long.

Boyle worked his heart out for Chelsea, and it was probably a disadvantage to him that he was effective at full-back as well as in midfield and also, on occasion, in a wide role. He wore nine different numbers in his Chelsea career, only needing 1,5 and 9 for the full set. Whatever job Sexton gave him he pursued with diligence, his tough-tackling, combative contributions much appreciated by his teammates. He was extremely unlucky that injury severely curtailed his 1969-70 season, thereby missing out on an FA Cup Winners Medal, making it still more pleasing that he played in both Athens games, and performed so creditably.

Charlie Cooke at his best bewitched his manager, his teammates and the supporters but on an off-day, he could equally bewilder and infuriate them. His dribbling skills were astonishing, but often, especially in his early days at the club, the end product failed to match up to expectations. He had weight issues when he first arrived at the club but trimmed down and became a more consistent and effective player as a result. A highly intelligent man who thought deeply about the game, he was a conundrum Sexton managed to largely solve, getting match-changing displays from him in big matches, sometimes using him wide, sometimes in the middle. His cross for Osgood's headed equaliser at Old Trafford is one of the most iconic moments in the club's history, capping an inspiring personal display, and his performances in Athens were of an equally high standard.

Brian Gaches captures Cooke's appeal to Chelsea supporters. 'He was brilliant on his day with the ability to run with the ball seemingly glued to his feet as he glided past defenders. If he had scored more goals he probably would have been more universally rated but to us Chelsea fans he was brilliant, entertaining, and more than made up for this (lack of goals) with the number of goals he created for others.

The Chelsea Football Book', published after the FA Cup win, included a feature on Cooke. 'It is individualists like Cooke the crowds still flock to watch...He has high-speed dribbling off to a degree that few have equalled...He thinks a lot, he broods about his own game...There is a theory he sometimes thinks and talks himself out of the team'. In *The Working Man's Ballet'* Alan Hudson eulogised about his colleague. 'When Cooke had the ball, if he was in the mood, it was almost an impossibility to get it off him', and in *'Ossie The Wizard'* Peter Osgood opined 'Charlie Cooke took his game very seriously, but never himself'.

The other winger Sexton inherited was Peter Houseman, who Tommy Docherty admitted deserved more chances under his stewardship. Unflashy, hard-working and under-appreciated, Houseman was probably the best crosser of a ball at the club and, within a year of the managerial change, deservedly a regular in the side. Sexton gave Houseman the opportunities he had lacked under Docherty. The *'Kings Of The King's Road'* explains how Houseman finally made the left-wing position his own in 1968-69, the manager appreciating his 'crossing, stamina, left-footedness and reliability'. Scapegoating by elements of the support occurred sporadically through much of his Chelsea career and was grossly unfair. Despite what he said publicly, it must have affected his confidence early on, and it is to Sexton's credit that he boosted that confidence and made him such a reliable cornerstone of the team.

Alan Hudson can polarise opinion among Chelsea supporters even today, and certainly his post-Athens career at the club was marked by bouts of underachievement, but in the period covered by this book, when fit, he was often as good a creative midfield talent as there was in the country. Sir Alf Ramsey rarely uttered untrammelled praise about players but made an exception in his case.

Sexton deserved enormous praise for his diligent coaching of the young Hudson and injecting him into the first-team mix at exactly the right time. As soon as he had a run in the side in late 1969 the player impressed. As he himself recalls in *'The Working Man's Ballet'*, by the time of the Palace FA Cup-tie in January 1970 Hudson was starting to get press coverage, with the King's Road link and 'the long-haired, trendy-clothes image'. He took time to get going in the 1970-71 season, severely affected by injury, but by season-end was able to make major contributions in key matches.

Supporter Barry Holmes remembers Hudson's early Chelsea career fondly. 'A great player to watch with his close control and eerily calm distribution, socks around his ankles and long hair on his hunched shoulders. I can remember an article on him after England were knocked out of the World Cup during that 1970 summer, predicting that he was so good that he would be leading the country to World Cup glory in 1974'. Cooke felt he had the rare ability to 'step up a gear at will'. Supporter Bob Barlow recalls that 'some of the intricate passing between Ossie, Houseman, Hutchinson and him on edge of the box was stunning'.

Brian Gaches opines 'I have no hesitation in saying that Alan

Hudson in the second half of the 1969-70 season was the most talented Chelsea player I have ever seen. Quite simply in many games he was unstoppable, a driving force in midfield, creative, imaginative with pace, power and youthful confidence to burn. He was brilliant until suffering the injury that kept him out of the FA Cup Final, and tragically for him I don't believe he was ever quite the same again'.

Terry Cassley is another supporter with fond memories of the midfield star. 'The first time I saw him play my jaw dropped. He had balance, control, strength and made the game look easy like all good footballers do. I thought he was world class and still do. It was such a pity he didn't play in the two matches against Leeds...For all the fantastic players I've seen in my 65 years of watching Chelsea the one footballer I would love to have played like is Alan Hudson'.

When Sexton signed Keith Weller, it was unclear whether he would play as a striker, as winger or even in midfield. In the end, the manager wanted him as a direct, goalscoring wide man. Becoming leading scorer in what turned out to be his only season at Chelsea speaks volumes about how quickly he took to Division One. A real crowd favourite, as Brian Gaches remembers, on form he was terrific with pace and power that many defences could not cope with. He had his own song '*Keithy Weller On The Wing*' sung by The Shed, no mean achievement for a man at the club for just over a year. He was also popular with his teammates, some of whom were completely confused and utterly mortified when he left in September 1971.

Strikers

Bobby Tambling, a true club loyalist and a top-class goalscorer at his peak, was the club's all-time leading scorer and was top scorer as late in his Chelsea career as 1968-69. Brian Gaches remembers 'it was sad to see such a fantastic and popular player leave the club in 1969-70 especially as he was only 28'. However injury had blunted his pace and sharpness. Given the establishment of Osgood, Hutchinson and Baldwin ahead of him in the pecking order, and the arrival of Weller, selling him was probably the right call. Gaches wonders 'if he had stayed, albeit with less game time, I always wondered how many goals he would have added to his 202 over the next 4 or 5 years'. Geoff Kimber thinks there ended up being so much forward competition that it made sense, eventually, for him to leave.

Peter Osgood was an enigma but is also, without a doubt, one of the most mercurial and gifted talents ever to wear a Chelsea shirt, with a happy knack of scoring crucial goals in key matches. There were times when he almost disappeared, and, as '*Back Home*' pointed out, he was not known for hard work when Chelsea were not in possession, but he had the talent to turn a match in an instant. Fed up with relentless fouling by hatchet-men he toughened up, but unfortunately a by-product was that his short fuse came to the fore and he was prone to acts of retaliation. The lack of protection players of his calibre received from referees in those days was a disgrace but, given it was the way it was, it is a shame he did not find a way to control his temper without diminishing his qualities. He spent most of 1968-69 in midfield and put in some excellent performances, but it was up front where he was most effective, especially when Hutchinson became a first-team regular.

Supporter Geoff Kimber thinks Osgood is 'one of the finest players I have ever seen play football. Some of his goals defied belief and it is just a shame that there was not such widespread TV coverage in those days meaning that same old goals are viewed again and again.' As Kimber argues, it is astonishing as much as it is absurd that he only got four England caps, two of those as substitutes in the 1970 World Cup campaign in Mexico, against Rumania and Czechoslovakia. If Osgood had started those games and played well in the matches against Brazil and West Germany, that tournament and indeed English footballing history could have looked a lot different.

Brian Gaches remembers Osgood as 'a football genius, a supreme dribbler with balance, pace and power. The fact he was a local lad who could look after himself on the pitch just added to the adoration every Chelsea fan had for him as our No.9'.

The dogged, hard-chasing Tommy Baldwin is sometimes portrayed as Chelsea's nearly man of the era, never establishing himself as a first-team regular for an extended period. Given he won two major cup medals, the 'nearly man' tag is unfair, even if he was only in the team for the FA Cup and Cup-Winners' Cup Finals because of injury (Hudson in 1970, Hollins a year later). Hudson, in *The Working Man's Ballet*, praised Baldwin's hard work and he was respected by his colleagues for his unselfish work, Osgood enthusing how well they worked together. In a team with its share of more mercurial but less energetic stars, the likes of Baldwin and Houseman were very necessary to close down opponents and win the ball. His use of the tabloid press to complain when he was omitted would not have endeared him to Sexton, but he was without doubt a key squad member and is still fondly remembered for his hard work by supporters to this day.

Sexton's first signing was Alan Birchenall, a tall, strong, hard worker, very left-footed, who quickly became a crowd favourite. His goal record, 20 in 75 Chelsea League games, was not top-rate and, with the rise of Hutchinson, particularly, it probably made sense for him to be sold on. Osgood was a fan. 'Birchenall was like a breath of fresh air when he came to the club. He was a superb player and it's a shame he didn't stay longer'.

The emergence of Ian Hutchinson as a first-team regular in March 1969 was a significant moment for Chelsea. They had acquired, for a ludicrous initial price of £2,500, a brave, direct, tireless old-school centre-forward with wonderful aerial ability and a happy knack of bringing his co-striker, usually Osgood, into the game. Supporter Brian Gaches eulogises about Hutchinson. 'Quite simply the bravest and unluckiest Chelsea player I have ever seen. His injuries...are well documented but less so was his ability as a quality striker who could finish with both feet, with power in the air, and possessing one of the longest throws in history. In *'Upfront With Chelsea'*, Liverpool boss Shankly described Hutch as 'a very brave man, very brave'. The book says he had regular cortisone injections to enable him to play when injured, which caused him trouble in later life, a problem shared with a number of other stars of his generation.

After his injury at Southampton in February 1971 Hutchinson did not make a first-team appearance for 22 months, as he suffered other problems on his road to recovery from the cartilage problem, including a broken leg. He was only to play 52 more League games for the club before being forced to retire in early 1976. Tragedy is an overused word in football, but it is valid to use it in this case. It is worth remembering that, because of fitness issues, Hutchinson only played 72 matches alongside Osgood in his career but despite that, they are without doubt one of the most fondly remembered striking partnerships in Chelsea's history.

In *'Upfront With Chelsea'* Osgood admitted 'my partnership with Hutch was the most effective I had at Chelsea. If he could have stayed fit, there's no end to what we could have achieved together'. 'He was...very brave, too brave'. Indeed.

International Appearances

Given the talent in Sexton's squad, it is surprising how few international appearances his players made, as this table shows.

Player	Full Caps (Total)	Full Caps (10/67- 6/71) with Chelsea	U-23 Caps (Total)	U-23 Caps (10/67- 6/71) with Chelsea
Tommy Baldwin	0	0	2	2
Alan Birchenall	0	0	4	3
Peter Bonetti	7	4	12	0
Charlie Cooke	16	10	4	0
John Dempsey	18	7	0	0
Ron Harris	0	0	4	4
Marvin Hinton	0	0	3	0
John Hollins	1	0	12	7
Stewart Houston	0	0	2	0

Tommy Hughes	0	0	2	2
Alan Hudson	2	0	9	1
Ian Hutchinson	0	0	2	2
Eddie McCreadie	23	12	0	0
Paddy Mulligan	50	5	1	0
Peter Osgood	4	3	6	6
John Phillips	3	0	3	0
Bobby Tambling	3	0	13	0
Keith Weller	4	0	0	0

Only six Chelsea players won full caps in the period covered by this book, and none were international regulars. There is a wider spread of under-23 caps, as international managers used such matches to experiment and try different youngsters out, given which it is remarkable that John Boyle and Peter Houseman never appeared in such a game.

Transfer Activity

Appendix B shows very clearly that Sexton was extremely efficient in the transfer market. In the period covered in the book he spent an estimated £367,500 but recouped an estimated £360,500, meaning he only ran up a tiny estimated deficit. He was in some ways working with one hand tied behind his back, given the quality of top players signed by their main rivals over this four-year period. Chelsea were not raising money through player sales in this period, unlike under Docherty and in the last three years of Sexton's reign, but they rarely 'speculated to accumulate' unlike their peers.

Bringing in Ian Hutchinson so cheaply was a master stroke. Sexton, Ron Suart and Frank Blunstone deserved huge credit for spotting him, taking a chance by signing such a raw talent and turning him into a feared top-flight striker inside a season.

Birchenall, Webb, Dempsey and Weller were all very decent signings but not in the top bracket in terms of price. When in February 1971 Derby County spent £170,000 on Colin Todd, a classy defender who would have improved Sexton's team (and indeed any English team), Chelsea's record fee paid for a defender was Dempsey at £100,000 less. Birchenall, at £100,000, was the joint record fee paid by Chelsea (equal to the 1966 signing of centre-forward Tony Hateley) but this was at a time when the very top echelon of striker (e.g. Allan Clarke) was going for £150,000+.

Sexton's record in the transfer market was good during this period, but would looser purse strings have enabled him to buy greater success? As detailed elsewhere, the side was short of a top-level full-back and, until Hudson emerged, a high-quality midfield passer and if the board had allowed him money to spend it would have in all likelihood been put to good use. As outlined elsewhere, if he had spent the money freed up when the Wilf Smith deal collapsed, the squad could only have been stronger.

Though sometimes happy to sell those not in his first-team plans, Sexton was probably pleased when John Boyle's planned move to Sheffield Wednesday fell through in September 1970 and Baldwin's various transfer requests never went anywhere. He actually sold remarkably few established players in his first four years at the club, and only Tambling of the long-term regulars at the end of the Docherty reign was not at the club four seasons later.

Appendix E lists every player Chelsea were supposedly interested in buying, taken from the columns of the *News Of The World*, *The People* and the *Sunday Mirror*, who never signed for the club. Some of these were genuine deals that almost worked (Wilf Smith being one example), others are almost certainly completely speculative. What is striking is that apart from Allan Clarke, for sale as Leicester City were relegated, there were no really top-class names listed. There were other very good players linked with a move to Stamford Bridge - Tony Green, Willie Morgan, Keith Newton, Jon Sammels, Terry Venables and the highly-promising John Toshack. It is instructive, however, that many of the most expensive names of the time like Ron Davies, Martin Chivers, Martin Peters, Terry Hennessey and Colin Todd were not talked about as Chelsea prospects.

Steve Earle and Les Barrett were listed so often I assume that whenever Suart or Sexton went down the road to watch their neighbours, or when it was a quiet news day, the story was run.

In terms of players moving on, all of the senior professionals at the club when Sexton arrived, except Ron Harris and Eddie McCreadie, were linked with a move although only Tambling actually left.

Attendances and Support

The following table details the average attendances for the four seasons covered in this book plus, for comparison purposes 1966-67, the season before. Figures for the average away League crowds are taken from the *Bounder Friardale* website.

	66-67	67-68	68-69	69-70	70-71
Average League Crowd	35,391	35,979	37,613	40,342	39,545
Ave. Increase / (Decline) On Previous Season	4,245	388	1,634	2,729	-797
% Increase / (Decline) On Previous Season	13.5%	1%	4.5%	7.3%	-2.0%
Ave. League Crowd Division 1 Ranking	5th	8th	5th	4th	5th
Home League Crowds over 35,000	10	9	12	15	13
Home League Crowds under 25,000	2	2	2	1	2
Average Away League crowd	33,404	36,203	31,875	34,772	34,957

As can be seen, League gates increased markedly for the first three seasons of Sexton's reign, though the falloff in 1970-71 is, in retrospect, a surprise, maybe due to the sheer number of cup-ties played that season. The board always thought 40,000 was a realistic average League attendance (but thought it should have been higher), and in 1969-70 figure that was achieved. Fourth place in the First Division average crowd list that season was a decent achievement and a sign that Chelsea were competing with the top echelon of English clubs.

Chelsea's away support grew significantly in the late 1960s, as it did at many clubs. Taking support of 10,000+ to cup-ties at Birmingham City (1968) and Manchester City (1971) gives an indication of the attraction of travelling to a big match. Special trains were easier to organise than 50 years later, which made transporting large numbers round the country more straightforward.

As can be evidenced when watching TV footage from the time, The Shed, despite being so far from the pitch, could still make a heck of a noise and the volume from the away support at Southampton in 1969 is astonishing.

The Stadium

Supporter Brian Gaches remembers the late 1960s Stamford Bridge well. 'At the time it was all we knew, so as fans we came to accept it despite its obvious drawbacks in being so far from the pitch and the loss of atmosphere. However we had The Shed and not only did it have a fearsome reputation, it could also help create a brilliant atmosphere in big games like Bruges in 1971'. Indeed. The stadium itself was showing severe signs of wear and tear, however, apart from the West Stand, only fully opened in 1966.

Supporter Julian Patten remembers that Alan Ball insisted that the Bridge had one of the best atmosphere's around when full, and thought other players were of the same view. He recalls that 'it was obviously dreadful with a sparse crowd. For me, with a capacity crowd, there was no other ground that could match it. It was different because it was away from the pitch and in the open, so you heard a constant hum. I thought it was unique. The other point is, it wasn't just about the noise, you could see the whole ground erupt when a goal was scored. Other grounds had a lot of restricted viewing' which is a good point.

Supporter Tony Foss rightly wonders 'what would have happened had we lost the 1970 FA Cup Final? There would have been no Cup-Winner's Cup Final, yet the ground was in desperate need of an upgrade'. What indeed. Stamford Bridge needed redeveloping and the board were right to commit to a plan. Whether it was the right plan, and exactly how it could and should have been funded are issues explored in *Stamford Bridge Is Falling Down*'.

What Happened Next...

Seeing the positivity in Summer 1971 it is hard to believe that within three years Peter Osgood, Alan Hudson and David Webb would have left the club and that in 1975 the club would be relegated, Sexton having been sacked after mediocre results and fall-outs with a number of squad members. As shocking was the off-field decline, with the club in an abject financial position, largely brought about by the self-same stadium redevelopment that seemed such a great idea at the turn of the decade. Athens was to be Chelsea's last major trophy for 26 years...

A full analysis of exactly how Chelsea went from Athens to anarchy is detailed in '*Stamford Bridge Is Falling Down*'.

APPENDICES

Appendix A
Player Profiles October 1967 – May 1971
(every player with 20+ appearances between 23/10/67 when Dave Sexton took over the end of the 70/71 season – 156 games.)

Tommy Baldwin
88+2 League games 23/10/67-01/05/71, 36 goals
(182+5 games, 74 goals in Chelsea League career)
Signed from: Arsenal, September 1966 (swap for George Graham)
Chelsea League Debut: Manchester City (A), 1/10/66
Left for: Gravesend & Northfleet, June 1975
England U23 International

Alan Birchenall
74+1 League games 23/10/67-01/05/71, 20 goals
(74+1 games, 20 goals in Chelsea League career)
Signed from: Sheffield United, November 1967
Chelsea League Debut: Sunderland (A), 2/12/67
Left for: Crystal Palace, June 1970
England U23 International

Peter Bonetti
133+0 League games 23/10/67-01/05/71, 0 goals
(600+0 games in Chelsea League career)
Signed from: Junior, April 1959
Chelsea League Debut: Manchester City (H), 2/4/60
Left for: Retired, June 1979
England International

John Boyle
83+3 League games 23/10/67-01/05/71, 4 goals
(188+10 games, 10 goals in Chelsea League career)
Signed from: Junior, August 1964
Chelsea League Debut: Leeds United (A), 23/1/65
Left for: Leyton Orient, December 1973
Scotland Youth International

Charlie Cooke
118+4 League games 23/10/67-01/05/71, 8 goals
(289+10 games, 22 goals in Chelsea League career)
Signed from: Dundee, April 1966
Chelsea League Debut: West Ham United (A), 20/8/66
Left for: Crystal Palace, September 1972
(re-signed Jan 1974, left for Memphis Rogues July 1978)
Scotland International

John Dempsey
81+2 League games 23/10/67-01/05/71, 3 goals
(161+4 games, 4 goals in Chelsea League career)
Signed from: Fulham, January 1969
Chelsea League Debut: Southampton (A), 1/2/69
Left for: Philadelphia Fury, March 1978
Eire International

Ron Harris
136+0 League games 23/10/67-01/05/71, 1 goal
(646+9 games, 13 goals in Chelsea League career)
Signed from: Junior, November 1961
Chelsea League Debut: Sheffield Wednesday (H) 24/2/62
Left for: Brentford May 1980
England U23 International

Marvin Hinton
75+4 League games 23/10/67-01/05/71, 0 goals
(257+8 games, 3 goals in Chelsea League career)
Signed from: Charlton Athletic, August 1963
Chelsea League Debut: Ipswich Town (A) 12/10/63
Left for: Barnet, June 1975
England U23 International

John Hollins
145+0 League games 23/10/67-01/05/71, 16 goals
(465 games, 48 goals in Chelsea League career)
Signed from: Junior, July 1963
Chelsea League Debut: Stoke City (A) 4/3/64
Left for: Queens Park Rangers, June 1975
(re-signed June 1983, retired June 1984, joined coaching staff)
England International

Peter Houseman
120+4 League games 23/10/67-01/05/71, 9 goals
(252+17 games, 20 goals in Chelsea League career)
Signed from: Junior, December 1962
Chelsea League Debut: Sheffield United (H) 21/12/63
Left for: Oxford United May 1975
International appearances: none

Alan Hudson
63+1 League games 23/10/67-01/05/71, 6 goals
(144+1 games, 10 goals in Chelsea League career)
Signed from: Junior, July 1978
Chelsea League Debut: v Southampton (A), 1/2/69
Left for: Stoke City, January 1974
(Re-signed August 1983, left for Stoke City February 1984)
England International

Ian Hutchinson
60+2 League games 23/10/67-01/05/71, 27 goals
(112+7 games, 44 goals in Chelsea League career)
Signed from: Cambridge United, August 1968
Chelsea League Debut: Ipswich Town (H), 5/10/68
Left for: Retired through injury, July 1976
England U23 International

Eddie McCreadie
108+2 League games 23/10/67-01/05/71, 0 goals
(327+4 games, 4 goals in Chelsea League career)
Signed from: East Stirling, April 1962
Chelsea League Debut: Rotherham United (A) 18/8/62
Left for: retired November 1974, joined coaching staff
Scotland International

Paddy Mulligan
22+3 League games 23/10/67-01/05/71, 1 goal
(55+3 games, 2 goals in Chelsea League career)
Signed from: Shamrock Rovers, October 1969
Chelsea League Debut: Manchester City (H), 20/12/69 (as substitute)
Left for: Crystal Palace, September 1972
Eire International

Peter Osgood
128+2 League games 23/10/67-01/05/71, 50 goals
(286+3 games, 105 goals in Chelsea League career)
Signed from: Junior, August 1964
Chelsea League Debut: Leicester City (H) 23/10/65
Left for: Southampton, March 1974
(re-signed Dec 1978, retired Dec 1979)
England International

Bobby Tambling
55+4 League games 23/10/67-01/05/71, 24 goals
(298+4 games, 164 goals in Chelsea League career)
Signed from: Juniors, September 1958
Chelsea League Debut: West Ham United (A), 7/2/59
Left for: Crystal Palace, June 1970
England International

David Webb
124+0 League games 23/10/67-01/05/71, 14 goals
(230 games, 21 goals in Chelsea League career)
Signed from: Southampton, February 1968
Chelsea League Debut: Manchester United (A), 2/3/68
Left for: Queens Park Rangers, May 1974
International appearances: none

Keith Weller
32+4 League games 23/10/67-01/05/71, 13 goals
(34+4 games, 14 goals in Chelsea League career)
Signed from: Millwall, May 1970
Chelsea League Debut: Derby County (H), 15/8/70
Left for: Leicester City, September 1971
England International

Appendix B
Total League Appearances and Goals For Each Player Under Sexton, from 23/10/67 to May 1971

156 League Games in period under review

Player	App	Sub	Goals
Hollins	145	0	16
Harris	136	0	1
Bonetti	133	0	0
Osgood	128	2	50
Webb	124	0	14
Houseman	120	4	9
Cooke	118	4	8
McCreadie	108	2	0
Baldwin	88	2	36
Boyle	83	3	4
Dempsey	81	2	3
Hinton	75	4	0
Birchenall	74	1	20
Hudson	63	1	6
Hutchinson	60	2	27
Tambling	55	4	24
Weller	32	4	13
Mulligan	22	3	1
Phillips	14	0	0
Kirkup	10	2	0
Smethurst	12	0	4
Hughes	9	0	0
Houston	6	3	0
Fascione	6	2	0
Butler	4	1	0
Lloyd	3	2	0
Droy	3	1	0
Thomson	2	2	0
Feely	2	0	1
Own Goal			6

Appendix C
1967-71 Season-By-Season Overall Record

	1967/68 (under Sexton)	1968/69	1969/70	1970/71
League	Division One	Division One	Division One	Division One
Home				
Won	10	11	13	12
Drew	2	7	7	6
Lost	2	3	1	3
Goals For	22	40	36	34
Goals Against	11	24	18	21
Points	22	29	33	30
Away				
Won	6	9	8	6
Drew	5	3	6	9
Lost	5	9	7	6
Goals For	25	33	34	18
Goals Against	25	29	32	21
Points	17	21	22	21
Total				
Won	16	20	21	18
Drew	7	10	13	15
Lost	7	12	8	9
Goals For	47	73	70	52
Goals Against	36	53	50	42
Points	39	50	55	51
Position 1st Sep	n/a	5	15	5
Position 1st Oct	n/a	6	12	18
Position 1st Nov	19	5	8	5
Position 1st Dec	18	6	6	4
Position 1st Jan	16	5	3	3
Position 1st Feb	14	5	3	4
Position 1st Mar	12	5	3	3
Position 1st Apr	9	5	4	3
End of season	6	5	3	6
Played in League	23	28	25	25
Most League Appearances	Cooke 30 Osgood 30 Baldwin Bonetti McCreadie all 28	Webb 42 Hollins 42 Harris 40	Hollins 42 Houseman 42 Osgood 38	Hollins 40 Harris 38 Houseman 37
Most Lge Goals	Osgood 13 Baldwin 12 Tambling 7	Tambling 17 Baldwin 16 Birchenall 12	Osgood 23 Hutchinson 16 Hollins 6	Weller 13 Hollins 6 Hutchinson 5 Osgood 5
FA Cup	Round 6	Round 6	Winners	Round 4
League Cup	Already Out	Round 3	Round 4	Round 4
Europe	n/a	(Fairs Cup) Round 2	n/a	(Cup Winners' Cup) winners
Ave Lge Crowd	39,038	37,613	40,342	39,545
Highest Lge Crowd	54,712 v Man Utd 25/11/67	60,436 v Man Utd 15/3/69	61,479 v Man Utd 21/3/70	61,277 v Tottenham H 14/11/70
Lowest Lge Crowd	23,494 v Burnley 22/4/68	17,639 v Coventry 10/3/69	24,904 v Burnley 17/9/69	14,356 v Burnley 26/4/71
POTY	Cooke	Webb	Hollins	Hollins

Appendix D
1967-71 Transfer Activity

1967-68 / 1969/70

67-68	Player from 23/10/67 onwards	Other Club	Players In £	Players Out £
10/67	Colin Waldron	Burnley		30,000
11/67	Alan Birchenall	Sheffield United	100,000	
01/68	Ian Hamilton	Juniors	0	
01/68	Ken Halliday	Juniors	0	
01/68	Geoff Butler	Sunderland		65,000
02/68	Paul McMillan	Retired (injury)		0
02/68	Joe Kirkup	Southampton		30,000
02/68	David Webb	Southampton	40,000	
03/68	Brian Brown	Millwall		0
06/68	Brian Goodwin	Hamilton Aca.		0
06/68	Geoff Idle	Guildford City		0
06/68	Roy Summers	Released		0
06/68	Warren Tennant	Guildford City		0
06/68	Kingsley Whiffen	Plymouth A (TRIAL)		0
Total 14		**Season Total**	**140,000**	**125,000**
68-69				
07/68	David Bibby	Juniors	0	
07/68	Alan Hudson	Juniors	0	
07/68	Brian Turner	New Zealand	0	
07/68	Ian Hutchinson	Cambridge Utd	2,500*	
08/68	George Luke	Durban City		0
09/68	Ian Hamilton	Southend Utd		5,000
09/68	Jim Thomson	Burnley		40,000
10/68	Derek Vaughan	Juniors	0	
12/68	Derek Smethurst	Durban City	1,000	
01/69	Ken Shellito	Retired (injury)**		0
01/69	Allan Young	Torquay Utd		8,000
01/69	John Dempsey	Fulham	70,000	
01/69	Barry Lloyd	Fulham		30,000
02/69	Michael Maskell	Juniors	0	
04/69	Alan Cocks	Juniors	0	
06/69	David Bibby	Released		0
06/69	Joe Fascione	Durban City		0
06/69	Ken Halliday	Released		0
06/69	Steve Hipwell	Released		0
06/69	Brian Turner	Portsmouth		0
Total 20		**Season Total**	**73,500**	**83,000**

* Ian Hutchinson transfer fee £2,500* (+ £2,000 after 10 1st team games and £2,500 after England U23 appearance.

** Ken Shellito joined Chelsea's coaching staff after retiring.

Appendix D (continued)
1967-71 Transfer Activity

1969-70 / 1970-71

	Player	Other Club	Players In £	Players Out £
69-70				
07/69	Alan Dovey	Juniors	0	
07/69	Tony Frewin	Juniors	0	
07/69	John Ware	Juniors	0	
10/69	Paddy Mulligan	Shamrock R.	17,500	
11/69	Alan Delacour	Portadown	4,500	
04/70	Peter Feely	Enfield	1,000	
05/70	Keith Weller	Millwall	100,000	
06/70	Alan Birchenall	Crystal Palace		100,000
06/70	Bobby Tambling	Crystal Palace		40,000
06/70	Alan Cocks	Southport		0
06/70	Roger Hawkins	Oxford Utd		0
06/70	Tim Haydon	Bournemouth		0
06/70	Joe Larkin	Shamrock R		0
06/70	Michael Maskell	Brentford		0
Total 14		*Season Total*	**123,000**	**140,000**
70-71				
06/70	Laurie Craker	Juniors	0	
06/70	Charlie Morrison	Juniors	0	
08/70	Tony Potrac	Juniors	0	
08/70	John Philips	Aston Villa	30,000	
10/70	Micky Droy	Slough Town	1,000	
01/71	Joe Cruickshank	Released		0
01/71	Tony Frewin	Released		0
01/71	Alan Dovey	Folkstone		Loan to Mar 71
03/71	Gary Stanley	Juniors	0	
01/71	Alan Dovey	Brighton &H.A.		Loan to May 71
05/71	Tommy Hughes	Aston Villa		12,500
06/71	Ian Delacour	Johannesburg*		0
Total 12		*Season Total*	**31,000**	**12,500**
		Total 1967-71	**367,500**	**360,500**
		Total Transfer Deficit	**7,000**	

* Johannesburg Jewish Guild

Additional Notes For Guidance:
Where disparity exists on reported fees, the most commonly reported version has been used.

For purchases from non-league and overseas clubs, in the absence of data a nominal fee of £1,000 has been given.

Appendix E
Listing of Chelsea transfer rumours

These are Chelsea-related transfer stories that appeared in the News Of The World, The People and Sunday Mirror and local newspapers (primarily *Chelsea News*) but never resulted in a purchase, loan or sale.

1967-68 – Incoming

Player	Club	Position
Peter Cormack	Hibernian	Forward
Len Glover	Charlton Atheltic	Winger
Arthur Duncan	Partick Thistle	Winger
Tommy McLean	Kilmarnock	Winger
Alex Edwards	Dunfermline	Winger
Bryan Conlon	Darlington	Forward
Terry Venables	Tottenham Hotspur	Midfield
Andy McFadden	St. Mirren	Defender
Graham Rowe	Blackpool	Defender
Malcolm Russell	Halfax Town	Defender
Ivan Hampton	Halifax Town	Defender
Derek Crampton	Spennymoor Utd	Goalkeeper
Brian Hill	Huddersfield Town	Winger
George McVitie	Carlisle Utd	Winger
Tommy Taylor	Orient	Defender
Dennis Bond	Tottenham Hotspur	Forward
Tony Green	Blackpool	Forward

1967-68 – Outgoing

Player	Club(s)
John Hollins	Notts. Forest
Joe Kirkup	Aston Villa
Peter Osgood	Notts. Forest
Allan Young	Brighton & H.A. / Northampton Town
Bobby Tambling	Arsenal / Coventry City / Manchester Utd
Joe Fascione	Aston Villa / Bristol City / Ipswich Town / Luton Town
Marvin Hinton	Queens Park Rangers / Southampton
Jim Thomson	Glasgow Rangers / Kilmarnock / Greenock Morton
Charlie Cooke	Newcastle Utd / Sheffield Utd
Geoff Butler	West Bromwich Albion

1968-69 – Incoming

Player	Club	Position
Jon Sammels	Arsenal	Midfield
Willie Morgan	Burnley	Winger
Lex Law	Queen of the South	Forward
Peter Cormack	Kilmarnock	Winger
Hugh Curran	Wolverhampton W	Forward
Harry Kirk	Darlington	Winger
John Galley	Bristol City	Forward
Paul Went	Charlton Athletic	Defender
Preben Arentoft	Greenock Morton	Midfield
Denis Rofe	Orient	Defender
Tommy Taylor	Orient	Defender
Jim Blair	St. Mirren	Forward
Les Barrett	Fulham	Winger
Alan Glover	Queens Park Rangers	Forward
John McHugh	Clyde	Winger
Danny Hegan	Ipswich Town	Winger
John Ritchie	Sheffield Wednesday	Forward
Joe Kinnear	Tottenham Hotspur	Defender
Allan Harris	Queens Park Rangers	Defender
Eric Winstanley	Bernsley	Defender
Terry Venables	Tottenham Hotspur	Midfield
Liam O'Kane	Derry City	Defender

1968-69 – Outgoing

Player	Club(s)
Tommy Hughes	Huddersfield Town
Peter Houseman	Norwich City
Marvin Hinton	Crystal Palace / Fulham / Queens Park Rangers
Joe Fascione	Brighton & H.A. / Luton Town / Charlton Athletic
Allan Young	Bristol City
Alan Birchenall	Sheffield Wednesday
Ian Hutchinson	Portsmouth
Peter Osgood	Liverpool / Tottenham Hotspur
Charlie Cooke	Aston Villa / Tottenham Hotspur

1969-70 – Incoming

Player	Club	Position
Terry Venables	Tottenham Hotspur	Midfield
Irwin McKibben	Cliftonville	Goalkeeper
Allan Clarke	Leicester City	Forward
Peter Cormack	Hibernian	Forward
Steve Earle	Fulham	Midfield
Keith Newton	Blackburn Rovers	Defender
Terry Fitzgerald	Barnsley	Defender
Trevor Storton	Tranmere Rovers	Defender
Jim Conway	Fulham	Winger
Danny Hegan	West Bromwich Albion	Winger
Alan Glover	West Bromwich Albion	Forward
Dick Malone	Ayr Utd	Defender
Jon Sammels	Arsenal	Midfield
Tommy Hutchinson	Blackpool	Winger
Laurie Churchill	Enfield	Forward

1969-70 – Outgoing

Player	Club(s)
Charlie Cooke	Aston Villa / Hibernian
Tommy Baldwin	Birmingham City / Crystal Palace Sheffield Wednesday / Newcastle Utd
Alan Birchenall	Birmingham City / Wolverhampton Wanderers Ipswich T / Newcastle Utd / Liverpool
Ian Hutchinson	Ipswich T / Liverpool
Peter Osgood	Liverpool
Peter Houseman	Leicester City / Southampton
Marvin Hinton	Reading

1970-71 – Incoming

Player	Club	Position
Wilf Smith	Sheffield Wednesday	Defender
Malcolm Partridge	Mansfield Town	Forward
John Toshack	Cardiff City	Forward
Bill Coulson	Consett Town	Forward
Joe Jopling	Aldershot	Defender
Dick Malone	Sunderland	Defender
Jim Hince	Tranmere Rovers	Forward
Steve Earle	Fulham	Midfield
Les Barrett	Fulham	Winger
John Fraser	Largs Thistle	Winger
George Ley	Portsmouth	Defender
Denis Rofe	Orient	Defender
Godfrey Briggs	Mansfield Town	Defender
Peter Allen	Orient	Midfield
Norman Whitehead	Rochdale	Winger
Bill Green	Hartlepool United	Defender
Alan Foggon	Newcastle United	Winger
Charlie Smith	Partick Thistle	Midfield
David Clunie	Hearts	Defender

1970-71 – Outgoing

Player	Club(s)
Charlie Cooke	Tottenham Hotspur
John Boyle	Crystal Palace / Sheffield Wednesday Everton / Tottenham Hotspur
Tommy Baldwin	Newcastle Utd / Liverpool / Notts. Forest Queens Park Rangers
Tommy Hughes	Blackpool / Brighton & H.A.
Marvin Hinton	Leeds United / Queens Park Rangers
Peter Bonetti	Leicester City / Southampton
John Hollins	Manchester United
John Dempsey	West Bromwich Albion

Appendix F
List of Televised Chelsea Games 1967-71

The sources of these listings are given in the bibliography.

All are Division One games unless stated. The *Star Soccer* games shown are the main games, i.e. those shown in London, for 1967-68. *The Big Match* games shown are the main games, i.e. those shown in London, from 1968-69 onwards.

This is not a fully comprehensive list. I could find no completely comprehensive listing for 1967-68 ITV games and the 1968-69, 1969-70 and 1970-71 ITV listings may be incomplete. No fully comprehensive listing could be found of BBC or ITV midweek domestic or European games shown. In addition brief highlights of some games were shown on BBC News and ITN (most famously the Ipswich game in 1970 with the 'phantom' Alan Hudson goal) but no listing of these could be found.

Some brief highlights of overseas European games were shown on Saturday lunchtime sports programmes, though no listing of these exists. '*Football Preview*' was the BBC offering, part of '*Grandstand*'. '*Soccer Round-Up*' from August to December 1968 and '*On The Ball*', from December 1968 onwards, were the ITV offerings, as part of '*World Of Sport*'.

Quite often, in the early rounds of European competition, there was no highlights programme. If such a programme was scheduled only one game was shown, and these were often European Cup games, meaning that coverage/footage of Chelsea's 1968-69 and 1970-71 European adventures is less comprehensive than would be hoped.

1967-68 (11 games) (*from 23/10/67 onwards*)

28/10/67 Chelsea 1 v West Ham United 3 (SS)
11/11/67 Chelsea 3 v Sheffield Wednesday 0 (SS)
25/11/67 Chelsea 1 v Manchester United 1 (MOTD)
30/12/67 Arsenal 1 v Chelsea 1 (SS)
06/01/68 Southampton 3 v Chelsea 5 (ITV)
27/01/68 Chelsea 3 v Ipswich Town 0 (FAC) (MOTD)
17/02/68 Chelsea 1 v Norwich City 0 (FAC) (SS)
09/03/68 Sheffield Wednesday 2 v Chelsea 2 (FAC) (MOTD)
30/03/68 Birmingham City 1 v Chelsea 0 (FAC) (MOTD)
23/03/68 West Ham United 0 v Chelsea 1 (SS)
13/04/68 Chelsea 2 v Tottenham Hotspur 0 (SS)

SEXTON FOR GOD

1968-69 (16 games)

01/09/68 Chelsea 2 v Tottenham Hotspur 2 (TBM)
07/09/68 Chelsea 1 v Everton 1 (MOTD)
22/09/68 Chelsea 1 v West Ham United 1 (TBM)
12/10/68 Wolverhampton Wanderers 1 v Chelsea 1 (MOTD)
19/10/68 Chelsea 3 v Leicester C 0 (TBM)
02/11/68 Chelsea 2 v Manchester City 0 (MOTD)
09/11/68 Liverpool 2 v Chelsea 1 (ITV)
24/11/68 Arsenal 0 v Chelsea 1 (TBM)
30/11/68 Chelsea 1 v Leeds United 1 (MOTD)
25/01/69 Preston North End 0 v Chelsea 0 (FAC) (MOTD)
02/02/69 Southampton 5 v Chelsea 0 (ITV)
12/02/69 Chelsea 3 v Stoke City 2 (FAC) (BBC)
15/02/69 Leeds United 1 v Chelsea 0 (MOTD)
01/03/69 Chelsea 1 v West Bromwich Albion 2 (FAC) (MOTD)
08/03/69 West Bromwich Albion 0 v Chelsea 3 (ITV)
15/03/69 Chelsea 3 v Manchester United 2 (MOTD)

1969-70 (24 games)

23/08/69 Southampton 2 v Chelsea 2 (MOTD)
30/08/69 Chelsea 1 Crystal Palace 1 (TBM)
07/09/69 Manchester City 0 v Chelsea 0 (ITV)
13/09/69 Chelsea 2 v Wolverhampton Wanderers 2 (MOTD)
20/09/69 Leeds United 2 v Chelsea 0 (MOTD)
27/09/69 Chelsea 3 Arsenal 0 (TBM)
11/10/69 Chelsea 2 v Derby County 2 (MOTD)
18/10/69 Chelsea 2 West Bromwich Albion 0 (TBM)
25/10/69 Newcastle United 0 v Chelsea 1 (ITV)
08/11/69 Sheffield Wednesday 1 v Chelsea 3 (MOTD)
16/11/69 Chelsea 1 Everton 1 (TBM)
06/12/69 Manchester United 0 v Chelsea 2 (ITV)
20/12/69 Chelsea 3 v Manchester City 1 (MOTD)
04/01/70 Chelsea 3 v Birmingham City 0 (FAC) (TBM)
10/01/70 Chelsea 2 v Leeds United 5 (MOTD)
17/01/70 Arsenal 0 Chelsea 3 (TBM)
24/01/70 Chelsea 2 v Burnley 2 (FAC) MOTD
07/02/70 Crystal Palace 1 Chelsea 4 (FAC) (TBM)

279

21/02/70 Queens Park Rangers 2 Chelsea 4 (FAC) (TBM)
14/03/70 Chelsea 5 Watford 1 (FAC) (TBM)
21/03/70 Chelsea 2 Man Utd 1 (TBM)
04/04/70 Chelsea 1 Tottenham Hotspur 0 (TBM)
11/04/70 Chelsea 2 Leeds 2 (FA Cup Final)*
29/04/70 Chelsea 2 v Leeds United 1 (FA Cup Final Replay)*
(*both games shown live in their entireties by BBC and ITV)

1970-71 (22 games)
(Chelsea banned The Big Match cameras from Stamford Bridge from Aug-Dec 1970 in a dispute about fees)

08/08/20 Chelsea 1 v Everton 2 (Charity Shield) (MOTD)
15/08/70 Chelsea 2 v Derby County 1 (MOTD)
22/08/70 West Ham United 2 Chelsea 2 (TBM)
29/08/70 Chelsea 2 Arsenal 1 (TBM)
06/09/70 Leeds United 1 v Chelsea 0 (ITV)
20/09/70 Coventry City 0 v Chelsea 1 (ITV)
30/09/70 Chelsea 5 v Aris Salonika 1 (ECWC) (ITV)
03/10/70 Liverpool 1 v Chelsea 0 (MOTD)
10/10/70 Chelsea 1 v Manchester City 1 (MOTD)
28/10/70 Manchester United 2 v Chelsea 1 (LC) (ITV)
05/12/70 Chelsea 1 v Newcastle United 0 (MOTD)
19/12/70 Chelsea 2 West Ham United 1 (TBM)
02/01/71 Crystal Palace 2 Chelsea 2 (FAC) (TBM)
06/01/71 Chelsea 2 v Crystal Palace 0 (FACR)
09/01/71 Chelsea 1 Man Utd 2 (TBM)
23/01/71 Chelsea 0 Man City 3 (FAC) (TBM)
30/01/71 Chelsea 4 v West Bromwich Albion 1 (MOTD)
20/02/71 Stoke City 1 v Chelsea 2 (ITV)
03/04/71 Arsenal 2 Chelsea 0 (TBM)
24/04/71 Chelsea 2 Coventry 1 (TBM)
28/04/71 Manchester City 0 v Chelsea 1 (ECWC) (ITV)
21/05/71 Chelsea 2 v Real Madrid 1 (ECWC Final Replay) (BBC*)
(*whole game live)

BIBLIOGRAPHY

Books

Some of these books have been used extensively in research, others for background or specific fact checking. Many are out of print, but all are worth seeking out and reading.

Bagchi, Rob and Rogerson, Paul. *The Unforgiven*. London. Aurum Press. 2002.
Batty, Clive. *Kings Of The King's Road*. London. Vision Sports Publishing. 2007.
Benson, Colin. *The Bridge*. London. Chelsea Football Club. 1987.
Birchenall, Alan. *Bring Back The Birch*. Polar Publishing. 2000.
Chelsea Chadder. *100 Memorable Matches* - London. Gate 17. 2018.
Cheshire, Scott. *Chelsea – An Illustrated History*. Derby. Breedon Books. 1997.
Cooke, Charlie with Knight, Martin. *The Bonnie Prince – My Football Life*. Edinburgh. Mainstream Publishing. 2006.
Dawson, Jeff. *Back Home - England And The 1970 World Cup*. London. Orion Books. 2001.
Dutton, Paul & Glanvill, Rick. *Chelsea - The Complete Record*. Liverpool. deCoubertin Books. 2015.
Finn, Ralph. *A History Of Chelsea*. London. The Sportsmans Book Club. 1970.
Fitzsimon, Neil. *A Deeper Shade Of Blue*. Worthing. Pitch Publishing. 2021.
Fitzsimon, Neil. *Rhapsody In Blue*. Worthing. Pitch Publishing. 2020.
Glanvill, Rick. *Chelsea – The Official Biography*. London. Headline. 2005.
Glanvill, Rick. *Chelsea Football Club – The Official History In Pictures*. London. Headline. 2006.
Glanvill, Rick. *Rhapsody In Blue – The Chelsea Dream Team*. London. Mainstream Publishing. 1996.
Harris, Harry. *Chelsea's Century*. London. John Blake Publishing. 2005.
Harris, Ron. *Soccer The Hard Way*. London. Pelham Books. 1970.
Hockings, Ron. *100 Year of the Blues. A Statistical History Of Chelsea*

Football Club. London. The Hockings Family. 2007.
Hudson, Alan. *The Working Man's Ballet*. London. London Books. 2017.
Hugman, Barry J. *Football League Players Records 1946-92*. Taunton. Tony Williams Publications. 1992.
King, Martin & Knight, Martin. *The Special Ones*. London. London Books. 2006.
Knight, David. J. *The Chelsea Experience*. London. 60 Minutes With.... 2008.
Mears, Brian with MacLeay, Ian. *Chelsea – Football Under The Blue Flag*. Edinburgh. Mainstream Publishing. 2001.
Mears, Brian with MacLeay, Ian. *Chelsea – The 100-Year History*. Edinburgh. Mainstream Publishing. 2004.
Mears, Brian. *Chelsea – The Real Story* London. Pelham Books. 1982.
Moynihan, John. *The Chelsea Story*. London. Arthur Baker. 1982.
Moynihan, John. *Soccer Focus*. London. Simon & Schuster. 1989.
Moynihan, Leo. *Chelsea's Cult Heroes*. Derby. Knowthescore Books. 2005.
News Of The World Football Annual 1971-72. London. News Of the World Ltd. 1971.
Osgood Peter. *Ossie The Wizard*. London. Stanley Paul. 1969.
Osgood, Peter with King, Martin & Knight, Martin. *Ossie – King Of Stamford Bridge*. Edinburgh. Mainstream Publishing. 2002.
Pawson, Tony. *100 Years Of The FA Cup*. London. William Heinemann. 1972.
Pawson, Tony. *The Football Managers*. London. Eyre Methuen. 1973.
Rollin, Jack (Ed). *Rothmans Football Yearbook 1971-72*. London. Queen Anne Press. 1971.
Rolls, Tim. *Diamonds, Dynamos and Devils*. London. Gate 17. 2017.
Rolls, Tim. *Stamford Bridge Is Falling Down*. London. Gate 17. 2019.
Sewell, Albert. *The Chelsea Football Book*. London. Stanley Paul & Co. 1970.
Sewell, Albert. *The Chelsea Football Book No.2*. London. Stanley Paul & Co. 1971.
Sewell, Albert. *The Chelsea Football Book No.3*. London. Stanley Paul & Co. 1972.
Smith, Neil with Johnstone, David. *Where Were You When We Were Shocking?* London. Gate 17. 2018.
Steen, Rob. *The Mavericks*. Edinburgh. Mainstream Publishing. 1995.
Tabner, Brian. *Through the Turnstiles*. Middlesex. Yore Publications. 1992.

Tesser, Greg. *Chelsea In The Swinging 60's*. Stroud. The History Press. 2013.
Tongue, Steve. *Turf Wars - A History Of London Football*. Worthing. Pitch Publishing. 2016.
Westcott, Chris. *Upfront With Chelsea*. Edinburgh. Mainstream Publishing. 2001.
Worrall, Mark. *Liquidator*. London. Gate 17. 2020.

Magazines and Programmes
Chelsea FC Magazines (various)
Chelsea FC home match programmes (1967-71)
Chelsea FC away match programmes (1967-71)
Football League Review (1967-71)
Football Monthly (1967-71)
Goal Magazine (1968-71)
Illustrated London News (1967-71)

Newspapers (accessed via the British Library Newsroom)
Various 1967-71 editions of:-
National Newspapers:- *Daily Express, Daily Mail, Daily Mirror, Daily Telegraph, News Of The World, The Observer, Sunday Mirror, The People, Sunday Telegraph*
Regional newspapers:- *Birmingham Daily Post, Coventry Evening Telegraph, Evening Standard, Liverpool Echo, Nottingham Football Post, Newcastle Evening Chronicle, Sports Argus (Birmingham)*
Local newspapers:- *Acton Gazette, Chelsea News, Fulham Chronicle, Kensington News, Kensington Post, Middlesex County Times*

Television Programmes (many of the games listed in Appendix D can be watched online, usually via YouTube)
'*Match Of The Day*' and other BBC Sport programmes
'*The Big Match*' and other ITV Sport programmes
'*Kicking And Screaming*' 1995 BBC Documentary series about the history of Association Football

Websites
www.bounder.friardale.co.uk *(for results, scorers and season summaries)*
www.chelseafc.com (*Chelsea FC official website*)
weaintgotnohistory.sbnation.com (Chelsea Supporter site)

https://thesefootballtimes.co/ (*general football site*)
www.worldfootball.net (*for leading scorers and other club appearances season-by-season*)
www.11v11.com (*for League tables during seasons*)
http://carousel.royalwebhosting.net/itv/ITVfootball55-68.html (*for ITV listings up to 1968*)
https://forums.digitalspy.com/discussion/499101/lwt-big-match-listings (*for The Big Match listings*)
http://carousel.royalwebhosting.net/itv/ITVfootball68-83.html (*for other ITV football listings*)
https://sites.google.com/site/motdlistings/ (*for Match Of The Day listings*).
Facebook Groups *Bygone Chelsea: 1905-99*; *Memories Of Going To Chelsea In The 50s, 60s and 70s*; *Memories Of Going To Chelsea FC In The Seventies*
Paul McParlan's entertaining reminiscences of the Jan 1970 Burnley FA Cup replay.
https://thesefootballtimes.co/2019/09/27/the-tortuous-trek-to-turf-moor-and-a-great-fa-cup-game-told-through-the-eyes-of-one-away-fan-in-1970/
Gary Thacker piece on the Old Trafford replay.
https://thesefootballtimes.co/2017/09/26/cry-havok-and-let-slip-the-dogs-of-war-the-1970-fa-cup-final/

Other Sources
Chelsea scrapbooks compiled by Gordon Sole, and kindly lent by his son Howard.

GATE 17
THE COMPLETE COLLECTION
(AUTUMN 2021)

CHELSEA

Over Land and Sea – Mark Worrall
Chelsea here, Chelsea There – Kelvin Barker, David Johnstone, Mark Worrall
Chelsea Football Fanzine – the best of cfcuk
One Man Went to Mow – Mark Worrall
Chelsea Chronicles (Five Volume Series) – Mark Worrall
Making History Not Reliving It –
Kelvin Barker, David Johnstone, Mark Worrall
Celery! Representing Chelsea in the 1980s – Kelvin Barker
Stuck On You, a year in the life of a Chelsea supporter – Walter Otton
Palpable Discord, a year of drama and dissent at Chelsea – Clayton Beerman
Rhyme and Treason – Carol Ann Wood
Eddie Mac Eddie Mac – Eddie McCreadie's Blue & White Army
The Italian Job, A Chelsea thriller starring Antonio Conte – Mark Worrall
Carefree! Chelsea Chants & Terrace Culture – Mark Worrall, Walter Otton
Diamonds, Dynamos and Devils – Tim Rolls
Arrivederci Antonio, The Italian Job (part two) – Mark Worrall
Where Were You When We Were Shocking? – Neil L. Smith
Chelsea, 100 Memorable Games – Chelsea Chadder
Bewitched, Bothered & Bewildered – Carol Ann Wood
Stamford Bridge Is Falling Down – Tim Rolls
Cult Fiction – Dean Mears
Chelsea, If Twitter Was Around When… – Chelsea Chadder
Blue Army – Vince Cooper
Liquidator 1969-70 A Chelsea Memoir – Mark Worrall
When Skies Are Grey, Super Frank, Chelsea And The Coronavirus Crisis – Mark Worrall
Tales Of The (Chelsea) Unexpected – David Johnstone & Neil L Smith
The Ultimate Unofficial Chelsea Quiz Book – Chelsea Chadder
Blue Days – Chris Wright
Let The Celery Decide – Walter Otton
Blue Hitmen – Paul Radcliffe
Sexton For God – Tim Rolls

FICTION

Blue Murder, Chelsea Till I Die – Mark Worrall
The Wrong Outfit – Al Gregg
The Red Hand Gang – Walter Otton
Coming Clean – Christopher Morgan
This Damnation – Mark Worrall
Poppy – Walter Otton

NON FICTION

Roe2Ro – Walter Otton
Shorts – Walter Otton
England International Football Team Quiz & Trivia Book – George Cross

www.gate17.co.uk

Printed in Poland
by Amazon Fulfillment
Poland Sp. z o.o., Wrocław